Advance Praise for *Pioneer in Tibet*

"*Pioneer in Tibet* opens a new window on the period in Asian history a century ago when the remoteness and supposed mysteries of Tibet and its border regions were a magnet for an endless stream of explorers, adventurers, free-booters, spies, and missionaries. Albert Shelton was one of the last Westerners to have actually lived there, and Douglas Wissing's account of his life is an engrossing narrative of how things once were in that evocative land, as well as of how much things have changed since."

—Orville Schell, author of Virtual Tibet *and Dean of the Graduate School of Journalism, UC Berkeley*

"Dr. Albert Shelton was the twentieth-century's David Livingston. Douglas Wissing's portrayal of this Disciples of Christ missionary is no hagiography. Shelton is presented in his human complexity as a healer, diplomat, collector and dealer in Tibetan artifacts, interpreter of Tibetan culture to Americans, as well as a courageous servant of God. In Wissing's words, Shelton possessed an 'adventurer heart and missionary soul' as his life's journey took him from the frontier border of Kansas to the frontier border of Tibet. Shelton's biographical portrait is well-positioned in Wissing's detailed descriptions of the machinations of the Chinese–Tibetan conflicts of the early twentieth century."

—Peter M. Morgan, President, Disciples of Christ Historical Society, Nashville, Tennessee

PIONEER IN TIBET

DOUGLAS A. WISSING

PIONEER IN TIBET
Copyright © Douglas A. Wissing, 2004.
All rights reserved. No part of this book may be used or reproduced in any manner
whatsoever without written permission except in the case of brief quotations embodied in
critical articles or reviews.

First published 2004 by
PALGRAVE MACMILLAN™
175 Fifth Avenue, New York, N.Y. 10010 and
Houndmills, Basingstoke, Hampshire, England RG21 6XS.
Companies and representatives throughout the world.

PALGRAVE MACMILLAN is the global academic imprint of the Palgrave Macmillan
division of St. Martin's Press, LLC and of Palgrave Macmillan Ltd. Macmillan® is a
registered trademark in the United States, United Kingdom and other countries. Palgrave
is a registered trademark in the European Union and other countries.

ISBN 1-4039-6328-2 hardcover

Library of Congress Cataloging-in-Publication Data
Wissing, Douglas A.
    Pioneer in Tibet : the life and perils of Dr. Albert Shelton / by Douglas A. Wissing.
        p. cm.
    Includes bibliographical references and index.
    ISBN 1-4039-6328-2 hardcover
    1. Shelton, A. L. (Albert Leroy), 1875–1922—Travel—China—Tibet. 2. Tibet
(China)—Description and travel.   I. Title: Life and perils of Dr. Albert Shelton.
II. Title.
DS785.W57   2004
951'.5035'092—dc22
[B]
                                                                                    2003058230

A catalogue record for this book is available from the British Library.

Design by Letra Libre, Inc.

First edition: March 2004
10 9 8 7 6 5 4 3 2 1
Printed in the United States of America.

For Clarence A. Stout

CONTENTS

ACKNOWLEDGMENTS

I owe a great debt of gratitude to the many experts who graciously guided me through the mazes of Dr. Albert Shelton's life and times. None, of course, bears any responsibility for my errors of fact or interpretation.

I would particularly like to acknowledge the late Dr. Robert M. Taylor of the Indiana Historical Society, who championed the award of a Clio Grant that supported my research in Kham, eastern Tibet, as well as the many worldwide archives. The society is an exemplary organization, and their support of this far-flung project is testimony to their vision. John Harris and Steve Cox of the IHS Education Division were able administrators for the grant. The Ragdale Foundation of Lake Forest, Illinois, provided a pastoral writer's retreat for me to complete the final work on the manuscript. My appreciation to Susan Page Tillett, Sylvia Brown, and Melissa Mosher. Thanks also to Dr. William Fierman, director of the Inner Asian and Uralic National Resource Center, and Jeff Pennington for the center's support of the Kham photographic exhibit. I would also like to thank His Holiness the Dalai Lama for his support of the project. Like him, I hope this book will bring greater attention to the oppressed and often forgotten eastern Tibetans who live outside the Tibetan Autonomous Region. Albert Shelton would like that.

Editor and friend Kent Calder provided important encouragement at an early stage of the project. Jim Canary, fellow Tibet enthusiast and Head of Conservation at Indiana University's Lilly Rare Book Library, offered critical insights into the importance of Dr. Shelton. Curator of Asian Collections Valrae Reynolds at the Newark Museum provided a wealth of information on Dr. Shelton and the Newark's extraordinary Tibetan collection. Her willingness to share her wide-ranging knowledge and the Newark's extensive archives opened a great door.

Gerry, Paula, and Charles Still of Scottsdale, Arizona, archivists of the Shelton family papers, allowed me to utilize diaries, letters, and family photos that brought Flora and Albert Shelton to life with their own words. I owe them my sincere thanks.

The staff members of the Disciples of Christ Historical Society in Nashville, Tennessee, were nothing less than superb. It still seems miraculous that the records of the tumultuous mission on the edge of China would be intact and well organized. I would like to thank President Peter Morgan, Director of Library and Archives David McWhirter, Clinton Holloway, Lynne Morgan, and Elaine Philpott, as well as Marcia Harns, archivist of the Division of Overseas Missionaries at the Disciples of Christ Headquarters in Indianapolis.

Curator of Asian Art Bennett Bronson at the Field Museum in Chicago provided his unpublished manuscript on Berthold Laufer's Tibetan expedition, which was instrumental to my understanding of Shelton's initial interest in collecting and the financial realities of acquisitions in the borderlands. I also appreciate the help given me by Registrar Dorren Martin-Ross and archivist Armand Esai. Thanks also to curators Steven Kossak and Alyson Moss at the Metropolitan Museum of Art and the American Museum of Natural History's Laurel Kendall and Laila Williamson for checking their collections for Shelton material.

A number of scholars selflessly took the time to assist me. Professor Elliot Sperling of Indiana University ably translated the Dalai Lama's invitation to Albert Shelton as well as provided insights into Tibetan diplomacy. After a remarkable lecture on Buddhist philosophy at the Bloomington, Indiana, Kalachakra event, Professor Robert Thurman shared his view of Khampa culture. Historian William Martin of the U.S. State Department provided his exceptional bibliography of mission work in Tibet that was a critical path into the subject. Honorary Secretary of the International Association of Ladakh Studies and Tibet mission historian John Bray offered vital contacts and his own impeccable scholarship. As former CIA operations officer for the secret Tibetan army in which Khampas played a large role, historian John Kenneth Knaus provided perspective on their warrior culture and additional Kham contacts. Thanks to Barbara Crossette of the *New York Times,* Father Dick Shelburn, the Trace Foundation's Ethan Goldings, and Jamyang Norbu of the Amnye Machen Institute for Himalayan mission information.

My wife Flavia and I spent a delightful day in Los Angeles with filmmakers John Basmajian and Bill Haren reviewing Basmajian's interview footage of the Shelton daughters, Dorris and Dorothy. Dining in one of the world's best Thai restaurants afterward was just a bonus. Dr. Enid Zimmerman of the Indiana University Department of Education graciously loaned me materials from an Indiana-Tibet exhibit. Dr. Suzanne Barnett of the University of Puget Sound aimed me toward some important missionary resources. Miller Professor of History James Madison of Indiana University clarified Hoosier issues. Steve Weinberger of the University of Virginia Tibetan program gave me incisive perspectives on Tibetan Buddhism and its contemporary American manifestations as we ate incendiary Sichuan hot pot near the Chengdu bus station. Trent

Pomplum of the University of Virginia offered information and resources on Desideri, and scholar Laurent Deshayes provided resources and translations relating to French Roman Catholic missionaries in Kham. Thanks to authors Paul Diebold and Julia Fangmeier of Indianapolis for introducing me to the College of Missions. Kim Siriporn at Baltimore's Calvert School informed me about home schooling materials used by foreign missionaries. Former Kham missionaries George Kraft and George Patterson shared their memories of the mid-twentieth century borderlands, and Marguerite Fairbrother, who was raised in Batang, provided a copy of her memoirs. Author Marian Duncan was also raised in Batang. Our conversations on her inside views of the TCM gave me a new perspective on this group of idealistic Americans in the back blocks of China. Research assistant Teresa Heinz did a stellar job of ferreting out elusive literature and being a scholarly jack-of-all-trades.

Biographers should maintain an eternal flame for research librarians, who patiently satisfy our insatiable appetite for minutiae. National Geographic Society Archives Manager Renee Braden provided a cache of correspondence that defined Shelton's important relationship with the institution, as William Peniston at the Newark Museum did with his. Thanks to Ian Baxter at the British Library Oriental and India Office for Political and Secret documents. Hum Thomas at the Royal Geographical Society found Albert Shelton's fellowship documents. Tom Rosenbaum of the Rockefeller Archives supplied a surprising file of letters that illustrated Shelton's missionary-dealer hybridity. At Indiana University, Lou Malcomb and Andrea Singer were enormously helpful with documents relating to Shelton's diplomatic history, while Carl Horne and Tom Lee helped illuminate the Tibetan milieu. The long-suffering librarians at the Monroe County Library in Bloomington satisfied some very arcane interlibrary requests and answered a host of obscure questions. Particular thanks to Amy Novick, Dirk Fraser, and Marla Gray. Ruth Eckerman at the Ruth Lilly Medical Library at Indiana University-Purdue University Indianapolis sorted out essential information on early-twentieth-century doctoring. David Bundy and Don Haymes at the Christian Theological Seminary in Indianapolis assisted me with their archives of Disciples of Christ missionary publications. Former missionary and CTS scholar Joe Smith told me the tale of Shelton's prayer-burnished yak-skin chaps. Librarians at the Indiana State Library, Diane Sharp, John Selch, Darrol Pierson, Martha Wright, and Andrea Hough, provided material on Indianapolis in Shelton's childhood and on the great migration to the West. Susan Sutton at the Indiana Historical Society helped me visualize the Indianapolis of 1875. Joann Sprague at the Ben-Hur Museum in Crawfordsville supplied information on Lew Wallace, whose writing flamed the romance of missionary life in Albert Shelton. Further thanks to Mark Stephen

Mir at the Ricci Institute for Chinese-Western Cultural History, Paul Streubenberg of the Yale University library, B. J. Gooch at Transylvania University, Leslie Cade at the Kansas State Historical Society, Barbara Robbins at the Emporia State University archives, Lin Frederickson of the University of Kansas Spencer Research Library, Carolyn McCaffrey and Mary Sullivan of the Grant County [Kansas] Public Library, University of Virginia Library Tibet Specialist Phillip McEldowney, Royal Asiatic Society's Michael Pollack, Reverend Joseph Wenniger, director of the Archives of the Christian and Missionary Alliance, Seventh Day Adventists Tim Poirier, Bert Halovich, and Jim Ford, Linda J. Long at the University of Oregon, and Camilla Berger and Gertrude Riggle in Pomona.

Albert Shelton's homesteader boyhood in Kansas clearly marked his life and accordingly needed to be thoroughly understood. During my research and journey through Kansas to the Shelton homesteads, a number of extraordinary Kansans helped my wife and me in endlessly considerate ways. I would like to thank Mary Lynn Stevenson and Don Banwart of Fort Scott and Chip and Ashley Walker and Susan Rathke of Emporia. Further thanks to the Anthony, Kansas folks, Barbara Wright, Gwen Warner, Sandy Trotter, and particularly Eldon Younce, who provided guide services to the site of Shelton's properties. Carol Peterson benevolently sent a number of Shelton letters that appeared in the Anthony paper. On the high plains, Director of the Grant County Chamber of Commerce, June Hart, squired us to the site of Shelton's boyhood soddie, and Ginger Anthony, Melanie Lee, and Catharine Anderson at the Historic Adobe Museum were wonderful interpreters of west Kansas life, as well as providers of an unexpected file of Shelton material.

My research expedition to Kham, eastern Tibet, took assistance that reached far beyond the academic. My deepest thanks to the Anyetsang family of Bloomington, Indiana, and Dahor Village. Thupten Anyetsang of Bloomington's Little Tibet Restaurant extended himself with information about his beloved homeland and arranged for his remarkable brother Kalsang to serve as my guide in Kham. Quite literally, the journey would not have accomplished its goals without Kalsang's fearless commitment. While in northern Kham, the Anyetsang family—Kalsang, Bhuko, Lhamo Ngodup, and Yamakhando—provided much needed succor in their beautiful village of Dahor in the Zachu River valley. The view of the glittering peaks of Zara Yachen and Zara Machen from their balcony is alight in my memory. I am also deeply appreciative of the unstinting assistance of Pamela Logan, president of the Kham Aid Foundation. My trip would have been far more eventful without the help of Wu Bangfu, Kham Aid's highly effective field man in Kangding. Thanks also to Lotendu, aide to Gyalten Tulku of Gyalten Monastery and delegate to China's National

Congress. I am appreciative of the warm hospitality provided to Kalsang and me by the Lobsang family of Batang, who took us off the road into their loving Tibetan home. Special thanks to the Ba Lama of Batang, a remarkable Khampa patriot and revered reincarnate, who reminisced about his friendship with Dr. Albert Shelton in a previous lifetime. Dinner with the Ba Lama was the penultimate moment in a very long trip. Thanks also to his effective secretary, Danduna, who poignantly related the travails of the Khampas. I also wish to recognize the Batang historian who felt compelled to remain nameless. This Khampa rescued Dr. Shelton's gravestone during the Cultural Revolution. Without his expert guidance, I never would have located the ruins of the Tibetan Christian Mission.

Thanks to Shareen Blair Brysac and Karl E. Meyer for their insights into central Asia and the publishing process, and Professor Kenneth Silverman of New York University for the opportunity to speak to the Biography Seminar on the Kham research trip. I owe a great debt to the enthusiasm of my agent, Giles Anderson, and editor Anthony Wahl. The book wouldn't be here without you.

There seems to be a trope of almost obligatory supplication that accompanies biographies, as the author attempts to make amends for years of preoccupation. I join that long line of scholars. To all my friends and family that I have benumbed with eternal Shelton chatter, I sincerely thank you. Special thanks to my children, Dylan, Seth, and Amanda, my sister Bunny Ostendorf, and Sandi Clark and Charlie Grannon for all their support. And a most heartfelt thanks to Dr. Flavia Bastos—my wife, great friend, and muse.

THE DALAI LAMA

MESSAGE

In the early years of the twentieth century Dr Albert Shelton established a mission in Batang in the western Chinese province of Szechuan close to the border with Tibet. From there he ventured into Kham, the easternmost of Tibet's three provinces, where his medical work and attempts to mediate in conflicts between Chinese and Tibetans won him many friends and an invitation from the Thirteenth Dalai Lama to visit Lhasa. His writings, photographs and lectures, in addition to his assemblage of Tibetan artefacts that form a significant part of the Newark Museum's fine Tibetan collection today, introduced the hitherto unknown people and nation of Tibet to the American public. This book, *Pioneering in Tibet: the Life and Times of Dr Albert Shelton* tells the story of this sturdy adventurer who worked in Kham from 1904 until 1922. It also provides an account of the Sino-Tibetan clashes then taking place in this turbulent region, a foretaste of the tragedy that was to befall the whole of Tibet three decades later.

August 26, 2002

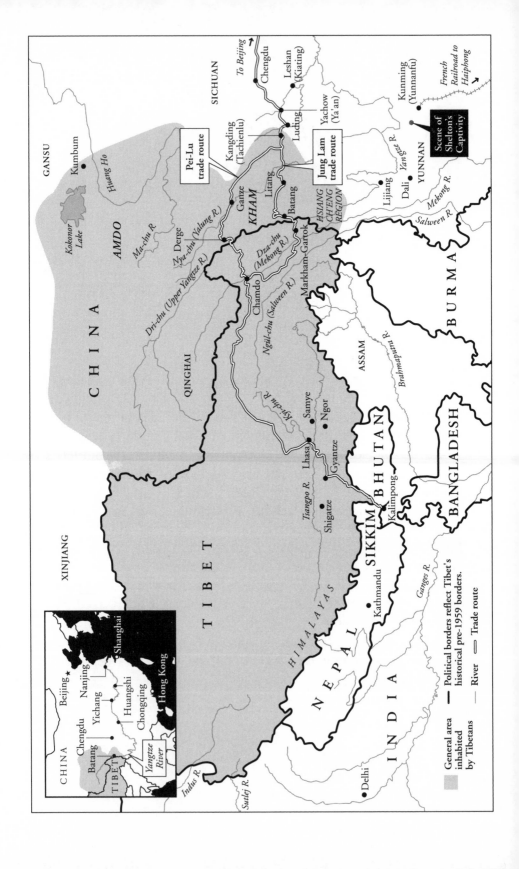

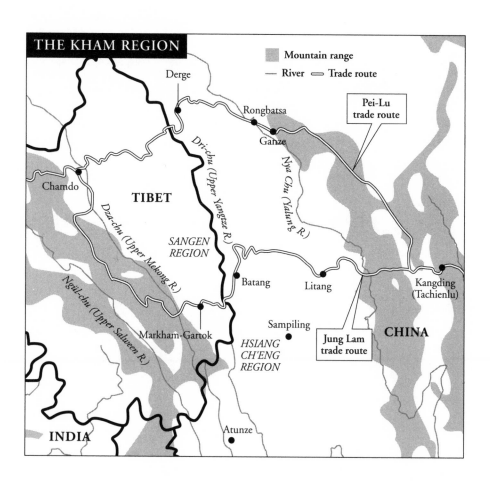

THE KHAM REGION

Mountain range
— River ⎯ Trade route

Derge

Rongbatsa

Ganze

Pei-Lu
trade route

Dri-chu (Upper Yangtze R.)

Nya Chu (Yalung R.)

Chamdo

TIBET

Dza-chu (Upper Mekong R.)

SANGEN
REGION

Batang

Litang

Kangding
(Tachienlu)

Ngül-chu (Upper Salween R.)

Markham-Gartok

Sampiling

HSIANG
CH'ENG
REGION

Jung Lam
trade route

CHINA

INDIA

Atunze

PROLOGUE

THE TRAIL TO TIBET, 1922

A man who can succeed is always the one sent. If there is nothing to be done, it does not matter who goes.[1]

—Tibetan Proverb

The Tibetan governor's emissary caught Dr. Albert Shelton's caravan waiting beside the swollen Yangtze River.[2] They were in the eastern Tibetan borderlands of Kham, a day's ride west of the Batang mission. Shelton was leading the caravan to Gartok to finalize his travel papers for Lhasa, the forbidden capital of Tibet.

The messenger explained that Lhasa sent new instructions, and the governor instructed his friend Shelton to turn back from the border. It was February 15, 1922. That night the group camped beside the turbulent river. The next morning Shelton turned his mule back toward Batang, accompanied by two Chinese soldiers, his Tibetan major domo, Gezong Ongdu, the deposed Prince of Batang's scion, Gwei Tsen Chi, and the Tibetan cook, Demnbajangtsen. Tibetan horsemen herded the pack mules with the jewels for the governor.

A land of soaring Himalayan mountains and deep river canyons, Kham was the fractious frontier between China and Tibet. Almost exclusively populated by bellicose Tibetan Khampa tribesmen, the California-sized region was the centuries-old battleground between the rulers of two ancient imperial cultures—the Manchu Emperor in Beijing's Forbidden City and the Dalai Lama in his thousand-room Potola Palace in Lhasa.

The Khampas were the holy warriors of Tibetan Buddhism. Until the imperial Chinese army invaded, Kham was an assemblage of more than thirty independent Tibetan kingdoms, principalities, and tribal and lama states. The unending conflict made Kham a wild and dangerous land where brigandage and battle were inextricably woven into a unique culture of warriors and monks. Decapitated heads ornamented the trees and gateposts. Severed hands festooned the government buildings. The Chinese and Tibetans skinned men alive, chopped them into chunks, boiled them to death in giant cauldrons.

In 1904, the Chinese launched a massive imperial offensive into Tibet. Dr. Albert Shelton and his schoolteacher wife Flora followed the Chinese bayonets into the eastern Tibetan borderlands, sent by a Christian missionary society. He was the first American doctor to serve the Tibetans, the only surgeon for many hundreds of miles. The Shelton daughters, Dorris and Dorothy, were born in the borderland, reared by Khampa nurses to speak Tibetan almost as their first language. Though Tibetan children were their playmates in the isolated Himalayas, the beribboned and primly starched Shelton girls were indistinguishable from their Midwestern counterparts half a world away.

In 1908, the Sheltons pioneered a mission in Batang, the town in west China nearest to Tibet. It was the most remote Christian mission on earth—six months' hard travel up the Yangtze River into the Himalayas from America. The mission post was also among the most dangerous, as Kham had long proved deadly to Christian missionaries. Incited by hostile Buddhist lamas, Tibetan tribesmen repeatedly attacked the mission stations. Time and again the Khampas tore the missions to the ground, leaving murdered missionaries in their wake.

But Dr. Albert Shelton was more than an extremely rural doctor with a very rough practice. He was also a famous adventurer. A homesteader boy who grew up in the frontier conflicts of the Great Plains, Shelton found the lawless hinterlands of Kham to be an oddly familiar environment. A native of Indiana, he descended from the rugged Scotch-Irish who pioneered both the bloody borderlands of the British Isles and America's violent Appalachian frontiers, another warrior tribe whose religion buttressed their martial zeal.

With his Stetson hat, Dr. Albert Shelton rode his faithful mule, Abe, more than fifteen thousand miles across Kham on journeys of exploration and medical relief. He and his entourage traveled heavily armed with rifles and revolvers. "Men not armed lose caste in Tibet," he said. All the while he chafed to get to the sacred city of Lhasa, barred to Christian missionaries for hundreds of years. Lhasa, nearly a thousand miles west of Kham, was the great unattainable goal of the foreign missionaries, "the last redoubt of Satan" where they ached to preach the Gospel.

By the time Shelton returned to the United States on furlough in 1910, the American public had already acclaimed him as an exotic missionary-explorer, comparing him to Africa's Dr. David Livingstone. While he lectured across America, throngs toured New Jersey's Newark Museum to view an exhibition of Tibetan "curios" that he acquired in war-ravaged Kham. The artifacts formed a stunning collection of Tibetan objects and religious art. Emboldened by the popular enthusiasm, the museum purchased Shelton's collection, inspiring him to continue his ethnologic work.

Following the Sheltons' return to Kham in 1913, the Batang mission grew to be a sprawling walled compound, anchored by the only hospital within seven hundred miles. It was a bastion of Western ideas in the heart of central Asia. Serving Chinese and Tibetans alike, Dr. Albert Shelton's gregarious nature and medical skill won him respect in both antagonistic camps. He counted as friends Chinese mandarins, Lhasa officials, and revered Tibetan lamas.

However, in the maelstrom of the borderlands, Albert Shelton still faced dangers. Tibetan bandits ceaselessly plundered travelers. Chinese brigands plotted abductions. Opium dealers whom Shelton had thwarted muttered threats of revenge. Cliques of Tibetan lamas were jealous of his growing power. British authorities in India plotted to keep missionaries out of Tibet at any cost. Endemic warfare between the Chinese and Tibetans threatened all in its range.

Yet another war erupted between the Chinese and the Tibetans in 1918. Trained and equipped by the British, the Dalai Lama's Tibetan army marched to the Chinese border to the wail of Scottish bagpipes. New Enfield rifles and mountain guns glistened in the high Himalayan sun.[3] The tattered Republican Chinese frontier army proved no match for the fierce and well-equipped Tibetan forces.

After a horrendous battle in the north of Kham, high Tibetan officials asked Shelton to hurry north to treat hundreds of wounded Chinese and Tibetan soldiers. Scores of surviving amputees soon testified to Shelton's marathon surgeries. He also helped facilitate a cease-fire between the warring sides. In recognition of his service, the thirteenth Dalai Lama sent a message permitting him to set up the first Western-style hospital in Lhasa—Dr. Albert Shelton's great dream.

Before Shelton could make his momentous journey to Lhasa, he needed to accompany his family to the China coast. Chaperoned by Flora, his now-adolescent daughters were returning to the United States for schooling. He also needed to escort his treasure trove of Tibetan artifacts through the anarchy of west China for shipment to America. After saying goodbye to his family in Shanghai, Dr. Albert Shelton intended to head to his destiny in Lhasa, but fate intervened.

During the family's months-long caravan trip through the disorder of Warlord-era western China, bandits kidnapped Dr. Shelton for ransom. As the Chinese army pursued the brigands through the Yunnan mountains, the kidnapping became an international sensation, front-page news around the globe.

When he returned to the United States for medical treatment, he was an international media star. The press and public acclaimed him a hero. Following his rehabilitation, he lectured to overflowing halls coast to coast, including enthusiastic audiences at the National Geographic Society. His book, *Pioneering in Tibet,* sold briskly, and the *National Geographic* made plans to publish Shelton's article, "Life Among the People of Eastern Tibet," illustrated with thirty-six of his photos.[4] When hundreds of Shelton's magnificent Tibetan objects arrived in New Jersey, the Newark Museum's curators planned an extravagant new exhibit. John D. Rockefeller, Jr. invited Shelton to a family dinner at his palatial Manhattan mansion, and Shelton capped the episode by selling the industrialist a thousand dollars worth of Tibetan jewelry.

The country feted Dr. Albert Shelton as an adventurer and explorer, an ethnologist and connoisseur, a devoted missionary and father—in short, a type of warrior-saint who embodied the sort of rough-and-ready, middle-class missionary militancy that America idealized. He was Daniel Boone, Wyatt Earp, and the apostle Paul rolled into one.

Financed in part by the sale of his collections, the Sheltons purchased an imposing home in the sunny southern California town of Pomona. Against the wishes of his wife, Albert Shelton again returned to Tibet, determined to reach Lhasa. Inspired by his example, four new missionaries traveled with him. After another arduous journey, Shelton's caravan reached Batang in late 1921.

Within a few weeks Shelton contacted the Tibetan governor, the Teji Markham, to arrange his Lhasa expedition. When Albert Shelton traveled to the governor's compound in Gartok, he hoped to get the final papers for his long-awaited trek to central Tibet. But Shelton never went where he wasn't permitted. When the Teji Markham instructed him to return, Shelton led his caravan back toward Batang.

Albert Shelton was at home again in the saddle, wearing his battered Stetson and old yak-skin riding pants, the seat worn from riding and the right knee polished from prayer. Ever ready for an impromptu hunt, his rifle rested in its worn leather scabbard. Sauntering along the high mountain trails, Shelton's big red mule scuffed up puffs of dust, now and again sending a stone skittering off the cliffs. In spite of the danger from bandits lurking on the mountainsides, the day wore on with the languor of a long ride. The local tribesmen valued his medical work, and Shelton had little fear of ambush.

Albert Shelton's life was in fine shape as he ambled along. Flora had overcome her initial terrors to forge a new life in Tibet. Nurturing a bond with Gezong Ongdu, she had devoted herself to Tibetan translation and was now in India to publish her work. Their daughters were safe in America getting an education. Only the day before he wrote an excited note to them about his upcoming Lhasa adventure, signing it, "love, Pappy." With his missionary work, journalism, and

Tibetan artifact-dealing, his family's finances were on a firm footing. The purchase of the southern California house gave the Sheltons a haven for retirement.

America was giving her best to him, groups secular and religious jostling to pay tribute. With the arrival of fresh missionaries, the future of his Tibetan Christian Mission was secure. Foremost on that day in February, Albert Shelton's obsession of ministering in Lhasa was soon to become a reality.

The caravan rode through the day, punctuating the ride with rest stops. About two o'clock they neared Khuyuk La pass, about six miles from Batang. After a stop, Albert Shelton mounted first and rode ahead of Demnbajangtsen. The trail started up the mountain, narrowing to a slender wisp high along a cliffside. As Albert Shelton climbed the mountainside to Khuyuk La pass, Demnbajangtsen wound through the little horseshoe-shaped Paimokou Valley below, about ten minutes behind.

Dr. Albert Shelton turned and whistled to Demnbajangtsen, waving for him to catch up. Demnbajangtsen signaled back and rode forward, but Shelton disappeared around a blind curve on the mountain. A minute later Demnbajangtsen heard three shots echo through the valley. Thinking the doctor had bagged some wild game on the mountainside, Demnbajangtsen cantered forward to help.

CHAPTER ONE

BLOOD OR BREAD

The Early Life of Albert Shelton, 1875–1880

There are lots of features about it that are lovely, but the racket and the rattle of it all is positively awful.[1]

—James Whitcomb Riley

On June 9, 1875, a young wife, Emma Shelton, gave birth to her first child, Albert, in an Indianapolis, Indiana working-class neighborhood. Her husband, Joseph O. Shelton, was a carpenter.[2] In his first years, Albert Leroy Shelton experienced the forces that dominated his life: the collusions and collisions of ethnicity, the turbulence of economic struggle, and the imperatives and compensations of frontier culture.

Indianapolis at the time was a taut little city on the prairie. Though dozens of smokestacks and church steeples picketed the skyline, the city gave way to farmland within a few miles of the downtown.[3] The population had swelled well past sixty thousand as European immigrants and displaced Indiana farmers migrated to the industrial city. The town was an amalgam of gracious neighborhoods and crowded worker's districts. On downtown Washington Street, slump-shouldered workmen passed silk-hatted nabobs. In the primrosed Northside households, domestics from Irish Hill cleaned as the fancy ladies sashayed out with their parasols and kid gloves.

The city had struggled through a rough winter with heavy snowfalls and plunging temperatures. Spring brought torrential rains and heavy flooding. It was a hot, dry, dusty summer, but Albert's mother had the good fortune to endure the last days of her pregnancy during a spate of mild weather. About a week after Albert was born, a sharp earthquake rattled the town.[4]

In 1875, Indianapolis was mired in the deep depression that followed the Panic of 1873, an economic paralysis that was thoroughly tarnishing the Gilded Age. The panic commenced a six-year depression that deflated prices and wages, the burden falling disproportionately on the working classes. In spite of the best efforts of national leaders, the panic rippled through the country including Indianapolis. It was a shock to a city grown accustomed to growth and prosperity.

The Civil War had irrevocably transformed Indianapolis from a sleepy agrarian state capital to a city intertwined with the fortunes of a rapidly industrializing nation. Indianapolis' central location and good railroad connections made it an essential hub of operation for the Union Army.[5] Indianapolis was a web of tracks, most heading east to civility and west toward the raw frontier. In 1869, archeologist Heinrich Schliemann, later the discoverer of ancient Troy, wrote, "12 great railroads come through this little town of 40,000 inhabitants and their number will increase to 15 before the end of the year. Three railroads go right by my house and the clanging of the trains arriving and departing continuously from early morning till late at night give evidence of the really colossal traffic on these."[6]

But the locomotives' shrill whistles also blew a dirge for Indiana's pioneer agrarian way of life.[7] With the railroads tying together the disparate markets of the United States, the market price for agricultural commodities was set hundreds, even thousands of miles away, subjecting independent farmers to the whims of a national market.[8] When farm produce prices rapidly declined and debt and interest rates mounted, many farmers abandoned the countryside and made their way to the cities.[9] Albert Shelton's parents were among them, joining a patchwork of diverse immigrants in Indianapolis. The streets of baby Albert Shelton's modest neighborhood were alive with a babel of brogues, drawls, and outlander accents. Over 70 percent of his neighborhood's population was foreign born, including Germans, Irish, English, Canadians, Scots, French, and Swiss.[10]

Something Close to Penury: The Panic of 1873

The Panic of 1873 began with a financial crisis in the money centers of the East and rapidly spread through the country. On September 25, 1873, the *Indianapolis Sentinel* headline read, "The Panic: The Wave Reaches Indianapolis."[11] Eventually a number of Indianapolis banks restricted withdrawals or closed.[12] In the Sheltons' working-class neighborhood a few miles to the south, it was a hardscrabble world of mean labor and miserly wages, devolving circumstances and hard choices. Families were evicted, reduced to eating cornmeal bought from feed mills and served without milk because there was none. By November a thousand men stood in the cold to apply for Indianapolis jobs, and throngs gathered to purchase cheap meat from the slaughterhouses, even refuse from the cutting tables. Workingmen's wages had doubled since the Civil War, but the panic quickly deflated them.

The Keynote of Courage:
The Disciples of Christ and Borderland Culture

A year prior to the crash, Albert's father, twenty-four-year-old Joseph O. Shelton, married sixteen-year-old Emma Rosabelles Belles in Morgan County, Indiana, where his family owned a farm. They said their vows before Minister John Phillips on March 14, 1872.[13]

Morgan County was an isolated region of rugged hills about thirty miles south of Indianapolis, a haven for yeoman farmers. It was just the latest stop for the peripatetic Sheltons, one of the westering families of the American experience. Starting in the East, the Sheltons, like Abraham Lincoln's family and thousands of other pioneer families, had steadily moved west generation after generation, crossing the Appalachians into the broad valleys and uplands of Kentucky and Tennessee. Joseph Shelton himself was born in Kentucky, as were his parents, before the family moved north to the rumpled hills of Morgan County in 1857.[14]

The Sheltons were devout Disciples of Christ, a denomination that rose out of the New Light Movement. It was a great revival of primitive evangelical Christian experience that ignited the central Ohio Valley around 1800. Disciples of Christ congregations had reached Morgan County by the late 1830s, becoming the leading church in some sections of the county.[15] The congregations were followers of evangelists Barton Stone and Alexander Campbell. Barton Stone was a Kentucky man with a slender face and prominent chin, a tousle of curly blond hair on his head. The Ohio Valley New Light revivals deeply influenced Stone. He promulgated a Christian ethos that was persistently primitivist, opposed to the corrupting influence of the contemporary world. Alexander Campbell was an anti-establishment Scotsman with deeply set, hooded eyes, sparse hair, and a patriarchal white beard framing a dour set of mouth. He incorporated a more rationalist viewpoint into his theology, mingling his Christian primitivism with a progressive outlook.[16]

The Disciples of Christ's antecedent, the New Light Movement, arose in the bloody borderlands of eighteenth-century Britain and Scotland. For almost seven hundred years, there was never fifty consecutive years of peace in the borderlands.[17] The centuries of warfare and violence shaped the culture, ethos, and social organization of the border folk.

Called Scotch-Irish when they came to pioneer the backwoods of America, the border folk of northern Ireland, the Scottish lowlands, and the barren hills and deep valleys of the British north country developed a warrior culture, buttressed by an agrarian economy and strong familial ties.[18] Given to an indulgent parenting and games of physical domination, the border people raised their male children with the aim of fostering a fierce pride, adamantine independence, and a warrior's determination.[19]

Calling themselves "People of the New Light," the border folk began gathering in the ferment of the early eighteenth century. Preaching their belief in "free grace" and prayer societies in open field meetings, they avowed an abiding faith in reform Christianity and a deep hostility toward the established churches and their clergy. The New Lighters' conflict with authority engendered a martial Christianity among the believers. With a bible in one hand and a weapon in the other, they successfully fought off the armies sent to suppress them.

By the eighteenth century, the border regions emptied as exile and emigration delivered a new style of immigrant to the docks of the mid-Atlantic American colonies—a people distinctly different from the Puritans and Cavaliers of earlier British migrations.[20] Soon the border people were heading for the back-country frontiers, where they served as a buffer between the Indians and the genteel, coast-clinging Quakers and Tidewater Virginians.

In time, the Scotch-Irish border people became dominant in a vast hill and mountain area that stretched from western Pennsylvania south to Georgia and west across the Carolina piedmont to the banks of the Mississippi. The Scotch-Irish continued their traditions of truculent independence in the southern uplands, their subsistence farms nurturing an obdurate streak of self-reliance. The American backcountry was contested territory when the borderers arrived, defended by the warrior tribes of Shawnee, Cherokee, Creek, Choctaw, and Chickasaw. The Revolutionary War added tinder to the fire, as the British used the tribes against the colonial interlopers threading through the Cumberland Gap. To the Scotch-Irish, the American hinterland was just another chaotic environment, not unlike the lawless one they had known in Britain and Ireland.

The martial spirit extended to the upper South's religion. Orthodox ministers bemoaned the disruption caused by the New Light believers. In their frontier evangelical camp meetings, the Scotch-Irish of the Appalachian hills interspersed prayers for vengeance and the conquest of enemies with sermons on the loving Nazarene. "Courage seems to me the keynote of our whole system of religious thought," one southern mountain woman stated.[21]

The Disciples of Christ in the upper South and lower Midwest eventually combined Barton Stone's and Alexander Campbell's two disparate streams of thought into an expansive world-affirming view.[22] In 1832, the Disciples of

Christ organized with the tenets of congregational governance, weekly observance of the Lord's Supper, and adult immersion baptism. There was a particular emphasis put on the liberty of the Christian individual and the autonomy of each congregation. The denomination called for preaching God's unconditional love for sinners as revealed in the teachings of Jesus Christ, unfettered by teachings outside the Bible such as Calvinist teachings of election and predestination. The Disciples believed that teachings received through faith ended the sinner's mutiny against God, which in time would result in Christian union, the worldwide conversion of unbelievers, and the beginning of Christ's millennial reign.[23]

In the course of commingling Campbell's and Stone's viewpoints, the denomination evolved distinctly ecumenical outlooks. Its members prized freedom and had a high forbearance for diversity and nonconformity. "In essentials, unity; in nonessentials, liberty; in all things, charity" was a characteristic Disciples phrase. Alexander Campbell's father, another Christian iconoclast, stated, "Where the Scriptures speak, we speak; where the scriptures are silent, we are silent."[24] Alexander Campbell once described his own work as a Disciples minister and editor as being part of "a species of non-descripts, oddities, and incongruities."[25] Ultimately the sect paid the price of tolerance with an exceptional amount of intradenominational strife over issues such as slavery, but the legacy of open-mindedness stood the Disciples in good stead as they encountered new and disparate groups.[26]

It was also a denomination that prized debate. In the early days of the denomination, the Disciples continually challenged their ecclesiastic counterparts—Methodists, Baptists, Universalists, Quakers, and Spiritualists—to engage in debate over a great number of theological questions. It was said Disciples converts carried as standard equipment a New Testament in their pocket and a chip on their shoulder. One Kentucky convert emerged from his baptismal immersion sputtering, "Now I'se ready for 'sputing.'"[27]

The lower Midwest, including the Ohio Valley regions of Kentucky, Indiana, Illinois, and Ohio, formed the core region for the Disciples of Christ. By the 1870s there were five Disciples congregations in Indianapolis, including the Third Christian Church attached to one of the denomination's colleges, which became Butler University in 1877. The university displayed the Disciples' increasing power and intellectual action, which included education, chautauquas, and an expanding Sunday school organization.

The Disciples' activities reflected the Gospel of the Middle Class promulgated by men such as the popular Protestant minister, Henry Ward Beecher, who mixed cultural activities, accreditation, and the accoutrements of the good bourgeois life into a Christian ideal.[28] In March 1876, Beecher presented his address, "The Ministry of Wealth," at the Indianapolis Opera House, trumpeting, "The whole tenor of the Old Testament pointed to the refining influence of wealth." Beecher declared that a man's wealth "should go first to benefit himself," to build a rich home, and to "bestow upon his wife and daughter and make a home of royalty. . . ." Later, Beecher declared a laborer should be ashamed if after twenty years of work he didn't own an unmortgaged home with carpets, china plates, pictures on the walls, and "some books nestling on the shelf [in] the sweetest place upon the earth."[29]

Blood or Bread: The Crisis of 1877

The aftermath of the Panic of 1873 proved to be an economic and social horror for Indianapolis.[30] Through Albert Shelton's infancy and early childhood, class tension and strife were endemic, strikes and lockouts common. Wages, days worked, and living standards plummeted, particularly among the working classes. Between 1873 and 1879, the average union carpenter in Indianapolis saw his wages fall from $2.40 to $1.43 a day.[31] Worse, laborers saw their work days drop dramatically as construction and industrial production declined.

Food and rent prices declined at a far slower rate than wage cuts, reducing the workers' already penurious standards of living.[32] The situation was particularly tough for working-class families with children. Childless working-class couples could maintain a comfortable if precarious lifestyle, but children changed the equation. Each succeeding birth brought increased deprivation.[33] Until their children reached working age, it was a rough existence. The Sheltons experienced firsthand the economic impact of a second child. Albert's younger brother, Fredrick, was born in 1879.[34]

As baby Albert celebrated his first birthday in the summer of 1876, Americans prepared to celebrate the centennial of liberty. Instead, the nation suffered continued trauma. The number of unemployed had risen to as many as three million, and, for the first time, America saw armies of as many as a million tramps and vagabonds drifting across the country. As the *Indianapolis Sentinel* dourly noted, "It was hard times yesterday, and will be tomorrow, but to-day is the Centennial Fourth of July."

But even as the newspapers lauded the celebrations the next day, they also reported the shocking news of the campaigns against the Indians out on the High Plains.[35] On July 5, 1876, the *Indianapolis News* had a telegraphed dispatch from Bismarck in the Dakotas headlined "Latest from Sioux Country," detailing the exploits of Generals Terry, Gibbons, and Custer on the trail of "about 3,000 Indians" in the Rosebud region. "The general impression prevails that the campaign will be a short, sharp, and hot one thereafter," the story read. "No serious casualties have occurred; the men and animals stand the march well, though the pack animals are badly chaffed."

But rather than leading another grand chase after bands of retreating Indians, General George Custer lay with his massacred and mutilated Seventh Cavalry on a sere hillside in Montana above the Little Bighorn, casualties of the immense body of Cheyenne and Sioux warriors assembled under Crazy Horse and Sitting Bull. On July 6, the paper reported "Custer's Disaster Confirmed."[36]

Economically, Indianapolis ended 1876 as badly as it started, with numerous failures and further wage declines. Even the State Fair failed financially, unable to pay the promised premiums to the ribbon winners.[37] But 1877 was even worse, proving to be the nadir of the depression. By 1877, eight railroads serving Indiana were in receivership.[38] Suicides increased, and the township trustees handed out relief money for food at a record pace.[39]

A few days before young Albert's second birthday, a crowd of five hundred laborers—some of whose families had not eaten in two days—gathered in the yard of the State House with radical rhetoric and calls for violence.[40] "Blood or Bread" was their cry.

Before the labor situation was defused, Indianapolis became an armed camp with thousands of troops and armed posses patrolling the streets. Sentries around the government buildings had to shoot. Infantryman dug ditches on the downtown Circle. Following the ban on open-air meetings, the cavalrymen cantered through eerily empty streets. After the hubbub, the city continued its dreary economic pace.[41] Wages had yet to cease spiraling downward, and life was getting harder for working families.[42] The reality was apparent: it was tough for a carpenter with a young family to get by in Indianapolis.

Health and Prosperity: The Call of Kansas

An alternative beckoned: the wide-open spaces of the American West, where there was bargain land for those who wanted to start a new life. The 1870s saw immense migrations to the West as cheap steamship travel and inexpensive railroad fares moved masses to America's thinly populated swaths.[43]

The Federal government's Homestead Act of 1862 granted 160 acres to any citizen, or even an aspiring one. With various preexemptions and legislative acts, homesteaders could acquire an additional 320 acres. The cost was a $10 filing fee and $1.25 an acre after six months. The homesteader had to establish residence within six months of filing and live on the acreage for five years.

In their great push across the country, the railroads had acquired immense plots of public land to support their investments, 400 million acres from the Land Grant Act alone.[44] In Kansas, the railroads held 10 million acres.[45] The rail companies knew they had to sell this land to create markets for freight and passengers to haul. In essence, the railroads became linear colonizers, peopling the endless strips of Western land with homesteaders dislodged by the Gilded Age's economic upheavals.

The railroads heavily promoted the virtues of the wide-open spaces of the West. They touted the salubrious, affluent life available for settlers there with periodicals, directories, tourist guides, timetables, and ever-persuasive representatives.[46]

Increasingly, the railroads through Indianapolis shifted their focus from hauling Eastern commerce to selling transportation and land to emigrants bound for the West. The Indianapolis and St. Louis Railroad advertised, "We carry our emigrants on fast express trains, in comfortable coaches," and provided Horton's reclining chair cars at no extra charge. The "Old Reliable Vandalia" line pledged, "Emigrants are carried on first-class trains, and are allowed two hundred pounds of free baggage to each ticket." In January 1879, a Kansas railroad, the Kansas City, Fort Scott, and Gulf, advertised land in eastern Kansas, "350,000 acres Comprising the Greater Part of What is Called the Cherokee Neutral Lands! In Bourbon, Crawford & Cherokee Counties, Kas." The brochure went on to read: "No other section in the West offers greater inducements to those seeking new homes and profitable investments. . . . Coal of Superior Quality and Inexhaustible in Quantity Found on almost every section, producing cheap fuel and an unfailing resource for profitable labor. . . . The climate is delightful, there is no better fruit region in the United States. Winter wheat, Corn, and all other Cereals, Tobacco, Hemp, Sweet and Irish Potatoes, and all other roots and vegetables grown in this latitude are produced here. School houses are already built in almost every school district, and churches are at convenient points."[47]

Presumably some part of the railroad's promotional plan must have reached Albert Shelton's father, because the 1880 Census enumerators found the Shelton family living on the eastern edge of Kansas in Pawnee Township, Bourbon County. The family settled on Cherokee Neutral Lands that J. O. Shelton purchased from the Kansas City, Fort Scott, and Gulf Railroad.[48]

Albert Shelton himself recalled precious little of his early life in Indiana and his first Kansas years. Years later he wrote, "When I was about five years old, my parents moved to Kansas, so I have no recollection of Indiana at that time at all except being in a boat one day with my father, and another time seeing a blacksmith shop." He recalled his father "who had gone through in a wagon, came down to meet my mother and us two children" when the family migrated to Kansas.[49]

Bert, as his family called him, his brother Fred, and their mother had traveled to Kansas by train, beginning their journey by passing through the columned porch that ran the length of the Indianapolis Union Depot, joining the other emigrants heading west on the Pennsylvania Railroad. They made the clackety, clattery, wind-blown journey to the Kansas border at the Missouri

River past a landscape of freshly broken farmland, interspersed now and again with the raw track-side views of railroad boomtowns. The West began just over the river.

During his Indiana years, Albert Shelton teethed, toddled, and grew into a boy among vibrantly different cultures. It was a period of violent economic and social conflicts. The disparities and differences of various peoples came with his mother's milk; the strife of class and race and hunger for land was part of his everyday experience. He grew up in an upwardly aspiring religious denomination that arose in the tumult of the frontiers. The Disciples gloried in cultural and religious differences as long as they had the opportunity to dispute and convince those with whom they differed. Born and bred in conflict, nurtured to expound the gospel, Albert Shelton was ready for his next lessons.

CHAPTER TWO

STRANGE COUNTRY

The Frontier Education of Albert Shelton, 1880–1893

Pioneers do not always go in lust of land; sometimes they go to satisfy their souls.[1]

—William Allen White

Like much of the American West, Kansas was a land of mythic romance and violent realities. Growing up as a Kansas pioneer boy, Albert Shelton spent his most formative years as the man of the house on an isolated high-plains homestead. From his youth, he knew the clashing conflicts and inspired borrowings of disparate cultures, as well as the soaring hopes and crushing defeats of life in an alien world. Ultimately, his boyhood experiences on America's last frontier prepared him for his wild life in the Tibetan borderlands.

The Sheltons experienced Kansas in all its variations, from the well-watered and timbered eastern edge to the high, stark, shortgrass country on the western border. The Sheltons' first Kansas home was about sixty miles south of Kansas City in Bourbon County, which abutted the Missouri-Kansas border at the eastern edge of the Flint Hills. About six hundred feet high, it was a land of broad river valleys and high uplands, with ample rainfall to water the silt soil and scattered forests, allowing an interplay of farm and town that resembled the Sheltons' Indiana life.

The Sheltons' Bourbon County land was twelve miles southeast of Fort Scott at Pawnee Station. Established by the Border Tier Railroad in 1871, the village stood on the former Cherokee Neutral Lands. Pawnee Station was a tiny knot of buildings perched on the prairie. The silver track curved in a great arc out of the village, coursing across an undulating empty green landscape. A low gray sky often hung overhead, carrying the rain that western Kansas settlers craved so badly in 1880. Eastern Kansas escaped the dreadful 1880 drought, though it desiccated the plains further west.[2] Bands of trees defined the fields and streams. Hillocks of rocks stood here and there on the landscape, harboring dens of rattlesnakes that sunned themselves on the stones.[3] The surrounding countryside was finely adapted to agriculture, making Pawnee Station a considerable entrepôt for the shipping of grain, hay, livestock, and produce. The bawling of cattle and steady knock of woodpeckers drifted in the rural quietude until the sound of the approaching train alerted the residents that civilization was on its way.[4]

Seven times a day, with remarkable punctuality, a Border Tier train whistled into Pawnee Station.[5] The railway station was a bastion of urbanism in a wholly rural setting; the train a rolling linear distributor of middle-class values—uniformity, orderliness, technological progress, and the structured rush of the industrial world.[6]

Pawnee Station, Kansas, where young Albert Shelton began his schooling, was the streets of southside Indianapolis writ small: the peoples of a heterogeneous world gathered in an unfamiliar place to make a new life together.[7] The one hundred inhabitants were mainly poor working people, many unsuccessful tenant farmers or laborers in their previous homes. While the majority of the Sheltons' neighbors were from the Midwest, settlers came from around the United States and Europe. The only ones native to Kansas were babes in arms and young children.[8]

The Sheltons' stay in Pawnee Station was a short one. Joseph Shelton bought his eighty acres of Kansas ground for $328 on August 18, 1881. Before he even traveled to Fort Scott to record his original deed and his mortgage to the Phoenix Mutual Life Insurance Company, Shelton sold the north forty acres to Mattie Muelin for $160 in December.

Less than four years later, on March 18, 1884, Shelton, his wife Emma, and Mattie Muelin sold the entire eighty acres—including the forty acres that was sold to Muelin—to Charles Chapin. The selling price was fifteen hundred dollars. The Shelton mortgage to Phoenix Mutual Life Insurance was paid off and released. Joseph Shelton had done all right as a land speculator.[9] By the time Charles Chapin recorded his deed, the Sheltons had already moved halfway across the state to Harper County on the border of Indian Territory.

Strange Country: Western Kansas

Throughout the last four decades of the nineteenth century, the western two-thirds of Kansas remained a separate place from the settled eastern counties, an austere land ravaged by frontier violence. Just west of the Flint Hills, the land began its shift from the well-watered climate of eastern Kansas to the semi-arid lowlands and plains of western Kansas, the tallgrass prairie giving way to the shortgrass of the high plains. The north-south axis at Wichita was the great dividing line of Kansas, past which rainfall was uncertain, nature less forgiving, and settlement precarious.[10]

When the railroad tracks inched across the grasslands in the 1860s, the western region was still the home of millions of buffalo and tribes of nomadic plains Indians. The Cheyenne, Kiowa, Kansas, Arapaho, and Comanche tribes battled to protect their homelands against the rising tide of white settlement. But the clang of spike hammers was the death knell of the tribes' nomadic culture.

The great buffalo herds of the plains, the key to Indian culture, became the fuel of the railroad work crews and the target of military men determined to defeat the tribes. In 1850, there were still at least twenty million buffalo on the Great Plains, and enormous herds still ranged the grasslands in the 1860s. As the railroad moved west, professional hunters contracted to supply meat to the construction crews, and the great buffalo slaughter was on. Buffalo Bill Cody, later famous for his Wild West show, alone killed 4,280 buffalo in eighteen months to feed railroad work crews. Hunters swarmed to the plains to decimate the herds, and the buffalo hides traveled back east to become the lap robes of America's Victorian-era gentry.

The Indians responded to the destruction of the bison herd and the growing settlements with violent raids. In spirals of increasing atrocity, white settlers defended their homesteads against Indian warriors defending their homeland. When Albert Shelton and his family arrived in Kansas, the strife between the Indian tribes and the white settlers was still part of plains life. The conflict wasn't a dry history that was a generation or two old as it was back east in Indiana and Kentucky.

Just four years prior to the Shelton family's move to western Kansas, tribal warfare again wracked the Kansas plains. By 1878, the buffalo slaughter and continued violations of treaty rights made western Kansas inhospitable to Plains Indian culture. The government had already removed most tribes to a bleak, arid banishment in Indian Territory. In the fall of 1878, Northern Cheyenne chiefs Dull Knife and Little Wolf escaped from their starving exile with a band of warriors and headed north to their homeland, hoping to reach the safety of western Canada. They cut across southwestern Kansas on their way to the northern plains, traveling as many as seventy miles a day.[11]

The Indians eventually killed forty-one, raped dozens of females from eight years old up, and destroyed property worth a hundred thousand dollars. The soldiers finally captured the Cheyenne band in western Nebraska, herding them into captivity at Fort Robinson, where sixty-four died in an escape attempt. The government eventually tried seven leaders and returned the remnant to the reservation. One Kansas victim, Margaret Smith, wrote Kansas governor John St.

John in 1881, "For I think it is pirty hard that I was brot out in a strange cuntry and my husband killed and taking my teem a way from me and left with a large family of children and nothing to seport them with it is hard for me to git a long now with out some help on the account of the drouht. . . . I neede something and I live in a place that everybody has all that they can do to take care of them self."[12]

In 1882, Indians escaping north from the reservations again galvanized Kansas. The state sent guns and ammunition to settlers, as government troops pursued the renegades. The Indians crossed the railroad west of Garden City headed for the Colorado border, where the soldiers forced their surrender. While the 1878 Cheyenne raid proved to be Kansas' last great Indian battle, the settlers continued to fear another uprising. The warfare scarred the state's psyche for many years, leaving a legacy of violence in western Kansas that prepared Albert Shelton for the brutality he encountered on the frontiers of inner Asia.

Hard Cases or the Better People: The Kansas Cattle-Drive Years

The slaughter of the buffalo also precipitated Kansas' fabled cattle-drive era, when frontier tumult captured the popular imagination. As the bison herds disappeared in the early 1870s, cowboys began herding Texas longhorn cattle north to the railheads strung along central Kansas. Bottled up by the Civil War, the Texas herd had grown to a prodigious size, and there was a burgeoning urban market in the East.

With the coming of the railroads to Kansas, a product and a market came together. A thousand dime novels were set in the cow towns of southwestern Kansas during years of the great drives, fixing the region in American mythology. When Illinois livestock shipper Joseph G. McCoy arrived in Abilene in 1867 to look for a central Kansas railhead, only one of the town's dozen log huts had a shingle roof, and the place was so poor the saloon keeper raised prairie dogs to supplement his income. Within four years, more than seven hundred thousand steers passed through the boomtown, and seventy-five bartenders worked around the clock seven days a week, with little time for prairie-dog breeding.[13]

The cow towns of the Kansas plains proceeded to sprout one after the other along the route of the railroad as railroad workers laid track across the state. As a river of cattle arrived beside their shiny new tracks, Abilene, Ellsworth, Caldwell, Wichita, Hunnewell, and Dodge City each in turn became the boomtown terminus. In May 1874, the *Wichita Eagle* described the typical cow town:

It is a motley crew you see. Broad-brimmed and spurred Texans, farmers, keen business men, real estate agents, land seekers, greasers, hungry lawyers, gamblers, women with white sun bonnets and shoes of a certain pattern, express wagons going pell mell, prairie schooners, farm wagons, and all rushing after the almighty dollar. The cattle season has not yet fully set in, but already there is a rush of gamblers and harlots who are "lying in wait" for the game which will soon begin to come up from the south. There was a struggle for awhile for which should run the city, the hard cases or the better people. The latter got the mastery, and have kept it only by holding a "tight grip." Pistols are as thick as blackberries.[14]

Kansans such as Wyatt Earp, Bat Masterson, and Doc Holliday served as lawmen in the rough Kansas cow towns, becoming fodder for the journalists' juicy stories as much as far-flung foreign missionaries such as Shelton did for another generation of newspapermen. English journalist Henry M. Stanley, famous for glorying missionary Dr. David Livingstone when he found him in "Darkest Africa" a few years later, was one of the roving reporters on the frontier looking for heroes.[15]

Civilization, religion, and the law crept into western Kansas in small, tottering steps. Dodge City was still a one-street plains town of prefabricated buildings when the Philadelphia *Record* editorialized in 1877, "Its best people are Puritanical and the rest Satanic—the one class being as disagreeable as the other is dangerous."[16] By 1882, Dodge City was a small city of twelve hundred with four churches, a two-story belfried school, an imposing courthouse, rival newspapers and hotels, and a few dozen blocks of residential neighborhoods neatly laid out with sturdy houses.[17]

When the Dodge City citizens of propriety began to enforce an 1883 "Ordinance for the suppression of Vice and Immorality within the city of Dodge" to eliminate prostitution and gambling, there was a furor at the Long Branch saloon. Owner Luke Short had a gunfight on Front Street with an arresting officer. Wyatt Earp and Bat Masterson, who both had drifted west after being Dodge City lawmen, returned to town to help their old friend Short. The two gunmen returned again at the next election to insure the good citizens didn't dominate the polls.[18] For Albert Shelton, this teeter-totter between law and disorder presaged the alternating cultural stability and anarchy of the Tibetan borderlands.

As the Sheltons made their way across the plains in 1884 to join the rising flood of homesteaders in west Kansas, the wildest days of the old West were over. The buffalo slaughter of the Great Plains herd was essentially complete, and with it the days of the free-ranging Plains Indians tribes. Alarmed by the rise in Texas Fever in the Kansas herd, the Kansas legislature prohibited in 1884 the further importation of Texas cattle during the traditional cattle-drive season, ending the Texas cattle drives. Homesteaders began to flock to southwestern Kansas and fence the immense open range.[19]

Tallgrass Home: Harper County

The first years of settlement were bleak for most of the homesteaders on the plains—most likely the most difficult homesteading experience on the entire American frontier.[20] It was the sparsest of settlements on the most monotonous of landscapes, and the intense isolation and unending vista were a heavy burden for people used to more populous and varied locales. Many settlers habitually climbed on their house roofs in hopes of seeing another soul from the high point.

Droughts parched the plains, followed by howling blizzards that froze both cattle and settlers. The relentless wind from the south gave the original Indian inhabitants their name, the Kansa—"people of the south wind." Fierce windstorms surged out of the plains and every part of the pioneers' fragile houses would groan.[21] Ignited by the lightening strikes, prairie fires regularly swept the land, traveling a hundred miles in walls of flames. Rain barrels and hope were the settlers' only weapons to defend their homes. Even walking on the plains could be a danger, as lightening and rogue storms could strike down the unwary.

Plagues of grasshoppers swept across Kansas, desolating immense swaths of the western regions.[22] Rattlesnakes were common. Children wandered off into the trackless plains, sometimes never to be seen again. Rampant disease carried away adult and child alike—diphtheria, dysentery, scarlet fever, cholera, even influenza were among the killers. Farm and gun accidents took their share. Rabid wolves, skunks, and dogs posed a constant threat.

In a rough borderland world dominated by men, women were the primary civilizers. Their appearance on the frontier was often seen as the beginnings of order and community. They were the moral arbiters, the educators, the precipitators of pioneer churches, camp meetings, and, as the pioneering phase gave way to settlement, denominational conventions. The women were often the most enthusiastic supporters of missionary societies, both home and foreign.[23]

The Sheltons arrived at their new home of Harper County a few years before the west Kansas boom. Railroads ignited a land rush, and populations doubled and redoubled during the next few years. The county sat at the western edge of the tallgrass prairie near the center of the state, with enough rainfall for sustainable agriculture. The years of 1886 and 1887 were abnormally wet years for western Kansas, and farmers harvested bumper crops. Wild speculation inflated the value of southwest Kansas land, and towns across the plains boomed. As the new towns mushroomed, so did the need for carpenters such as Joseph Shelton.

Albert Shelton and his family lived for five years in Harper County. On January 21, 1885, Joseph and Emma Shelton filed a land office receipt at the courthouse in Anthony for a homestead claim of 160 acres near the tiny hamlet of

Ruella, about eleven miles southwest of Anthony. They paid $200 in cash for the land.[24] The farm was on generally level ground with gentle swales and broad open vistas of the prairie around it. A band of trees followed the meander of Plum Creek that ran just adjacent to the Shelton property. The altitude colored the skies a brilliant blue in the blazing summers. Winters brought snow that dusted the bare gray landscape.

Like Pawnee Station, Ruella was on the railroad. Four times a day passenger trains arrived at the large depot. There was a store, blacksmith shop, post office, and several residences.[25] A few years after their arrival, the Sheltons' farmhouse was still the only structure on their property.[26] Other neighbors had prospered with barns and orchards and multiple houses for tenants set in rows of catalpa trees.

Bert Shelton continued his education in a country school near the hamlet. To some extent, his attendance was testimony to the importance his family placed in education. In Harper County's twenty-four frame schoolhouses, fewer than half of the schoolage children attended classes.[27] As in many rural regions, a local girl about sixteen years old served as schoolteacher.

Later Bert Shelton was part of a small gang of ten- and eleven-year-old-boys whom the young teacher had trouble handling. "One day," Shelton wrote, "she told us not to go near the creek, which was near the schoolhouse, but five of us slipped off and went in swimming." Frontier discipline prevailed, and the teacher sent an older girl to gather switches. "We considered that she got them unnecessarily large," Shelton wrote. With the five transgressors laid out on the floor, the teacher proceeded to switch the first. "When she drew back the switch the boy let out a tremendous yell which frightened her and so took her from her frame of mind that she only gave him four licks. As she had only given him four licks she could only give the rest of us four licks, so we got off easily." Shelton's father wasn't so easily deflected and he promised the boys they would get a like amount of licks at home each time they received them at school. "This promise he faithfully kept," Shelton recorded.[28]

As Albert Shelton learned his letters, the novel *Ben-Hur: A Tale of Christ*, written by Hoosier General Lew Wallace, was setting records for sales. Published in 1880, the book was the story of a Christian missionary in the pagan world of ancient Rome. With its vivid scenes of chariot races, "a Roman orgie," suppurating lepers, "the arts of Cleopatra," and pilgrims and martyrs, the book tantalized and titillated hundreds of thousands with visions of foreign lands and Christian glory. By 1893, 88 percent of public librarians across America still ranked *Ben-Hur* as the most-requested book. It went on to become the best-selling novel of the nineteenth century.[29] Bert Shelton was among the avid readers who traveled through the book to the Jewish, Roman, Antiochean, and

Christian worlds of the Mediterranean and discovered the romantic possibilities of the missionary life.[30]

By the middle of the nineteenth century, missionaries were popular heroes.
When Dr. David Livingstone returned from the heart of Africa, he received a
gold medal from the Royal Geographical Society and spoke to overflow crowds
at lecture halls across England. His every activity was headline news. The inspiration to become a missionary often came not from the Bible but rather from romantic biographies and tales of travel to remote and exotic lands. *The Last Voyages
of Captain Cook* inspired William Carey, the father of British missions, to become
a foreign missionary.[31] In the late nineteenth century, publishers cranked out
dozens of highly embellished missionary adventures, such as *Adventures of Missionary Explorers* and *Bishop Patteson of the Cannibal Island.*[32] Martyrdom and suffering were glorified.[33] The highly colored tales popularized the missions and
spurred countless adventurers into the field. Though Christianity was central to
their worldview, missionary volunteers were seldom religious zealots. Rather, they
were often enthusiastic young people who were attracted to an exciting life in a
far-off land, far from their mundane lot back home.[34]

The Sheltons found Disciples of Christ on the plains. The Disciples of Christ
had gone west with the frontier, arriving in Kansas in 1855 and holding their
first state convention two years later, where they formed the Territorial Missionary Society.[35] The Harper County seat of Anthony also had a Disciples of
Christ congregation, which began in 1882 with services in the town's one-room
schoolhouse.

The winter of 1886 was legendary on the plains, bankrupting cattlemen
across western Kansas as blizzard after blizzard left carcasses piled in the aftermath. It was "the most perilous experience prairie people ever encountered," the
Wichita Eagle wrote. The Sheltons just missed the economic crash. Wheeling
and dealing, J. O. Shelton sold their farm and used the profits to purchase more
Ruella land.

The Last Frontiers: The Shortgrass Country

When Bert Shelton was about twelve, his family headed further west, traveling
by covered wagon from Harper County to a homestead in far southwestern
Kansas' Grant County. "It was great fun for us children," Shelton remembered.
"We had four horses to the wagon and just before leaving my uncle completed
my happiness by giving me a little Flobert rifle and a thousand rounds of ammunition. So far as I could see there was nothing else to wish for in this life, and
under my father's direction I was allowed to shoot morning and night at such
things as might be available around camp."[36]

It was two hundred miles from Harper County to the shortgrass country of the west Kansas borderlands, partially along the meandering wagon tracks of the old Santa Fe Trail.[37] With high hazy clouds floating overhead in a bowl of blue sky, the Sheltons traveled through the immense landscape of the Cimarron River region, the thin strip of river purling past red rock formations and pale-brown bluffs.

Only a decade before, southwestern Kansas was still the buffalo commons, crisscrossed with deep ruts of the migrating herds. Buffalo wallows, where the herds rolled to shed their woolly coats, still dotted the plains, becoming sparkling little lakes after the occasional rains. Gnarled cottonwoods followed the riverbeds. Partridges and quail exploded from the brush. Wildflowers burst into bloom and painted the earth. Josiah Copley, who traveled through western Kansas in 1867, pronounced the landscape "as unique is it is stupendous."[38] Albert Shelton, who seldom waxed lyrical about a landscape, wrote that west Kansas was "a very beautiful country, perfectly level, covered with a solid mat of buffalo grass, and not a tree within many miles."[39]

The high plains of western Kansas were part of America's last frontier.[40] The U.S. Census defined the frontier as the margin of settlement with a density of two or more people per square mile at the edge of free land, and by 1880 it found there were few places left in the country that met that standard. With its meager population and available homesteading land, Grant County, Kansas, was still the frontier in the late 1880s.

As with many aspects of the American West, academics and journalists saw great import in the frontier. Historian Frederick Jackson Turner gave his momentous address, "The Significance of the Frontier in American History," in 1893. "The frontier is the line of the most rapid and effective Americanization," Turner wrote. Even as he prematurely proclaimed the frontier closed, Turner and his many popularists saw in that narrow zone the crucible of the American character. "It strips off the garments of civilization and arrays him in the hunting shirt and moccasin," he said of the frontier's impact on the pioneers, who, in Turner's view, used their American competency and frontier skills to wrest a civilization from the wilderness.

Turner's short address became a paradigm of American thinking, influencing a wide spectrum of politicians, editors, and theorists who incorporated it into the canon of popular thought. As the nineteenth century waned, American imperialists searching for a credo brushed Turner's frontier thesis onto a global canvas. They saw modern American pioneers prepared to civilize the world and in turn maintain their own cultural virility.

While Turner explained the frontier's impact on man, he failed to comprehend the repercussions of men on the frontier. In a larger ecological sense, the arrival of the railroad and the destruction of the buffalo impacted the Great Plains far more than the relatively small numbers of humans who migrated there. Shaped by his Anglo-Saxon viewpoint, Turner couldn't visualize the human tragedy of failed European and Eastern American technologies and social structures. In a real and wrenching way, the Sheltons experienced the failure of pioneering life in a land environmentally hostile to it.

The Sheltons also experienced the frontier confluences that Turner failed to see, the commingling of people and culture in a land where terms such as mestizo, mixed-blood, and half-breed were part of the everyday parlance. The West was a scene of great borrowing and sharing, interchange and cultural evolutions. In the process, the frontier both destroyed and fertilized cultures. The Plains Indians owed the flourishing of their horse culture to escaped Spanish horses. American cowboys melded the horse-based expertise of Hispanic *vaqueros* with imported Yankee technology. Dressed in their *chaparajos,* the cowpokes rounded up cattle with their *la riata* into corrals, aided by Yankee-manufactured barbed wire, windmills, and the quintessential American tool, the Colt .45 from Hartford, Connecticut.[41]

While the far west of Kansas in the late 1880s was one of the few places left in America for homesteaders yearning for free government land, it was a horrendous place to try to wrest a living from the earth—pioneering at its abysmal worst.[42] The settlers faced the problems of choosing the right land, fighting an intractable bureaucracy, and fending off rapacious merchants, bankers, and railroadmen. Homes on the treeless plains were most often "soddies"—upturned sod walls of buffalo grass stacked around a hole dug into the ground. The environment of Southwest Kansas was semi-arid, unsuited to Eastern agriculture as settlers practiced it. Even sod busting the buffalo grass took special heavy-duty plows. The high plains were far too dry, occasionally too wet, and always too unpredictable to make life easy. Add to that the physical rigors of finding fuel and farming under an unmerciful sun in a harsh desiccating wind, and homesteading was a recipe for heartache.

The new Shelton homestead was eleven miles northeast of Ulysses, the primary town of the region.[43] George Earp, first cousin to the lawman Wyatt, organized Ulysses in 1885, giving away the town lots for free or close to it in the early days.[44] By 1887, the brand new town was scattered about on the buffalo grass plain. There were fifteen hundred people in the town, four hotels, twelve restaurants, twelve saloons, six gambling establishments, an opera house, a bank, and a collection of houses in various states of becoming—another boomtown for carpenter J. O. Shelton. "Hundreds of Buildings Being Erected in Ulysses—A Large Number of Carpenters in Great Demand," the Grant County *Republican* headlined in May 1887.

Ulysses was the raw frontier and determined gentility mixed together. Over at the two-story Hotel Edwards, mounted cowboys with Montana hats and lassos on their saddles chatted with rifle-toting Gibson Girls lounging on the ginger-breaded porch.[45] The Palace Pool Parlor sold fine brands of cigars, along with crab-apple cider, though a sign warned, "No intoxicants sold." The Grant County Meat Market had fresh and salt meats on hand, as well as antelope, buffalo, and game. The Cyclone Daily Stage Line advertised its routes, "Stopping at Wonderful, Astonishment, Surprise, Amazement, Ulysses for dinner, Zionsville, and Woodsdale, arriving at Hugoton at 6:00 P.M." Purcell, Carr, and Co. of Lakin, Kansas, touted homestead mortgages: "Money to loan on final proofs!"[46]

The Grant County *Republican* trumpeted the wonders of Ulysses, a local prejudice that was pervasive among west Kansas papers. "Lots still Going and More Influence and Wealth tacked on the banner of Ulysses, the Embryo County Seat of Grant and the Shining Star of the Southwest," a February 1887 headline breathlessly read.[47] "Seventeen Business Houses to Be Erected in Ulysses within Thirty Days," the paper crowed in early 1887. "Ulysses! Gaining Rapidly in Growth and Population. Hotels Crowded—the Excitement Does Not Abate," read a headline in April 1887.

But it was a cruel winter in 1887-1888, with the temperature at thirty below in January. In mid-March a wild blizzard blew in from the north and froze the quails, robins, snowbirds, and meadowlarks that had been lured north by a thaw. Come spring the children found the frozen corpses in the hedgerows.[48] Undeterred by the weather, the local citizens petitioned the state of Kansas to incorporate itself as Grant County in 1888. The petition stated that there were twenty-five-hundred bona fide citizens and four hundred were householders. Among the signatures was that of J. O. Shelton.[49]

The Shelton homestead was located at the nearly uninhabited eastern edge of Grant County on an endless vista of softly curving earth. The four thousand feet of altitude gave a sharp tang to the air. No watercourse or trees interrupted the view. In the spring, green grass stretched as far as the eye could see, dotted with millions of wildflowers. There was the smell of earth under a pale blue sky, and the endless south wind carried the calls of the birds. Antelope and a few wild herds of mustangs still raced across the landscape.[50]

Water was a constant problem on the plains, with watercourses dry most of the year and little water close to the surface. The Shelton homestead was no different. "During the years spent on this Homestead," Albert Shelton wrote, "I was growing very rapidly and took a share of the work. One of my jobs was to haul water. We could not afford a well, as it was some two hundred and fifty feet to water and cost a great deal of money to dig, so I hauled water from Conductor, a little town some six miles to the west, where there was a township well."

Shelton drove a team of two oxen to the well, hauling five of the family's water barrels. Sometimes as many as twenty or thirty teams awaited access to the well. And many times, races to the well determined who waited and who hauled their water home. "It is not easy racing with an ox team but it can be done," Shelton confided.[51]

Perhaps nearby Conductor was a hopeful name, because the railroad never came through Grant County while the Sheltons lived there. Given the Sheltons' previous choices of land near the railroads, perhaps J. O. Shelton speculated the tracks would arrive. Each year the newspaper boomed that the railroad was just over the hill, but like so many things promised in west Kansas in the late 1800s, it never came to be.[52]

While waiting for the train to arrive, J. O. Shelton spent the week working as a carpenter in Ulysses. The responsibilities of the farm fell to his wife, Emma. Many homesteader women in their dugout houses found the life abhorrent. A west Kansas woman wrote: "The awful monotony was killing. There was nothing to do, nothing to see, and no where to go, and should we have attempted to go anywhere we would have become lost, for there were only a few dim trails leading to the claims of a few settlers, so we women crept about from house to house. There was no hurry; we had all the time there was. Our conversation each day was a repetition of that of the day before and always concerned the awfulness of living in such a desert, when the wind and sun had full sweep. . . . It was a time to try women's souls. I never heard the men complain, and as a sect, I was sure they did not require much to satisfy them."[53]

Bert Shelton was a pioneer boy, focused on the small world of his family and the homestead. The children of the plains were often blithely unaware of the discomforts and travails, seeing the land as a source of wonder and delight, not an empty cask of failed dreams. They quickly adapted to their new lives and, like Albert Shelton, cherished the memories of their west Kansas childhoods. "The pleasantest recollection I have of pioneer days in Western Kansas," wrote an elderly lady who was a child on the plains in the 1880s, "is the memory of the prairie in springtime with the green grass as far as one could see dotted here and there with millions of beautiful wildflowers."[54]

With the men often gone from the farms, homesteading on the west Kansas plains melded gender roles and gave children extraordinary responsibilities and flexibility. Tales of twelve-year-old girls helping their mother give birth were not uncommon. Life was hard, but the plains experience often gifted children with iron wills and a faith in their abilities.

Young Bert spent his free time hunting small game for the bounty that was paid. Gophers, ground squirrels, skunks, jackrabbits, and coyotes fell to his little Flobert rifle, and Shelton earned a bounty of five cents for smaller game to a dollar for the coyotes. He wrote, "There were one or two occasions when I took my scalps to town on Saturday and to bring my father home after his week's work in town at carpentry, on which my earnings for the week were equal to my father, which made me very proud."[55]

Unwelcome guests often shared the homesteaders' dugouts—bedbugs, fleas, and snakes, including the thick-bodied, short-tempered prairie rattlesnakes that occasionally dropped from the ceiling onto the kitchen tables.[56] Luckily, Bert Shelton had a hobby: "My avocation in those days was killing rattlesnakes. There were a great many and I saved all the rattles, at one time having a cigar box full."[57]

His schooling continued on the high empty plains. He would leave before daybreak in the wintertime, walking four miles to the neighborhood school through the cold, cutting wind. Later, the Sheltons and neighboring home-steaders organized a dugout school, presided over by a local girl.

J. O. Shelton continued to speculate in land, but after two years of good rain in 1886-1887, the drought began in 1888 and continued in 1889. Crops failed and banks went bust. By the summer of 1889, the bottom had dropped out of the west Kansas land boom, and the region's newspapers were filled with columns of delinquent tax rolls. Mortgages were in arrears, and most real estate taxes in the county were delinquent. As it did to many Kansans, the de-pression pulled the Sheltons into court. In April 1890, the mortgage holder on the Shelton's old homestead in Ruella sued Joseph and Emma Shelton in Harper County. When the Sheltons had sold their farm, they passed their mortgage to the new owner, who couldn't make the payments. They lost the land to foreclosure.[58]

As homesteaders abandoned the land, populations plummeted, some coun-ties losing half their population in four years. Settlers flooded back east "to see the wife's folks," as the saying went. Grant County rapidly lost people—the local paper claimed the "boodlers" and "boomers" of 1888 had moved on.[59] From the apex of 2,500 during the boom in 1888, 1,308 residents remained in Grant County in 1890. When the 1900 census came through, only 422 were left.

Hard times continued in Grant County as people fled crushing mortgages and bad memories.[60] After a few years of heady speculation and growth, west Kansas settlers suffered the bitter realities. Nature reasserted her hegemony—the semi-arid environment of western Kansas could not support a large farming population with Eastern-style agriculture.[61] Western Kansas appeared best suited for the vast migrating herds of American buffalo and the nomadic peo-ples who followed them.

In the midst of the maelstrom, Bert Shelton spent a few winters studying in a Ulysses school, "which had given me a greater desire than I ever had before to attend school." He also lived one winter with his maternal grandmother in Anthony, probably another case of "going to visit the wife's folks." While in Anthony, he studied under a schoolteacher named Miss Preston, who made a lasting impression on him. For ambitious young people like Albert Shelton, teaching in a country school was often the only path open to higher education and the professions. Teachers encouraged their best students to pursue the certification necessary to teach in the one-room schools that dotted the plains.[62]

The summer following his seventeenth birthday, Shelton graduated from the county Teachers' Normal Institute, one of the bare-bones programs in which teachers learned the basics. Self-supporting through modest state funding, the county institutes were extremely cheap, allowing poor farm boys like Bert Shelton to gain proximity to education and the ideals of professionalism. Albert Shelton did just fine in the teachers' institute, passing his exam on July 1891 with grades that ranged from 40 for Grammar to 90 in Arithmetic, Physiology, and Hygiene. In August 1892, he took the exam again, raising his score to an average of 80 with an 85 in Grammar.[63]

By 1892, Bert Shelton was already active in Christian activities. An 1892 letter from the Ulysses First Presbyterian Y.P.S.C.E. recommended him: "You will find him to be a genial warm heart, an earnest character, and has a sincere desire to show his colors on the Lord's side. . . . He has been an interesting, useful and consistent member of the Y.P.S.C.E. . . . We trust he may find an ample opportunity to continue in the work of Christian endeavor wherever he may cast his lot."[64]

Early in Grant County's settlement, Disciples of Christ erected a sod Sunday school. As the bust devastated the settlers, they abandoned their soddie for church meetings in various locales.[65] In the winter of 1892, Disciples evangelist Eric Newby and his son H. W. held a revival meeting in the Ulysses schoolhouse. They faced a dispirited and cynical group. It was two weeks before the first sinner stumbled forward for confession. Eric Newby was so discouraged that he cried when he returned to his lodging that night, convinced the meeting should close the following night. His son implored him to go on for another week. During the next two weeks, eighty-five Christians came forward for baptism. Albert Shelton and his brother were among them.[66] On January 28, 1893, the congregation gathered on the cold plains outside of town at a bend of the Cimarron and witnessed a missionary minister immerse Albert Shelton and the others in baptism.[67]

The next winter Albert Shelton taught his first school in the Cimarron grasslands about twenty-five miles south of Ulysses. Morton County paid Albert Shelton $25 a month for the four-month term. School boards often preferred male teachers to handle the winter term when the older boys arrived for their schooling.[68] For the first time in his life, Albert Shelton was in position of some authority and esteem, second in respect only to the local judge and ministers in his frontier world.[69]

Shelton taught the standard curriculum of reading, arithmetic, writing, and spelling, with lessons in grammar, history, geography, literature, and physiology in a murmur of overlapping recitations, with the older children helping the younger ones with their lessons. *McGuffey's Reader,* with its combination of morality, history, and classical learning, played heavily in the construct of rural education.[70] Naturally, some of the learning was "taught to the tune of the hickory stick."[71]

Once a month, when weather allowed, Bert Shelton walked the twenty-five miles back home to Ulysses, leaving after he dismissed the students in the afternoon.[72] Following his first year of teaching, Shelton clerked for his uncle sixty miles north of Grant County in the tiny town of Leoti, spending his free time hunting antelopes and chasing wild horses.[73]

But Albert Shelton was not to be a small town merchant or a high plains schoolteacher. The lessons of self-sufficiency and resolute respectability took hold. In the fall of 1895, when he was twenty years old, Bert Shelton left the shortgrass country for the Kansas State Teachers' College in Emporia. He later wrote, "It was a great undertaking and no one knew what would be the outcome."[74]

CHAPTER THREE

GOOD TOWNS AND
TIBETAN DREAMS

Respectability and Romance, 1895–1903

My life is not worth too much and even if it was it couldn't be given for a better cause.[1]

—Albert Shelton

Bert Shelton arrived in 1895 at Kansas State Normal in Emporia with $9.25 in his pocket—"That lasted me for eight years," he wrote. The 1895–1896 K.S.N. catalogue listed Albert Leroy Shelton from Ulysses, Grant County, in the C Class. To his fellow students, he was "Shelly," a friendly, hard-working rustic who favored a wide-brimmed hat with a red bandanna around his neck. Though he was a frontier homesteader, his classmates considered him a genteel fellow, never rough in speech or manners.

Emporia in eastern Kansas was a plump prosperous town, the townspeople pleased with their accomplishments and sure of their values. Writer and town newspaper editor William Allen White wrote a facetious essay summarizing Emporia for the State Normal yearbook, *The Kodak:* "Every town in Kansas is noted for something. Topeka is noted for her boarding houses. Atchison for her smart men. Wichita for her joints, Lawrence for her history, but Emporia is noted for being a *good town.* There are ten thousand people—more or less—in Emporia, and there is not, among the ten thousand, a confirmed drunkard, not a budding criminal. The police court has not contained the name of a woman on the record of office for three years. There has not been enough money collected by the police department to pay for the axle grease of the fire department." White concluded his Emporia homily by stating, "It rises at eight and goes to bed at nine, never is happy unless asleep."[2]

The town maintained an inordinate pride in its two institutions of higher education. The College of Emporia, a Presbyterian school, opened in 1882. The state legislature founded the Kansas State Teachers' College in 1865, which became Kansas State Normal. K.S.N. was a "Normal" school, adhering to a teacher-training curriculum that had its roots in France. The term referred to the teachers' acquisition of society's highest standards of behavior, or "norms."[3]

The main college building housed eighty steam-heated rooms that were lit by gas and electricity and guarded by an electric watchman system. Enormous windows flooded natural light into the building's high-ceilinged, airy rooms that included drawing and music rooms, a well-equipped gymnasium, and new laboratories for the natural sciences. The college boasted a library housing over twelve thousand volumes and touted the Albert Taylor Hall as "the finest auditorium in the state."[4] A local and long-distance phone system connected the campus to Emporia and the world. It was a far cry from the dugouts and rough-sawn, one-room schoolhouses of Shelton's experience.

After the genial though impecunious young man arrived from the shortgrass country, one of Kansas' famous storms blew the roof off the main college building on September 8, 1895. The storm caved in the upper part of the north wall and deluged the building with over eight inches of rain in the next few hours. The lower floors flooded with water, and then the plaster fell with a sodden thud. Everyone was pressed into service to clean up. Bert Shelton stayed on the job all night, leaving just in time to change his clothes for 8:40 chapel.[5]

By the mid-1890s, the school was relatively flush with state appropriations. The college offered free tuition to all students such as Shelton in the teaching, or Normal Department, and a rebate to the student if his or her railway fare exceeded $3. The college contended it was a "fine temple for the instruction of teachers of common schools" that promoted "the highest welfare of the student, physical, mental, and moral" with a "firm but mild and parental" administration.[6] The school's 1,735 students could find furnished rooms renting from $4 to $6 a month, and board in nearby private houses for about $3 a week. To stay in school, Bert Shelton needed to find about $35 to $75 each semester for books, board, fuel, and laundry, a substantial amount for a poor farm boy.[7]

Albert Shelton wrote, "During the years while I was in Emporia, I carried the *Kansas City Star*, I did janitorial work, I cut corn, I took care of cows, I took care of furnaces for some of the professors, and after I had finished the course in mathematics, I did a great deal of tutoring for Professor Bailey."[8] The student newspaper remembered that Shelton always "worked with untiring zeal even though many times he was entirely warnout [sic] with the long days of work. He often worked into the night and started again at three o'clock in the morning."[9]

Bert Shelton had a soft heart for helpless animals. At one point, he took care of eight cats that he rescued from the Normal physiology classes, feeding them in the back yard of a local woman he knew through the Christian Church. Even as a young man, people noted Albert Shelton's concern for others. One of his bosses, C. A. Boyles, recalled, "He always said he wanted to be a missionary to the hardest field in the world—some place where no one else had gone."[10]

The Kodak yearbook of 1898 captured the German Club, two dozen students clustered together for the camera. Most looked to the foreground or away from the cameraman, except one dark-haired dandy in the second row, curtly identified as "16. Shelton," who looked forthrightly at the lens. His hair was fashionably slicked into a small pompadour, and he sported a large black mustache that dashed past his lower lip—a desperado's mustache, or perhaps that of an adventurous sheriff.

Come Back Next Winter: War and Romance

The K.S.N. spring term began on February 2, 1898. Bert Shelton took time from his studies to write a letter to a young woman named Flora Flavia Beal, with whom he had been corresponding for a few months. A fellow Hoosier whose family had also migrated to Kansas, Flora Beal was the daughter of a prosperous farmer. The family farm was located near Parsons in the region of ample water in southeastern Kansas. She was a few years older than Albert, born on September 28, 1871.

As a child she was baptized into the Presbyterian Church and later was baptized into the Brethren Church. She continued her sectarian journey by being baptized into the Methodist Church as well. Like Albert Shelton, Flora Beal's early education was in Kansas's country schools. She attended high school in Cherrydale and Independence, Kansas before attending K.S.N. Like Shelton, Flora was also a Kansas schoolteacher.[11]

Bert wrote to Flora, who was teaching the winter term back in her home county, "I rec'd your letter several days ago and how glad I was to get it. . . . I read it twice without stopping and I won't tell how many times I've read it since then but more than a few." Anxiously he inquired about her plans: "Will you come back next winter? I hope you will for I expect I will be here until I am 80 or 90 years old probably."

Albert Shelton was twenty-three years old, in his third year of juggling several jobs to pay for his room, board, and books while slowly making his way through college. His grades were excellent, ranging from the high nineties in math- and science-related subjects to the low eighties in Music, Latin, and Penmanship. He was active in his church and a host of student clubs.

Early in 1896, a nasty struggle between Cuban rebels and their Spanish colonial overlords began to catch America's attention. For various reasons—political, humanitarian, and economic among them—increasing numbers of Americans decided it was their job to intervene. President McKinley, always ready to lead by following the crowd, gave Congress the opening it wanted to declare war in 1898. Led by the jingoism of the yellow press, Americans quickly caught war fever, as did Bert Shelton. "During those strenuous years, in 1898," Shelton wrote, "the war with Spain came on. Against the advice of friends and professors I enlisted in Company H of the 22nd Kansas, which company consisted of students from the three State institutions." According to the roster, one Albert L. Shelton of Anthony enlisted on May 6, 1898.[12]

Before leaving for active duty, Bert wrote a short note to Flora, and handdelivered it to her in Emporia. He wrote, "My Dear Flora, I have your dear flowers here by my side now as I write. . . . I will see you again so I can give you what I have for you. Will you promise to take it Flo? It's no snake!" A smitten swain, he signed off, "From one unworthy but who will strive to ever be true, Yours, Bert."

Two days later Flora wrote to her soldier fiancé, "Such a strange beautiful world you have led me into, I have been trying to realize that I am *myself*." A few times she referred to "my little ring and I." As her beau trundled toward the war, she wrote, "The thunder is sounding out of doors and it makes me think of *cannon;* merciful heaven why cannot such questions be settled without the surrender of human life & the shedding of human blood!"

The same day Albert wrote to Flora's parents asking for her daughter's hand in marriage: "Well, I never could make a speech so I'll not try it now. But here's what I want. Won't you please grant it? Flo promised to be my wife at some future time and now I want your consent and blessing for me. . . . Hoping to receive a favorable answer at no very distant date. I am yours, Bert Shelton."

Amidst her rhapsodies, Flora began a refrain that lasted through much of their life together: "Oh, Bert, please don't make so much of my little life, it was such a wee thing to give to a noble man that I haven't gotten it into my head yet, why he wanted me, and what he ever intended to do with me after he gets me." Bert was equally in love, writing from Camp Leedy in Topeka: "I knew my eyes were looking right out from my soul but I couldn't help it. And yet I didn't want you to know I loved you for I was afraid you would surely be pained and that it would put an end to our delightful friendship instead of drawing us closer. . . . But O Flo I could hardly believe my ears as I looked into your dear eyes and heard your words. And O Flo I do hope I can teach you to love me just a little as the days go by."[13]

Kansas contributed four regiments to the "splendid little war," including the Twentieth Kansas Volunteers, who fought Emilio Aguinaldo's Filipino insurrectionists in the postwar actions. The regiment returned to Kansas in glory, marching into Topeka to a thirteen-gun salute, a nine-band parade, and a reception and banquet reportedly "staged by 75,000 persons."[14]

Albert Shelton's Twenty-second Regiment began its military career by traveling by train to Topeka's Camp Leedy, where officers mustered the men into the army. Bert Shelton wrote the college company cheer to Flora Beal:

> O! Manilla Dead and gone!
> O! Manilla Come no more!
> O! Manilla Why didn't you run
> When you saw old Dewey with his gatling gun
> O Cuba! you shall be free
> When?!!!
> In the morning!!!

Now an urbane college man, Shelton intimated to his fiancée that the "farm boys" couldn't do the concerted yell: "it sounds so funny to hear them try."[15]

In late May, Bert wrote Flora about marching off to picket duty to the sound of martial music: "The band is playing now I can imagine men marching to the music to meet in deadly battle. . . . But who couldn't go to death to the 'wild grand music of war.'" Putting aside his fear and foreboding, he wrote the coda of his life: "The only thing to do when on duty is to obey orders." At the end

Figure 3.1   During the Spanish–American War, Albert Shelton served in H Company of the 22nd Kansas Regiment, comprised of volunteers from Kansas colleges. Photograph courtesy the Still Family Archive. Reprinted with permission.

of August, he wrote to Flora on tiny scraps ripped from a small ledger book: "You ask 'why will I enlist?' Because Flo I want to always be on the sides of the oppressed and helpless people and I couldn't stay at home and do nothing when I have a chance to lift my arms in defense of some poor half starved man woman or child of Cuba. Stay? NEVER! . . . My life is not worth too much and even if it was it couldn't be given for a better cause."[16]

Discussions of mission work began to creep into their letters. Flora mentioned Shelton's letter to the missionary supporter publication, *Christian Endeavor.* He wrote to her about Christian missionaries in the biblical novel, *Quo Vadis,* and a self-sacrificing Christian doctor in a lachrymose little volume entitled *Beside the Bonnie Briar Bush.* "Dr. McClure in the 'Bonnie Briar Bush' is the richest man I ever read of," he told her. The missions held less allure for Flora Beal. She wrote about friends in the Salvation Army: "I would much rather stay at home than stand down there on the street."[17]

At the end of May, Shelton's company entrained for Camp Alger, Virginia, but the war was already receding as Spain rapidly collapsed. The citadel of Santiago fell in mid-June. For a generation of young men raised on their fathers' Civil War exploits, it was a bitter disappointment to miss the defining moments of battle.

After the regiment underwent two months of incessant drill and other military instruction at Camp Alger, the troops marched fifty miles through the Virginia countryside to Thoroughfare, Virginia, camping on the way at Burke's Station, Bull Run, and Bristow. Albert Shelton wrote of "weary steps."[18] Officials held the Twenty-first and Twenty-second regiments in readiness, but events outpaced the troops. By late August, the regiment was on the move again, but away from the war. After about six months of enlistment, the army mustered Shelton's regiment out of service. Demoralized by the lack of glory, Shelton dispiritedly wrote Flora about his discharge without action. He told her he had sold his pistol, "so you needn't be afraid I'll shoot myself."[19]

By September 9, 1898, the regiment was back in Kansas at Fort Leavenworth, where the officers gave the soldiers thirty days leave. On November 3, 1898, the Twenty-second Regiment, Kansas Volunteer Infantry, was discharged, including Albert L. Shelton of Anthony.[20] Shelton returned to Emporia with some military training, transcontinental travel experience, and about a hundred dollars in savings.

The Adventurous Professional Man

Albert Shelton prepared to complete his college education with a little monetary cushion. "I put it in the First National Bank on Friday and on Monday the president shot himself, the bank having failed. However, I was in no worse condition than I had always been," Shelton recounted. He wrote a perky note to Flora, who was then living and teaching back home in Labette County: "The First Nat. Bank failed today at 12:30 that was interesting for Mr. Boyles and his brother had all their money in and sweetheart it also got mine for I had deposited there as soon as I got to Emporia Ho Ha! Not a very safe place was it?" He went on to describe the bank president closing the doors and driving out to his farm where he put a .38 caliber Smith & Wesson revolver to his temple and pulled the trigger. "Poor man he could not face poverty among those by whom he had been known as the wealthiest man in the community. It's awful awful but enough of this." Only then did Shelton mention he had no money to visit her at Thanksgiving.[21]

The loss of money must not have disheartened him, because the next spring the couple completed plans for their wedding. On April 21, 1899, he wrote Flora, "Unless something of which I do not know now happens this is the last letter I'll ever write to Flo Beal."[22] Later that week he took two days off to travel to Parsons, Kansas, where he married Miss Flora Flavia Beal on April 27, 1899.[23] Their wedding photo showed a slender bride in a high-necked crêpe de chine dress with wire-rimmed glasses perched on her serious face. A youthful groom with a pompadour and handlebar mustache looked expectantly at the camera.[24]

The young couple returned on the evening train to Emporia, where a crowd of four hundred students awaited them at the station, having "mysteriously" heard about the wedding. "Amongst them were three or four of my former comrades in Company H, armed with a blanket," Shelton remembered, "and they proceeded to blanket me right there on the platform." Blanketing consisted of flinging Shelton ten or twelve feet in the air and letting him fall back in the blanket. Unfortunately, they failed to make a catch and Shelton fell to the floor, stunned but no worse for wear. After the friends succeeded in injuring the bridegroom, they proceeded to devour the balance of the wedding cake the new Mrs. Shelton had brought, while "embarrassing us to the limits of their ability." The schoolmates made it up to the newlyweds by presenting them with two rocking chairs.[25]

In 1900, Shelton obtained a scholarship though the good graces of K.S.N. President A. R. Taylor to attend the medical department of Kentucky University in Louisville. Unfortunately, Shelton was in such financial straits, he couldn't take advantage of the scholarship. One day as Shelton worked at his school janitorial job, his supervisor, C. A. Boyle, asked, "Well, Shelly, what are you going to do about that Medical School?" Shelton replied, "Well, Boss, it isn't any use thinking about it because it can't be done." That afternoon Boyle appeared

Figure 3.2 Albert Leroy Shelton and Flora Flavia Beal married in Parsons, Kansas on April 27, 1899. Photograph courtesy the Still Family Archive. Reprinted with permission.

in the little room where Shelton was working and laid a check for $100 on the table. "Now get out of here," he said. "I don't want to see you around here any more." C. A. Boyle wrote a letter of reference for Albert Shelton, which read, "He is faithful and strictly honest and will do whatever he is told to do."[26]

The summer following graduation from K.S.N., Shelton put in hard labor to pay back the money he owed C. A. Boyle. Traveling like a tramp in boxcars, he had to borrow money from a friend to get home after he was thrown off a train. "But the big thing was done—I was out of debt again."

Shelton's medical school, Kentucky University, was an outgrowth of Bacon College in Georgetown, Kentucky, the first institution of higher education founded by the Disciples of Christ. The medical school had a faculty of sixteen, who, the school bulletin assured, were all "thoroughly competent, harmonious, and industrious." The school claimed its medical courses were taught with "the latest and best appliances and apparatus for laboratory work." The catalogue's Board of Curators' statement read, "It assures the medical profession, as well as the general public, of its hearty cooperation and support of its faculty to it untiring efforts to elevate the standard of the medical education."[27]

The study of medicine was Shelton's second choice. He wrote, "During these early years, I had a desire to be a preacher, but I had decided I wasn't good enough to be a preacher, so I had decided to be a doctor, the alternative as I thought, and the next best thing by which to live a life of usefulness."[28]

Flora had good cause to be wary of missionary life, particularly in China, which had the greatest concentration of American foreign missionaries. The nation's press thundered about the increasingly rebellious Chinese, and ministers bemoaned the depredations visited upon the Christian missionaries. The American consul wired Washington that Chinese were stalking the missions to spear sleeping women and children.[29]

The anti-foreign Boxer Rebellion began to convulse north China in 1899. The next spring, a Boxer placard appeared near Beijing's crowded foreign quarter that read in part: "The will of heaven is that the telegraph wires shall be first cut, then the railways torn up, and then shall the foreign devils be decapitated. In this day shall the hour of their calamities come."[30]

From all over northern China, missionaries and Chinese converts fled to the high walls of the Beijing foreign legation. Thousands of Chinese soon assailed the legation, where five hundred foreigners defended several thousand Chinese and foreign civilians. It eventually took twenty thousand foreign military to lift the two-month siege. Across China, the Boxers killed two hundred and fifty foreign missionaries, including fifty children, as well as thirty-two thousand Chinese Christian converts.[31] America's inflamed media smeared the gory details across the nation's front pages.

With his hopes for Spanish-American War heroism thwarted, Albert Shelton saw the foreign missions as offering him a substitute test of courage. Flora accepted his need, writing, "I do not fear your ever telling that you have lost all your manhood for you will *never* do that. And Bertie please don't let me be always alone, I will not, could not let you go alone, either the downward road or one of advancement. O darling please take me with you 'ever the ends of the earth. . . . '"

Albert did well in his first years of medical school, receiving high grades in Chemistry, Anatomy, and Materia Medica, though struggling a bit with Physiology, Morbid Histology, and Clinical Pathology. His senior year, he had stellar grades: all A's except for a B in Gynecology.[32] He paid his way through medical school with the aid of the scholarship and by tutoring chemistry. Flora taught for two of the years Shelton was in medical school.[33]

In October 1902, Albert and Flora Shelton traveled to Omaha, Nebraska, to attend the Disciples of Christ international convention. The keynote speaker was the famous missionary adventurer, Dr. Susie Rijnhart, who talked about her arduous escape from Tibet four years before. When she returned to America in May 1899 to trumpet Christian evangelization in Tibet, Rijnhart quickly became a celebrity.[34] Churches and conventions clamored for her lectures, and in 1901 the missionary publisher, Fleming H. Revell, published her book, *With the Tibetans in Tent and Temple,* to widespread sales.[35]

Tibet and the Travails of Dr. Susie Rijnhart

To the Christian missionaries at the turn of the century, Tibet represented the great apostolic challenge, a satanic coven of mythic dimensions that shimmered in their imaginations. For more than five hundred years, the impenetrable city of Lhasa was their grand obsession, their idée fixe, the itch they couldn't scratch. Long before Western emissaries and military men braved the Himalayan passes onto the high plateau, their religious compatriots had pioneered the routes through Tibet, enduring horrific hardships and risking martyrdom to preach there. From the west, the missionaries struggled through the Indian Himalayas to try to pierce the cordon that surrounded Lhasa. From the east, they struck from Silk Road caravan cities in China's far northwest, plodding across the bleak wastes of northern Tibet toward the city of dreams. From China's southwestern provinces, the missionaries planned their most dangerous approaches, daring the violent trade routes that ran across the wild eastern Tibetan region of Kham—the passage that Dr. Susie Rijnhart survived.

That night in October 1902 Rijnhart told her rapt audience about her adventures in Tibet, a harrowing mission that changed her life forever. A Canadian medical doctor, prim, pale Rijnhart had dreamed of becoming a foreign missionary. In 1895, she and her husband, Petrus, opened a Christian mission on the northwestern Chinese border with Tibet, near the immense Tibetan lamasery of Kumbum. While on an arduous caravan journey to forbidden Lhasa, she, her husband, and their year-old son, Charlie, encountered tragedy. First, baby Charlie died of altitude sickness. They buried his tiny body with his hands clutching a bunch of wild asters and blue poppies at the foot of the bleak Dang La mountains.

After being turned back by Tibetan guards a few days from Lhasa, the Rijnharts stumbled back toward China through anarchic eastern Tibet. Tibetan brigands attacked them and drove off their horses. The next day, Petrus spotted a nomad camp across a river and decided to swim across for help. Changing clothes, he walked toward the river. "Then he followed a little path around the rocks that had obstructed our way the day before, until out of sight," Rijnhart recounted, "and *I never saw him again.*"[36]

Susie Rijnhart made it back to China, surviving the privations and dangers of the long journey with pluck and periodic brandishing of her large revolver. When she arrived at a recently established Christian mission in the border town of Tachienlu, she was barely recognizable as a woman or a Westerner.

At the talk, she recounted the funeral of baby Charlie: "Around the little grave we three gathered, and with a burial service in the native language the body of the first Christian child was committed to the bosom of bleak Tibet." Rijnhart glorified her husband's death: "Unknowingly he went to his death, for he was murdered by those from whom he hoped for help. Brave and good, devoted to the people, his martyr's death has been a benediction to many, and a missionary incentive to thousands who have, through his tragic death, heard for the first time, of the needs of Tibet."

She concluded with a ringing cry for support: "The first work of the Disciples of Christ is to give the Gospel to a lost world. . . . Our societies have both the opportunity and fidelity, but they must have the support of a great people to do their work. We have one million three hundred thousand members. . . . This will probably be my last appeal to a large body of Disciples. A year from now, if not in less time, I hope to be among the nomads of Tibet. Both opportunity and fidelity are my possessions through Him whose work I do. Yours is the opportunity also. The fidelity, is it yours, too?"[37] One can only imagine the impact of the speech on Albert Shelton's missionary dreams and his wife's attendant fears.[38]

The Disciples of Christ and its Foreign Christian Missionary Society responded with a ringing endorsement. The missionary society gave Dr. Susie Rijnhart an appointment to Tibet in November 1902, and the Iowa State Disciples Convention presented her with $600 for surgical equipment for her medical work. Missionary society leader C. T. Paul wrote in 1903 about Rijnhart's mission: "She will open a hospital and school at Ta-Chien-Lu, an important town on the Chino-Tibetan boundary, having mail facilities and a telegraph office."[39] In February 1903, the *Christian-Evangelist* reported, "The Foreign Society is to open a pioneer mission among the Tibetans this year. This work needs the hearty support of the brethren. May I ask that the readers of the Evangelist will, on the Sunday in March, remember this needy field prayerfully and liberally."[40]

C. T. Paul announced Dr. Susie Rijnhart's mission in the *Christian-Evangelist* in May 1903: "It is hoped that the foreign society will be able to complete the Tibetan party by August, and that Dr. Rijnhart and her co-workers will set out on their long journey to Ta-chien-lu, an important town on the Chino-Tibetan boundary, where they will at once begin their ministrations in the cause of the gospel. Gradually, it is hoped, they will be able to establish other stations in the interior, along the great caravan route to Lhassa."[41]

Albert Shelton again pondered the call to a life of Christian action—this time as a medical missionary. There continued to be resistance from his wife. In May 1903 he wrote a note to Flora Shelton about the call to mission: "You do not like the peoples, etc. Yet they have the spark of the divine and are beautiful in there."[42] During his third year in medical school, he applied to the Disciples' Foreign Christian Missionary Society in Cincinnati, a leading American missionary organization. The society president, Archibald McLean, informed the Sheltons by letter that it was impossible to send any more missionaries into the foreign fields that year.

Albert Shelton graduated from the Kentucky University Medical Department in 1903 with an Allopathy degree, the medical system that utilized a variety of disease treatments. Dr. Albert L. Shelton's medical school graduation picture shows a confident young man, dressed in a tuxedo and white tie, still looking clear-eyed and forthright at the camera.[43] With the door to medical missionary work in China closed, Dr. Albert Shelton determined to form a medical partnership with Dr. J. H. Henson of Mound Valley, Kentucky, and strike out on his career.[44]

But his path soon changed. Shelton sent a letter in June 1903 from Louisville to his friends back in Grant County, Kansas, offering warm greetings. He then wrote, "As you see I will graduate in Medicine July 3rd, and then I will return to Kansas for two months. Then I will go to China where I've been appointed as a medical missionary to take charge of our hospitals there. I wish I could visit Grant County before I have to go but I suppose it will be impossible to do so."[45]

The Perfect Apprenticeship

Albert Shelton had the ideal education for his life on the Tibetan border. Of course, his medical training gave him a profession in great demand in the remote hinterlands. But his learning extended far beyond school subjects. His boyhood and early manhood had helped him to accept hard labor and strenuous physical activity and sometimes to revel in it. He learned a broad range of skills—construction, farming, foraging, hunting, soldiering, and teaching among them—and a philosophy of self-reliance to go with it. He saw diverse cultures annealed together in conflict and cooperation.

The triumph of the Spanish-American War gave Albert Shelton faith in the rising glory of the West, and America's celebration of middle-class respectability gave him an ideal to strive toward. The Disciples' expansive style of frontier religion gave Albert Shelton a model of evangelism, and his parents' militant

Christian activism offered him a vision that would sustain him his entire life. Kansas also gave him his life mate, a woman of the prairie who knew hard work and who accepted his romantic dreams of a mission.

Shelton learned adaptability on the plains of Kansas, and knew the human tragedy of inappropriate cultural forms in an inhospitable land. If the high plains gave him nothing else, they gave him a tolerance for ambiguity and the streak of stubbornness that characterized those who eked out a living there. Albert Shelton had earned his spurs on the frontier of the American West, and in the process had developed a taste for the wild parts of the world.

JOURNEY TO THE BORDERLANDS

From the Midwest to the Himalayas

Up and up we go, and to the Kansas bred the mountains seem very high.[1]

—Flora Beal Shelton

The Foreign Christian Missionary Society appointed Albert Shelton as a medical missionary with the words, "Well, Doctor, you're going to China." His first post was Nanking (Nanjing), a bustling inland port on the Yangtze River.[2] Still excited by Dr. Susie Rijnhart's exhortations for Tibet, the posting deflated Shelton a bit, but FCMS secretary F. M. Rains told him, "Don't get discouraged. Remember the Lord's not dead yet."[3]

When Dr. Albert Shelton accepted his post as medical missionary to China, he joined a select company. From ports of the South China Sea to the western frontier of the Himalayas, from the bleak plains and Great Wall of northern China down to the steaming rice paddies of the south, there were only three hundred medical missionaries in the country.[4] Yet Shelton became part of a vast, centuries-old, intercontinental enterprise involving thousands of missionary workers in the field and supported by millions of Christians in Europe and the United States.

Christianity in China dated back to the Nestorian Christians, who arrived from Syria via the Silk Road early in the seventh century. After two hundred years, there were a few thousand converts, mostly foreign traders along the frontiers.[5] It wasn't until late in the sixteenth century that Western curiosity and technological breakthroughs precipitated organized missionary work.[6] The Jesuits were the first to proselytize at the Manchu imperial court in Beijing.[7] Only a half-century before, the Manchus had overthrown the decaying Ming dynasty and founded the dynasty known as Qing—"pure."[8] Using Western scientific discoveries as an entrée, the Jesuits came to hold high technical and scholarly positions in the Manchu government.

The emperor officially approved Christianity in 1692, though his successor revoked consent in 1724. For the next century and a quarter, Christianity in China functioned as a secret religion. There were estimated to be three hundred thousand practicing Christians in 1705, dwindling by 1830 to less than two hundred and fifty thousand despite a massive increase in the Chinese population. Without an evangelical upsurge, Chinese Christianity probably would have drifted into oblivion within a few generations.[9]

In 1807, Robert Morrison of the London Missionary Society stepped on the docks of Canton (Guangzhou) as the first Protestant missionary. Americans began arriving in Canton in the 1830s, still fired by the Second Great Awakening that had ignited the Ohio Valley and the founders of the Disciples of Christ. Confined to the trading ports of Canton, Macao, and Hong Kong, the Protestant missionaries had baptized only about a hundred Chinese by 1840—primarily mission employees or students.

The treaties following the Opium Wars of the 1840s dramatically changed the missionaries' situation as they happily followed the Western bayonets with their bibles. While the Opium Wars treaties contained no provisions that directly addressed missionaries, they benefited from certain clauses. The British annexation of Hong Kong and the opening of five treaty ports allowed the missionaries to expand on the mainland, and extraterritoriality gave missionaries immunity from Chinese laws. While missionary work in the interior was still illegal, the worst an arrested missionary could suffer was transport to the nearest consul.[10]

With the protection of the unequal treaties, the foreign missions expanded through the 1850s. After the French military invasions of 1857–1860, the Chinese signed the Treaty of Tientsin, part of which removed all strictures against Christianity from Chinese law. Because of the most-favored-nation clauses in the treaties, the Protestant missionaries, though barely on speaking terms with the Roman Catholic priests, were able to take advantage of the same rights.[11] Once the mission societies planted themselves on Chinese soil, they became small bastions to be defended with all of the Westerners' powers.

By the last years of the century, the industrialized powers had effectively carved up China into spheres of influence with the "Open Door" policy that allowed all outside powers equal access to the booty. The American advance into the Far East after the Spanish-American War further captured the imagination of the American missionary public. The missionaries took advantage of the opening. Using Western organizational expertise, the mission societies transformed themselves into the first modern large-scale multinational corporations, with China as their largest market.[12] Throughout the nineteenth century, Western missionary investment in China far outstripped merchant investment.[13] Americans alone were contributing more than $5 million annually by the turn of the twentieth century to spread the Christian gospel to the Chinese.[14] At the time, there were four times more American missionaries in China than there were other Americans.[15] "Whenever on pagan shores the voice of the American missionary is heard," said the American missionary leader J. H. Barlow, "there is fulfilled the manifest destiny of the Christian Republic."[16]

By the time Flora and Albert Shelton headed for the Orient, a swarm of Christian religions and denominations competed for Chinese converts. Five Roman Catholic orders divided China, while sixty-nine different Protestant sects maintained China missions, including the Disciples of Christ, which arrived in 1886.[17] By 1905 the Protestant societies supported a total of 3,445 missionaries in China, 90 percent of whom were British or American. Despite a century of enormous investments and heartrending work, the Chinese continued to resist the call of the missionaries. By 1900, there were only about a hundred thousand Protestant and seven hundred thousand Roman Catholic converts in China—far less than 1 percent of the total population.[18]

American missionaries like the Sheltons were primarily products of small towns and rural backgrounds. They found China shared much with their previous lives: an illiterate peasantry, a mixture of peoples, and an agricultural pace that coexisted with a bustling urban one. But with little knowledge of the East save lurid tales, Sunday school homilies, and perhaps a traveling performance of *The Mikado,* missionaries were hard pressed to see China as little but a Sodom and Gomorrah of heathen idolaters.

As a college-educated medical man, Dr. Albert Shelton joined a new breed of missionaries who incorporated the new scientific discoveries into a more modernist theology.[19] Seldom philosophers or theoreticians, missionaries were practical people, determined to Christianize the Chinese one way or another. Aggressive and self-confident, they hurled their Western challenges at the ancient creeds and customs of the Orient.[20]

To the Tibet Border

While visiting with Flora's family in Kansas before leaving for China, a letter from F. M. Rains caught up with them, asking if they would accompany Dr. Susie Rijnhart to the Tibetan border instead of taking the post in Nanjing.[21] "As a matter of fact, Tachienlu sounded little farther than Nankin to us," Flora Shelton recalled, "and we telegraphed we would go."[22]

Dr. Albert Shelton must have seemed an ideal candidate for the difficult Tibetan post—young, dedicated, and hardened by the American frontier. His FCMS medical examination confirmed his robust condition, and the doctor said, "If this man's qualifications in other lines are as good as they are physically, he'll be all right, because he's the best animal I've seen in a long time."[23] Flora Shelton was less certain about the missionary appointment, favoring her husband's proposed medical partnership in Kentucky. She had recently learned she could not bear children and was trying to persuade her husband to adopt. Given the uncertainties to be found there, Bert Shelton contended that it was impractical to take a child to the Orient. His stand dismayed her, but Flora nonetheless supported her husband's decision.[24]

The Sheltons arrived in San Francisco in late September 1903, where they met their traveling companion to Tibet, Dr. Susie Rijnhart. As the group had no ordained minister, a Disciples minister ordained Dr. Albert Shelton at the First Christian Church in San Francisco. Following the common practice of medical missionaries, Shelton received no theological training prior to the ordination.

The SS *China* sailed out of the Golden Gates on September 29, 1903, bound for the Orient. Flora Shelton recalled the maladies of ocean travel: "As the steamship *China* left the pier and we realized that we were out in that big, big water and America was fading way, it seemed very lonely, indeed, and we, that is, I, was dreadfully homesick, but it soon changed to another kind of sickness which kept us dreadfully occupied for a while."[25]

Before the Sheltons even reached China, they encountered exotic lands. Flora wrote: "The island of Hawaii was the first stopping place, and the many new impressions came thick and fast to the country-bred folk from Kansas. Tropical sea birds and vegetation were seen. New and queer things were found to eat."[26] Japan offered contrasting views. Flora thought the island country looked "like a perfect jewel in its setting of sea and sky that is seen in no other place in the world," while Albert stated, "The impressions of Japan were terrible."[27] In spite of his homesteading boyhood on the Great Plains where women shared the hard work, Albert expressed discomfort at the sight of Japanese women doing manual labor:[28]

Leaving Japan, the Sheltons took the short steam across the Yellow Sea, tinged by yellow silt pouring from the mouth of the Yangtze River near Shanghai. Almost four thousand miles long, the Yangtze stretched across China to the mountains of Tibet.

When the Sheltons' ship eased into the Shanghai harbor on October 23, 1903, Shanghai was in full lascivious flower.[29] Lorcas, scows, and tiny dinghies flitted around the fleet of Western gunboats hunkered in the harbor, their brass polished and glittering, cannons and machine guns at the ready.[30]

The quayside Bund was another bulwark of the Western world. Opulent hotels such as the Palace and Victor Sassoon's Cathay stood alongside prestigious banks, trading houses, and men's clubs like the Shanghai Club. With their classically styled columns and pediments, the buildings of the Bund would have looked at home in London's Mayfair. Crisp white bungalows, brick *godowns* (warehouses), belching smokestacks, and steepled churches dotted the foreigners' trading enclave that stretched back from the Bund. At the docks, half-starved beggars pleaded for a few coppers as prostitutes hailed sailors veering toward the available charms of Blood Alley. Bare-chested coolies jogged by with bamboo poles supporting baskets filled with everything from piles of vegetables to honking geese. Rickshaw pullers yowled for passage and workmen with wheelbarrows dodged the trundling trams ringing out warnings. Street vendors cried out their wares as blind men rapped their presence on small pieces of wood.

But Shanghai was also the exotic Cathay of Western fantasy and leering legend: dragon-roofed temples and soaring pagodas, courtesans teetering on "lily feet" over arch-backed marble bridges, luxurious silk and ceramics, ancient courts of esoteric ritual and staggering wealth.[31] It was a cacophony of unfamiliar sounds, a blizzard of strange smells, a world wholly unlike anything the Sheltons had ever experienced. Shelton wrote his hometown paper: "The streets everywhere were so densely crowded that required pushing to get through, and were exceedingly filthy; hogs, dogs, cats, chickens, and ducks mingling promiscuously with the people. . . . We were also taken to one of the large opium dens which were new to us then but which we see daily now, and which is one of the terrible curses of China. . . . We were invited to have a pipe, which we politely refused."[32]

By the turn of the twentieth century, Shanghai was reputed to be the most decadent, licentious, sin-ridden, and corrupt city on the planet—"the Whore of Asia." One missionary stated, "If God lets Shanghai endure, he owes an apology to Sodom and Gomorrah."[33] This sense endured in spite of the city harboring "the biggest evangelical army in Christendom" from the entire panoply of missionary groups, all earnestly proselytizing their particular cant.

Yangtze Journey: Mission Life in China

By the arrival of the Sheltons, the influence of the West extended far into the interior of China. Flooded with capital from the Industrial Revolution, foreign companies busily laid railroad track, constructed harbors and commercial buildings, opened mines, and jostled for the best chance throughout the Celestial Kingdom's vast market. Across China, Christian missionaries strode out of their walled compounds with religious tracts in hand to bring Jesus to the Chinese. As they had for fifty years, foreigners depended on the industrialized powers' military might to protect their commercial and ecclesiastic forays.

From the Opium Wars on, the gunboats of the United States, Britain, Germany, Japan, and other Western powers cruised the Yangtze as far inland as Chungking (Chongqing), thirteen hundred miles from the sea, keeping the waterway open for Western commerce and Christianity. Missionaries were always at the forefront of the Western military and economic penetration of China's interior. When the first British navy steamships churned up the Yangtze, an American missionary fluent in Chinese, a Mr. Schereschewsky, went along to translate, becoming the first American to see the rapids and gorges of the upper river. By the time the Sheltons headed up the river, American warships had been patrolling deep in the heart of China for a half-century.[34]

The Sheltons took a small steamer to the treaty port of Nanjing where the Foreign Christian Missionary Society Central China Mission had its headquarters. The FCMS station in Nanjing was a typical urban mission on the navigable rivers and eastern seaboard of China. Inside the mission's high-walled compound, a multitude of Chinese servants looked after the comfortable American-style buildings and well-tended gardens. (As the missionaries tended to lament the hardships of expatriate life for folks back home, the subject of servants was a touchy one.) Inside the compound, the missionaries ran both a day school and a boarding school for boys. Aided by Chinese assistants, two missionary doctors ran the dispensary and a small hospital. Seeing Western medicine and hygiene as an essential tool of evangelism, the missionaries often crowed that they were "conquering China at the point of a lancet." By Chinese standards, the walled mission was a very posh environment. With extraterritoriality, it was a little bit of America where no Chinese magistrate would dare enforce his country's laws.[35]

The Sheltons encountered some flustered missionaries at Nanjing. "The missionaries were expecting Dr. Shelton to stay in Nankin," Flora Shelton wrote, "and were filled with consternation when they found he was going on with Dr. Rijnhart to the Tibetan border."[36] Nonetheless, the headquarters assigned two southern Chinese men to accompany them to the group's Tibetan frontier post at Tachienlu (Kangding). Because of the Chinese military presence and ostensible sovereignty in the border areas, Westerners preferred to use Chinese as guides.

One of the Tibet-bound party's escorts, Mr. Yang, was an English-speaking Chinese scholar and Christian convert. "He was a most valuable man," Flora Shelton wrote. "His preaching was the finest that ever had been heard in Nankin, and great crowds came to hear him." An English-speaking cook, Chang

Shao-yu, whom the missionaries nicknamed Johnny, completed the party.[37] Doubts began to creep into the Sheltons' minds. Flora wrote, "Nankin seemed very far from anywhere; what would farther on seem like?"

The party's journey six hundred miles up the river to Hankou (Huangshi) was a simple run by steamer. Even ocean liners could navigate the Yangtze that far, and river steamers could sail for a thousand miles more.[38] At Huangshi, FCMS missionaries from Wuhan joined the Sheltons' party when it transferred to a small steamer for the upriver trip to Yichang.

Yichang was another squalid, sprawling Chinese city, stinking of odorous mud.[39] At Yichang, Dr. Rijnhart and the Sheltons rented a Chinese junk with a missionary couple for the British and Foreign Bible Society. Having loaded their baggage on board the junk, the party began the long haul through the dramatic gorges of the Upper Yangtze to Chongqing.

"Square-nosed it was, like the rest of them," Flora Shelton wrote about their boat, "high in the back somewhat resembling a duck, and a little room at the rear the captain and his wife dwelt. The middle part was partitioned off into three or four rooms for the rest of the party, while the long deck in front was where the coolies stretched at night."[40] Yangtze houseboats tended to be somewhat similar on that stretch of the river. Made of pine and cypress slathered periodically with tung oil, they were from forty to one hundred twenty feet long and could carry as much as a hundred tons. The Sheltons' junk was about forty feet long and fifteen feet wide, with a typical ribbed oblong sail, patched with a hundred scraps. The four-foot-high deck provided a fair amount of headroom underneath. The interiors were also oiled, giving them a neat and attractive appearance.[41]

With the ritual dispatch of a rooster, the Sheltons' houseboat cast off on its dangerous upriver journey. The voyage took them through deep gorges churning with rampaging rapids. Hull-gashing rocks and immense sucking whirlpools picketed the channel. Between Yichang and Chongqing there were thirteen large and seventy-two smaller rapids. Giant waves beat against the cockle skin of the boat; jagged rocks passed a few feet from the wooden hulls. The Chinese estimated one in twenty boats were destroyed annually. Each year one boat in ten was stranded on the rocks and sandbars.[42]

The three-hundred-mile trip through the Yangtze gorges to Chongqing was a determined tug against wild water that was codified and organized by Yangtze riverfolk over hundreds of years. The Sheltons' voyage was indistinguishable from travel centuries earlier. Forty coolies trod the shoreline trail, hauling the junk's thick bamboo rope through deep grooves worn in the rock by centuries of friction, crossing from bank to bank to "clamber on paths that seem impossible . . . where even a goat would find it hard to get a foothold," Flora wrote.[43]

Paths were often a few feet wide and twenty feet above the river. Occasionally, the trackers were on paths so high they looked no bigger than flies as they tugged over a thousand feet of hawser along the cliffside trails.[44]

In the perilous stretches, the missionaries disembarked, carefully carrying their valuables with them. The gang bosses yelled and howled, and the trackers bent double with the calls of "Ayah! Ayah!" Clutching rocks and earth for purchase against the unrelenting current rushing down from half a million miles of Chinese hills and Tibetan peaks, the coolies slowly pulled upriver. When the coolies' towing ropes broke, as they commonly did, the boats went spinning down the river to disaster.[45]

While the Sheltons highlighted the lurid aspects of Yangtze travel for their American audience, the reality was somewhat more prosaic. There were thousands of junks on the upper Yangtze, and more than a million people who built them, manned them, supplied them, and towed them up the river.[46] Most often attached to riverside towns and villages, the junkmen and trackers were organized by guilds. Wages for the long slog up the valley and back was a few shillings and large bowls of greasy rice. Many of the trackers assuaged their arduous work with the comfort of the opium pipe. When the trackers hooked themselves to their yokes and began their distinctive arm-swinging, short-stepped gait, they were hauling centuries of culture up the stream with them.

It took a month to travel from Yichang to Chongqing, during which the Sheltons crossed into Sichuan, the west China province that was to be their home. The unique inland province stretched from the stark empty yak pastures of the Tibetan Himalayas east through the low hills and rolling plains that formed the teeming rice bowl of China. About the size of France, the wealthy province was a crucial part of the empire. Irrigated since 100 B.C., Sichuan's name, "Four Rivers," came from the powerful rivers, the Minjiang, Tuojiang, Fujiang, and Jialing Jiang that wound across the province. With wealth and water transport came practiced facility at trade and commerce. It gave the Sichuanese a reputation for being extremely polite—and equally shrewd and quarrelsome.[47]

Located at the end of the gorges, Chongqing was one of the sprawling metropolises of interior China. Sited on a high rocky promontory between two rivers, the streets were so steep no wheeled vehicles were allowed inside the city walls. Coolies carrying sedan chairs called for passage. Countless water-carriers hauled buckets of water up the broad stone steps from the river. Splashing through the looming city gates, they scattered the pigs, dogs, chickens, and children in the dark noisy streets. In 1904, foreigners were still a great curiosity in inland China. Crowds pressed round at every stop. With the crush of onlookers, their cooks could barely serve. The Chinese even followed Westerners into their bedrooms, "exhibiting the curiosity of overgrown children," according to one missionary.[48]

As with most of their fellow missionaries, the Sheltons found little to value in traditional Chinese culture. Albert wrote, "I think my greatest trial was to see the utter indifference to human suffering and the cheapness of life in the Orient."[49] They noted the trade in young girls as concubines. Chinese hygiene and health appalled them. Flora wrote: "Mercy seems to have gone from the earth; all things seem pitiless and men most of all always and always, wherever we went there were misery and pain and suffering, especially among the women and children, and there was just one thing to aid. That was opium, and it was everywhere."[50]

Transferring to a smaller junk, the Sheltons took another three weeks to travel up the Yangtze from Chongqing to Kiating (Leshan). They boated along the great bend in the river through the Red Basin, an immensely fertile region that rises toward the distant Himalayas. At Leshan, Dr. Shelton began his Tibetan medical career, doctoring the first Tibetan he met—the king of Chala, whose capital at Tachienlu was the Sheltons' destination. The king fortuitously happened to be in Leshan while on a pilgrimage to the sacred Buddhist mountain of Emeishan near Chengdu. His traveling companion was China Inland Mission worker Theodore Sorensen, one of the missionaries Dr. Susie Rijnhart had encountered in Tachienlu when she stumbled out of Tibet five years earlier. Dr. Shelton recalled that he treated the king for a minor ailment. "It was thus that I had my first Tibetan patient, and thus began a friendship which had lasted throughout all these years."[51]

At Leshan, coolies transferred the missionary baggage to bamboo rafts for a voyage up a tributary of the Yangtze, a clear little river named the Taito-ho or Tung (Dadu River) to Yachow (Ya'an).[52] The missionaries gratefully left the water to transfer to coolie-hauled sedan chairs. Dr. Shelton wrote, "This was too much for me. I didn't mind having people work for me, but to be carried by them was just a little too much, so I had the chair carried along, but I walked most of the way."[53] His decision to hoof it may have partly been due to the dubious pleasure of the sedan chair. When William Gill traveled through Sichuan thirty years earlier, he wrote, "I found the dignity and discomfort were in about equal proportions, for one unaccustomed, the motion, especially in hilly country is very disagreeable."[54]

The Sheltons' transport and accommodation was a well-codified arrangement. A Chinese specialist that Westerners termed a "coolie-master" drew up an elaborate agreement that specified each parties' responsibilities, such as destinations, places and periods of rest, and pay.[55] Every two or three days, the coolies received a portion of their wages to pay for their fodder of corn cakes and day's ration of opium, which they rolled into pills for smoking during stops. Sedan-chair-bearers walked single file, two in front and two in the rear, each with a straw hat or turban on his head and spare straw sandals tied to his belt. The pole that rested on their callused shoulders was tied to two ten- to sixteen-foot poles that ran alongside the sedan chair. With a singsong cadence, the bearers pattered down the trail, the lead man calling out obstacles in the road ahead. Each day's stage terminated at an inn, where the coolies retired for a hot meal and opium. As the servants hung screens and prepared the missionaries' hot bath and dinner, the missionaries wrote letters or caught up with their diaries.[56]

The group took four days to travel to Ya'an, arriving in early March.[57] In some ways the Sheltons began seeing a familiar landscape. Flora wrote, "We were indeed glad that the land looked and felt as it did in dear old Kansas, though most of it did not smell the same."[58] The sight of familiar crops like mustard and beans growing in the small, tidy Chinese farmsteads charmed her. She wrote, "Such a beautiful land it is!"[59]

The earthen houses of far western Sichuan were akin to the west Kansas homesteaders' soddies, and the primary food of the region was corn, surely a homey remembrance for the Sheltons after the long journey through rice-eating southern China. For months after the autumn harvest, enormous wreaths and clutches of dried corn festooned the Sichuan mountain houses in an exuberance of edible folk art.[60]

The Brick Tea Route: The Jung Lam

After a few days' rest, the group started into the Himalayas.[61] The journey began in the verdant tea-growing region around Ya'an, where patches of green fields fit together like a living jigsaw puzzle. The last purely Chinese town before the Tibetan borderlands, Ya'an was an important entrepôt for the tea trade.[62] The missionaries traveled along a caravan route named the Jung Lam—the Brick Tea Route. The Jung Lam was part of the great central Asian trade route that commenced in Beijing and crossed China and the high Tibetan plateau to India. Fifteen hundred years old, it was the route of emissaries and merchants making the exhausting eight-month journey between Beijing and Lhasa.

The Brick Tea Route segment of the road began in Ya'an and climbed into the Himalayas to the Tibetan frontier town of Tachienlu. It then crossed the anarchic Kham region of eastern Tibet and the high desolate central Tibetan plateau to the Indian trading town of Kalimpong, a journey of six months.

A conduit of central Asian trade, the Jung Lam was vital to both the Chinese and the Tibetans. Commerce moved in an unending river along the winding route. Countless goods made their way via this route, but by far the most important was tea.[63] Tea was China's most valuable export to the Tibetan, Turkic, and Mongolian peoples who formed an arc at the periphery of the Celestial Kingdom. The brick tea trade was integral to Chinese-Tibetan commerce, politics, military history, and social intercourse. The trade dated back to the late Tang Dynasty (618–907), when the first loads of tea wound along perilous Himalayan trails to Tibet. Brick tea became a vital part of Tibetan culture, so much so that for centuries it was used as currency. For Tibetans, a steaming bowl of yak-butter tea represented sustenance, social intercourse, and sustained culture. Tibetans across the high plateau dropped chunks of brick tea into slender wooden barrels that resembled pioneer butter churns, adding hunks of golden yak butter and handfuls of salt, churning it with a sucking sound into a thickish salty brew. Each day the average Tibetan drank dozens of cups of yak-butter tea. American explorer and diplomat William Rockhill estimated the average Tibetan used five pounds of tea a month.[64] Villagers and townsfolk drank it around their low tea tables in kitchens and parlors. Nomads sipped tea bowls in their black yak-hair tents. Novice monks in the densely populated Tibetan Buddhist monasteries ferried unending pots of tea to warm monks in study and at worship. Yak-butter brick tea was fluid, caffeine, calories, and replenishing salt all in one.[65]

Many of the British travelers who passed through the frontier regions of southwestern China were mercantile scouts sniffing around the borderlands. They were attempting to determine if the Chinese monopoly on the Tibetan tea trade could be supplanted with tea from the British Indian fields in Assam.[66] The British obsessed over Tibet, attempting to block Imperial Russia's rising central Asian ambitions as Chinese political influence waxed and waned in Lhasa. The machinations and maneuverings of the two powers came to be known as the Great Game, which eventually ravaged the stability of eastern Tibet. Given the commercial advantages of the tea trade to the monasteries, the Tibetan authorities saw little reason to exchange the relatively loose laissez-faire control of the Chinese for the far more intense and expansive control of the British Indian colonial government.[67]

The brick tea moved up into the Tibetan regions in a dramatic fashion—in enormous packs on the backs of men. The grotesquely burdened tea coolies who transported the brick tea over the mountainous one hundred and forty miles from Ya'an to Tachienlu never failed to catch the attention of traveling foreigners. "If one loaded a mule as heavily he would undoubtedly break down," British explorer Henry Davies wrote. "Mules are occasionally seen with a load of tea on them, but it is an accepted fact that an animal's load has to be much lighter than what would be carried by a man." Davies noted the typical loads were approximately two hundred pounds per man, and he saw two men with seventeen tea packages apiece, three hundred and sixty-three pounds carried in towering loads on their backs.[68]

With short, slow steps, thousands of tea coolies hauled their massive loads over the hills and mountains between Ya'an and Tachienlu, one hundred yards between rests. The coolies marked their transit with a long, low whistle akin to a mournful sigh, the sound of exhaling breath through half-closed teeth before they gasped yet another deep breath.[69] For their portage of twenty days through the mountains, the coolies received a payment of four hundred cash Chinese, about one shilling.[70]

When they left Ya'an, the Sheltons were eight days from their destination in Tachienlu. In that transit they passed from a Chinese world to a Tibetan one. As they moved west, the landscape abruptly shifted into a Himalayan environment of scree and cloud-tearing mountains. Alpine plants replaced the lush agrarian landscape of southern Sichuan.

To the Chinese, Kham and its Tibetan population was a land beyond the borders of the Middle Kingdom that the Chinese entered only with enticements or under duress. The Chinese termed the Khampas, "Mantzu," considering them descendants of the original ancient occupants of Sichuan.[71] The ethnocentric Han Chinese tended to view the Tibetans as an inferior people, and accordingly, most Chinese records from the beginning of history refer to the Khampas with a variety of Chinese words that describe barbaric and uncivilized tribes.[72] While under the Qing Empire's suzerain since the early eighteenth century, the Chinese saw Kham as the harshest of postings, a station of hardship and tears.[73]

The Sheltons' passage on the tea road crossed the country to Lutingchow (Luding) where a three-hundred-year-old iron chain bridge crossed the roiling Dadu River to Kham. Constructed of thirteen stout chains with planks laid on top on nine of them, the bridge was a swaying, precarious passage to the Tibetan region. Almost four hundred feet long, the bridge swung fifty feet above the turbulent river. At certain times of the day, when the wind howled down the valley, the bridge was uncrossable. When the wind was down, special coolies accustomed to the sway carried over loads and helped passengers and solid-ground coolies with the tipsy crossing.[74]

The Luding Bridge was a traditional farewell point where Chinese men and their Tibetan wives said their final goodbyes, as few Tibetans could survive the steamy summers and damp, misty winters of lowland China. Tuberculosis often took those who tried a life on the plains.[75] The Tibetans refused to allow any Chinese woman to pass into Kham, not even the wives of the high ministers to Lhasa. William Gill noted the rationale behind the custom: "The officials and soldiers . . . when in Tibet, take to themselves Tibetan wives. The children thus become entirely Tibetan. . . . The Tibetans in this are wise in their own generation,

Figure 4.1   Brick tea, the penultimate Chinese–Tibetan trade item, traveled into the Himalayas on the backs of Chinese tea porters, who carried loads of up to 363 pounds. Albert Shelton photograph, courtesy the Collection of The Newark Museum. Reprinted with permission.

for if they permitted the Chinese to bring their wives with them, and raise Chinese families, the country would soon become altogether Chinese."[76]

With as many as one-third of the Tibetan males in monasteries, there was an imbalance between the sexes. The Chinese men who were posted to Tibet provided a provisional alternative for Tibetan women. A Tibetan proverb contrasted the marital arrangements: "To be a wife of a Chinese is like the burning of thorns; To be a wife of a Tibetan is like burning oak wood."[77]

There were two roads from Ya'an toward Kham, the shorter one crossing two high passes that included the breath-wrenching climb over soaring Erlang Mountain. Once across the Dadu River, the primary road to Tachienlu led up the course of a tumbling mountain river, over difficult nine- and ten-thousand-foot passes slick with ice and snow. Flora wrote: "Leaving the tropical ferns and bamboos, we go on up the mountain road of stone steps, climbing slowly, the chair-men swinging the chair with a kind of rhythm. The bamboos grow smaller and smaller, the ferns disappear; it is cold, and snow is on the ground."[78] As the party climbed toward the top of the pass, the wind rose, the chair tops blew off, and the forever-chatting coolies grew quiet, afraid of rousing the wind devils that inhabited the pass. Flora feared being blown off the sere trail into the treetops and cloudbanks below. "Up and up we go, and to the Kansas bred the mountains seem very high," she wrote.[79]

As the Sheltons continued on the road, they passed old stone Tibetan fortifications in the river valleys, the remains of Tibetan hegemony that reached in historic times all the way east to Ya'an. The mountain pines and rhododendron of the region near Erlang Mountain gave way to bare scree and steep austere slopes. One day from Tachienlu, the party rested in a trailside inn tucked between huge mountains. It was to be their last respite from high altitude, as the next day they climbed from the tiny village at three thousand feet up to Tachienlu in the clouds.

"The next morning we were out bright and early and on our way," Dr. Shelton wrote. "After we had dinner at the half-way place we were on again, and about four o'clock in the afternoon, in a heavy snow-storm, we were met by Mr. Moyes, who had come out a mile or so to meet us."[80] James Moyes was one of the China Inland Mission missionaries who had given succor to Dr. Susie Rijnhart when she stumbled into Tachienlu over five years earlier, and he had been wooing her by post ever since.[81] The chairmen stepped quickly through the falling snow toward their long-awaited destination. "Tachienlu at last," Flora Shelton exulted.[82] The Foreign Christian Missionary Society party arrived in Tachienlu on March 15, 1904, five and half months after sailing from San Francisco, almost three and a half months after leaving Nanjing for their trip across the breadth of China to the Tibetan border.

CHAPTER FIVE

THE PORTAL

Tachienlu and the Challenge of Kham

A religious atmosphere pervades Tibet and gives it a singular sense of novelty.[1]

—Isabella Bird Bishop

Tachienlu was like few places on earth, a point where two distinct and mutually antagonistic societies abruptly transitioned. After traveling two thousand miles across the vast bulk of the Chinese Empire, the Sheltons quite suddenly found themselves in the Tibetan world of yaks and Buddhist monks and the snow-covered Himalayas. Tachienlu was the juncture beyond which China was only a colonizing presence, and the culture and religion of the high Tibetan plateau held sway.

The Sheltons and Dr. Rijnhart first found shelter in one of the local inns that was primarily inhabited by Tibetan lamas and yak-caravan drovers. A man in love, missionary James Moyes arranged for the walls to be freshly papered, though the landlady couldn't condone washing the dirt-encrusted floor.[2] The housecleaning didn't abate the bane of the travelers' inns—bedbugs. Fleas and lice plagued the inns and virtually everyone in Tibet. When caravans stopped for a rest, a good many of the travelers engaged in impromptu louse hunts—one Englishman claimed it was the only blood sport in which the hunter provided the blood.[3] "Did I ever have bugs on me?" Flora Shelton wrote her folks back home. "Yes, fleas and lice. The lice poisoned me and made me nearly wild; they got on my right arm, (there might have been only one) but it bit from the wrist to the elbow and itched like 10,000 chigger bites, when I had it scratched. I got Bert to pour ammonia on it. It burned like fire, but felt better than the bites. I don't know if they are in my head again or not."[4]

Tachienlu was a little frontier city hustling with commerce. The exhausted tea porters arrived at Tachienlu's eastern gate to pay duty before tottering on to the city's dozens of tea-packing houses. As the tea workers prepared the tea for shipment, tea traders from Ya'an bargained with the Tibetan merchants. Chinese merchants called out their wares from their small stalls and shops. Tibetan yak-caravan drivers stumped through the streets with hands on knife hilts. Tibetan women ferrying tea loads called for passage. Tibet-bound Chinese soldiers and officials walked the lanes, soaking up the last bits of China they would see for a while.

The Tibetan brick tea trade was Tachienlu's raison d'être and the lure for the legions of Tibetans attracted to the town. Two major central Asian trade routes passed through the trading post, and at eighty-five hundred feet, the town was the lowest point the Tibetans would drive their yak herds. The highland animals could not survive lower altitudes and could handle Tachienlu's relatively low altitude only for short periods, making Tachienlu the axis of the trade. The Chinese hauled the trade goods to Tachienlu by human power, and the Tibetans carried it onward by yak, horse, and mule.

Tachienlu was the major Chinese portal into central Tibet. The Pei-lu, or Northern Route, ran from Tachienlu through the northern Kham provinces of Hor and Derge to Chamdo and on to Lhasa. The second trail was the Jung Lam, the brick tea route, which ran from Tachienlu across Kham through the monastery town of Litang to the ancient Chinese-Tibetan border near Batang. Depending on season, avalanches, bandits, and wars, the two trails carried the majority of the trade between China and Tibet.[5]

With emissaries and couriers in constant passage, the town was also a way stop on the route of diplomacy.[6] Every three years the Chinese *ambans* passed through Tachienlu en route between Lhasa and Beijing, traveling with enormous trains of goods, returning laden with the wares of Tibet.[7] Likewise, the Nepalese ambassador to the Imperial Court crossed Kham every twelve years with his large retinue. Following the eighteenth-century defeat of the Nepali army, the Chinese demanded an ambassador bearing tribute to traverse China to kowtow to the Emperor. The Nepalese sagely turned the demand into an extended trading opportunity and took years to make their passage slowly across China, doing business all the way.[8]

Tachienlu had been an entrepôt on the edge of the Chinese empire for centuries. By 1696 the Dalai Lama sanctioned a tea trade market in Tachienlu, and the business grew from there. Traders paid duty on ten million pounds of tea at Tachienlu in 1879, and additionally Chinese officials smuggled enormous amounts. By 1895 Tachienlu contributed 79 percent of Sichuan's entire tea export duty to the imperial coffers.[9] As the Sheltons began their mission, fifty-four hundred tons of tea entered Tachienlu annually.[10]

The Chinese traded tea, silk, and hardware to Tibet, and opium for the Chinese workers stationed there. The Tibetans were so wary of Chinese currency sold by weight that they traded with Indian rupees emblazoned with the crowned likeness of Queen Victoria, which they called "Lama tob-du" (vagabond lama), believing the queen's crown was the headgear of a religious mendicant.[11] Coins were cut into halves, quarters, and smaller for change, along with beads of turquoise and coral.

The Tibetans also traded horses, wool, fox, lynx, leopard, and lamb skins, musk, borax, gold, medicinal plants such as yellow root and rhubarb, and large quantities of yak tails. After tea, musk was the most valuable trade item in town.[12] For centuries, yak tails were a prime export item to the West, used on the London stage for facial hair and in Europe and the United States for Santa Claus beards. Beyond products of Tibet, the Tibetans also traded the goods of India and east Asia such as pearls and precious stones, soap, and Kashmiri saffron.[13]

There were almost ninety packinghouses and warehouses for brick tea in Tachienlu. At the packinghouses, workers broke the tea porters' loads of bamboo-wrapped yard-long blocks of tea into bricks called *parka* that were nine by seven by three inches long. They then sewed them into yak-skin packages called *gams* that weighed about forty-five pounds each.[14] Before packing the *gams,* the workers soaked the yak skins in water, which stiffened into cases that were hard as horn. Tough cases were essential, as yaks had an instinctive ability to shed their loads on the most precipitous of trails, and a well-prepared yak case bounced like a football down the slopes and cliffs. No self-respecting yak could be convinced to carry more than two *gams,* far lighter loads than the average tea coolie hauled up from Ya'an.[15]

As their husbands were gone most of the year on caravan work to Lhasa, Tibetan women commonly owned and operated the caravansaries. The inns were large structures with ample courtyards for the horses and mules and one or two wings to allow the storage of Tibetan trade goods. Often, the women served as brokers and traders, rivaling the men as moneymakers.[16]

Once the traders made their deals, the caravan men herded the yaks from the mountain pastures to the city gates where the tea porters deposited the loads. Pegged beside the gates, the hairy brown and black beasts stolidly awaited their loads. The drovers quickly roped the *gams* onto the yaks' rough wooden saddles and whistled the caravan off for the high plateau. Not long after arriving in Tachienlu, Albert Shelton inadvertently stumbled into thirty or forty loaded yaks awaiting their drivers. He was momentarily taken aback until he realized they were quite docile.[17] Being herd animals, the yaks tended to be aimed rather than driven, making the six-month journey to central Tibet more of a long grass-cropping meander than a hurried drive.[18]

*Figure 5.1   Yaks carried the brick tea from Tachienlu across the Tibetan plateau. The yaks were in-
dispensable to the Tibetans, providing food, clothing, shelter, transport, and fuel. Albert Shelton photograph, courtesy the Collection of The Newark Museum. Reprinted with permission.*

   In a high, hard climate with a soil that was primarily stony and infertile, the
yak was invaluable to the Tibetans, providing food, clothing, shelter, and fuel.[19]
As the buffalo herds were vital to the life of the Plains Indians, the yaks were
critical for human survival in much of the Tibetan region. Through their milk,
butter, and meat, yaks were a primary source of food. The nomad women made
clothing from the hide and wool, weaving the yak hair into fabric for the low
black tents that hunkered across the plateau like enormous black spiders. Yak
horns carried the Khampas' snuff and powder; the tail was a fly chaser and saddle tassel. Equally important, yak dung was the indispensable fuel for the nomads, gathered and dried as the Great Plains Indians and homesteaders did with
buffalo manure, to make a quick-burning, blue-flamed fuel.[20]
   The Sheltons' new home of Tachienlu had about eight hundred Tibetan-style
wood-and-stone houses crammed among the stalls, warehouses, and inns.[21] It
sat in a steep-sloped valley at the confluence of the Dar and Tse rivers, giving the
town its Tibetan name, Dartsendo. Minya Konka soared 24,900 feet into the
sky above the town, and a palisade of lesser snow-capped peaks surrounded the
forested valley.[22] A massive earthquake in 1820 loosed a glacier that obliterated
the town in a deluge of water and debris. The new town, never quite as large or
prosperous as the first, rose a half-mile further down the valley.[23]

The town had about nine thousand Tibetan and Chinese inhabitants, augmented by a floating population of traders, travelers, tea coolies, nomads, officials, and soldiers. Eight lamaseries with eight hundred lamas and acolytes were scattered through the valley. The population was a mixture of Tibetans, Chinese men, and various blends of the two. There were very few pure Han Chinese women to be found in Tachienlu.[24]

In ancient times Tachienlu was known as the kingdom of Mao-nui.[25] In the early fifteenth century, the king came under the influence of the Ming Dynasty, which decreed him a second-class native official. The Manchu Dynasty continued the relationship, though it awarded the chief only a third-class native official position. In spite of the imperial downgrade, the king of Chala, the native chief whom Dr. Albert Shelton treated for illness in Leshan, still controlled six subsidiary chiefs, one chiliarch, and forty-eight centurions in a territory that stretched far into eastern Kham.[26] The king was independent until the 1870s, when he had to seek Chinese military assistance during an insurrection. In exchange, the Chinese demanded the king wear a queue and dress in Chinese fashion.

British plant hunter and explorer E. H. Wilson found little charm in the trading town, writing, "Notwithstanding its great political and commercial importance Tachienlu is a meanly built and filthy city. It is without a surrounding wall, save for a fragment which runs near the south gate, and it has no west gate. The narrow, uneven streets are paved with stones in which pure marble largely figures, though this is only evident after some heavy downpour has washed away the usual covering of mud and filth."[27]

By "filth," Wilson probably was referring to the human and animal manure that dotted the lanes. Toilets and privies were unknown to the Tibetans, and they relieved themselves wherever they felt the urge. Accordingly, people trod warily down the lanes off the main street in fear of a misstep.[28]

Despite unsanitary streets, Tachienlu's shade trees, snow, and blustery spring weather reminded the Sheltons of Kansas. "I would rather live here than in any of the lower cities for we don't have the awful heat and have some winter and there are mountains all around the town, and I can get to the snow almost any times," Flora wrote.[29]

Language acquisition became the Sheltons' first priority, which began soon after they arrived. The Sheltons secured a teacher from Chengdu, most likely a down-on-his-luck Mandarin scholar. "Our Chinese teacher wears great big glasses and looks like an owl and seems very learned to us when he reads so readily those mixed-up Chinese characters," Flora wrote.[30] Missionaries commonly spent five to ten hours a day studying, initially focusing on the vernacular tongue, with the first preached sermon serving as a graduation ceremony of sorts. Literacy lessons followed. After two years of focused study, missionaries were expected to master written classical Chinese, spoken Mandarin, and the local dialect that had from four to eight tonalities depending on the region. A photo of the day portrayed the Sheltons and Susie Rijnhart dressed in Chinese garb. Dr. Shelton wore a Mandarin outfit with a Chinese cap, looking serious and a touch uncomfortable.[31]

Language was the great divide for missionaries. Those who learned the language could proceed with their work of evangelization and social work. Those who couldn't absorb the new tongue either returned to their home country or worked under a terrible handicap. In treaty ports and other areas where Westerners congregated, a rudimentary hybrid language emerged, "pidgin" or "business" English, and practitioners could be found across the country. But missionaries had to learn the language to do their jobs, as interpreters were rare.[32]

Because of its tonal system that varied from region to region, students needed to learn spoken Chinese where it was heard in day-to-day usage. Mandarin, for instance, had four tones while Cantonese had eight. While Mandarin was official language of the country and the common language north of the Yangtze and in some of the south, it was unintelligible to native speakers from Guangzhou or Shanghai. In part, the Foreign Christian Missionary Society chose Nanjing for its China headquarters because the local dialect was understood in fifteen of the eighteen provinces of China.[33] There were no formal language schools or protocols, the missionaries instead depending on trial and error for grammar and the elusive tonalities.[34] Transliteration from Chinese to English was haphazard. Interpreters used arbitrary systems of spelling, which lent a conjectural quality to a portion of translated material.

However tidy they tried to make the Tachienlu inn, it was not a hospitable place for the Sheltons. Flora Shelton became quite ill, perhaps from the insect bites. Albert continually bumped his head on the low doorways and tripped on the rough floorboards. Not long after arriving, they rented a house, Dr. Shelton supervising local men hired to clean and remodel.[35]

Set on a narrow dirt lane, the Shelton's first house was a two-story wooden and stone structure that was weathered dark.[36] The Sheltons began to adapt local foods to their tastes, procuring fresh yak butter to replace the rancid, well-aged cake they had received as a gift and refining the black Tibetan salt into a product they could stomach. "You see, we are like pioneers in America," Flora boasted to her in-laws.[37] A charcoal brazier provided heat, and Chinese carpenters constructed furniture. "Strange chairs and strange beds and dressers, made by the Chinese carpenters, but with matting on the floor and curtains at the tiny window, we felt clean and ready for the new guest," Flora Shelton wrote.[38]

The new guest, daughter Dorris Evangeline Shelton, joined the missionary couple on August 25, 1904, in spite of the Kansas doctors' assurances that Flora was incapable of bearing children. Dr. Shelton delivered the baby, assisted by Dr. Susie Rijnhart. Dorris was born less than a year after the Sheltons left San Francisco on September 29, 1903. A change of scenery appeared to have worked wonders for the couple.

A Picturesque People: The Khampas

Many Tibetans in Tachienlu spoke some Chinese, but it was essential for the Sheltons to learn Tibetan to work with Khampas from the interior who spoke no Chinese. Dr. Susie Rijnhart began her Tibetan language study on the northern borders with her husband Petrus. She wrote, "As the lamas are the sole possessors of Tibetan letters, the great masses of the lay population being unable to either to read or write, they were not pleased with the thought of communicating their sacred language to 'foreign devils,' and we had great difficulty in persuading any one to teach us." Eventually they secured a young lama, "rather good looking," according to Rijnhart, who agreed to tutor them.

The Sheltons hired a Tibetan to teach them. Spoken Tibetan eluded Albert Shelton as Chinese had not. His teachers happily translated into Chinese any forgotten Tibetan words, but his progress flagged. In hopes of accelerating his language acquisition, Shelton made his first foray into the Tibetan hinterlands: "I went three days back into the country where there were no Chinese and where it was necessary to speak Tibetan or not at all, and spent some weeks in this way. During this time I learned the language as it was spoken."[39]

E. H. Wilson described the Tibetans who thronged Tachienlu as "a picturesque people."[40] By inner Asian standards, the Khampas were very tall, the men averaging a little under six feet, their slim waists, muscular chests, and powerful shoulders accentuating their height and strength.[41] The men wore their long black hair in a queue wound around their head, into which they wove hunks of silver, turquoise, orange-colored coral, and elephant tusks. Both sexes dressed in long robes called *chuba* that hung to their knees, belted to form a pouch from which unending objects seemed to emerge—bowls and implements and bags of food. During the day the Khampas tied their *chuba* like a kilt, leaving their shoulders exposed. At night, they wrapped themselves in its folds to sleep.

Like most Tibetan people, the Khampa population divided themselves between *drokpa*, nomadic pastoral people, and *rongpa*, valley people who were sedentary agricultural people. The Khampa farmers raised a variety of crops, depending on the altitude and weather of their particular land. Up to 9,500 feet, the first crop was barley and wheat and the second planting was millet and buckwheat. Between 9,500 feet and 10,500 feet, farmers could still harvest two plantings, the first being barley and the second turnips. Above 10,500 feet, only one planting of barley and buckwheat could survive.[42] Roasted barley, *tsampa,* was the staple food. Tibetans hulled the harvested barley with flails and then parched it in an iron skillet, stirring the grains with a small whisk made of twigs. When the tan husk split, the cook cleaned grain of the husk and ground it. The Tibetans then stirred the rough barley flour into cups of yak-butter tea and rolled the mixture into edible balls the size of walnuts.

Far more than costume or cuisine, the Buddhist religion was the great definer of Tibet. Isabella Bird Bishop stated pithily, "A religious atmosphere pervades Tibet and gives it a singular sense of novelty."[43] The Sheltons faced a formidable adversary in Tibetan Buddhism. A deeply rooted and acculturated religion, Buddhism was the equal of Christianity in messianic and evangelical energy. The Khampas were among the most devout of Tibetan Buddhists, supporting hundreds of monasteries and thousands of lamas. Their religious power extended even to the great teaching colleges in central Tibet, where eastern Tibetans were respected scholars, high lamas, and revered reincarnates including Dalai Lamas. William Rockhill wrote of the Khampas' monastic and domestic devotion: "As night falls lamps are lit on the altars of every Buddhist temple, and a short service is chanted, while lamas on the porch play a rather mournful hymn on long copper horns and clarinets. This is the signal for the housewives to light bundles of juniper boughs in the ovens made for the purpose on the roofs of their homes, and as the fragrant smoke ascends to heaven they sing a hymn of litany in which the men of the house also join, the deep voices of the latter and the clear high notes of the former blending most agreeably with the distant music of the lamaseries."[44]

Buddhism arrived in Tibet in the late eighth century, brought by the Indian Adept Padmasambhava (also known as Guru Rimpoche).[45] Padmasambhava "tamed" the indigenous Tibetan gods, harnessing their powers to the needs and uses of the Buddhist *dharma,* though they remained only half-willing, a manifestation of the strong shamanist strain of Tibetan Buddhism, rooted in the old nature gods of hearth, mountain, lake, and stream.

Long after the arrival of Buddhism, Tibetans moved from folk religion deities to the Buddhist pantheon to the ministrations of pre-Buddhist Bön priests, utilizing whatever worked to assuage their worldly pains and desires, while attempting to improve their karmic lot and reach enlightenment. The pre-Buddhist gods included deities of the water, trees, soil, rocks, failed kings, and evil monks. *Düd,* malevolent spirits who had been opposed to *dharma* in previous lives, fed on human flesh and opposed the tantric practitioners.

Mamo were ferocious goddesses who congregated in charnel grounds, while *iha,* white gods who were well disposed to humans, counterbalanced the evil deities.

Gods of the Buddhist heavens formed the karmic system of rebirth that was the Buddhist moral structure. These gods helped Buddhists with their past and future lives. Based on the ideology of merit, the conditions of future lives depended on the actions of their present one. Tantric meditation gods such as Tara and Avolakitesvara were the preeminent deities of the tantric religion, used by meditating practitioners to manifest the celestial beings within themselves.

By Albert Shelton's time, there were four main orders in the Tibetan Buddhist tradition—Nyingma (the Ancient), Sakya (named after a monastery), Kagyu (Oral Tradition), and Geluk (Virtue Tradition), with each having its monasteries, lineages, lamas, and immense canons of liturgy. In some cases, competing schools and even rival reincarnated lamas within the same monasteries waged war against other factions. The monasteries' large populations, and in some cases, extensive armories, made them the dominant institutions in major areas of Tibet.[46] Each order arose during a historical resurgence of Buddhist vitality—a series of great religious revivals that canonized in turn the four orders and codified Tibetan Buddhism's unique synthesis of clerical and shamanist thought.

The Nyingma order was the first Tibetan order, contemporaneous with Buddhism's arrival in the eighth century. While Nyingma was still developing, the Sakya order began in the valley of Sakya in the southern province of Tsang. A guru, Konchok Gyalpo, and twenty-five disciples founded a monastery in 1073 to practice newly evolved tantric techniques. Tibet's union of spiritual and political power emerged in the Sakya order.

A layman, Marpa, founded the Kagyu order in the early eleventh century after traveling to India several times to study under the renowned Adept, Naropa. Milarepa, a beloved Tibetan Buddhist *bodhisattva* and poet was the best known of the Kayugpas, considered to be the first ordinary Tibetan to reach enlightenment in one lifetime.

The Geluk order, the most clerical of the four, arose in the eleventh century during the same time period as Sakya and Kagyu. In the early fifteenth century, the Geluk order built its great teaching monasteries (*gompas*) of Ganden, Drepung, and Sera near Lhasa. Centered on the three influential institutions near Lhasa (there were twenty-one thousand monks in the three *gompas*), the Geluk order spread through Tibet and became the most powerful order in the Tibetan world.

The Mongols and the Geluk lamas formed an alliance, and in 1577 the Mongol leader Altan Khan proclaimed the Geluk leader, Sonam Gyatso, to be the third Dalai Lama. (The Geluks and Mongols recognized the first two reincarnations retroactively.)

In the mid-seventeenth century, the fifth Dalai Lama played off various threats to the Geluk order by forming an alliance with the Qoshot Mongols led by Gushri Khan. Following the war, the Khan declared the fifth Dalai Lama to be the spiritual and temporal leader of Tibet. It was the first time the Dalai Lama merged the role of monk-sage with that of secular political leader. His power extended from the high desert of the Koko Nor region in the north to the Himalayan ramparts in the south, and from Ladakh in the west to Tachienlu at the eastern edge of Kham. The fifth Dalai Lama proceeded to build the thousand-room Potola Palace on Red Mountain above Lhasa as a combination monastery, temple, fortress, and office building.[47]

At the turn of the twentieth century, perhaps 10 to 15 percent of the Tibetan men were monks, with a smaller percentage being nuns.[48] There were large Geluk monasteries with thousands of monks in agricultural areas adjacent to trade routes, controlling estates as large as twenty-one thousand acres. Some of the largest teaching monasteries, such as Kumbum in eastern Tibet, existed at the edge of a nomadic area, providing religious services for a wide, sparsely populated area as well as educating monks from all over the Tibetan world. Many of the larger monasteries had several reincarnated lamas, with attendant devotees and students operating in communities almost independent of one another. Some monasteries, particularly the larger ones adjacent to trade routes, became heavily involved in trade. The major monasteries and the noble class associated with them controlled a large proportion of the arable land in Tibet.[49]

Best Killers, Greatest Saints: The Khampa Warriors

While the Khampas were clearly devout Tibetan Buddhists, they were also among the most bellicose tribes of central Asia. As unarmed men were considered almost undressed, Khampa men generally brandished daggers, swords, spears, and matchlock rifles.[50] One Khampa warrior, Aten, related:

> In a land as lawless and uncertain as ours, a rifle was an essential part of a man's life. This was due to a fear of bandits, who were bold and numerous, but also because of a prevalence of interminable and bloody feuds. . . . Our people were like that—they couldn't resist a good fight. There is an old saying that gives a fair idea of how the people of Nyarong (and other parts of eastern Tibet) behaved:
>
>> A blow on the nose of a hated enemy,
>> Is surely more satisfying,
>> Than listening to the advice
>> Of benevolent parties.[51]

The dozens of political states in Kham were often entangled in internecine raids, wars, and general strife, making violence a near-constant part of the region's life and culture. Warrior monks with well-stocked armories added to the tensions. Kham was also the friction point between the Chinese empire and central Tibet. However connected Khampas were to the larger Tibetan religious and cultural mores, their remoteness from Lhasa and Beijing engendered a fierce sense of independence and belligerence. Kham evolved into a society of devout Buddhist warriors. Lhasa Tibetans said Khampas made the best killers and the greatest saints.

As with Shelton's Scotch-Irish forebears in the borderlands, the Khampas' violent nature emerged from their uncertain life on the frontier. Not only did they need to defend themselves from the periodic wars with the Chinese, they also were endlessly engaged in factional disputes with neighboring tribes, albeit sometimes incited by the Chinese authorities.

Over the centuries, brigandage developed into an off-season occupation for many Khampas. Most raids against travelers and caravans were in the winter when the nomads' yak and sheep herds were safe in encampments and the autumn-fattened horses were ready for hard riding.[52] Travelers on the central Asian trade routes that bisected Kham considered the region to be a wild and lawless place, riven with bandits and extreme danger. Bandit attacks along the trails of Kham were so common as to be almost obligatory among Western travelers' tales.

French traveler Andre Migot's account of his robbery in a Kham inn was typical. He was accosted by "by a gang of swashbucklers of an unmistakably criminal appearance; they were armed to the teeth and were busily engaged in ransacking my luggage." The band of fifty Khampas helped themselves to all of Migot's things, including his jacket and shoes. Migot wrote, "From time to time some of the bandits would come back and run their hands over me, to make quite sure that nothing had been overlooked; one of them gazed long and wistfully at my trousers, almost made up his mind to take them, but finally decided (they were in a very dilapidated state) that I might as well be allowed to keep them."[53]

Kham: The Land of Deep Corrosions

With their devout Buddhist militancy and strong cultural cohesion, the Khampas ruled a high region of sweeping grasslands ringed by ragged mountains and cleft by raging rivers. The Tibetans called Kham *Ngam-grog-chi*—"the Land of Deep Corrosions," a wild, turbulent place that was the collision point of geology and culture.[54] Sitting astride the Himalayas where the Indian subcontinent rammed the Asian continent 45 million years ago, Kham was a jumble of mountains where four major Asian rivers—the Salween, Mekong, Yangtze, and its tributary, the Yalung—ran in deep, chasmed trenches parallel to one another.[55] The great rivers crossed Kham for a hundred and thirty miles, racing through gorges only fifty miles apart before splitting apart to water a broad landscape of southeast Asia. Explorer J. W. Gregory compared the rivers' unique approach, convergence, and dispersal to "the fasces of thunderbolts in the hand of Jove."[56]

The general Eurasian east-west pattern of rivers, deserts, and mountain ranges channeled the movement of people and ideas along the same axis. In contrast, Kham's rivers and ranges ran with a north-south grain, making it the corner of central Asia where cultures from Burma to Mongolia flowed in a vast stream.[57]

When Albert Shelton arrived, nearly three dozen different semi-independent states governed Kham—congeries of Tibetan states, nomadic tribes, and lamas' principalities. The Khampas asserted a bristly autonomy in the face of pressure from both China and central Tibet. The history of Kham's political relationships with imperial China and the Dalai Lama's Lhasa government was complex and subject to competing interpretations.

By the mid-eighteenth century the Manchu Chinese control over Lhasa and central Tibet was weak, though the Chinese reasserted their power for a short period following an invasion to expel a Nepalese Gurkha army. Accordingly, the Chinese control of Kham in the eighteenth and nineteenth centuries was very loose, and the rulers and inhabitants of Kham were independent of both the central Tibetan and Chinese governments. Indicative of the complicated power and control in the region, the Chinese authorities paid five thousand taels from the Tachienlu customs to the Dalai Lama annually. The Khampas continued to pay religious obeisance to Dalai Lama, though religion in Tibetan eyes was not clearly distinguishable from political alliances. Until the end of the nineteenth century, the Lhasa government generally cooperated with the Chinese suzerainty in eastern Tibet. However, between the two nominal overlords, the Khampas asserted a bristly independence.

In 1894, the Qing Dynasty suffered embarrassing reverses at the hands of the Japanese, who seized most of Korea, the naval bases of Port Arthur and Darien, and eventually the island of Formosa. It set into play a series of uprisings by border peoples culminating in anti-Chinese riots in Lhasa and uprisings in eastern Tibet.[58] In the upheaval that followed, the nomadic people of Nyarong invaded the kingdom of Chala near the eastern border, precipitating Chinese troops to restore order between the Khampas. Warfare spread to neighboring Derge, where the local prince was preparing for war with his youngest son, who had decided to accelerate succession.[59] When Susie Rijnhart traveled through Kham a few years later, local strife was still rampant.[60]

At the turn of the twentieth century, Kham consisted of twenty-six different eastern Tibetan states that were nominally under Chinese protection.[61] Another nine Khampa states west of the Yangtze fell under Lhasa's sphere of influence.[62] The political delineations generally related only to the collection of "tribute" or taxes. Both the Chinese imperial government and the Lhasa government administered outlying regions minimally as long as the taxes continued to roll.[63]

West of the Yangtze River, the Khampa states included pastoralist kingdoms in the north, Lhat'og and Gyandé, five of which were ruled by revered Tibetan lamas. Four lamaist states—Dragyab, Riwoche, Pagshöd, and Chamdo—were in the center of Kham. A reincarnate lama known as Phagpa Lha, who was the abbot of a large Geluk monastery founded in 1437, ruled Chamdo, the largest town west of the Yangtze. Markham and Gonjo were in the southwestern corner of Kham. The southernmost state was the cantankerous state of Powo, whose hereditary monarch, the Kanam Depa, chafed under Lhasa's rule.

A hereditary king or *gyelpo* ruled the kingdom of Derge, the largest of the Kham states. Located in the northwest of Kham, it was the richest agricultural and manufacturing state in the region, home to 32,000 people.[64] Derge was intransigently independent from both China and central Tibet, the populace demonstrating a particular antipathy toward the Chinese who tried to take residence. The main town was famous for its sacred printing house that reproduced Buddhist texts of all the major Tibetan sects. Derge was also renowned for the quality of metalwork produced by its craftsmen, who forged highly valued swords, guns, saddles, teapots, tinderboxes, seals, and bells.

North of the Yangtze River in northeastern Kham there were pastoral states outside of Lhasa's oversight, such as Lingts'ang on the Yalung River and Nangch'en with its busy capital of Jyekundo, where Chinese and Mongol traded yak hides, lambskins, musk, gold, deer horns, and wool.[65] The five wealthy Hor states were east of Derge, the boundaries overlapping as the rulers oversaw families, not territory. The Hor states were the largest in size and wealth next to Derge. As in other parts of Kham, Chinese administration consisted of a few scattered outposts manned by dispirited officers and ragged soldiers with little real power except as intelligence gatherers and courier-post guardians.[66]

East and northeast of the Hor states, the Gyelrong states were a collection of small, partly Tibetanized states, variously enumerated as eighteen to six. There were an additional five states in the region, including Sert'a, a Golok territory. The nomadic Goloks were notorious for their violent, independent ways and intense dislike of travelers.[67] Commingling piety with their warlike nature, the Goloks supported more than two thousand monks and one of the largest Nyingma monasteries in Tibet.

Another tribal area with a history of prickly independence was Nyarong, which led a Kham unification movement. Most other states east of the Yangtse were independent of Lhasa, including the kingdom of Chala with its capital of Tachienlu. The major states were Chala, Batang, Litang, Nagch'en, Mili, and the Gyelrong states. Kings also ruled the kingdoms of Chala, Nangch'en, Lhat'og, and Lingts'ang, the largest of which was Chala. Most of the other states also had secular rulers titled *depa* or *pönpo*.

The Last Stronghold of Satan: Christian Missionaries in Tibet

In March 1905, Dr. Shelton wrote the Foreign Christian Missionary Society requesting medical supplies for the dispensary, "which are needed very badly." His request included more than fifty drugs such as adrenaline, balsam copobia, castor and cod liver oil, potassium bromide, and quinine. He also asked for five pounds of chloroform, two hundred yards of gauze, ten spools of adhesive plaster, and fifty pounds of plaster of Paris.[68] By American standards, the medical fees Shelton received were laughable—about a nickel for everything from a sword wound to a leg amputation. One year Shelton's fees totaled a quantity of eggs, meat, yak butter, gunnysack cloth, a few wolf skins, and ninety-six rupees—less than twenty-five dollars.[69]

At first, Dr. Susie Rijnhart had treated patients while Shelton continued his Chinese language study.[70] However, emergencies soon flooded in the door, pressing Shelton into immediate service. He wrote, "Many cases of frost bite and consequent gangrene were coming in at this time, sword cuts, gunshot wounds, and attempted suicide by opium all were things that could not be let go, so it was necessary to combine work with study."[71] One afternoon a band of frostbitten Chinese soldiers came to the dispensary. That day Shelton amputated thirty-one fingers and toes.[72] For many reasons, medicine was the only Christian work that the Tachienlu people would accept. While the new gospel was unwelcome, the locals were more than willing to accept Western medicine when ill or wounded.[73]

Christian missionaries had been evangelizing Tibet for nearly three centuries. In 1625, two Jesuits, Antonio de Andrade and Manuel Marques, established a mission in the remote western Tibetan kingdom of Guge.[74] Initially, the king tolerated the priests, perhaps viewing them as Western-born *bodhisattvas*.[75] Over the next few years, as many as a hundred baptisms took place, but when Andrade tried to expand further into Tibet, a revolt ended the Guge dynasty. The mission closed in 1635.[76]

In 1716, twenty-seven-year-old Italian Jesuit Ippolito Desideri arrived in Lhasa after an eighteen-month journey across western Tibet. Desideri lived in the monasteries, studying language and religion to "arm myself to launch a war."[77] He wrote a book refuting certain Buddhist teachings, which the lamas found of great interest.[78]

Lhasa at the time was in immense upheaval with conflict between the lamas and the royal family. Allied with lamas of the Geluk order, a six-thousand-man Mongolian army took Lhasa on December 1, 1717. To protect the empire from the growing power of the Mongolians, the Chinese invaded Tibet in 1720. After heavy fighting and thousands of casualties, the Chinese captured Lhasa and Tibet. With the victory, the Chinese established a claim of suzerainty, which they solidified with resident political officers called *ambans* and strong contingents of Chinese soldiers.

In 1724, the Dalai Lama permitted the Capuchins to establish a monastery and church, most likely as a reward for their medical work.[79] However, the following year the Tibetans besieged the Christian mission, the friars barely escaping with their lives. Eight years later, the friars withdrew from Tibet but returned to Lhasa in the early 1740s to find the Chinese *amban* in attendance at the Potola Palace exercising Manchu power through the titular control of the Dalai Lama.[80] Within a year, the Tibetans yoked Christian converts into wooden cangues and flogged those who didn't recant. Besieged on every side, the three remaining Capuchins withdrew from Lhasa in April 1745. With the agreement of its Chinese suzerain, Tibet then closed its doors to Western visitors. Tibet became the great shadowy land of magical Buddhism, ruled by a mysterious god-king and forbidden to all who approached.

Lhasa remained barred to Christian missionaries until two French Lazarist priests, Evariste Huc and Joseph Gabet, arrived from northwestern China in 1846. The Chinese *amban* harried them out of Lhasa a few months after their arrival.[81] Their journey back to China took them through the heart of Kham. Once back in China, Huc wrote his widely translated *Souvenirs d'un voyage dans la Tartarie et Thibet*. His book helped convince the next generation of Christian missionaries that the eastern Tibetan ramparts along the Chinese border provided the best point for launching assaults on the cloistered city of Lhasa.

In the last half of the nineteenth century, Protestant missionary groups began to assail the high Tibetan bastion of Buddhism. The Moravians were the first, beginning to preach in the Indian Himalayas in 1856. The Church of Scotland missionaries began evangelizing Tibetans around Darjeeling and Kalimpong in 1870. In 1892, the Scandinavian Alliance Mission established a mission on the Indian-Nepalese border, the first American group aimed at the Tibetans.[82] The American-based Christian and Missionary Alliance established a mission in northwestern China's Tibetan border region.[83] The China Inland Mission began reconnoitering eastern Tibet in 1877. Twenty years later the China Inland Mission opened station in Tachienlu, just prior to Susie Rijnhart's dramatic arrival.[84]

By the beginning of the twentieth century there was great optimism among the missionary societies arrayed at the perimeter of Tibet. Missionary William Carey wrote about the future of Christianity in Tibet: "This apparently impregnable Gibraltar of modern missions is now invested on all sides but one, and the siege is being prosecuted with vigour by several societies, working independently of one another, but directed by a common aim and all cheered by the not distant hope of scaling the impenetrable walls and gaining the confidence of the people."[85]

To a great extent, the Chinese and Tibetans received Christian evangelization in different ways. Though resistant, the Chinese better tolerated Christian missionaries, as they understood the benefits, such as legal assistance, that accrued to converts. With their pragmatic ideas about religion, the Chinese often mixed several faiths together. Espousing an exclusive and aggressively evangelical religion, the Christian missionaries found this mix-and-match attitude abhorrent, using the term "rice Christians" to describe some of their less spiritually committed converts.[86]

Far more than the Chinese, the Tibetans resented the missionary cant, seeing it as a distinct cultural threat. Missionary James Edgar was typical when he wrote, "The religion of Tibet is based on false ideas of man, God, and natural operations, hence, it is a fountain of superstition and magic. The fanatical belief in malignant influences and evil spirits has blighted the national life of the Tibetans as an unseasonable frost withers their flowering wheat." He described a Tibetan temple, "It seems that the mind of man could hardly conceive anything so flagrantly obscene as the idols and decorations of this temple. . . ."[87]

As missionary newcomers in Tibet, the Sheltons thought little different. Flora contended the lamas were "the strangest mixture of cunning, avarice, and superstition and religion I ever saw or read of."[88] She wrote of novice monks placed by their families in monasteries under the care of "the big course men residing there": "They are taught to chant prayers from memory, or to read Tibetan meaninglessly, taught superstition to the highest degree, and given charms to keep away disease and evil. It is not much wonder their lives are foul, for pure thought has no soil in which to be born."[89]

Tibetan converts to Christianity were few and far between. During their first seventeen years in Lhasa, the Capuchins had only seven Tibetan converts.[90] In the western Himalayas, the few converts were either mission servants or orphans.[91] Even British traveler and missionary enthusiast Isabella Bird Bishop had to pronounce the evangelical mission unsuccessful, writing that a lama told a missionary, "'When you came here people were quite indifferent about their religion, but since it has been attacked they have become zealous, and now they *know.*'"[92]

The French Roman Catholics also had little success in their five decades of ministry in Kham, suffering instead ferocious attacks by Khampa tribesmen in 1865 and 1873.[93] An 1881 uprising in southern Kham destroyed missions and cost French missionaries their lives, including Father Briex who died in Batang. In 1887, another general uprising ravaged the missions in Kham. William Rockhill noted the Khampa rage even extended into the grave: "At Bat'ang the lamas took from the grave the bones of Father Briex, killed in 1881, filled their place with ordure, and made a drinking-cup of his skull."[94] In 1900, the Tibetans again visited destruction and violence on the Kham missions.[95] After the Khampa villagers of Thom Bundo near Jyekundo killed French explorer Dutreuil de Rhins in 1894, the French insisted that the Chinese exact revenge. The imperial officials roused themselves to behead three Tibetan villagers and a lama and then demanded the villagers pay reparations to the French. Not long after, Susie Rijnhart's husband lost his life in the same area.[96]

CHAPTER SIX

BAYONETS TO KHAM

Chao Erh-feng and the Christian Missionaries

This is a different work and must be done in a different way.[1]

—James Ogden

As the Sheltons accustomed themselves to family life in the borderlands, open rebellion erupted in western Kham. On March 26, 1905, rioting broke out in Batang. Led by armed lamas, a crowd of over five hundred enraged Khampas attacked a field where Chinese farmers were working, killing those they found there. The Khampas burned down several buildings in town as Chinese troops vainly tried to restore order.[2] Incited by the monks, a crowd of thirty-five hundred Tibetans pillaged the French Roman Catholic mission on the night of April 2, 1905. Capturing a French priest, Father Mussot, the Tibetans scourged him with thorns before shooting him point blank. Later, they nailed his head and hands to the monastery door.[3]

As the night wore on the Khampas killed Chinese traders and soldiers, including the local garrison commander. The imperial Chinese official, assistant *amban* for Kham, Feng Ch'uan, was in residence in Batang. Fleeing the outraged mob, he and his men sought refuge in the compound of one of the Tibetan chiefs. But the chief had already allied himself with the rampaging Tibetans, and the horde quickly surrounded the house.[4] On April 5, 1905, Feng and a contingent of soldiers and officials broke out of the compound to flee to Tachienlu. Not far from Batang, the Tibetans ambushed Feng's party in a narrow gorge. When the massacre was over, a hundred soldiers and twenty officials lay dead in the defile.[5] Word soon reached the Sheltons in Tachienlu that the Tibetans cut Feng's body into pieces and threw them in the river.[6]

The revolt spread through western Kham, including Batang, Chamdo, Nyarong, Sangen, and Litang. The Tibetans pledged "to exterminate all inhabitants . . . even the dogs and chickens, up to the least blade of grass."[7] Another priest, Father Soulié, lost his life at nearby Yaragong when a band of fifty Tibetans captured him in early April and killed him ten days later, burying his corpse under a pile of rocks. A few months later, Tibetans in southwestern Kham murdered Pérés Dubernard and Bourdonnec, bringing Bourdonnec's liver and head back to the large monastery at Atunze, south of Batang.[8] The Tibetans killed Christian converts who didn't recant, including some they sewed inside of fresh yak-skins, which squeezed out their lives under the drying sun.[9]

Younghusband and the Chinese Forward Policy in Kham

The Khampa rebellion of 1905 had its origins in the final years of the nineteenth century, when the Chinese imperial government became increasingly sensitive about its central Asian land frontiers. Embarrassed by the foreign powers' penetration of their country, the Chinese were determined to avoid further subjugation by the imperial powers that encircled them—Great Britain's India, France's Indochina, Russia's encroaching central Asian conquests, and Japan's new territories to the northeast. Seen through the lens of Chinese history, the concern was justified: Asian nomads had repeatedly ravaged China when dynasties lost power and allowed their land defenses to weaken. There was no greater indication of declining dynastic power than weakness in Chinese Inner Asia.[10]

In the post-Opium War era, China maintained influence in the non-Han Chinese native districts through native chiefs (t'u-ssu), a system the Manchus inherited from the Mongols. But as the Western governments' power continued to grow, the traditional system of ruling frontier regions through local chieftains, kings, and lama-controlled states began to look like a foolhardy system, leaving China open to further despoliation.

As a result, the Chinese government initiated its new frontier policies beginning in Mongolia. The Chinese authorities attempted to absorb the border regions culturally and politically into the greater Chinese polity through economic development and educational schemes and the encouragement of Mongolian intermarriage with Chinese immigrants.

The Chinese were not the only imperial power concerned about their frontiers. In 1902, the British officials in New Delhi became alarmed by reports that the Czarist Russians were gaining influence in Lhasa. The British were fearful the Russians would continue their relentless expansion into central Asia, which would have dire implications for British-held India. Accordingly, the British

Foreign Office approved a "trade expedition" to Tibet. On December 12, 1903, Col. Francis Younghusband crossed the border between British Imperial India and Tibet, riding at the head of a seasoned colonial army of British, Gurkha, and Sikh soldiers. The campaign has been called "the last forward move of the Great Game," part of Britain and Czarist Russia's decades-long machinations for control over central Asia and the theoretically strategic high ground of Tibet.[11] The dynamic thirteenth Dalai Lama ruled Lhasa and central Tibet at the time—the first Dalai Lama to rule in his own right since 1757.

The Younghusband expedition advanced halfway to its objective of Gyantse without shedding blood, the Tibetans withdrawing in the face of overwhelming odds. But at the small village of Guru, fifteen hundred fighting monks from Lhasa stood ready to do battle, armed with swords, bows and arrows, matchlocks, and magic amulets blessed by the Dalai Lama to render them bulletproof.[12] Surrounding them, the British began wresting weapons from the befuddled monks' hands. The Tibetan commander drew his revolver in frustration and shot off the jaw of a nearby Indian soldier.

The subsequent carnage disproved the efficacy of the monks' amulets. When the British finished firing four minutes later, seven hundred monks lay bleeding or dead on the Tibetan plain, some shot as they wandered off in shock. One soldier wrote, "I hope I never have to shoot down men *walking* away again."[13] The uproar in England was without parallel, one of the most unpopular moments in the British Empire's long history of unequal warfare against the natives.

The British army marched relentlessly on, encountering their only stiff opposition at the *dzong* (fort) that towered over Gyantse. After finally subduing the Gyantse fort, Younghusband and his troops marched forward to arrive in Lhasa in August 1904, becoming the first Westerners in hundreds of years to enter openly the forbidden city. The Dalai Lama fled to Mongolia.

As Younghusband and his army climbed into Tibet, the Chinese coincidentally embarked on a policy in Kham designed to bringing the recalcitrant border region under their control. The provincial Governor of Sichuan petitioned the Emperor to give consideration to developing Kham with agriculture and mining, utilizing Chinese colonists from overcrowded eastern Sichuan. The Chinese governor foresaw Khampa resistance as the major obstacle, writing, "It is very hard to show them reason and entice them with advantages because of their arrogant nature. Military force must be used to suppress them; sternness and favors both used."[14] The governor recommended that Batang in western Kham be the first area developed with Chinese farmers, since it was situated in a relatively low, protected valley that already had Chinese officials in place.

In response to Younghusband's initiatives, the imperial government also appointed an assistant Chinese *amban* to Chamdo in western Kham, Feng

Ch'uan.[15] Instead of traveling to his assigned post in Chamdo, which was beyond effective Chinese power, Feng made his headquarters in Batang. Concerned with the influx of Chinese colonists, the head lama of Batang's enormous Buddhist monastery protested loudly, saying the land chosen for farming was suitable only for grazing. In spite of the Tibetans' objections, Feng impetuously began to implement the imperial government's plan. A group of Chinese farmers arrived and began tilling a small field.

As Feng's moves inflamed the Khampas, he desperately needed seasoned soldiers. While Feng led a troop of Chinese soldiers trained in the latest foreign military techniques, they were newly trained and untested in combat. Hoping to buttress his forces, Feng organized a militia of local men, led by a Christian convert. Oblivious to the growing unrest, Feng proceeded with plans to develop Kham, including mines and the farming of ten thousand acres within three or four years. As a final insult, Feng gave the French Roman Catholic missionaries a land grant in Batang.[16]

Feng responded to the lamas' protests by decreeing there could be no more than three hundred lamas in the town's monasteries and imposing a twenty-year hiatus on new monks. With their large concentrated populations, arsenals, and tea-trade importance, the monasteries served as a locus of Khampa religious, economic, political, and military power. Any who refused to leave the monastic life would be decapitated.[17]

There were officially eighteen hundred monks in Batang, though Feng estimated there to actually be five thousand. Terming them "the parasites of the population," who sheltered the worst outlaws in the region, he attacked the monastery in mid-March, but the local people drove him off. Late that month he breached the outer wall of the monastery and killed a number of monks.[18]

Feng was still in Batang when Younghusband imposed his new treaty on the Lhasa Tibetans. On the strength of his military expedition, Younghusband forced the Tibetan regent to sign a new convention with the British on September 7, 1904, which recognized British hegemony in Sikkim, opened trade relations with India, and assented to previously unenforced treaties signed by Britain and China.[19] As the Chinese were relatively powerless in both eastern and central Tibet, they had little ability to enforce any treaties relating to Tibet. However the subsequent European disgust with the Younghusband campaign forced the British Foreign Office to demure on any further political initiatives. This ultimately opened the door for China to reassert itself in Tibet.

The Lhasa agreements abruptly changed the situation for the Chinese government, unintentionally unleashing a firestorm in eastern Tibet.[20] Where the Chinese previously saw Kham as a place for economic development, they now saw it as a line of defense against European colonialism. While Chinese power in Kham had clearly declined from the mid-nineteenth century, the imperial throne still maintained loose suzerainty.[21] With the British having their way a few hundred miles away in central Tibet, the Chinese determined to change fundamentally their strategy towards Kham by attempting to bring the region under their direct control.[22] As part of this plan, the Chinese aimed to shape the culture and polity of the Tibetan borderlands, with the intent of finally bringing the independent Khampa tribesmen to heel.[23]

Obstinate and short-tempered, assistant *amban* Feng quickly proceeded to annex Nyarong, a rebellious state northeast of Batang previously under the control of Lhasa.[24] With a maximum of saber rattling, Feng evicted of all Tibetan officials from the state and continued with his plans of conquest.[25] The moves precipitated the Khampa revolt the Sheltons encountered in 1905 that cost the imperious assistant *amban* his life.

Chao Erh-feng and the Kham Offensive

The Chinese quickly responded to the Khampa revolt of 1905. The viceroy of Sichuan appointed two men to bring the rebels under control: provincial Commander-in-Chief Ma Wei-ch'i, and Chao Erh-feng, a magistrate in Ya'an, who served as Ma's reinforcement. Ma Wei-chi mercilessly attempted to suppress the revolt in western Kham. The Tibetans retaliated by killing Chinese officials and soldiers and massacring an English botanist.[26] Wounded Chinese and deserters fleeing back to China filled the Foreign Christian Missionary Society (FCMS) dispensary. Flora wrote, "These would come into the dispensary literally soaked with blood, as one punishment was to cut off both ears close to the head."[27]

Chao Erh-feng arrived in Tachienlu in late May 1905. A Manchu bannerman from an influential family, the austere Chao was a formidable opponent for the Khampas to confront. Chao and his column marched out of Tachienlu in mid-July to join Ma Wei-ch'i against the rebellious Batang Khampas.

Arriving in Batang in mid-summer, Ma Wei-ch'i rapidly overcame the local resistance. He summarily executed the two rebel princes and exiled their families to Chengdu. To protect Ma Wei-ch'i's supply lines, Chao Erh-feng halted halfway across the Jung Lam at Litang, reputedly the highest and dirtiest town in the world. Situated on an enormous treeless plain at over thirteen thousand feet high, Litang had a population of three hundred families. An immense monastery with three thousand monks loomed on a hill above the town, golden spires glinting in the cloudless blue sky. Litang simmered with rebellion. When the local officials refused to provide transportation for Ma's supplies, they jeopardized the Chinese campaign.[28]

In the face of the Litang Tibetans' refusal, Chao had an easy remedy. He quickly executed the recalcitrant officials and jailed the local *t'u-ssu*. Supplies moved along quite briskly following Chao's enforcement. The transport problem solved, Chao moved forward to Batang, arriving two months after Ma.

Ma and Chao collaborated on a harsh pacification in Batang. In a shady grove near the monastery, Chao's efficient executioners beheaded local officials, Batang's chief lama, and scores of Khampas.[29] The Chinese buried some Khampas alive and boiled others to death in the monastery's enormous brass tea cauldrons. Monks received up to fifteen hundred blows with a bamboo flail, effectively flaying them to death. The Chinese pillaged and razed the monastery, using the Buddhist scriptures to resole their shoes. Turning to the surrounding countryside, the Chinese proceeded with further destruction.[30]

With Batang momentarily subdued, Ma withdrew the bulk of his troops back to Sichuan proper, leaving Chao to campaign against the remaining rebels. Never stinting in aggressive action, Chao soon launched attacks on Khampa strongholds in the mountains around Batang.

Back to China: The New Evangelist

As the carnage roiled Kham a few hundred miles to the west, the young Shelton family headed back to China. Bert led the way on horseback as Flora followed in a sedan chair with baby Dorris in her lap. After eighteen months in Tachienlu, the Sheltons returned to China to escort a new evangelist and his wife, James and Minnie Ogden, to Tachienlu. The FCMS board posted the Ogdens to Tachienlu as Dr. Susie Rijnhart's fragile health was rapidly failing in the high altitude.

The new mission's first year and a half had gone fairly well. Dr. Shelton gave his first sermon in 1905. The missionaries operated a chapel, dispensary, and school for ten boys. Besides her medical work, Rijnhart gave midwife training, women's bible classes, and industrial classes for women and children, as well as preaching in the countryside. Rijnhart and evangelist Yang held nightly prayer meetings for a few dozen Chinese and Chinese-Tibetans, some with hopes of getting help with lawsuits or private quarrels. They baptized three people in August 1905. Three days later Yang was on his way back to Nanjing, leaving the FCMS missionaries on their own.[31]

Over four years, the FCMS Tachienlu mission baptized about a dozen Chinese and Chinese-Tibetan people, as well as running a school for the same group.[32] There were no conversions among the pure Tibetan population.[33] Missionaries commonly adopted orphans to serve as bridges into the local communities. The Sheltons employed this stratagem, adopting a pair of orphan boys, thirteen-year-old Li Gway Gwang and his six-year-old brother, Li Gway Yuin. They were Chinese-Tibetan children, sons of a minor Chinese official and his Tibetan wife who both had died. Vermin-ridden, filthy, and undernourished when they arrived, the Sheltons intended to raise the boys for mission work. "We took him [Li Gway Gwang] in, had him shaved and washed, put clean clothes on him, and kept him," Flora wrote.[34]

In spite of its isolation, the foreign contingent of Tachienlu still had its social moments as it continued to serve as local experts and a haven for passing Western travelers. British botanist E. H. Wilson was a guest of the Sheltons in 1904, and he left a botanical memento of his visit: *Rhododendron sheltonae,* a variety of rhododendron that covered the mountain slopes around Tachienlu. "A very neat species," Wilson wrote, "common on scrub-clad mountains near Tachienlu. Named in compliment to Mrs. Shelton, wife of Dr. Shelton, missionary at Tachienlu, to both of whom I am indebted for kind hospitality in 1904."[35]

The U.S. Consul at Chongqing, Mason Mitchell, also made a visit to Tachienlu in search of hunting trophies. Hunting bonded Shelton and the sporting foreigners who traipsed through Kham. The daily bag of game filled the travelogues of the touring Westerners, and it was a rare day when at least a brace of grouse wasn't noted.

After eight days of travel down to China to fetch the new evangelist couple, the Shelton family parted at the tea town of Ya'an. Flora and the baby traveled on another four days to Chengdu while Bert and a servant floated down the Dadu River on an enormous bamboo raft. Sixty feet long and eighty feet wide, the raft bobbed over a hundred miles of rapids in four days. At Leshan Shelton and his servant switched to a small boat for the perilous journey down the Yangtze rapids to Chongqing, writing, "many times the boat was lost control of and we went around and around like a top, but fortunately we struck no rocks."[36] Shelton boarded a steamer at Yichang to travel the last thousand miles to Shanghai. The twenty-four-day journey down the river to Yichang would require nine or ten weeks of hard up-river travel on the return trip.

In Shanghai he located the Ogdens, who were somewhat overwhelmed by China. James and Minnie Ogden were Kentucky graduates of Transylvania College, an affiliate of Dr. Shelton's medical alma mater, Kentucky University.[37] Albert and the Ogdens prepared for the long journey home. "We trust, however, that we shall have no serious mishap and will arrive safely in Ta Chien Lu some time in February," Shelton wrote the missionary society.[38]

The Sheltons reunited in Leshan and continued on to Tachienlu. After an absence of almost five months, the caravan arrived back in Tachienlu on February 3, 1906. Their retinue of sedan chairs and baggage included a church organ that Dr. Shelton purchased in Shanghai. Slung between two poles, the organ made

its ponderous way to Kham on the shoulders of coolies. The instrument represented the Sheltons' more liberal affinities. Conservative Disciples of Christ ab-
horred the use of instrumental accompaniment, as they found none in the
accounts of Jesus and the apostles.[39]

The Siege of Sampiling and Chao Erh-feng's Policies in Kham

As the Sheltons made their way back to China, Batang again ignited in rebellion. The new upheaval forced Chao to appeal to Ma Wei-ch'i for fresh soldiers
from Sichuan in November 1906. After Chao again conquered Batang, he
moved against the particularly aggressive Khampas of the Hsiang-ch'eng (Xi-
angcheng) region south of Litang. With the independence-minded lamas of the
fortified Sampiling monastery providing political and military leadership, the
large nomadic state was a center of resistance to both the Chinese and the central Tibetans.[40] A region of precipitous mountain trails leading to high remote
grasslands, the Hsiang-ch'eng was so unexplored that it was a blank on most
maps. The region sat strategically astride the Tachienlu-Batang Jung Lam trail,
allowing the tribesmen to cut the Chinese communication and supply lines almost at will.

The Chinese had not dared enter the area since 1902, when they made a
punitive foray into the Hsiang-ch'eng to avenge the murder of a Chinese officer
and his son eight years before. Capturing the commander of the 1902 expedition, the Khampas flayed him alive, exhibiting his skin "in the Lamasery Museum of curios and wild animals," according to missionary J. H. Edgar.[41]

Many monks who survived the Chinese retribution joined the militant
monks at the Sampiling monastery, a vast walled compound that sprawled on a
remote tableland deep in the Hsiang-ch'eng. Chao invaded the Hsiang-ch'eng
in January 1906 with a troop of two thousand seasoned soldiers trained in Western-style military methods. Chao's army was equipped with German-made rifles
and four Krupp field guns. After fighting several engagements with Hsiang-
ch'eng renegade tribesmen and fighting monks, Chao forced them to retreat to
Sampiling. With its twenty-foot-high, four-foot-thick walls and two thousand
monks, the monastery was particularly well suited to defense.

The combatants settled down for a long siege, the monastery proceeding with
daily worship as the Chinese languished on the barren plain.[42] The siege was a
stalemate for several months until a captured Tibetan disclosed the source of the
monastery's water supply, which Chao quickly interrupted. By June the
monastery's situation was desperate. The monks dispatched a courier to plead
for reinforcement from another monastery, but Chao captured him. Recognizing the lamas would be expecting relief, Chao sent men disguised as Tibetan

warriors to the monastery. One of the Chinese soldiers managed to convince the defenders to open the gate, and Chao's men rushed in. After fierce fighting between the monks and the Chinese troops, Sampiling fell on June 19, 1906. Chao ordered the surviving rebels be put to the sword. The slaughter of the monks became legendary among the Khampas, who gave Chao his nickname, "Butcher Chao."[43]

With the Sampiling revolt crushed, Chao effectively ended the Khampa rebellion. He had ranged undefeated through much of southwestern Kham, in the process earning a reputation for cruelty and severity across all of eastern Tibet.[44] By the end of his first Kham campaigns, Chao had such a gory reputation that Tibetan folklore began to embellish his already violent punishments.[45] British Lt. Col. F. M. Bailey recounted one hyperbolic folktale: "Chao had killed a Tibetan at Batang by tying him up, cutting away the flesh and skin covering his stomach, and nailing a flap of this to his chest while he amused himself with watching his heart and interior workings until he expired; after which he ate his head!"[46] Chao wasn't ruthless just with the rebellious Khampas. He executed eighteen hundred of his own men during the siege of Sampiling alone.

Once back in Chengdu, the Chinese officials bestowed high military honors on Chao Erh-feng and confirmed his designation as Frontier Commissioner of Sichuan and Yunnan with the rank of vice-president of a Beijing board, an appointment announced to be equivalent to that of the *ambans* in Lhasa.

China no longer saw Kham as a wild, near-useless borderland inhabited by grudgingly subordinate barbarians. Rather, Beijing now understood that Kham needed to be controlled and developed in a Chinese manner. Chao accordingly promulgated a set of forty-three regulations in April 1906 regarding Chinese colonization and economic development. First posting the regulations in Batang and the Hsiang-ch'eng, Chao intended Chinese development to spread from his pilot projects there, eventually Sinicizing all of Kham's Tibetan culture. The regulations declared the local population was subject to the emperor in Beijing. Chinese officials had already replaced the local Tibetan authorities. The local officials who remained reported only to Chinese authority. The regulations stripped the lamas of much of their power and sharply reduced the populations in the Buddhist monasteries. The Chinese permitted only three hundred monks in the Batang monasteries and completely proscribed the monks of the Hsiang-ch'eng region from living in monastic communities.

The regulations decreed major cultural changes among the Tibetans. Marriages had to be monogamous. Funerals, particularly those involving parents who the filially devout Chinese held in high esteem, had to be according to the Chinese custom. Tibetan children were required to wear Chinese-style pants, and adults were urged also to wear pants to increase sexual chastity. Cleanliness and civic sanitation were encouraged with the construction of public toilets. The regulations required Tibetans to adopt Chinese names and for the Tibetan men to wear their in Chinese-style queues—"no one will be permitted to have his hair in the disheveled state hitherto the custom, which makes men resemble living demons."[47]

Journey to Batang: The First Itineration

Chao Erh-feng was still in the Hsiang-ch'eng in the autumn of 1906 when Albert Shelton and James Ogden followed behind his bayonets. Lured by the dream of a station on the Tibetan border, the two missionaries left Tachienlu on September 3, 1906, on a five-week trip to reconnoiter Batang. They rode mules across the Jung Lam, with yaks carrying their provisions.[48] Batang was four hundred and sixty miles from Tachienlu, over fourteen high mountain passes that were fourteen thousand to seventeen thousand feet high. It was the longest journey Albert Shelton had made in Kham, the previous being only three days from Tachienlu.[49]

Within an hour of Tachienlu, the Chinese presence vanished and Tibetans thinly settled the countryside—no more than twenty dwellings to be seen in the next two days. Tiny villages and scattered tents populated the balance of the stages to the high monastery town of Litang.[50] In the final days to Batang, the missionaries encountered only about a hundred huts along the trail. When they arrived in Batang, Shelton and Ogden found a small Tibetan-speaking town with about three hundred and fifty families. Except for a Chinese temple, all of the architecture was Tibetan. "The large Lamasery, which was nearly as large as the rest of Batang and had over 2000 Lamas, has been destroyed by the Chinese, and all the Lamas driven out except about 200."[51] Shelton wrote, "The Chinese had been absolutely ruthless in their punishments. The innocent and guilty suffered alike, and executions would sometimes run into forty and fifty in a day."[52] While the prince of Batang was among the victims, his son welcomed Shelton and Ogden, as did the local Chinese official, eager as they were to obtain Shelton's medical services.

Batang sat in a broad valley that was sheltered from the harsh weather by surrounding peaks.[53] As with most missionary enterprises, finances were a vital concern. Shelton and Ogden thoroughly investigated Batang's cost of living.[54] They found rent, land, and building materials to be cheaper than in Tachienlu, though provisions raised in the valley were 50 percent higher. Manufactured provisions such as canned goods, candles, coal oil, and matting couldn't be purchased at any price, and would have to be hauled in. Ogden wrote the FCMS that it would cost 20 percent more to relocate the mission to Batang.[55]

Notwithstanding the additional costs and obvious danger, the missionaries petitioned to move the station to Batang. Once back in Tachienlu, James Ogden made the case: "It has not as many people as here, but it is in the main Tibetan, the language Tibetan, and it is located on the main road leading into Tibet, and is on the border. . . . The population is nearly all Tibetan and this district is as populous as any portion of Tibet except a district in the southern part where missionaries are not allowed to go."

Batang didn't have any Protestant missionaries, which was another plus. Missionary societies in China generally divided territory into evangelical fiefdoms, and territorial overlap and Christian evangelical competition were frowned upon.[56] The evangelism problems of Tachienlu would also be ameliorated, as there were far fewer Chinese in Batang. Flora Shelton wrote, "The situation in Tachienlu was very difficult. The Chinese were the rulers, and monopolized the services, and the Tibetans refused to come and mix with them at all, for several reasons. One was the position in which they were held by the Chinese, and the other, their hatred of them."[57] James Ogden was not flippant about the challenges in Batang: "Should we go to Batang, or any place else, we are going to find Tibetan work very difficult. . . . Tibetans will not assemble in a hall to hear the gospel as the Chinese, Japanese, Indians, or Africans. This is a different work and must be done in a different way."[58]

Illness and altitude problems plagued the Tachienlu missionaries.[59] Theodore Sorensen and his child contracted smallpox. James Moyes suffered a life-threatening bout with dreaded typhoid fever, nearly dying before Dr. Shelton stimulated his heart by injecting syringes of whiskey behind his breastbone. Shortly after returning from their journey down to China, Flora also came down with typhus, an endemic disease in China and central Asia.[60] Albert wrote: "It appeared impossible that she should recover, but at last, after two days and nights, during which time, at intervals of fifteen minutes, she had been given a teaspoonful of water to prevent her choking as she lay unconscious, she began to show improvement."[61] Flora also developed an alarming paralysis of the arms. For treatment, she retreated with her baby and Dr. Susie Rijnhart to the lower altitude and warmer climes of a village further east on the trail to Luding.

In the fall of 1906, a cable from the FCMS arrived in Tachienlu via China, responding to the missionaries' Batang request. The society requested the Tachienlu mission to close the station and relocate back to east China, citing the perils of the road, the remoteness of the mission, and the difficulty in finding missionaries willing to be stationed there. In reply the missionaries cabled back to the FCMS headquarters in St. Louis, "We'll go in, not out; forward not back."[62]

The Feasible Plan: Chao Erh-feng and the Christian Missionaries

In February 1907, Chao published a proclamation to all the district magistrates in Sichuan, inviting settlement in the frontier region. "The over-populated state of Szechuan renders the struggle for existence very difficult," the proclamation read, "Why then do you not hasten to this promising land?" Like the glossy promises of land promotions back in Kansas, Chao's proclamation painted glowing prospects for homesteaders on the Tibetan frontier. Kham was inexpensive and fertile, awaiting the superior farming skills of the Chinese. Likewise the hard-working Tibetan women: "A native girl taken as a wife will prove of great assistance in the work, for these women perform all the carrying of water, cooking of food, hoeing of the ground, and cutting of firewood. Nor is any dowry necessary, for all that is needed is garments in which to clothe her."

Acknowledging the dangers of Kham, Chao assured the potential settlers that the region was now secure: "Armed posts have been established everywhere, and death was meted out last year to a great number of thieves and robbers, so little danger of violence is to be anticipated from these gentry."[63]

Chao's occupying army at times reached six thousand men. It was essential to his strategy of controlling the Tibetans so Kham could be a defensive bulwark against the encroaching British Empire. Kham also provided a forward position to take Lhasa, an objective the Chinese saw as attainable in the post-Younghusband political vacuum.[64]

With an inhospitable climate and a hostile populace, Kham was a wrenching pioneer experience for the Chinese settlers. Chao shared his true thoughts about Kham's potential for Chinese settlement on July 20, 1907. Kham was a difficult area, he wrote, "truly a wilderness to be opened for the first time." He admitted, "When setters first arrive, they need vast reserves to fill their stomachs. Otherwise there will be disastrous starvation."[65]

Discouraged by the poor agricultural prospects in Kham, Chao turned to mining for development capital. Working from Chengdu from late 1906 to the autumn of 1908, Chao organized the conquered states of Batang, Litang, and the Hsiang-ch'eng into Chinese counties called *hsien*, governed by Chinese officials. By the end of 1908, the situation in eastern Tibetan borderland looked favorable to the Chinese imperial government. A broad band of southern Kham from Tachienlu to Batang was relatively quiescent. Colonization and administrative initiatives were in place. The British advance was checked, and the final Chinese advance to Lhasa appeared imminent.[66]

The Western missionaries saw Chao as a great conquering hero, a man who could at last subdue the Tibetans and allow them to transmit word of the West and its Christian God. Emissaries of a martial, muscular brand of Christianity, the missionaries trailed the Chinese army into eastern Tibet, dreaming they would accompany the Chinese legions into forbidden Lhasa.[67] Lauding Chao's draconian policies as essential to his success against the unruly Khampas, missionary J. H. Edgar gave glowing reports of the effects of Chao's conquests: "Now the outcome of all this is a confidence in the Government, which is highly beneficial to the Chinese and the Tibetans. Business is increasing rapidly; trees are being planted in the waste lands; telegraph communication connects the city [Litang] with Peking; and the Roman Catholics have bought buildings for missionary purposes. All this suggests that Litang has entered a new era—an era with orderly government, uninfluenced by Lamaism."[68]

Like the other Tibet missionaries, the Sheltons were enthusiastic supporters of Chao's initiatives. Dr. Albert Shelton had few illusions about the Chinese advance. When he filled out an FCMS questionnaire, he acknowledged their brutal enforcement, noting the Chinese shut up three-quarters of the Tibetan Buddhist monasteries and compelled the children "to worship Confucius." However, when asked if the Chinese administration was beneficial, he answered, "Yes (with some few exceptions)."[69]

Naturally, the Khampas disagreed with the Westerners' sentiments. They saw their homeland as independent of both Lhasa and Beijing but wholly and totally part of the Tibetan world. One Tibetan governor provided a mass of material proving Kham was inextricably part of Tibet and stated, "All Eastern Tibet is inhabited by Tibetans, and the Eastern Tibetan is as much a Tibetan as a Yorkshireman is an Englishman."[70]

There were clear indications that Kham was far from pacified. In spite of the total destruction of Sampiling, raiders continued to sweep out of the Hsiang-ch'eng. J. H. Edgar noted, "Although large numbers have been caught, travelers within the last few days have been robbed, and at Lamaya, sixty li distant, success is only in its initial stages, for both the Embassy and the Lhassa Amban have been pillage. . . ."[71]

One morning a messenger arrived to tell Dr. Shelton that a high Chinese official in the Tylin gold fields a hundred miles and five days to the north was wounded and in urgent need of his services after a battle with the Tibetans. Quickly mounting, Shelton and his guide rode through the rainy night and on into the morning, arriving in Tylin at noon the following day.

The Chinese had opened the gold field in the face of Tibetan opposition. Using primitive mining techniques, the Chinese miners shoveled dirt from holes beside the stream into baskets and then washed it in the rushing stream for dust and tiny nuggets. The lamas objected to the mining, contending it would disturb the nature gods. At the urging of the monks, the Tibetans drove out the Chinese gold miners. When Chinese soldiers retook the field, the war settled down to a series of bloody skirmishes that filled Shelton's dispensary with wounded men.[72]

Once at Tylin, Shelton treated the officer's gunshot wound and spent ten days treating the ailments of the camp. When it came time for Albert to leave, the official gave him two hundred rupees, a very large sum for the time. The official also presented Shelton with a fine black mule, along with saddle and tack. "This was the largest fee I had ever received," Shelton wrote, naming the mule Abe, after Abraham Cory, his stubborn FCMS friend who led many fund-raising campaigns.[73] In the years to come, he rode his beloved Abe many thousands of miles across Kham, and the mule became famous in America as a symbol of Shelton's pioneering ways.

A New Home: The Sheltons in Kham

In the three years since their arrival in Kham, missionary life had transformed the Sheltons. Albert was now a father and a frontier doctor, struggling to deal with two new, distinctly different cultures and languages. With Dr. Susie Rijn-hart gone, he was also the senior FCMS missionary in a turbulent and chaotic war zone.

His paternal duties soon increased. On May 27, 1907, Flora gave birth in Tachienlu to the Sheltons' second daughter, Dorothy Madelon Shelton.[74] Flora found Tachienlu a hard post and continued to wrestle with the travails of the remote station: "The snow falls early, and stays late, and it rains almost everyday in the summer time. A dreadful shut-in place it seemed to those who had seen only plains and broad fields."[75] She faced the challenges of new motherhood without the comfort of her family. "I was homesick, deathly homesick yesterday," she wrote in her diary. "I wanted to take my babies in my arms & run home for a few minutes, to see the farm & pappa & let him hold my dear little baby."[76] She often lamented her husband's absence while he was away on missionary work. She wrote, "Bert has been gone 4 days and it seems like a month. & there are still 2 weeks yet until he expects to return to us."[77]

With the arrival of the new baby, Dorris became "Daddy's little girl," accompanying him everywhere in his work. Flora wrote, "She orders him to play bear sometimes, and growl like a baby bear she saw; then he must be a horse, down on all fours while she rides; next with a *tsampa* bowl she is a whining beggar, and her father is putting cash in the bowl."[78]

With the constant stimulus of Tibetan and Chinese domestic help, the two girls learned the native tongues almost as their first language—"the children speak it just as naturally as the natives and learn it more readily that they do English, and more correctly," Albert reported.[79]

Figure 6.1   Albert and Flora with babies Dorris and Dorothy. Both Shelton daughters were born in the Tibetan town of Tachienlu. Dorris arrived on August 25, 1904 and Dorothy on May 27, 1907. Photograph courtesy the Still Family Archive. Reprinted with permission.

His early years in the Tibetan borderlands had a dramatic effect on Albert Shelton. In many ways, Albert Shelton already knew the life of the frontier. He knew hunting and riding from his life on the Western frontier. The Jung Lam was just the high Asian version of the Santa Fe Trail. The mud and wood houses were reminiscent of Plains soddies. The Tibetans' nomadic culture was reminiscent of the Plains Indians' migrating ways, and the confluence of Chinese and Tibetan culture resembled the commingling of the American West. The endemic violence of Kham was a replay of the tales of his High Plains frontier boyhood. Failed homesteading was something he knew to the core of his being.

Tibet was a conservative migration for Shelton, almost a romantic attempt to reverse time back to his homesteader youth. He again felt the freedom of the frontier, where jack-of-all-trades self-reliance and the ability to think independently were vital skills. Yet he was also a highly trained physician and an exemplar of his society. It created an internal tension. Shelton was a borderman operating in the interstice between the wildness of the frontier and Western imperial values. As with most frontiersmen, he had to maintain his link to his homeland, or he would simply melt into the native culture. Though he was a sojourner in Tibet, Albert Shelton had come back home again, halfway around the world.[80]

Dr. Albert L. Shelton

Figure 6.2 Shelton on Abe. His early years in the Tibetan borderlands transformed Shelton into a rugged pioneer doctor. Photograph courtesy the Collection of The Newark Museum. Reprinted with permission.

A photograph captured the transformation of Dr. Albert Shelton. He sat on his tall, muscular mule, looking confidently into the camera, a rustic sophisticate. His battered Stetson and worn boots were dusty with the Himalayan trails, his saddlebags and bedroll behind him. A rifle hung from the saddle in an old scabbard. Barren Tibetan hills formed the backdrop. Albert Shelton was no longer a genteel aspiring doctor from the Midwest. He was the head of a pioneering family; an adventurer on the Tibetan border.[81]

CHAPTER SEVEN

THE DOCTOR IN KHAM, 1908-1909

Medicine is given out left and right, while hot shots of gospel are put in between doses of colomel and santonine.[1]

—Flora B. Shelton

After the mission society rejected the proposed Batang station, the Sheltons settled down in Tachienlu. Albert's medical practice found a ready clientele in the war-torn region, and Flora managed their busy household. Though Chinese came for Christian services, evangelization among the Tibetans continued to yield thin harvests. Albert Shelton and James Ogden searched Tachienlu for buildings to rent for the mission. Finding none suitable, they petitioned the mission board in St. Louis for permission to build.

Correspondence was slow between Tachienlu and the FCMS headquarters, letters and their reply often taking several months for exchange. So the reply from the society president surprised the missionaries. Instead of responding to the Tachienlu plans for construction, the president wrote that the society board approved opening Batang as a mission station. Back in America, the board had acquiesced to Shelton's emotional "we'll go in, not out" telegram of a few months before.

The Mission to Batang

On July 7, 1908, the Sheltons' small caravan left for Batang. As he rode toward the farthest edge of the Chinese empire, Albert Shelton was just one more spear-carrier in the grand campaign to take Christianity and the West to the world. It was a heady time for Americans and their global mission. The same year

Theodore Roosevelt exhorted America and its missionaries to push to the farthest ends of the Orient: "The work of the missionaries tends to avert revolutionary disturbances in China. . . . *Now* is the time for the West to implant its ideals in such a manner as to minimize the chance of a dreadful future clash between the two radically different civilizations."[2]

The Sheltons traveled on Kham's northern trade route two days around the wide shoulder of Ta-pai-shan mountain that stood north of Tachienlu. The two Shelton babies were in one palanquin, Flora in the other. While sedan chairs were relatively uncommon west of Tachienlu, Chinese officials and Christian ladies hired chairs and coolies to haul them west through the mountains.[3] Albert rode his mule, Abe. Dr. Shelton had requested two hundred dollars from the FCMS for "a caravan of twelve animals and a man to care for the same, to carry silver, mail, medical, and other supplies."[4]

The northern route was one of three great trails across western China to Tibet, but it was the only one usable at the time. The intractable Hsiang-ch'eng tribesmen blocked the southern Jung Lam route. The far northern trail through Gansu to Lhasa was a most roundabout route to Batang, and one subject to attacks by Mongolian tribesmen. The conditions left the northern route as the preferred trail.

The trade routes across Kham were perennially difficult and dangerous for travelers, particularly those journeying under the aegis of the Chinese authorities. One traveler reported, "We were told of robbers here who have a habit that must be especially unpleasant in cold weather, of robbing a man of everything, down to the last rag on his back, and leaving him absolutely naked." Bandits were so thorough that in one case they cut a naked Tibetan's plait off to get his hair ornament.[5] So generations of travelers nervously scanned the heights and gingerly rounded the cliffside trails, always expecting to hear the "Ahhehehehe!" of Khampa war cries followed by a volley of gunfire.[6]

The roads through mountainous Kham were themselves precarious. In Shelton's day, they were little different from the trails earlier missionaries described: "fearful chasms from which the most intrepid traveler must recoil in horror," where "a single step spelt annihilation on the jagged rocks below."[7] Old Chinese guidebooks discussed the difficult roads through the mountains. One read, "The way is blocked by the great mountain Hsiao-kuan, in the profound gorges of which heavy torrents of rain continually fall, and the flanks of which are always clothed in mist and fog."[8]

The caravan journeyed west through wildflower-strewn meadows and mountainsides for several days before turning south to Litang on the Jung Lam. The great monastery town of Litang stood on its high plain. Chao's depredations had reduced the population of monks considerably, and the once-proud monastery was now tumbledown and derelict.[9] A Tibetan folktale told of a Litang lama Chao had beheaded. Another head miraculously appeared in place of the old one. This was also severed, only to have another grow in its place. The Chinese executioner persevered through multiple heads, and, after incessant chopping, the monk gave up.[10]

Each night the Sheltons stopped at the flat-roofed stone rest stations the Chinese had built after Chao's conquest. As their cook scurried to prepare supper, washpans and combs emerged for the crucial family cleanup. Khampa caravan teamsters formed a U with the unloaded baggage to protect them from the cold mountain winds. While one drew water and another gathered dried yak dung for fuel, a third constructed a fire ring of stones. One man sparked a fire with dried moss and then used a huge leather bellows to keep the yak-dung chips glowing with a clear steady blue flame.[11] Mornings brought the reverse of the evening unpacking. After morning toilets and breakfast, the caravan mounted for another stage across Kham, pausing at midday for the Sheltons' lunch break and opium for the chair coolies.

Trading caravans between China and central Tibet shared the roads. Shaggy black yaks and long-horned yak-cattle hybrids called *dzos* meandered down the trail carrying Tibetan wool, medicinal herbs, Chinese silk, and brick tea. Herdsmen with swords and matchlocks goaded their malingering pack mules and ponies forward. Pilgrims bound for Lhasa ambled by with prayer wheels awhirl.[12]

West of Litang, the Shelton's caravan failed to cross the high Whangtogang pass during the day's travel. Whangtogang pass, which translated as "the abomination of desolation," was a misery for travelers. That night the high altitude prevented any sleep. Albert wrote, "We were simply like fish out of water. There was not enough oxygen to in the air to sustain one at a retarded rate of respiration, so we sat up and managed to get through the night; but at three o'clock got breakfast and were ready to move on."[13]

A Challenging Oasis, Batang

The Sheltons arrived in Batang on July 24, 1908. Batang, meaning "Plain of Cows," was a fertile valley, sheltered by high mountains. The Chitsuen River hugged the western mountain and the Taso River ran through the center of the valley. Irrigation canals sparkled across the plain.[14] The relatively low altitude of 8,500 feet, good soil, and consistent water supply made the town an agricultural haven—so intensely cultivated there was scarcely any room for trees.[15] The fields produced two crops a year, including oats, wheat, maize, barley, and buckwheat, and the gardens abounded with vegetables that were exceptional in size and flavor. In arid Tibet, Batang was renowned for its fruit and nuts, including peaches, pears, grapes, and walnuts. Fresh meat, eggs, and milk were available daily.[16]

Farmers and herders brought their produce for barter and sale to the Batang market, where central Tibetans and Mongolians traded borax, gold, furs, and musk for tea and snuff.[17] The market was on the main paved thoroughfare, which was about half a mile long, with several side streets and lanes for three hundred or so houses branching from it. The two- and three-story Tibetan houses were made of pounded yellow mud akin to adobe.[18] Notched logs served as stairways between the floors.

The climate was remarkably genial for Tibet. Though snow often filled the passes in winter, isolating the valley, it was a rarity in the town. Spring and the fall brought vivid blue skies and mountainsides of wild color. While verdant, it was often hot and stifling in the summertime. The Tibetans considered Batang to be such a propitious place that they used the town in a proverb representing two lovers:

> In the happy country of Bathang,
> There are two crops in the summer time;
> Where religion spreads in the cloister,
> Whose cedar trees circle to the right.[19]

It was a rough start. The Sheltons' cook had preceded them to Batang a few months prior to rent and prepare rooms.[20] He had difficulty finding a place, as no one wanted to rent to the Westerners. Eventually, the Chinese officials requisitioned rooms for them, "the missionaries paying liberal rent to console the unwilling landlords."[21] The missionaries couldn't go out at night for fear of attack. If they took some air on the roof of their house, Tibetans threw rocks at them. Five months after arriving, the Sheltons found an old mill property to rent. Perched beside the river that flowed past Batang, the property was near the town's southwestern gate.

The Sheltons arrived in Batang at the nadir of Tibetan Buddhist power. The great Batang monastery with its gilded roof and towers was demolished, the rich Buddhist religious art looted or destroyed. The nine-acre courtyard inside the monastery walls became a drilling ground for the twelve hundred Chinese soldiers posted in the town. Chao turned the grove of cedar trees surrounding the monastery into the execution grounds where weekly beheadings and floggings took place.[22] With the lamasery in ruins, the most imposing structure in town was the Chinese *yamen* (city hall) that Chao ordered built in the spring of 1907. It was to be capital of his provincial administration of Kham, the center of a separate Chinese province with thirty-six sub-prefectures.[23]

Knocking on the Iron Gates

With its proximity to the Tibetan border, the missionaries felt Batang was a prime center for evangelization. The region had a relatively large permanent population of seven thousand families, and substantial numbers of Tibetan traders passed through. Tibetan towns such as Draya were within itinerating distance.[24] Batang had adequate provisions, and a livable altitude for foreigners, and as a Chinese garrison town, it was defensible. There was even the hope for rapid communication back to China. In the period after Chao's triumphs, the Chinese strung telegraph wire from China proper all the way across Kham to Batang.[25]

The Sheltons' Foreign Christian Missionary Society station was the first permanent Protestant mission in Batang. After a half-century of Protestant evangelism, the FCMS mission in Batang was the nearest outpost to Lhasa. Dr. Albert Shelton was "knocking on the Iron Gates."

However promising Batang appeared to be as a center for Christian evangelism, the missionaries faced a daunting task. Batang remained the most remote mission on earth, two to three months by mule and sedan chair from river ports or railheads, and then many hundreds of miles further to the coast. Even the famously inaccessible New Guinea mission of Ononge was only a week by pack train from the coast.[26] The China Inland Mission in Tachienlu was the closest Western presence to Batang, eighteen days travel to the east.

Beyond the remoteness of the region and the rigors of the high altitude, the missionaries had to deal with the traumas of living in an active war zone and the ongoing violence of the Tibetans. Jealousies divided Catholics and Protestants, and there was confraternal squabbling among the rival Protestant groups. Missionaries spoke of "diversities of operations but the same spirit"; nevertheless, negotiations over evangelical territories were often tense.[27] Internally, the FCMS missionaries in Batang also faced the tensions endemic to a small group operating in isolation. The quirks and idiosyncrasies of normal life often became magnified under the strain of life on the frontier.

Most critically, the missionaries faced the opposition of the Tibetan lamas. While Chao had executed and dispersed the Batang monastery's monks, the lamas retained political and moral power in the town. In spite of the oppression, the Tibetans continued their Buddhist devotions. The rooftop chimney altars still smoked each evening with the offerings of green twigs and evergreen branches. The town still resonated to the dull beat of monks' drums and chants of "Om Mani Padme Hum."

In spite of their hostility to the lamas, the missionaries had to come to a mutual understanding with them. Without it, the mission simply couldn't survive.

Albert wrote, "In these conditions, work was very difficult because in a way were looked upon as being the friends of the Chinese. But we never made any change in our attitude so far as it was possible to maintain it, telling them that we were there to do good to every one, whether Chinese, Tibetan or half-caste, insisting at all times, both to the Chinese and the Tibetans, that all men were brothers."[28]

In many ways, the missionaries' entrance into Batang was eased by the intercession of Gezong Ongdu, a wealthy Tibetan trader whom Albert Shelton recruited in 1908 to be his Tibetan language teacher and native agent. A sturdy Khampa with a shaven head, open manner, and eyes creased with smile lines, Ongdu was the former headman of the deposed prince of Batang.[29] On Shelton's behest, Ongdu traveled to Batang several times to plead the missionaries' case with the Chinese officials and head lama of the battered Batang monastery, emphasizing Shelton's value as a doctor.[30]

Shelton and Ongdu became firm friends. "It has somewhat difficult at first to secure a teacher," Albert wrote, "I was almost desperate and one day one of my Tibetan friends came to visit me and I said to him, 'Gezong Ondu, I am in an awful fix. Why can't you help me out with this Tibetan a little?' He said, 'Yes, I'll help you out a little.'" At the end of the month, Shelton stuffed what he thought to be an appropriate amount of money into Ongdu's *chuba*. Shelton wrote that Ongdu said, "'All right, if you don't want to be friends any more I'll take it; but if you want us to be friends and want me to come back, you will have to take your money back.' Thus I was forced to accede to his terms because I could not get along without him."[31]

Dr. Shelton and Tibetan Medicine

Two days after his arrival in Batang, Dr. Albert Shelton performed his first local operation. A man from Yunnan followed Shelton five hundred miles across Kham from Tachienlu. The man had traveled to Tachienlu seeking Shelton's surgical skills, but the doctor had already shipped his instruments to Batang. He told the patient he would need to travel to Batang if he wished to have surgery. Once in Batang, an old door on two benches became the operating table, and an open part of the Sheltons' house served as the theater. Theater was a particularly appropriate term given the operation's considerable audience.[32]

Shelton performed the operation under the close scrutiny of the crowd. "Every one thought the man must be dead as he lay so still and uttered no moan while the operation was performed," Shelton wrote, "and it was with great surprise that they saw him at last wake up."[33] The man recovered and returned to his home twenty-five days south in northern Yunnan, a round trip of seventy days for medical treatment.

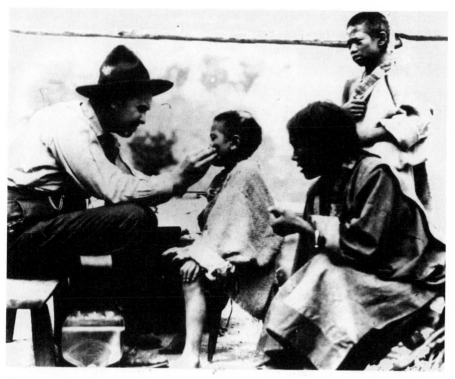

Figure 7.1   Dr. Shelton treating a Tibetan boy. The Sheltons and other foreign missionaries were deeply aware of the power of Western medicine. Photograph courtesy the Collection of The Newark Museum. Reprinted with permission.

After Shelton opened a dispensary near the south gate of the city, he was called to operate on a road worker whose skull had been crushed by a falling rock. Shelton initially declined to operate as he thought the wound was fatal, but the man's friends insisted. After the delicate operation in another makeshift theater, the man was barely breathing. "It appeared as if he would not live," Shelton wrote. "But that man got well, when by all the laws of medicine he ought to have died." Within three weeks, the patient recovered and walked home. Shelton credited divine intervention. "But 'Man's extremity is God's opportunity,'" he wrote. Later the man's parents traveled to Batang to express their gratitude. Dr. Shelton found them beside the road on their knees bowing their head to the ground in thanks. When he tried to stop them, they presented him with gifts the man withdrew from his *chuba*. "My fee was one old rooster, one piece of dirty butter, and six eggs, but, you know, it was one of the best fees I have ever received. Gratitude of people to whom we have been able to be of service is one of the greatest compensations."[34]

As with Tachienlu, much of Dr. Shelton's practice related to wounds, opium, and various epidemic diseases such as cholera, dysentery, typhus, and typhoid, a result of Batang's polluted water.[35] Smallpox epidemics were common. Living in a high, dry environment where few bacteria could flourish, Tibetans had low resistance to disease. While smallpox vaccinations barely "took" with lowland Chinese, Tibetans often had reactions that approached smallpox itself.[36] In iodine-poor Tibet, many suffered from goiters, a massive swelling of the thyroid gland. Some grew so large the sufferers looked like three-headed monsters. A simple treatment of potassium iodide was an almost immediate cure.

The Sheltons were deeply aware of the power of Western healing. Flora wrote, "Perhaps the first thing of any importance that brought a knowledge of foreign medicine to the Tibetans was the slight operation on the hand of a big lama belonging to one of the lamaseries in Tachienlu." The lama arrived with a needle broken off in the fleshy part of his hand just below the thumb. Dr. Shelton numbed the lama's hand with cocaine and prepared to cut open his hand to extract the needle. The lama protested that it was going to hurt, and Shelton assured him it would be painless. "While the lama's eyes grew bigger and bigger and those standing around groaned and asked if it didn't hurt, he said, 'No, it didn't, but just look at the blood.' This small operation drove another small wedge into this land in the shape of a needle," Flora wrote.[37]

The missionaries to Tibet had divergent views of the traditional Tibetan medicine that the lama-doctors practiced. One was appalled to discover the curative pills the Tibetans sought were composed of the Dalai Lama's excrement.[38] Others saw the Tibetan doctors as rigorous clinicians.[39] British mission enthusiast Isabella Bird Bishop was dogmatic: "Sorcery is largely used in the treatment of the sick. . . . The doctors know the virtues of many of the plants of the country, the quantities of which they mix up together while reciting magical formulas."[40] Susie Rijnhart found few good things to write about Tibetan medicine: "The Tibetans themselves having no medical science worthy the name, the treatment given by the native doctors generally means an increase of agony to the patient."[41] Flora concurred: "Perhaps there is no nation on the globe knowing so much of the construction of the human body as the Tibetans, and who have so little medical knowledge or so few remedies."[42] Dr. Shelton had a more sanguine opinion, acknowledging a boundary between his medical work and that of the Tibetan lamas: "For work of a more purely medical nature such as fever, etc., I was not so much in demand, as they had methods of their own for treating things, among which are the calling in of some eight or ten priests and the reading of prayers, the ringing of bells, the blowing of horns, and the beating of drums, in order to drive out the devils."[43]

Tibetan medicine combined aspects of both Chinese and Indian systems of medicine, mixed with a strong dose of karmic Buddhist teaching. The larger monasteries provided multi-year courses of study, during which monks learned

Buddhist medical teachings, herbal and mineral remedies, a sophisticated system of pulse and urine examination, and the manufacture of blessed pills made of ground-up prayers and bodily composites.[44] There was no surgery in Tibetan medicine, a proscription that began when an eighth-century Tibetan king banned procedures after his mother died during an operation.[45] The Tibetans had a brutal realism about medical care. A proverb stated, "A first class doctor heals one at once, a second class doctor heals in three months, but a third class doctor brings you other ailments." Even more succinctly, another Tibetan proverb advised, "Those without an illness, do not call a doctor."[46]

Call to the Badlands

Medicine was Dr. Shelton's bridge to the lamas. The Jo Lama, a revered figure in Batang, asked Shelton to journey two days into the backcountry to treat victims of a house collapse.[47] The accident was in the Sangen, the lawless badlands that stretched along the east bank of the Yangtze north of Batang. The Sangen people had been notorious bandits for two hundred and fifty years, ravaging the

Figure 7.2   The Jo Lama picnicking with the Sheltons. The Jo Lama, considered a reincarnate manifestation of the Buddha by the Tibetans, was one of Shelton's most important allies. Photograph courtesy the Collection of The Newark Museum. Reprinted with permission.

trade routes and defending their territory against interlopers.[48] "The people are wild and fierce, and live by robbing travelers," a Chinese guidebook stated.[49]

Despite this, Shelton agreed. The Jo Lama was the spiritual head of the large monastery in Atunze before the Chinese destroyed it and exiled him to Batang.[50] The muscular, square-headed Khampa was another important contact for Shelton. While he had married and renounced his vows as a monk, the Tibetans considered him a reincarnate manifestation of the Buddha known as a *tulku*.[51] While traveling with Shelton, Khampas lined the trails to get his blessings.[52]

Shelton and the Jo Lama's party started for the Sangen before daybreak. Teetering along a cliffside trail two thousand feet above the Yangtze, the riders reached the village at nightfall. The villagers insisted Shelton wait until the next morning to see the wounded men. As they had been on the trail all day, the travelers were sure to be carrying a multitude of road devils who could injure the patients.

That night the men retired to a small room on the third floor of a Tibetan house. Rain poured through the mud roof, and they huddled under oilcloth that sheltered the bed. "After a night spent in discussing the different problems of the Tibetans with the Ju Lama, morning came at last," Shelton wrote. "Ju Lama has been a good friend to me through all the years."[53] A photo of the time recorded the Jo Lama at a family picnic with two bored-looking Shelton girls in floppy hats sitting at his feet. Wearing a fedora on the back of his head, Dr. Shelton sat smiling beside him.[54]

In short order, Albert Shelton had situated his family and begun his work. Naturally gregarious, he found allies among both the Chinese and Tibetan communities. With his medical skills and willingness to take them into the hinterlands, Albert Shelton had an entrée into the Tibetan world.

CHAPTER EIGHT

CONQUESTS, CURIOS, AND CONVERSIONS

Batang, 1909–1910

Finest week I ever had—traveling and making friends with many, many people.[1]

—Dr. Albert Shelton

Dr. Albert Shelton's trip into the Sangen was the opening foray of his campaign. With Lhasa as his ultimate goal, he planned to travel deep into the mountains of Kham dispensing medical treatment and the gospel—itinerations the missionaries called the journeys. He anticipated long periods away from the mission. To free Shelton for his journeys, the Foreign Christian Missionary Society dispatched a second Disciple physician to Batang, Dr. Z. S. Loftis. He was born in Tennessee and raised in Kansas before moving to Texas. After working as a pharmacist for several years, Loftis decided to devote his life to the Christian missions. He graduated from Vanderbilt University's medical school in June 1908. Three months later he sailed on the SS *Mongolia* for China, finally arriving in Batang on June 17, 1909 after a torturous journey up the Yangtze and across Sichuan.[2]

He quickly immersed himself in the mission activities. A heavy rain washed out the planned July Fourth picnic, but singing Chinese hymns in the mission church service and dispensing Sunday school cards cheered Loftis considerably. He made friends with members of the great Nepalese embassy returning home from Beijing as they waited for their immense convoy of eight hundred yaks, horses, and mules to be assembled.[3] Soon after his arrival, Loftis began his medical work.

On the political front, Chao Erh-feng's colonization plans unraveled almost as soon as they began. Chao promised Chinese settlers oxen, seed, and plows to be repaid over three years at easy interest. He further offered land tax exemptions, paid travel expenses, and critically, protection from the Tibetans.[4]

In spite of Chao's efforts, by 1909 only two hundred Sichuan farmers took the offer of Batang land. A year later eighty had died and another hundred returned to China proper.[5] Chao had wildly overestimated the fertility of the soil and mildness of the climate. With the exception of a few river valleys, Kham was more suited to lightly peopled nomadic herding than it was to Chinese agriculture, and most of the best land for farming was already occupied. After a decline from Chao's ruthless executions and depredations, the Tibetan population in western Kham rapidly rebounded. Even in the Hsiang-ch'eng, the population soon returned to pre-invasion numbers.[6]

The Chinese settlers faced the unending enmity of the Tibetans, who resented the Chinese colonization.[7] The Tibetan lamas led much of the opposition. Nomadic tribespeople of Kham provided the primary financial support for the monasteries, where the monks educated nomad sons and stored their collective wealth. The continuation of the traditional nomadic-agricultural mix was essential to the entire Tibetan way of life.[8]

Nonetheless the Chinese authorities continued their attempts to strengthen their hold on the region. When the British signed the Anglo-Chinese Convention of 1906, they retained only trade rights and reaffirmed Chinese hegemony over Tibet. To increase their power, the Chinese extended their direct control of eastern Tibet with plans to create new Chinese provinces. Chinese officials in Lhasa began to overhaul the Tibetan government with Chinese-style boards of mines, communications, agriculture, commerce, war, revenue, education, and the like. Endeavoring to undermine the monasteries' power, the Manchu officials began organizing a modern forty-thousand-man Tibetan army. The Chinese imperial diplomats also decided to force the Dalai Lama to accept reduced power in the Manchu hierarchy, while initiating a campaign to undermine British prestige in central Asia by making claims on British-dominated Nepal and Bhutan.[9]

The Dalai Lama, who had been in exile in Mongolia and Amdo since Younghusband's invasion of Lhasa, was unsuccessful in his attempts to form alliances with the Russians or consensus with critical elements of the Tibetan hierarchy. He decided to seek rapprochement with the Chinese while simultaneously improving relations with the British authorities in India. When the Dalai Lama arrived in Beijing in September 1908, he hoped to address the emperor directly rather than through the *ambans* as before. The Chinese made it clear they viewed him not as a sovereign ruler but as another subordinate member of the imperial polity—albeit a revered and powerful one. After the Chinese forced him to accept his new status, the Dalai Lama left Beijing in an immense entourage and slowly made his way back to Lhasa.

In 1909, Chao Erh-feng launched another massive offensive in western Kham with six thousand of his veteran soldiers. By 1910 Chao occupied Derge, Gonshon, Chamdo, Draya, and Markam, all located across the 1727 frontier line in Tibet proper. War news began filtering down the mountain trails to the missionaries in Batang: eighty lamas and forty Chinese soldiers were killed in battle in northern Kham; the great Draya monastery was destroyed; atrocities were rife across the battle zone.[10]

As the Dalai Lama made his way back to Lhasa, it was apparent the Chinese intended to re-occupy his capital and take control. A month earlier the Chinese even had the temerity to petition for passage of two thousand troops through Calcutta and India to invade Tibet, though the British government quickly denied the request. While still en route to Lhasa, the Dalai Lama pleaded with both Great Britain and China to rein in Chao, who was advancing on Lhasa.[11]

When Chao's vanguard of forty cavalrymen and two hundred infantry marched in one Lhasa gate on February 12, 1910, the Dalai Lama fled out another, this time escaping to the British in India.[12] While the Raj authorities gave him safe haven in Darjeeling, their hospitality didn't stop the British government from recognizing the puppet government the Chinese set up in Lhasa. The Chinese deposed the Dalai Lama and took control of the country.[13] Sir Charles Bell, the sagacious consular official who handled British diplomacy in the Indian Himalayas, wrote, "The Tibetans were abandoned to Chinese aggression, and aggression for which the British Military Expedition to Lhasa and subsequent retreat were primarily responsible."[14]

The British strategy regarding Tibet was a dismal failure. Instead of protecting the flank of British India, the Younghusband expedition had galvanized the Chinese into an expansive military and political offensive. With Chao's conquests, China controlled eastern and central Tibet. To the great consternation of British officials, the Chinese frontier was now in the Indian Himalayas. "China, in a word, has come to the gates of India, and the fact has to be reckoned with," one British journalist wrote. "It is to be hoped that the Indian Government will do what they can to retrieve the position, and use the presence of the Dalai Lama [in India] as a lever for securing from the Chinese Government some concessions in frontier rectification."[15]

With Lhasa removed as a potential deterrent, Chao was free to secure eastern Tibet under Chinese rule. He quickly subjugated Derge in December 1909, exiling the deposed prince of Derge and his highborn Lhasa wife to Batang.[16] With the Jo Lama and Ba Lama, the progeny of the executed prince of Batang, and now the prince of Derge, the little town of Batang had more than its share of eastern Tibetan aristocrats and notables. One by one, Dr. Albert Shelton added them to the list of Kham personages who became his friends and colleagues.

In the aftermath of his triumph in western Kham, Chao appointed Chinese to positions across the district and opened 105 primary schools, located wherever twenty or more students could be found.[17] The policy eased the way for the FCMS missionaries to open their own primary and industrial school in Batang.[18] However, Chao's campaign ravaged Kham's cultural and religious institutions. The vast majority of the taxes and revenues that previously went to the Buddhist monasteries now went to the Chinese officials in the region. With the region's monasteries destroyed and the monks killed or dispersed, most Tibetan families were unable to send their sons for education and training. Instead they stayed with their agrarian and nomadic families, or became part of Batang's floating population of orphans left in the wake of the Chinese invasion.[19]

Mission-Keeping in Batang

A few months after arriving in Batang, Albert Shelton began construction of new mission buildings. After he secured the local magistrate's permission, Shelton hired fifteen Chinese woodsmen to begin felling trees about fifteen miles away, transporting the lumber to Batang by mule and donkey, the larger pieces on men's backs. He also hired workers to build two large kilns for the firing of bricks and roof tiles. Shelton chafed at being tied down: "I do not want to be the rest of my life building a house so I am doing all I can to get things moving."[20]

While waiting for her mission house, Flora concentrated on bringing Midwestern order to her rented Himalayan home. "The floors were scalded and scraped, and scalded and scraped again," she wrote. Servants whitewashed the walls and papered them with pale brown Chinese wallpaper. Chinese-Tibetan carpenters crafted furniture to their liking, based on designs cribbed from the Montgomery Ward catalogue.

The missionaries purchased two cows so they could have milk and butter to their taste rather than in the Tibetan style. "At first we used their butter," Flora sniffed, "but had to cook it and strain out hairs, etc., and it wasn't very good. They don't wash the churns, either, so the butter does not smell very fresh; no salt is used in it, and the cakes are patted out with bare hands."[21] The Sheltons' food the first year in Batang was heavy on cabbage, yak meat, and *tsampa*. By the second year, gardens grown with American seeds flourished and the family ate peas, beans, corn, and potatoes.[22]

Supervising her Tibetan maids, Flora maintained rigorous standards, including crisply starched clothes for the family. Strict American-style housekeeping, the gospel of stringent cleanliness, was a recurring theme in Flora's writing. Through her control of an immaculate household on the Tibetan border, she also exerted her female moral authority in both the domestic and social arenas. Her determined domestic hygiene in the midst of an anarchic war zone provided a distinctly different mode of living to the local population.[23] With her patronizing views of the Tibetans, she mirrored many of the attitudes of Kansas homesteaders and missionaries to the Plains Indian reservations.[24]

Seldom traveling outside the mission, Flora lived in a narrow world. Banned from a traditional economic marketplace and supplanted by her domestic help from household duties that would have occupied her in America, Flora Shelton searched for new meaning in her life. Increasingly, she commingled domestic management and motherhood with spiritual work such as Tibetan translation to gain a sustaining sense of accomplishment.

Sundays were the day for the Christian gospel, with a preaching service and Sunday school in the morning and a small prayer meeting for the missionaries in the evening. James Ogden taught the Chinese on one side of the room; Dr. Shelton led the Tibetans on the other. After a few songs, Millie Ogden taught the women in one room, while James Ogden instructed the Chinese men. Flora recounted, "Dr. Shelton is in another room, sitting on the floor or on a low stool, and thirty-five or forty dirty little children are squatted around him." In the mission school, teachers taught religion and reading in the Tibetan language, augmented by illustrations clipped from periodicals such as *Ladies' Home Journal.* The school also employed a Chinese scholar to teach the Chinese students the Confucian classics, "or they can never hope to be employed by the Chinese government," Flora noted.[25] The first Batang Sunday school consisted of ten adults, thirteen local children cloaked in dirty robes, and two little blond Shelton girls with starched white dresses.[26]

Christmas 1909 was festive for the missionaries. The crowd of Chinese and Tibetans who gathered for holiday largesse cheered them immensely. Flora wrote her father-in-law back in Kansas: "On Christmas Day we fed about a hundred beggars in our courtyard. I wish you could have seen the old, and sore, and blind, and dirty, and ragged, but all so well behaved. We fed them beef soup, tsamba, and a big buckwheat cake each. We had two hind quarters of beef and chopped it up and made soup. It was good to see them eat."[27]

After the meal, the missionaries passed out religious cards to the crowd and Albert played Dr. Loftis' phonograph for them. Shelton and Ogden told the crowd in Chinese and Tibetan, "This is Jesus' birthday and he loves you."[28] After the meal, the crowd stretched out in the sunshine beside the mission gate and went to sleep.[29]

As with Tachienlu, converts were made more easily among the Chinese than the Tibetans. With her interweaving of Christian gospel and cleanliness, Flora, like many missionaries, saw attempts to "clean up" as the first sign of interest in the Christian teaching: "If the convert is a Chinaman, he will likely put a clean gown over a dirty one, but it doesn't matter, he is trying." She found the Tibetans more recalcitrant. "The Tibetans are a little slower learning to clean up than the Chinese, perhaps because they have fewer clothes, and washing is such a foreign element in their lives."[30]

Curios and Itinerations: Albert Shelton as a Missionary Collector

As the Sheltons packed for Batang in the spring of 1909, an ambitious German anthropologist, Berthold Laufer, had arrived in Tachienlu.[31] He was on a major expedition, collecting Tibetan artifacts for Chicago's Field Museum. With an enormous acquisition budget of more than forty thousand dollars, he'd already collected thousands of objects in India and China. Mandarin-dressed, meerschaum-smoking Laufer quickly recruited two China Inland Mission missionaries in Tachienlu, Theodore Sorensen and John Muir, to guide him and acquire objects. In the Himalayas, fine Tibetan *tangka* paintings went for two to five dollars. A bronze statue of Padmasambhava cost about twelve dollars. A copper image of Tara in Derge cost less than fifteen cents. For a hundred dollars, Laufer collected an enormous sacred book printed in Derge, the Ashtashasrikapprajnaparmita, which weighed over ninety-three pounds. The further into the Tibetan hinterlands that Laufer traveled, the less expensive the objects became.

Before returning to China, Laufer hired Muir to acquire Tibetan artifacts, giving him a thousand taels (the standard Chinese currency, which was not a coin, but one Chinese ounce of silver) to purchase the objects, a substantial amount of money for an impecunious missionary in a war-impoverished region.[32] In the small closed world of foreign missionaries, Laufer and his museum-funded munificence was sure to catch the ears of the entire community, including Albert Shelton's.[33]

As Laufer trudged across northern Kham, Dr. Shelton and evangelist Ogden left on July 5 for a long itineration southeast of Batang into the Hsiang-ch'eng—"the home of the fiercest tribe in all Eastern Tibet," Shelton wrote. The region was relatively pacified after Chao Erh-feng's campaigns, though bands of robbers and rebels still made the journey a precarious one. Shelton and Ogden made a great loop, riding through mountainous country on difficult trails. On the return journey, they traveled west until they hit the ancient salt-making city of Yenjin on the Yangtze and then turned north to Batang. Shelton's friend, the

Jo Lama, accompanied the missionaries, making the passage of the party an auspicious one.[34]

The Hsiang-ch'eng journey was a grand camping trip, with Shelton's medical
treatments and Ogden's preaching punctuating the days of discovery among the
black-tent nomads. Shelton exulted in his travel diary, "Finest week I ever had—
traveling and making friends with many, many people."[35] In the course of the
journey, Shelton treated six hundred patients.[36] He treated sore eyes with boric
acid and a salve of yellow oxide; stitched up a harelip; doctored a man suffering
from a yak-goring; a Tibetan woman whose eye was gouged out by Chinese soldiers billeted in her house; a man whom the Chinese had beaten with bamboo
flails until the flesh was flayed from his bones. "Medicine is given out left and
right," Flora wrote, "while hot shots of Gospel are put in between doses of
calomel and santonine."[37]

Albert Shelton began to enthusiastically collect Tibetan artifacts or "curios,"
as he termed them. They included fine Buddhist *tangkas* (religious paintings on
fabric), manuscripts, silver and bronze statues, and everyday items. The diary of
his trip in the Hsiang-ch'eng noted acquisitions among his descriptions of landscapes and people. "Bought a bracelet and bowl," Shelton wrote on July 17.
"Bought charm box from lama today for twelve rupees," he noted a few days
later. Later he purchased a Tibetan musket and accepted the gift of a Tibetan
holy-water vase from a Chinese official posted to the Hsiang-ch'eng. His collection included a belt taken from one of the Sampiling monastery's religious statues and a beheading knife acquired from a Chinese officer.[38] Shelton also
included in his travel diary a description and inventory of the Buddhist
monastery in Yaragong (Yahaikung), located three days' south of Batang, that
the Chinese had also pillaged. Shelton acquired a number of objects at
Yaragong, including a Tibetan *tangka* that Shelton described as "Painting representing some of the licentious gods of the Tibetans."[39]

Kham was an ideal place to commence a Tibetan collection on a missionary
budget. Being a devout, relatively prosperous region on the Tibetan trade routes,
Kham was a major repository of Tibetan cultural objects. Shelton purchased material from local people including Gezong Ongdu, the Jo Lama, mendicant
priests and lamas in the Batang monastery, even the Ba Lama—"The Living
Buddha of Batang, the most exalted personage among the Tibetans in Eastern
Tibet," Shelton wrote.[40]

But as other Western collectors discovered, it wasn't an easy task to acquire
Tibetan artifacts, particularly sacred objects such as statues and liturgical texts.
William Gill related, "As we were now almost out of Tibet I was very anxious
to buy a prayer cylinder, but the people had a superstitious objection to parting with them, and it was difficult to prevail on anyone to sell one."[41] Even

non-religious objects could be difficult to acquire. William Gill wrote, "They have a curious superstition also about their wooden bowls; they say that if they sold the bowls from which they had eaten to a foreigner, their country would fall into hands of a nation whose representative had bought them."[42] A Tibetan woman near Litang also refused him. "The wife was always so gorgeously arrayed with strings of beads, from which great gold and silver ornaments were suspended. . . . We wanted to buy the complete set, but she would not part with them, because she said it would be like dying before her time, and very unlucky."[43]

The Tibetans' reluctance to part with artifacts was offset by circumstance and their love of trade, particularly after Chao's conquest.[44] The Chinese destroyed many of the Buddhist monasteries and looted their religious artifacts and treasure. As a result, there was plenty of booty in circulation. When not buying from Chinese officers, Albert Shelton used Gezong Ongdu and the Jo Lama as intermediaries for many of his purchases from the impoverished monks.

Albert Shelton wasn't unique as a missionary-collector in Tibet or most other places in the foreign field. Ethnologic collecting was almost a cottage industry among missionaries, a way for them to gather gold and glory far from home. At the urging of the Vatican, Catholic missionaries were avid collectors for the church museums.[45] Dr. Susie Rijnhart and her husband Petrus were collectors. "We traded some Tankar boots for the kind used in the locale," she wrote about her journey toward Lhasa, noting her retainer bought a prayer wheel made with silver set with coral and stones.[46] American missionary and scholar D. S. Dye collected thousands of objects from southwestern Chinese and Tibetan ethnic groups, later forming the bulk of the Sichuan University Museum. A few missionaries became such ardent traders that there trading overshadowed their ostensible work. One Yunnan missionary "spent his early mornings trading horses and rifles and after 10:00 A.M., was too exhausted for anything else."[47]

Missionaries collected "curios" for a range of reasons. Ethnic material helped them understand the cultures they hoped to convert, serving as an academic cache for philosophic and theological deconstructions. Cultural artifacts also served as lurid attractions for missionaries supporting audiences back home, objects that could spice up a fund-raising meeting back in America and Britain. And for foreign missionaries living on sparse salaries, collecting also offered a way to pick up some extra cash from nouveau-riche Western museums and wealthy collectors who had a taste for the exotic.

While Dr. Albert Shelton was a medical missionary who was intrigued by new scenes and people, he was not an explorer in a geographic sense. He kept little record of his journeys beyond patients treated and gospels delivered. But even those notes added to the Western knowledge of the Chinese-Tibetan borderlands. Rather than exploration, Dr. Albert Shelton focused on medical treatment and Christian conversion. Geographic matters related mainly to that goal. Shelton shared the focus of most Protestant missionaries to Tibet. China Inland Mission's James Edgar was characteristic when he quoted the bible to explain the role of exploration in the missions: "Every place whereon the sole of your feet shall tread shall be yours." Edgar asked, "For is not the pioneer missionary to the Mission Boards what the scouts are to the armies?"[48] In their unrelenting search for new souls, the missionaries sometimes uncovered new wonders. After all, they were adventuresome, inquisitive people.[49] Edward Amundsen discovered the great bend of the Yangtze while on an itineration in northern Yunnan. James Edgar is credited with being the first white man to see a panda.[50] In 1907, Edgar and Muir became the first Westerners to see the great Sampiling monastery in the Hsiang-ch'eng.

Broken-Hearted Mission

While Shelton and Ogden doctored and evangelized on the trails, Dr. Z. S. Loftis treated a normal retinue of patients back in Batang. After treating an opium overdose, Loftis noted in his journal, "This morning the fellow was up, sober and repentant. Another life saved by my being here."[51] As the mission awaited Shelton and Ogden's return from the Hsiang-ch'eng, CIM missionary Theodore Sorensen entered Batang on a long journey through Kham, and he later recalled, "I shall never forget the kindness shown me by Dr. Lofties [*sic*] who came in the rain and met me, and insisted upon me going to stay with him in the hospital where he was living at the time."[52] That same night Loftis took ill. A new virulent strain of smallpox had broken out in Batang, and though Loftis had been vaccinated a number of times, he contracted the disease from infected patients. He was already suffering from dysentery and malaria. As he weakened, typhus fever attacked.

Dr. Shelton returned from his journey and isolated himself with Loftis. Ogden retreated to the mountains with his family to try to escape the smallpox plague. Ogden assured Shelton that with divine assistance Loftis was sure to survive. Shelton wrote, "I was with him night and day and did in all in my power, but when the secondary stage of the smallpox—the pustular stage—came on, it was more than mortal could bear and he died unconscious, at 4 P.M., August 12th, not having been here two months."[53]

Flora wrote of their despair: "I heard Dr. Shelton sobbing in the yard, and he called me, telling that Dr. Loftis had gone. I could not go to him, and he dare not come to us. I could only hug my two little girls and cry. To say that we are broken-hearted and that our work has seemingly come to a halt, is saying very little."[54] Ogden came down from the mountain about midnight in the midst of a storm saying, "I didn't believe the Lord would let him die. We've waited and waited and waited for his coming. But there he is."[55]

Loftis' death was a wrenching disappointment for Shelton.[56] Shelton yearned to be breaking new ground, reconnoitering for his great race to Lhasa. Isolated as Batang was, even its domesticity chafed him. With Loftis gone, Dr. Shelton was again anchored to the mission station; the Shelton family could not even return to America for their scheduled seventh-year furlough. "We cannot come home unless another doctor comes," Shelton wrote, "for we dare not leave the station without a medical man, for here typhus, smallpox, and dysentery find a thriving ground all year round."[57]

Responding to the pleas from the Batang missionaries to replace Loftis, in June 1910 the FCMS dispatched another physician, Dr. William M. Hardy. He was a Disciple from Kentucky who received his medical education at the University of Tennessee. Now the Sheltons could return home for furlough. The Sheltons timed their departure to rendezvous with Dr. Hardy in Tachienlu on their way home.[58]

It was a clear, bright autumn day on October 8, 1910, when the Sheltons' caravan ambled out of the Batang walls headed for America, seven years after they initially sailed for China. Flora Shelton couldn't walk, so bearers carried her down the steps of her home to the waiting sedan chair. Earlier she and a horse tumbled down a mountain gully, and the animal had smashed her leg when it rolled over her. While the mending leg made the journey difficult, the furlough was vital as she needed an operation in America.[59]

On their way out of Batang, the Sheltons passed through a gauntlet of well-wishers. Tibetan women stood along the road crying and offering the teetotaling Sheltons gifts of milk rather than the customary wine. Further down the road, James Ogden waved with the schoolboys, and another few miles down the trail Gezong Ongdu waited. Albert remembered, "I rode up, got off my mule, and said, 'Well, good-bye, Gezong.' He then held out of his hand, but tears came to his eyes and he couldn't speak, so I just got on my mule and rode away."[60]

Going Home

The Sheltons' caravan arrived in Tachienlu two days before Dr. Hardy's sedan chair made it up the mountain from Luding. The three missionaries spent a day becoming acquainted before the Sheltons headed east and Hardy began his journey across Kham.[61]

The Sheltons retraced their steps to the China coast, taking eight days to reach Ya'an. The first stage was a wild raft ride of a hundred miles downstream on the Dadu River.[62] The Sheltons moved back down the Yangtze River, visiting with missionary friends at Chongqing and Yibin. When the hosts brought oil lamps into their bedroom, Flora Shelton became alarmed that they might explode and blew them out. She had become so accustomed to candles, the only illumination available in the backcountry, that oil lamps seemed frightening.[63]

CHAPTER NINE

THIS GREAT AWFUL CITY

Furlough, 1910–1913

I think no man ever made a deeper impression upon those with whom he had to do.[1]

—Archibald McLean

In December 1910, the Sheltons strolled on deck as the SS *Mongolia* steamed from Shanghai toward America.[2] Dorris and Dorothy flaunted large hair bows and Flora sported a fancy hat. Albert was rakish in his Stetson and dark turtleneck.[3] The *Mongolia* sailed to Yokohama to take on additional passengers, including Edward N. Crane, the vice-president of a booming bathroom fixtures and toiletries company in Newark, New Jersey. Crane was also a trustee of the recently established Newark Museum. On board the luxury liner, Crane and Dr. Shelton struck up a friendship. When Albert talked of his Tibetan curios, Crane immediately saw the possibilities for a Newark exhibit while Shelton arranged a final home for his collection.

After eighty-nine continuous days of travel from Batang, the Sheltons arrived on the West Coast in early January 1911.[4] America had changed in the seven years since the Sheltons departed for China. The country had added 10 million new citizens since they left, growing to over 92 million Americans.[5] America continued to evolve from a laissez-faire society overseen by a self-selecting elite to a country run from Washington.[6] The ongoing war between labor and capital sharpened. Endemic strikes swept the country, accompanied by violence and disorder. Industrialization and urbanization continued their frantic pace. As Albert crisscrossed the country speaking to church groups, the frenetic syncopation of ragtime issued from the nation's player pianos and the avant-garde tangoed and turkey-trotted. Vaudevillians and proto-flappers with turbans, bobbed hair, and lipstick-smudged cigarette holders began to set the fashion tone for the Roaring Twenties. America was on the cusp of the Jazz Era.[7]

Manual for Young Missionaries recommended a nine-month furlough every four years, but because of the length of the journey from remote Batang, the Sheltons had waited seven long years before their year of furlough. It was supposed to be a period for rest, family obligations, additional training for the field, and fund-raising work.[8] Ultimately, most of the missionaries' furlough time was absorbed by fund-raising, which became a source of internal criticism. An independent board formed to investigate the conditions of the foreign missions chided the societies for their exploitative fund-raising expectations and their failure to plan or finance the furloughs, forcing missionaries to depend on their own families for help during their home leave.[9] Missionaries on leave often stayed with relatives, sometimes moving from one to the other in a string of forced hospitality. After years of decorous mission life with a plethora of servants, the home-leave missionaries suddenly found themselves living on the road in endless lecture tours and fund-raising campaigns. Some missionaries broke under the strain of the expectations.[10]

Dr. Albert Shelton soon joined the ranks of foreign missionaries crossing America on promotional tours.[11] During 1911 Dr. Shelton worked with the Million Dollar Campaign, headed by FCMS leader Abraham Cory, the namesake of Abe, Albert Shelton's beloved mule.[12] The campaign was an outgrowth of the missionary society's inability to raise enough funds for larger capital projects in China. The goal eventually became $6,300,000 and a thousand workers in the foreign mission field. By the end of the campaign, the monetary goal was met and over eight thousand young people had signed commitments to consider missionary work.[13]

Stephen J. Corey, the secretary of the Foreign Christian Missionary Society, wrote Flora about her husband's fund-raising efforts: "Shelton's a good chap. He stirs the people up greatly in the rally campaigns. A modest, sturdy, two-fisted fellow that talks right from the shoulder and gets down to 'brass tacks.'"[14]

Crowds and Curios: The Newark Museum

While Albert Shelton was on the missionary circuit, the upcoming Newark Museum exhibit that Edward N. Crane had arranged was on his mind.[15] The exhibit of his Tibetan curios took place in the recently constituted Newark Museum, located in two rooms on the fourth floor of the Newark Public Library. The Tibetan exhibit was the third one held in the new museum. It was an immediate success. From February 14, 1911, to the closing a little more than four months later on June 22, more than two hundred people a day thronged the museum to peer at the exotica from the Forbidden Kingdom.

The Tibetan exhibit had barely opened when Crane and the board of trustees began strategizing to purchase Shelton's collection, understanding they might have competition. Shelton evidently mentioned the Field Museum as a likely purchaser. On February 18, 1911, Edward Crane wrote to John Cotton Dana about a letter from Shelton, "You can see from his letter that it is fortunate that we acted quickly and had the articles sent on to us without delay, and you will also notice that the Field Museum people lost no time after they heard about it from China sources, to write to Dr. Shelton and ask that they be given a chance to acquire them." Crane urged quick action. "I do not think we can act too quickly in the matter and believe we can arrange terms of payment satisfactorily if it is the desire of our people to acquire the exhibit, although nothing has been said to Shelton along these lines."[16] Shelton responded to Crane's subsequent inquiry about terms, "I have no desire to go into this business about the curios in a commercial spirit whatever. My only object in bringing the artifacts to this country at all was that they might go to some *American* institution."[17]

As the Newark trustees scrambled to place a value on the esoteric Tibetan material, they consulted the Metropolitan, the American Natural History Museum, Columbia University, Chicago's Newberry Library, and the Library of Congress.[18] The institutions directed the Newark to Berthold Laufer at the Field Museum as the only authority on Tibetan material in America.[19] When contacted, Laufer confirmed the importance of Shelton's artifacts and indicated the price was reasonable given the "great difficulty" of collecting in Tibet and the high cost of shipment.[20]

With the Newark exhibit nearing the end of its run, the Newark and Shelton jockeyed for position. Crane wrote Dana, "I have just received word from Mr. Shelton stating it will be all right regarding the payment for the Tibetan articles being deferred somewhat. That it doesn't matter *if* the museum people want them, and he states it would be no use to re-ship them under these circumstances. His idea was that there should be some decision made either for or against, so he will know what to do."[21]

But fate intervened. Edward N. Crane unexpectedly died in the summer of 1911. His widow and son considered purchasing the collection as a memorial. On September 21, 1911, Dana, writing as the Newark Museum director, sent a letter to the widow, Cordelia M. Crane. In the letter he assured her of the museum's permanency and specified the conditions of the proposed gift, which included the agreement the collection would always be exhibited under the name of the "Edward N. Crane Memorial." The museum agreed to return the collection to the eldest male Crane descendant should the museum ever disband. On October 16, 1911, the Cranes signed the gift document giving the Newark Museum the collection of "curios, paintings, books, and other objects assembled by

Dr. Albert L. Shelton, in Tibet, illustrating the life of the people of that little known country, and secured as a loan of the Museum by the late Edward N. Crane of this city, to be known as the Edward N. Crane Memorial, on the conditions hereinafter mentioned."[22] Albert Shelton received two thousand dollars for the collection.

The Newark Museum incorporated the one hundred and fifty Tibetan artifacts as part of its permanent collection. Tibetan religious objects formed about two-thirds of the group. The artifacts included skull drums, ritual clothing, prayer wheels, a bell and *dorje* (ritual thunderbolt), butter lamps, and charm boxes. Many of the objects listed the "Living Buddha of Batang," Shelton's identification for the Jo Lama, as the source. Shelton also listed as sources "mendicant priests," "priests at the lamasery at Batang," and "a half-breed interpreter, resident in Batang," his term for Gezong Ondu. A number of objects Shelton noted as coming from the "Lamasery at Yaragong," without identification of a person.

The great treasure of the collection was the ornate silver Wheel of the Law Shelton bought from the Jo Lama. The wheel was an ancient Buddhist emblem of royal sovereignty. Almost two feet high, wrought of pure Chinese silver, the wheel depicted in repoussé sixteen rays emanating from a spinning sun. The wheel sat on a pedestal of lotus petals that was slightly collapsed by the weight of silver above it. The Jo Lama told Shelton it was the symbol of authority of a Tibetan king who ruled under the Dalai Lama and was stolen from the king's palace during the Nepalese invasion of the late eighteenth century.[23]

The household objects ranged from bowls and pen cases to teapots and wine flasks. Personal objects such as jewelry, gowns, boots, belts, and aprons also formed part of the collection. Under the heading "Implements of Warfare and Justice," the collection included a yak-hair rope used to tie the hands of condemned men and a beheading knife that Shelton obtained from a Chinese officer in the Hsiang-Ch'eng.

Dr. Albert Shelton also provided two hundred negatives to the museum for photographic printing. Using a large, boxy tripod-mounted Graflex camera, Shelton found photography to be another enveloping activity, with Gezong Ongdu often serving as his assistant.[24] The photos exhibited the range of Shelton's interests in Kham. They included photos of Khampa life such as holiday scenes, nomad tents, pilgrims, lamas, women washing clothes, and a beggar by his cave. He photographed Tibetan houses, monasteries, inns, and bridges, as well as yaks, pack donkeys, and coracles. Scenes of eastern Tibet included villages, mountains, streams, and grazing herds. Exhibit photographs included a baptism, Shelton sewing up a harelip, and numerous pictures of Shelton with Tibetans noble and common.

Battle Creek and the Missionary Hustings

Albert Shelton continued negotiations with the Newark while he had an operation at J. H. Kellogg's celebrated Battle Creek Sanitarium in Michigan.[25] The retreat was suffused with an air of sober morality that contrasted with the high-life spas such as Sarasota Springs, New York or French Lick, Indiana. Dr. Kellogg was the inventor of modern breakfast cereal, as well as a popular author on nutrition and various moral philosophies. His surgical skills, particularly relating to the gastrointestinal system, were renowned. By Dr. Shelton's visit, the Battle Creek Sanitarium had grown into a combination medical boardinghouse, hospital, religious retreat, country club, chautauqua, and spa—a vast, six-story Italian Renaissance resort for the prosperously infirm (or nearly so).[26] With its elegant Christian setting and proximity to potential donors, Battle Creek was a favorite of foreign missionaries.

In May 1911, Shelton was back in Anthony, Kansas, where his parents had settled. Perhaps based on his father's advice, Albert and Flora Shelton purchased 160 acres in Harper County, Kansas, mortgaging it for six hundred dollars. In November 1911, after the sale of his collection to the Newark Museum, the Sheltons went back into the real estate market, purchasing several properties in Anthony.[27]

Albert Shelton returned to the missionary hustings. In July 1911 he spoke at the General Convention of the Disciples of Christ in Portland, Oregon about the "last heathen nation of earth," where benighted Tibetans suffered under the lamas.[28] In the early fall Dr. Albert Shelton was on the road again to New York, receiving specialized medical training at the New York Postgraduate Medical School for his impeding return to Batang.

Bedlam in the Borderland: The Chinese Revolution

However, the Sheltons were not to return to Batang on schedule, as the situation in China and Tibet dramatically changed. "In the early fall of 1911," Flora wrote, "Dr. Sun Yat Sen at last succeeded in bringing about the revolution he had spent so many years in instigating. The Chinese were successful in overthrowing the Manchu dynasty that had ruled absolutely for almost three hundred years."[29] China was in chaos, ultimately precipitating a major shift of power in eastern Tibet.

The October 1911 Chinese revolution swiftly changed the situation in Tibet and the borderlands. When the Republican revolt broke out, the Chinese garrison in Lhasa mutinied and attacked the *amban's* residence, capturing him. They called on their fellow soldiers in Tibet to mutiny as well and return to Lhasa.

From his exile in India, the Dalai Lama organized a secret War Department and urged armed rebellion against the Chinese. Eastern Tibet soon rose against the Chinese. Several Chinese garrisons mutinied, including one in Litang that looted the town and monastery. The Hsiang-ch'eng tribesmen again thundered out of their high grasslands in revolt.

A few days after Sun Yat Sen's revolution began, the Chinese magistrate in Batang advanced funds for the missionaries to leave immediately for the coast. With telegraph lines down and rebellious tribesmen controlling the trade routes, Batang was isolated from Sichuan proper. Tachienlu's China Inland Mission workers and Roman Catholic priests and nuns fled to Batang for safety, but the disorder had already preceded them. "Whippings, executions, and punishments of all kinds were occurring daily under our eyes in the city," James Ogden wrote.[30] With China in bedlam, the U.S. consul urged all inland American residents to move to places of safety, primarily foreign enclaves along the coast. The FCMS missionaries in Batang had ten days to secure their belongings and abandon the town. Gezong Ondu brought yak-skin boxes for storage, and the missionaries assigned a Tibetan caretaker to each house. Li Gway Gwang, the Chinese-Tibetan boy the Sheltons had adopted, remained behind.

The missionaries traveled south by horseback and sedan chair through rugged robber country. It was a harrowing journey as they continued south, finally reaching the French Indochinese port at Haiphong. There the missionaries made their way to Hong Kong, where they caught a steamer to Shanghai. Exhausted by their experience, the Ogdens sailed for America on Christmas Day, 1911. Within the year James Ogden was also a patient at the Battle Creek Sanitarium, a victim of a nervous breakdown from the stress of mission promotion tours.[31] Dr. William Hardy remained in China, working with the Red Cross and a Presbyterian mission.

Furlough Travels and New Institutions

Given the chaotic situation in Kham, the Sheltons chose to remain in the United States until some order returned. Flora and the girls stayed in Kansas as Bert again took to the rails, traveling across the country with his tales of the Tibetan frontier. He told his transfixed audiences, "Tibet is the last hermit nation on earth. It is sometimes called the roof of the world, the football of the nations, the keystone of the arch of Asia, the home of the pope of Buddhism. Nobody wants it, yet nobody wants any one else to have it. There is lies, the last stronghold of Satan, where paganism is making its last stand against the onward march of the gospel."[32]

Shelton shared his personal philosophy in a "Laughter is a Medicine and Must be Taken" lecture. "There are two things about which I will never worry my self. They are yesterday and tomorrow." He concluded by saying, "If you wish to talk to me of your troubles, very well, I'll do so. But never ask me to talk of mine, for I won't do it! Never!"[33]

Albert Shelton's diary in January 1912 illustrated his life on the missionary circuit. His journey began just after the New Year. When he arrived in Marion, Indiana on January 5 at midnight, he had already spoken in Muncie and Chicago. On January 6 he spoke in Daleville and on January 8 he was Cleveland. On the tenth, he was in Hartford City, Indiana, and on the twelfth he rode a sleigh to Washington, Illinois through two-below-zero weather to give a talk.[34]

After seven years of living in the wild nature of eastern Tibet, the Sheltons found the modern life of America a major departure. Flora wrote, "We were not used to moving faster than a man could walk, and we had traveled through country where absolute stillness reigned, unless it was the roar of a river or the slide of an avalanche."[35] In place of his vibrant life on the Tibetan frontier, Albert Shelton entered the world of the hurried urban man. Paunchy from banquet food and sedentary furlough life, he appeared stiff and dyspeptic.[36] He wrote Flora from a hotel room in Pittsburgh about a local woman dying in childbirth, calling it, "the tragedy of this great awful city."[37]

Albert spent most of the early spring at Foreign Christian Missionary Society headquarters in Cincinnati.[38] Flora joined him for the annual convention downriver in Louisville, where Albert spoke on "The Tibetan Field."[39] The upper South and lower Midwest continued to be the bastion of the Disciples of Christ. With the Disciples' Butler University and the Christian Woman's of Missions (CWBM) headquarters, Indianapolis was a major center. In 1910 Shelton's Foreign Christian Mission Society and the Christian Woman's Board of Missions jointly opened the imposing College of Missions on the Butler campus.[40] The college trained missionaries for the foreign field with courses in Oriental languages and culture, including Tibetan. Indianapolis, Indiana became one of the first places in America where students learned to speak Tibetan

Through 1912 Albert continued to fund-raise across the country at the same breakneck pace. He wrote his wife from the Montrose hotel in Cedar Rapids, Iowa in September 1912, "Went with a banker to country club for supper and stayed till 10 o'clock then caught sleeper to Chicago. Waited in Chicago from 7 to 9:30 A.M. and then got here at 3:25 P.M." With the relentless cycle of fund-raising, he began to revise his worth as a speaker and leader. He found a new status as a celebrated missionary whose homesteader background and future on the Tibetan frontier deeply affected his rapt audiences. He wrote to Flora about a fund-raising event, "They never heard of a missionary till last Sunday though last night we took their breath away."[41]

When not on the road, Albert Shelton stayed with Flora and the girls in Kansas. Dorris had sprouted into a long, skinny blond nine-year-old girl, a playmate for five-year-old Dorothy. Flora was far from idle during the furlough. Beyond mothering the girls, she wrote two books. Early in the furlough she organized and wrote an introduction to *A Message from Batang,* Dr. Z. S. Loftis' diary, which missionary publisher Fleming H. Revell published in 1911. On April 13, 1911, FCMS secretary Archibald McLean wrote to Flora, "Revell is getting out Dr. Loftis journal. That should have a good sale; it will if it does not cost too much. But you should write your book also. That also will do good."[42] She took his advice, writing *Sunshine and Shadow on the Tibetan Border,* which the Foreign Christian Missionary Society published in 1912. The influence of Kansas domesticity was obvious in her use of an old Midwestern quilt pattern, Sunshine and Shadow, as part of the book's title.

Dr. Shelton also hoped to write a book while on furlough, perhaps before he understood the demands of the lecture and mission promotion tours. By the fall of 1912, Albert Shelton was much more reticent about writing a book. He wrote to his wife about a Pennsylvania Secretary of Education who urged him to do a book after hearing him speak, "I appreciated his interest but told him when my words were put on paper they were not the same, etc."[43]

Missionaries generally wrote different types of material shaped for different audiences. First, missionaries wrote relatively candid reports and letters to the secretaries and boards of their mission societies. In these reports, they discussed the goals, accomplishments, problems, and internal conflicts of the mission.

Missionaries also wrote for mission board publications aimed at their supporting churches and churchgoers. Like other missionaries, Shelton generally reported a lurid and anecdotal portrait of his life in Asia that contained little of the ordinary and prosaic parts of daily reality. In this regard, he gave the supporters back home what they wanted: a titillating slice of the wild and barbaric Orient.[44]

While the missionaries used the language and techniques of early twentieth-century business systems, such as enumerations of converts, medical visits, and Sunday school attendance, to communicate with their boards, the information imparted in the non-board writing was highly anecdotal. Self-criticism or airing of internal mission disorder in church-oriented or general-public writing was so rare as to be extraordinary. The writers and editors crafted the writing to appeal emotionally to the readers' hearts and pocketbooks. As with other foreign missionaries engaged in collecting artifacts in the field, Dr. Albert Shelton also maintained an extensive correspondence that related to his museum and ethnographic work.[45] Though collecting constituted a significant part of their time, the Sheltons rarely mentioned it in their mission-related writing.

Bert also maintained extensive correspondence with Flora when separated from her. He was a romantic and deeply in love. From his early courtship missives to furlough campaign letters a dozen years later, he closed most often with a heartfelt message. "I love you beloved wife—I just want to take you in my arms and kiss you and look into your arms and kiss you and look into your eyes. With all my hearts love my Flo I love you." he wrote in 1912.[46] Flora, in turn, deeply loved her husband, though she was insecure about herself throughout their marriage and fearful of their life on the Tibetan border.

On February 11, 1913, Albert Shelton wrote to Flora to try to calm her: "I don't know why you're having to suffer as you do. . . . I'll never never leave you if God don't want me to go either. You know I want to go but I can say to you now Sweetheart what perhaps I could not 2 months ago. That if you're not to go back Sweetheart I can stay at home without a pang."[47]

Kham in Revolt: 1912–1913

During the furlough, the political situation in central Tibet and Kham became even more disordered. When Albert Shelton clopped out of Batang for America in October 1910, China was still the dominant player in Tibet, with large garrisons in Lhasa and other major Tibetan towns. The Dalai Lama was in exile in India. The imperial government controlled western Kham with contingents of Sichuan soldiers. By April 1912, the Tibetans succeeded in driving the Chinese from Lhasa, and three thousand Chinese survivors marched to India to await repatriation. Compelled by the dramatic shift of power, the Chinese Republicans telegrammed the Dalai Lama in exile in India to apologize for the excesses of the Chinese troops and to restore his Chinese titles. The Dalai Lama retorted he hadn't requested his former Chinese rank and announced he was going to exercise temporal and religious authority in Tibet without reference to the Chinese government. In January 1913, the Dalai Lama reentered Lhasa, free of Chinese troops and officials for the first time since the eighteenth century.

Soon after his return to Lhasa, the Dalai Lama proclaimed Tibet's independence and outlined the new relationship between China and Tibet. Noting the historic cooperation between the two countries dating back to Genghis Khan, he wrote, "A few years ago, the Chinese authorities in Szechuan and Yunnan endeavored to colonize our territory. They brought in large numbers of troops on the pretext of policing trade marts." Noting his flight to exile in India, the Dalai Lama explained his attempts to convince the Manchu emperor that the relationship between the countries was that of priest and patron and not one of subordination of one to the other. "I, too, returned safely to my rightful and country," the Dalai Lama wrote, "and I am now in the process of driving out the remnants of Chinese troops from Do Kham in eastern Tibet."[48]

The news of the Chinese revolution had ignited rebellion all across Kham by 1912, in spite of the Sichuan government's ill-advised strategy of circulating photographs of Chao Erh-feng's severed head around the region to prove the republic's legitimacy. Instead, the Hsiang-ch'eng tribesmen revolted and drove out most of the Chinese soldiers. In 1912 they attacked Batang in some force, but the Chinese forces held them off.[49] Monks and tribesmen revolted in the Sangen, Draya, Gonjo, and Markam. In Chamdo, three thousand monks of the immense monastery there besieged the Chinese garrison from a commanding bluff above the town. The Khampas cut the Chinese communication lines from the Mekong River all the way back to the Sichuan border at Tachienlu. Armed nomads harried Chinese couriers and traffic along the trade routes.

Recognizing the danger, the Chinese Republican authorities determined to gain control of eastern Tibet. In June 1912, the successor to Chao Erh-feng, Yin Ch'ang-heng, ordered the invasion of Kham by a vanguard of seven hundred Sichuan troops, part of an eventual army of eight thousand sent to pacify Kham. When the Chinese populace gathered in Chengdu to send off the troops, Yin Ch'ang-heng decreed himself and his army to be invincible. He told the crowd he was the vanquisher of Chao Erh-feng and had little to fear from the barbarian rabble in Kham. "I exposed the head of Butcher Chao in front of the army," he shouted.

By late July, Yin took Tachienlu with four thousand troops. The soldiers engaged in an orgy of destruction, looting the royal palace of the previously deposed king of Chala and wreaking havoc around the city.[50] The king retreated to tribal havens in the interior of his former state. The Chinese commander at Chamdo weathered the attacks of the monks and took the monastery, destroying it wholly. The destruction of the Chamdo monastery, one of the Tibetans' most important religious institutions, was never forgotten or forgiven.[51] In place of Chao's strict discipline, Yin's men were unrestrained by their officers. Their depredations left a particularly resentful legacy among the Tibetans.[52]

In early September, Yin reported to Republican officials that the main roads east of Batang were open and he anticipated pacifying the country west of Batang in short order. Yin, however, was not entirely candid. He lacked sufficient men to execute his strategy effectively against a hostile populace, and rivalries with other provincial warlords prevented reinforcement from Yunnan. British consul Louis King informed his government that Chinese control was far from unchallenged even in the environs of Tachienlu. By the end of 1912, repeated sorties by armed nomads had bogged down Yin's offensive. Armed with modern rifles captured from the Chinese, the Hsiang-ch'eng tribesmen again controlled the Jung Lam, where Yin faced not only the insurgent Tibetans, but Chinese troops still loyal to the Manchu imperial authorities.

Bowing to the realities of the situation, the Chinese abandoned hope of re-taking Lhasa. Instead, they revived Chao's dream of establishing the new Chinese province of Sikang (Xikang), which would encompass Kham and extend far into central Tibetan territory previously considered to be the bailiwick of the Dalai Lama's government. But the Chinese had little reason to believe they could even hold the entirety of Kham.

The Tibetan fortunes, on the other hand, were improving. Prior to 1913, there were only about three thousand soldiers in the Tibetan army, for the most part untrained in modern techniques and equipped with distinctly out-of-date equipment. As part of an overall program of modernization, the Dalai Lama ordered the expansion and upgrading of the army. He dispatched four regiments to Kham under the command of the Kalon Lama to repel the Chinese forces. He also gave instructions to raise local militia from among the Khampa tribesmen. In the military actions that followed, the Chinese were driven back from their forward positions in the eastern reaches of central Tibet to a rough frontier line at the western edge of Kham. It was clear that the insurrection in Kham and the Chinese attempt to suppress it had escalated into a war between the Dalai Lama's army and the weakened Chinese forces.[53] After the opening actions, a stalemate emerged in eastern Tibet. Along the western border of Kham, the two belligerents faced one another. The Chinese defended a line defined by their garrison towns at Chamdo and Batang while the Tibetans held a line to the west on the divide between the Salween and Mekong rivers.[54]

Back in America, Albert and Flora Shelton faced some harsh realities as they debated their return to Kham. The situation had radically changed. Chinese authority in eastern Tibet that the missionaries previously depended upon had eroded to the point of impotence. The FCMS missionaries had to reach an understanding with ascendant Tibetans if they were going to reach their great goal of Lhasa—or even continue their station in Batang.

Return to Tibet

In spite of her misgivings, Flora acceded once again to her husband's yearnings for Tibet.[55] As Albert Shelton prepared to return to Tibet, he began to order the mountain of supplies to sustain them in the far hinterlands. The missionaries had also decided to construct houses and a hospital on eight acres of land that Ogden and Hardy leased from the local Chinese official in 1911.[56] Dr. Shelton related, "We were to build and it had become necessary to provide the glass, hinges, screws, nails, roof, paint, etc., which could not be secured in the field. I also took back with me at the time furnishings for the hospital—beds, an operating-table, medicine, etc."[57] While in Chicago on a fund-raising swing, Shelton arranged for the massive shipments from Montgomery Ward, the China missionaries' great purveyor.

America was good to Flora and Albert Shelton. Crowds thronged his lectures. With the publication of her two books and missionary periodical articles, Flora Shelton had the verification she needed to continue her writing and translation work. Albert Shelton's photography and Tibetan artifact collection opened new doors. Not only did he have access to cultured museum people and a wealthy group of collectors, the sale of his objects also brought his family some degree of previously unattainable financial security. During Dr. Shelton's three-year furlough, his image changed. He was now a missionary-hero, revered and respected by the good Christian people of America, who opened their hearts and checkbooks to his message of Tibet. Shelton's past as a homesteader boy harkened back to deeply held myths of the American frontier. His life as a pioneer missionary doctor in Tibet resonated with their hopes for an expansive American future.

CHAPTER TEN

SHATTERED CHARMS
AND NEW PERSPECTIVES

Batang, 1914—1917

We're under war conditions and worse.[1]

—Albert Shelton

Wrapped in a sheet, Dr. Albert Shelton spent his first night back in China toss-
ing and turning on the lawn of a Shanghai mission. Traveling in advance of his
family, who were visiting with relatives on the West Coast, Shelton arrived in
Shanghai in the torrid heat of mid-August. The east China heat drove him onto
the front lawn for some relief, but he found little there either: "Every mosquito
in Eastern China, hearing that I had just returned from America in rather a cor-
pulent state, came to have a feast."[2] The years of fund-raising dinners and train
travel had broadened the formerly trim frontier doctor considerably.

After only one night in Shanghai, he fled to the cool heights of Kuling
(today's Lushan), a summer resort that perched at about thirty-five hundred feet
in the mountains of Jiangxi Province. A bit of the West in the Chinese mountains, Kuling was a foreign hill station of quaint limestone cottages, south German houses, little French-style churches, guesthouses such as the Fairy Glen
Hotel, and classic Victorian wooden manses encrusted with elaborate ginger-
bread trim. Thousands of missionary families and prosperous expatriates made
it their summer home, sequestering themselves by denomination and national-
ity into discrete enclaves.

Shelton rendezvoused in Kuling with his Batang colleague, Dr. William
Hardy. Hardy brought his new wife, Nina Palmer Hardy, a Disciple of Christ

missionary he met while working in eastern China. Inspired by the heroic tales of Dr. Susie Rijnhart, Nina Palmer attempted to volunteer for missionary work to Tibet, but single missionary women weren't allowed in remote stations such as Batang.[3] Another FCMS missionary couple bound for Batang, Harold and Josephine Baker, joined the group at Kuling. The Bakers had volunteered for Tibet duty in Nashville, Tennessee, traveling to China in 1912 to begin their language study.[4] Dr. Shelton's cook-cum-medical assistant, Johnny, also arrived in Kuling, returning to the mission after a stint as a Chinese army doctor.[5]

The Republican revolution continued to roil China into 1913. Republican president Yuan Shih-k'ai, a former imperial military man and head of the most effective Republican army, dissolved the Republican parliament in early 1913, replacing the democratic body with an administrative council. In spite of his moves, Yuan retained the approval of the Christian missionary community. Ever smitten by an iron fist, the missionaries saw Yuan as a powerful military link to the Manchu government's Westernizing reforms.

Though the Republican revolution profoundly altered Chinese society and politics, it had little effect on Chinese policies or attitudes toward Tibet. The year prior, Yuan Shih-k'ai had decreed his concept of the "Five Races": Chinese, Manchu, Mongol, Muslim, and Tibetan together peopling the territory of greater China. Yuan stated the Chinese would stop oppressing the Mongols and Tibetans and would institute a policy of strict egalitarianism. In turn, Yuan demanded, "Mongolia and Tibet should therefore all the more follow the wishes of the people as a whole, and should maintain peace and good order." In August 1912, the Chinese government revived Chao Erh-feng's dream of establishing the new province of Xikang in the eastern Tibetan borderlands.

On August 25, 1913, the Batang missionaries convened the organizational meeting of the Tibetan Christian Mission (TCM), as they named the reconstituted FCMS Batang station. From China Inland Mission workers in Kham, they learned Chinese soldiers had looted the dispensary and the Ogdens' house in Batang. "If this is true," Dr. Hardy wrote to Archibald McLean, "it means that all of our instruments are gone—a very serious loss indeed—and also our stock of drugs as well as Mr. Ogden's house personal belongings."[6] The group debated returning to Batang, eventually deciding scouts should proceed with care to Tachienlu.[7] A few days later, Dr. Hardy wrote the American consul apprising him that the Shelton and Hardy families were returning to Tachienlu, as they couldn't assess conditions from Kuling.[8]

In October 1913, Flora and the girls arrived in Kuling. A few days later, the Hardy and Shelton party began the grueling trip back to Tibet. The Bakers lingered behind as their young baby was too frail to travel.[9] The missionaries steamed the thousand miles up the Yangtze to Yichang, where they alighted to await the mountain of baggage and freight. Their thirty tons of cargo included their personal belongings, materials for the new hospital, two dwellings, and the immense quantity of supplies for years on the frontier. During their Yichang stay, one of the large warehouses in the foreign treaty port burned, threatening all of their belongings. The missionaries carried their steamer trunks from the blaze and sat on them to prevent theft while watching the firefighters. Flora rejoiced, "the invaluable flannel underwear for ourselves and babies, which could not be bought for love nor money in the interior, were still with us."[10]

Western technology had conquered the Yangtze rapids in the interim since their first ascent of the river, and the Sheltons took a small steamer, cutting the journey from thirty days of junk travel to five by steamboat. However, the slow cargo boats necessitated a two-month stay in Chongqing to await their baggage. In January 1914, Albert wrote from Chongqing to a Disciple in America, "Lots of executions these days here over 100 decapitations this month so far. We hope to get to Batang before April."[11]

The Simla Convention and the New Tibetan Army

With the Chinese-Tibetan borderland in bedlam and the political situation in Tibet in uncertain flux, the British attempted to become ostensible mediators in the Chinese-Tibetan dispute. The British hoped to calm a situation on their Indian flank by forcing the Chinese to clarify their rights and intents in Tibet, particularly in regard to the borders between China, Tibet, and Assam. Accordingly, the British proposed a tripartite conference composed of China, Tibet, and Britain. Tibet readily agreed to the conference in mid-1913. With some reluctance from the Chinese, all three arranged to attend the conference at Simla in British India.

In October 1913, the three governments' envoys convened at Simla. The military situation had dramatically changed since the summer. Undermanned and harassed, the Chinese army was on the defensive in Kham. Expansive after their triumphs in eastern Tibet, the Tibetans at the Simla conference demanded complete control of their internal affairs. With the exception of bona-fide merchants, all Chinese were to be barred from Tibet, even the *ambans* and their escort. The Tibetans further claimed territorial administration over Kham all the way to Tachienlu, thousands of square miles of land the Chinese had controlled for more than a century.

The Chinese envoy, Chen I-fan, countered with terms that included a claim on Tibet "as an integral part of the Republic of China." Tibet should have no bilateral foreign relations except through the Chinese government. Further, the Chinese retained the right to station an *amban* in Tibet with an escort of twenty-six hundred soldiers. The Chinese also contended the Chinese-Tibetan boundary should be at Giamda, a bare hundred miles east of Lhasa. East to west, the two claims for the territorial boundary differed by about a thousand miles.[12]

The British and Tibetan interests overlapped in many regards but differed in some important ones. The British had little interest in a truly independent Tibet that could form unilateral alliances with countries such as Russia, favoring instead a self-governing Tibet that was nominally under a tightly circumscribed Chinese influence. Seeing Tibet as some sort of medieval Himalayan Switzerland whose faux neutrality they could control, the British wanted to be Tibet's exclusive Western relation. To accomplish their goals, Britain sought to maintain a paternal oversight over Tibet, filtering in appropriate news of the outside world, keeping a watchful eye out for unhealthy intrigues, and discouraging disruptive guests such as sportsmen and missionaries.[13]

Initially the British government supported the Tibetans' boundary line just west of Batang. Senior British diplomat Sir Henry McMahon proposed a boundary line between China and the Dalai Lama-controlled Tibet that was along the east bank of the Salween to the west of Batang. In turn, the Chinese would give up religious control in southern Kham, with the monasteries at Litang and Batang regaining their authority. The British home government approved McMahon's territorial concepts, but the proposals were less appealing to the Tibetans and Chinese.

McMahon managed to keep the Chinese at the bargaining table only by noting the Tibetans' desire to return to combat in eastern Tibet (perhaps with British aid). McMahon further insinuated the British intent to negotiate a bilateral agreement with Tibet should the Chinese withdraw from the conference. By the end of April 1914, after months of fruitless negotiations over boundaries, the hopes for the tripartite conference came to naught. When the Chinese stuck to their original territorial claims, the Tibetans withdrew some of their previous concessions. In spite of last-minute British maneuvering, the Chinese foreign office repudiated the agreement and boundary line that emerged from the conference, which British and Tibetan envoys had signed and the Chinese envoy initialed.

The British persevered with their diplomatic efforts into July 1914, signing the trade agreements with the Tibetans along with an understanding relating to the Tibetan-Assam border. Ever the mercantilists, the British left the Simla conference with some commercial rewards. The Tibetans agreed to allow British trade agents to carry on their business throughout the country. The agreement established market towns in Tibet that acted much like extraterritorial inland treaty ports, Lhasa implicitly permitting Indian tea to be imported. The nineteenth-century British tea scouts had at last undermined the ancient Chinese brick tea monopoly.[14]

However, a bilateral agreement was not going to be sufficient in the long term. To build a strong, ostensibly independent Tibet capable of resisting the Chinese and acting as a buffer state for the Indian border, McMahon recommended the British supply the Tibetans with several thousand rifles and a half-million rounds of ammunition. McMahon further suggested the British send military instructors to train the Lhasa army, along with British surveyors, geologists, and physicians.[15] By September 1914, the arms and instructors were on the way to Lhasa. Soon a revitalized and well-equipped Tibetan army marched east to Kham. It was a uniquely Tibetan-British model. Dressed in British uniforms with puttees, pith helmets, and polished Sam Browne belts, British- and Indian-trained Tibetan officers barked commands in English. Scottish bagpipes swirled out the marching music for the Tibetan conscripts shouldering their new British rifles.[16] However, the traditional yak trains of wives, children, and household baggage still accompanied the Tibetan forces, which resembled "a migrating Tartar horde," according to one British officer.[17]

With the Kalon Lama, the governor of eastern Tibet and commander of the Tibetan army, at loggerheads with the Sichuan forces in Kham, the British recognized that to be the flash point. To keep tabs on the region, consular official relied on the missionaries to be intelligence gatherers in the borderlands, just as the U.S. War and State departments used the Batang missionaries to keep an eye on the frontier.[18]

Missionary-spies were not such a startling idea given the interweave of militarism, trade, and religion that characterized Western imperialism in China. From the early days of Western colonialism in China, missionaries served as interpreters and guides for diplomats and military men. As with the central Asian explorers, missionaries were a hybrid species who served, depending on the circumstances, as geographers, political agents, commercial scouts, linguists, diplomats, soldiers, and spies. Given Kham's location on the outskirts of the Chinese empire, the Western foreign services depended on the missionaries for regular appraisals of political and military conditions. The few Western diplomatic and military men sent into the Tibetan marches relied heavily on missionaries to act as guides and translators.[19]

The Road Home to Kham

The upper Yangtze remained intractable as ever as the Sheltons took houseboats from Chongqing to Leshan. At Ya'an, they transferred to sedan chairs for the up-country journey to Tachienlu, followed by three hundred coolies toting the mission's thirty tons of freight.[20] Crossing the great iron link bridge at Luding, they turned west over the snow-covered passes. Flora recorded in her journal, "Snow cold & lonesomeness everywhere but withal grandeur untellable: We reached Tachienlu March 17th & were glad to get there."[21]

"It was like going back home," she wrote.[22] But Tachienlu was a different home with a new name—the Republicans had renamed the town Kangding. Arriving in the wake of the Republican Chinese invasion, the missionaries found parts of the city burned and the king's palace in ruins. In addition, British consul Louis King, who pioneered Kham for the Foreign Service, had taken up residence. Initially sent to Chengdu, with secret instructions to travel to Tachienlu and report on Chinese troop movements, King opened the Tachienlu station in 1913. He traveled widely in the marches intelligence gathering.[23] Flora wrote, "Mr. King the English Consul located at Tachienlu is a queer piece indeed."[24] Suspicious of Britain's incursions into Tibetan affairs, the missionaries feared the British might close their eastern gateway into Tibet as they had done on the Indian side.

The entire mission finally assembled in Tachienlu when the Ogdens and Bakers arrived about a month later. Slowed by convalescences, the Ogdens hadn't sailed from the United States until January 1914. Without the impediment of the mission freight, however, the Ogdens and Bakers had traveled much faster than the Sheltons and Hardys.

On June 15, 1914, the Tibetan Christian Mission convened for a meeting, electing James Ogden president and Nina Hardy again to be secretary. With his new language skills, Harold Baker took the task of Chinese evangelism while James Ogden assumed responsibility for Tibetan evangelism, the school, and direction of language study. Minnie Ogden took the assignment for work with the Batang women. Fettered by their lack of early language training, the Hardys were assigned language study. Flora took responsibility for teaching the missionary children and music. Albert was put in charge of medical work and house repair, and he received approval to itinerate for a year.[25]

A substantial missionary contingent was returning to Batang. Whereas only two families worked in temporary quarters before, eight adults and five children were now planning to be in a large mission post constructed to their specifications. But given the problems of transport and dangers of the road, it was too large a group to travel together. "It was decided that one family at a time should go over the road, because of the number of men and the size of the caravan, and the smallness of the rest houses," Flora wrote. The Sheltons prepared to go by the northern route again. Albert noted it was the only alternative, "as the Chinese officials absolutely refused permission to travel by the southern route, one of the French Fathers having been killed near Litang by robbers the day previous. He was not only killed, but his body was badly mutilated."[26]

Accompanied by Chinese soldiers, the Sheltons and Hardys slowly proceeded west by muleback and sedan chair.[27] It was a hard trip for the Chinese coolies. Unused to the high altitudes, they had only thin clothes and no bedding or covers. James Baker wrote, "We gave them everything we could spare, but they still had to sleep at the end of the hard day's work with nothing on their bodies save one thickness of summer clothes. On the other hand we had woolen blankets and bedding in abundance, so much, in fact, that at times its weight made sleeping uncomfortable."[28]

The mission's freight caravan of 169 yaks was sent the shorter southern route. Men and transport animals conscripted under the *ula* system provided the baggage transport. *Ula* was a Tibetan system that required each locale along Kham's trails to provide a predetermined number of pack animals and tenders for a nominal sum (often less than half of the true value) to officials and travelers who held government permits. A British official noted, "Missionaries and other foreign travelers in Chinese Tibet often employ *ula,* for unless they employ their own caravans no other means of locomotion are available. This does not tend to increase their popularity with the natives."[29]

It was a lurching, spasmodic journey to Batang, filled with trepidation. In one village, they encountered a French priest who had survived being tied to a monastery gate for eighteen days. Caravan workers told them about tortures the Tibetans inflicted on Chinese prisoners: "Some were skinned alive. Others cut in pieces when they were alive & fed to the birds & others rolled in a green skin & laid in the sun."[30] At one monastery town, Flora quaked when she found herself surrounded and without Albert. "I was truly frightened, for hundreds of lamas come around the doors and gateways, staring at the queer white people."[31]

Nina Hardy suffered a particularly hard passage. Her chairmen ran off after six days, and she had to ride a horse. Unable to handle the horse, the missionaries hired Tibetans to carry her chair, but that failed. Eventually the missionaries made a seat out of a washboard and suspended it from poles. She rode the washboard the last three hundred miles to Batang.[32]

After twenty-nine days of travel across Kham, the Sheltons arrived in Batang on July 17, 1914. They had been gone almost four years. "We were home once more," Flora wrote, "but there was dust and dirt everywhere." The baggage also arrived safely, with the exception of Flora's new cook stove, which robbers captured. Flora wrote, "I presume they thought it was ammunition and strewed it all over the mountainside. All that reached Batang were the lids, legs, and lifter."[33] There had been fighting around the city, and thieves had looted the Shelton house of everything except books and pictures.[34] The robbers, primarily Chinese soldiers, also stole the medical supplies and dispensary instruments. Following precedents dating back to the unequal treaties after the Opium Wars, the missionaries petitioned to the Chinese government for reparations, which the Chinese government eventually paid after the missionaries withheld tax payments.[35]

The Sheltons moved back into the mill house beside the river, and the other missionaries scattered through town in rented quarters. Once back in Batang dealing with house rehabilitation, Shelton's aversion to construction must have resurfaced. At the November 2, 1914 meeting, the Tibetan Christian Mission resolved, "That Dr. Shelton be released from repairing Tibetan houses."[36]

Disorder in the Borderlands

A serious revolt broke out in Draya in the summer of 1914, coinciding with another uprising in the Hsiang-ch'eng. The Chinese suppressed both revolts. They used particular brutality in Draya, where they surrounded the large monastery of Yemdo and burned it, exterminating a mass of Tibetans taking refuge there. Following their conquest, the Chinese laid waste to the surrounding villages and countryside.[37] At the request of a Chinese general, Dr. Shelton traveled ten days to the northwest to Draya, where many were wounded. Anxious to move quickly, Shelton requested a fast-moving escort of fifty Chinese soldiers. Unwilling to wait for one swollen river to recede, Shelton's group crossed the river behind a breakwater of a hundred yaks driven into the stream by villagers to break the current.

Once he arrived in Draya, Shelton performed operations for ten days.[38] He was practicing medicine in a medieval war zone. Around him were the horrors of vicious warfare. Heads of victims dangled from tree branches, and the Chinese had used a giant iron tea cauldron to boil three Tibetans to death.[39] "Three of them had one after another been placed in this cauldron in cold water, tied hand and foot, but with their heads propped up, and then a fire built under the cauldron and slowly brought to a boil. The skeletons were lying bare on the stones near by, the flesh having all been eaten by the dogs." Some of the Tibetan prisoners had been covered in oil and burned to death; others were drawn and quartered by yaks hitched to arms and legs. The Chinese had sent the balance of the Tibetan prisoners back with their hands cut off.

While returning home to Batang, Shelton encountered a caravan worker whom robbers had attacked a half-hour before. The man was beside the road with a long deep gash in his head where a knife had passed through his skull, leaving his throbbing brain in plain sight. Shelton cleaned and sewed the wound, leaving him lying on the grass where they found him. "Such is some of the medical work that a doctor in this outpost, with no other doctor within seven hundred miles, is called upon to do."[40]

Kham was not the only part of the Tibetan-Chinese frontier in upheaval, nor were the Tibetan Christian Mission workers the only missionaries in peril. In the Gansu grasslands to the north, Muslims revolted against Chinese Republican rule and attempted to form alliances with the Tibetans along the northwestern border with China. In the Tibetan ethnic region of Amdo, William Christie and his Christian & Missionary Alliance missionaries suffered the attacks of the warlord White Wolf's renegade army during his half-year rampage. Besieged by White Wolf's men in a mission compound, William Christie escaped death only when a Chinese Christian woman gave herself to the bandits. The Chinese Republican army killed White Wolf by chance in 1914, and his brigand army melted away. The same year the Chinese sent a punitive column into Amdo after a bandit raid by a Tibetan tribe, an action that threatened to escalate the dispute into a northern border war. Acting as an intermediary, missionary Christie was instrumental in negotiating a cease-fire.[41]

By the end of 1914, Sichuan Viceroy Yin Ch'ang-heng was no longer a factor in the Tibetan marches. Republican officials summoned Yin to Beijing, where they summarily deposed him. His successor was Chang Yi, another warlord whom the Republican government expected to light a fire under the Chinese forces in eastern Tibet. Instead, Yi was notable in his timidity. Ten thousand freshly trained and well-equipped Tibetan troops stood along the eastern Tibetan border facing a demoralized and bedraggled Chinese army.[42]

The Chinese continued to control major parts of Kham, dispatching officers who proved to be interested in little but feathering their nests with onerous taxes on the Tibetans.[43] With some precarious order in central and eastern Kham, the Chinese enticed the Tibetans to the conference table in Tachienlu, though little came from the talks. During the summer, the Chinese foreign office in Beijing also approached British diplomats with an offer to sign the Simla draft agreement earlier worked out. After considering the offer, the senior British diplomats chose not to reopen the discussions. Failing to convince the British to open negotiations, the Chinese again approached the Tibetans, particularly in eastern Tibet. The Chinese overtures in eastern Tibet alarmed the Dalai Lama's government officials, who didn't want to give up their military advantage until they had resolved the boundary issues with the Chinese.[44]

The Pure Air of Japoding

In spite of the simmering hostilities along the border, the Tibetan Christian Mission began settling down, except for the itinerating Albert Shelton. "The year began as many do," Flora wrote in her diary, "Bert not at home as he had gone to Atunze on Dec. 29th."[45] Bert traveled south to Atunze to get cash, as currency could be transported only with large and heavily armed escorts from the faraway money centers. Local merchants in Atunze, Tachienlu, and Batang would take promissory notes in exchange for cash, except when bandit tribes swarmed the roads.[46] Flora wrote in her diary, "Hope the time he is away has no excitements. I do not care for anything out of the ordinary, but would like to live a very uneventful life with no rash doings intermixed."[47]

Albert started the journey by whirling down the rushing Yangtze in a large yak-skin coracle, a round boat made of a frame of lashed branches covered with skins. In two hours, he traveled farther than he could have in five or six hours on horseback. The second day he climbed out of the valley. "At that time of year it is very cold but the sun is usually bright and the air dry, so that it is very pleasant," he recalled.[48] Atunze, the monastery town where the Jo Lama had previously lived, was a caravan town, where trails crossed from south in Yunnan and west to Lhasa. On the trail, Shelton encountered some of the violence plaguing the country—a young child bayoneted and thrown to the side; a partially burned grandmother lying dead, one of a dozen family members slaughtered in a tribal feud. The road through the Mekong canyon was sometimes a hundred feet above the river, nothing more than rough planks laid on stakes driven into the stone. "Occasionally a man goes over, horse and all, and when he does, there is just the plunk," Albert wrote.[49]

Hungry for a change from their monotonous diet, the missionaries especially welcomed Shelton's return to Batang. He brought "some fruit, oranges, raisins, beans & rice," his wife noted. In June the mission voted to buy the Shelton's mill house from the Chinese official.[50] They also decided to move forward with the great building project on Japoding Hill, which included a hospital and two residences.

Shelton again managed a crew of woodcutters in the forests above Batang, as well as twenty mud builders, cement makers, lime burners, plasterers, and carpenters. The problems of construction again bedeviled Albert Shelton. Flora Shelton confided to her diary, "Housebuilding is too much for Bert's nerves, & he has just about to quit sleeping. They are so worrisome & steal so much of the wood."[51] A few days later she wrote, "Bert is up in the mountains for a day's rest to see if he could forget a few cares while he is gone."[52]

Through the spring of 1915, the construction on Japoding Hill continued. The missionaries arranged to build their Christian bastion on an old Chinese cemetery.[53] Ogden and Hardy had the graves dug out of the jumble of rocks and brambles before the fleeing from the revolution. During the revolution, more bodies were buried there. In early May 1916, the missionaries sought estimates from the Chinese official to disinter the new graves.[54] The Westerners use of old cemeteries was another source of tension in China. In 1874 there was a riot in

Shanghai when the French attempted to put a road through a cemetery. Similar brawls erupted when foreign railroads tried to drive tracks through Chinese graveyards. In the Chinese view, foreign desecration of a cemetery disturbed the bones of venerated ancestors, a sin as heinous as disrupting the omnipresent *feng-shui.*

The missionaries contracted for workmen to grade and terrace the hillside, leveling it into small fields, building sites, and gardens.[55] As the hill was without natural water (which indeed was one of the reasons the Chinese authorities were willing to lease it), the missionaries arranged for a flume to be built from a tributary of the Batang River that was more than a mile away. For the cost of under a thousand dollars, the builders curled the wooden water race around a cliff face and spanned gullies and washes with wooden aqueducts to bring water to the compound. The watercourse ran right in front of the hospital. From there, the mission workers hauled the water into the buildings.[56] The water quickly raised the value of the land and allowed the missionaries to cultivate lawns of Kentucky bluegrass, ornamental shrubs, and an orchard of apple trees that later became the basis of one of the valley's major cash crops.

On the advice of an English missionary Shelton met while steaming up the Yangtze, the TCM decided to build in a somewhat amended Tibetan style. The missionaries posited the buildings would be more familiar to the local people, who would theoretically then be amenable to visiting the mission for services. The missionaries also felt their construction techniques would teach lessons in Western sanitation, aesthetics, and building.

High mud walls began to rise on Japoding Hill as Tibetan workers swarmed the scaffolds, pounding adobe into wooden forms. In place of the much-maligned Tibetan mud roofs, the missionaries erected Chinese-style tile roofs and metal roofs hauled from the United States. Glass windows, carefully shipped from America, filled the wooden window frames. The Tibetan Christian Mission was a Western outpost on the far Tibetan frontier, another expression of the grand presumptuousness and unfettered idealism that characterized so much missionary business in China. "What a change from the stench of the streets to the pure air of Japoding!" Minnie Ogden wrote. "Presses to hang your clothes in, cupboards in the kitchen, a pantry, and a bath room!"[57]

The missionaries began a number of programs. They included a kindergarten and Women's and Children's Work, which involved home visits by Minnie Ogden and a local woman to new mothers and babies. James Ogden ran the mission school for thirty-two students, teaching basics and industrial training in coloring, soap- and shoe-making. Harold Baker established a rug-making business with the idea of developing a self-sustaining business. By the summer of 1915 there were over two hundred rugs in inventory—evidence of high production and low demand. The annual report stated, "Mrs. Shelton did an excellent job translating. A booklet on wine-drinking has been printed."

Baker and Ogden continued their evangelical work in the valley. Harold Baker focused on distributing tracts to local Tibetan leaders, both lamas and laymen, and gave Sunday services in Chinese, attended by sixty to one hundred people, most soldiers from the fort. The annual report noted, "50 have a desire to become Christians, mostly merchants and working men, but they have ulterior thoughts."[58] Flora reflected on the missionaries' attempts to regiment the Tibetan children with Sunday school, "Such a lot of Tibetan kids as we get at S.S. We are trying to teach them to march but its like getting a swarm of bees to keep time to music."

The TCM also funded Dr. Shelton's travels, with Dr. Hardy taking over all Batang medical work so Shelton could concentrate on itineration.[59] His journeys took him through areas where no Westerner had ever set foot, doctoring, collecting artifacts, and dispensing the gospel in equal measure. His retinue most often included his teacher-interpreter Gezong Ongdu and Li Gway Gwang. Once encamped, the missionaries erected a large white tent with Tibetan characters on the side and began healing and preaching.[60] With his native language skills, Li could preach in either lucid Tibetan or Chinese.[61]

By the fall of 1915, the hospital construction became daunting. A buckwheat harvest the missionaries had counted on for construction wages failed due to an early frost, necessitating a slowdown in work. In November Shelton's medical assistant, Johnny, resigned, the first of a number of instances in which he or the assistant Bu quit his position. By December, in spite of the labors of 300 coolies and 169 yaks, the builders began to run short on materials.

In spite of new quarters, Batang continued to be a perilous post. A sharp earthquake shook the town in 1915. Led by a rebel Chinese officer, Hsiang-ch'eng tribesmen and mutinying Chinese soldiers revolted again at the end of 1914. The winter brought no respite, as the Hsing-ch'eng used the traditional raiding season to attack the trade routes. In the spring, they broke out of the Hsiang-ch'eng and captured Tachienlu. Louis King and two CIM missionaries stepped forward to negotiate with the rebels who swept down the Jung Lam. The rebels responded by firing several rounds in their direction and kidnapping them. When the rebel leader threatened them with death, King archly advised him of "the inadvisability of allowing the expression of such opinions." Negotiations were successful. Tachienlu escaped major destruction and the Foreign Service lauded King for his daring. But once again the foreigners were pawns in the complex games of the border.[62]

The rebel force continued east on the Jung Lam from Tachienlu into Sichuan proper, eventually dissipating into the bands of brigands who preyed on the riches of the Sichuan plains. When the rebel force finally dispersed, the Chinese retook Tachienlu and the trade routes, more by default than by force.[63]

Batang faced more than the renegade Tibetan tribesmen and newly strengthened Tibetan army. The Republican soldiers in Batang, perennially unpaid and restive, revolted against a Republican officer. Perhaps seeking some peace from the unrest, Flora gloried in the aftermath: "Some 200 of the military men in the artillery rebelled against the usurper, he got the best of them & beheaded the whole 200! Such ability is worthy of Chao Er Feng!"[64]

In the summer, the Chinese authorities recalled many of their officers out of the Khampa country and the Tibetan army officials incited the tribesmen to revolt, fraying a few missionary nerves in the process.[65] As in other parts of China, the threat of kidnapping hung over the mission. The Catholic mission in Batang once again burned, driving the aging French priest into a fit of terror. Flora wrote, "The poor distracted old priest was being held by the Chinese soldiers so that he could not throw himself in the flames and be destroyed." Concerned that the fire might frighten Flora as her husband was away, the Chinese commander sent eight men to reassure her. When they found the gate barred, they broke it down to ask if she was afraid. "With my teeth chattering, I assured them that I was not, but the truth is I was more afraid of them than of the Tibetans or of the fire either."[66]

The local Chinese garrison proved to be a seasonal menace. Long before the harvest each year, the starving Chinese soldiers predictably threatened mutiny unless the town gave them grain or cash or preferably both. And each year the missionaries and town leaders scurried to round up the provisions to quiet the unrest.[67]

The Chinese official asked Shelton to travel to Derge with the Chinese army to treat wounded soldiers, which he did on June 3 in spite of Josephine Baker's typhus and advanced pregnancy. The day after he left, the Baker child was born prematurely, dying the next day. A few days later, the Sheltons' cow died. Flora fulminated in her diary. "This is Bert's 40th birthday & he goes serenely on not knowing of the cow or Mrs. Baker or anything but what he is doing. . . ."[68] A week later the mission sent a messenger to retrieve Shelton, though Josephine Baker had recovered by his return. In August, Shelton again traveled to Derge, in spite of a heavy bout with malaria. "Bert getting ready to go on his trip but is very ill. It seems impossible to get the malaria out of liver at all."[69] The group returned two weeks later.[70]

In the summer of 1917, Shelton traveled north two hundred miles to the monastery town of Peheu (Pelyul). Like some Cubist hive of Buddhist sanctity, the monastery's flat-roofed dwellings were stacked on top of one another as they rose up the mountainside to the apex of a three-story temple.[71] Shelton doctored about two hundred people on the trip and encountered a few robbers, though he didn't encounter serious trouble. It was also a profitable trip for Shelton, as he collected a number of fine Tibetan artifacts in the war-torn town and monastery.[72]

The incessant travel took its tolls. "Bert came home ill & has been very bad all day . . . can't tell what is the matter with Bert," Flora wrote. He was bedridden for days with an undiagnosed illness. "Doesn't eat a bite & is under morphine most all day."[73]

Flora Shelton also suffered from a variety of ailments. Her failing eyesight kept her from language study, and neuralgia plagued her.[74] Her broken leg never set correctly and left her with a distinct limp. Already a big woman, Flora Shelton was growing heavier, adding to her health problems in the stress and tumult of the high-altitude war zone.

Sichuan: The Devil's Cave

In 1916, the telegraph between Tachienlu and Batang went down again—always an omen of disorder—destined this time to remain out of commission for five years.[75] Republican president Yuan Shih-k'ai died the same year in Yunnan after his failed attempt to restore the Chinese monarchy by naming himself as the new dynastic emperor. The monarchist coup defeated, the Republicans reaffirmed their government under a new constitution. The new intrasocietal upheaval prevented the Chinese from attempting to resolve the Tibetan frontier questions, and the Khampa borderlands remained in contentious dispute. Bound by the Simla agreement that prohibited offensive action unless the Chinese first broke the truce, the Kalon Lama held his army in check west of Chamdo through 1915 and 1916, declining to exploit China's political and military weakness.[76]

In the wake of Yuan Shih-k'ai's death, Yunnanese warlords began to dominate Sichuan. A Yunnan frontier commissioner commanding a troop of Yunnan soldiers took over administration of Tachienlu in October 1916. By mid-1917, the two neighboring provinces were locked in a violent civil war, with Yunnan troops burning Chengdu before withdrawing to Yunnan. Sichuan had a long reputation for disorder. The Sichuanese were famous in China for their aggression and independent nature. Isolated deep in the interior of China with its wild terrain, riven with civil and tribal warfare, the province earned its post-revolution nickname, "The Devil's Cave."[77]

In the Tibetan marches, the Sichuan-Yunnan war had disastrous repercussions for the Chinese administration, which divided Kham into independent and mutually suspicious bodies. Chinese generals beholden to Sichuan commanded at Batang and Chamdo. Yunnan controlled Tachienlu. When the Yun-nan army retreated back home, the Yunnan commissioner and his soldiers in Tachienlu were forced to flee to northern Yunnan. The remaining Chinese gar-risons were isolated and left without provisions or ammunition "As a result," British consul Eric Teichman wrote, "they had degenerated into little better than brigands, helping themselves to food and money by plundering the natives of the localities where they chanced to be stationed."[78]

In February 1916, the Tibetan Christian Mission elected Harold Baker over Albert Shelton for chairman. The group then voted to suspend hospital con-struction for ten months while waiting for funds and materials. They arranged to begin construction on a tall stone and mud fence that eventually walled the compound. As was the case in most mission meetings, finances dominated the discussions.

Two months later, Dr. Albert Shelton resigned his elected office as treasurer. The missionaries refused his resignation, but he "declined to act." Like most for-eign mission groups, the TCM suffered from dissension and internal tension, perhaps natural to a group of well-educated, zealous people living in a powder keg far from home. Albert Shelton was a willful man who had his own sense of mission. William Hardy termed himself a grouch, and his letters were marvels of irascibility. Flora Shelton wrote in her journal that Harold Baker was an ass for his machinations.[79] Most likely suffering from a bipolar disorder, James Ogden was often in a rage, occasionally beating his wife. Flora wrote, "Another week begins & opened up with mission meeting. But I'm afraid I don't like them very well, they are too strenuous."[80]

Batang seethed with intrigues. Starving Republican soldiers plotted mutiny. Anti-Chinese secret societies and Hsiang-ch'eng rebels conspired with officials, lamas, and townspeople in cabals of increasing complexity.[81] At the outskirts of the little city, renegade tribesmen ravaged the roads and attacked any caravans foolish enough to travel. In four years, only three Westerners attempted to travel the Jung Lam east to Tachienlu, and one was killed in a bandit attack.[82] To the west and north, the conflict between the Chinese Republican forces and the Dalai Lama's Tibetan army was about to flare into full-scale war.

Reading, Writing, and Accumulating

With the help of Gezong Ongdu and the Jo Lama, Shelton had become an ag-gressive collector. The Newark Museum had contracted with Shelton to con-tinue his acquisitions, advancing him two hundred dollars. Other foreign collectors began to seek him out. Flora helped out with translating and organiz-ing.[83] She recorded, "Finished 11 of Bert's big Tibetan books, that is finished reading and listing their contents in all in which the contents are listed. It's interesting work."[84] Her translation work was both curatorial and evangelical, as the translation introduced her to Buddhist concepts for eventual Christian rebuttal. "Began reading the Kanjur today . . . it is like the bible & they say their religion is just like ours!" she wrote.[85]

Collecting from the Tibetans continued to be challenging. Flora wrote: "It is a difficult matter to purchase things from the Tibetans, as they keep them hidden away, and seldom bring them out for anyone to see. If they have anything to sell, they usually bring it hidden in their gowns, or after night." Albert Shelton and the other missionaries were wealthy people in the backcountry of China. As such, they were one of the only potential sources of cash for those that needed it, whether for food, land, or opium.[86] Increasingly, Shelton's acquisitions came to him in Batang, rather than being found on itinerations, as the growing warfare made collection difficult.[87] Even Batang was not secure. Dr. Shelton reported to the mission that robbers broke into a shipment of Tibetan artifacts he had collected and stole a quantity of objects. In May 1916, Shelton wrote to John Cotton Dana about the lost objects. "I had to send you the later letter saying they [Tibetan objects] could not be sent. We're under war conditions and worse. Robbery is everywhere. I lost a good part of the collection."[88]

In spite of the difficulties of collection and losses to theft, the Newark Museum purchased twenty secular objects from Shelton in 1914. The objects included a sheepskin coat, a yak-butter tea churn, and household objects such as bowls.[89]

Later in his second Batang posting, Shelton acquired two official documents of great historical and religious significance to Batang, magnificent yellow satin scrolls that he shipped to Newark.[90] One scroll came from the Batang Monastery. It was an early nineteenth-century imperial court document sent from Beijing by the third Changya Huktuku, a learned lama and advisor to the emperor. The decree congratulated the monastery for its excellent teachers and high level of Buddhist study. Paintings decorated the perimeter of the scroll, including a lama in Chinese robes and Mongolian-style pointed hat, and an image of Lhamo, patron goddess of Tibet, astride a mule framed by flames hovering above the waves of an ocean of blood.[91]

Shelton obtained the second scroll from the scion of the deposed and executed prince of Batang. Though he was a recidivist opium smoker and alcoholic, the Sheltons sheltered the well-connected young man for about a year. The second scroll was a decree from the Lhasa government to the second prince of Batang in 1680. Issued in the name of the fifth Dalai Lama by his regent Sangye Gyatso with the approval of the emperor of China, the document reflected a chapter of the historical relationship between China and Tibet, as well as the endemic disorder of the borderland. The scroll was addressed to: "all men of the snowy kingdom, to all followers of Tsong-kha-pa, to priests, to all Chinese, Tibetans and wild tribes . . . to land-holders, to those who holds the fields (for the clergy), to all who are in power, to everyone who is born or walks, to soldiers, bandits, travellers, merchants, pilgrims. . . . All officials under the second prince of Batang, receiving his authority from the Dalai Lama who is now in his fifth reincarnation." It noted the Chinese emperor sent a Beijing official to quell the border strife in Kham when he heard of conflicts over land and local governance, and he outlined the prince's authority and responsibility.[92]

In 1916, Albert Shelton began an important relationship with the National Geographic Society, when it purchased a collection of his Tibet photographs, arranged through a missionary supporter and friend of Shelton's, O. A. Rosboro.[93] The cachet of his Tibetan collection and experiences began to shift Albert Shelton's self-image. Accordingly, he sought out organizations of exploration and geography that reflected his new persona. In 1916 he joined the Royal Asiatic Society of Great Britain and Ireland, which was dedicated in 1823 to "enquiring into the History, civil and natural, the Antiquities, Arts, Sciences, and literature of Asia." In November 1916, he became a fellow of the Royal Geographical Society in London, the preeminent club of explorers, joining storied adventurers such as Sir Richard Burton, Mountstuart Elphinstone, and Lord Curzon, viceroy of India.[94] The society application listed Shelton as a "Medical Missionary and Traveler."[95]

The Western Temple: The Hospital

In the spring of 1916, the laborers completed the Shelton home on Japoding Hill, and in the summer the family moved into their new house. Their previous mill house home became the mission school. Perched near the brow of the hill, the new Shelton home was a large, two-story timber and adobe house in the Tibetan style. A shady columned porch and second-floor veranda overlooked the Batang Valley. Following Tibetan custom, the Sheltons set aside the lower floors of the house for storage. Albert also had his photographic darkroom there. The Sheltons lived upstairs in six comfortable rooms where Tibetan rugs lay on dark polished wood floors. Framed lithographs from America decorated whitewashed plaster walls crowned with a frieze of elaborate Arts-and-Crafts wallpaper. Wicker lounge chairs and a curio cabinet with a bronze Buddha on top stood beside a pump organ and music stand. High Himalayan light flooded in the long windows.[96]

By the fall of 1916, the Sheltons had neighbors when the Ogdens moved into their new house. The Bakers and Hardys continued to live near one another in

Figure 10.1   The Sheltons' Tibetan-style house had a cozy American-style parlor with a pump organ, popular lithographs, and Tibetan rugs and art.

the Jaranong neighborhood across town from the mission compound, a long walk around the town walls after the soldiers shut the city gates. Given threats that the near-besieged town faced, the gates shut promptly each evening and remained closed through the night. In the face of growing anarchy, the missionaries soldiered on with their work.

In the summer of 1917, as the Chinese garrison at Chamdo planned its great drive to Lhasa, the TCM missionaries prepared for the long-awaited opening of their hospital. The medical facility was a near-incomprehensible expression of Western technology wrought on the wildest frontier in central Asia. Visitors to the hospital compound climbed up the hill from the Batang River to the east gate of the walled compound where a gateman vetted guests. As they walked up the compound road past the tidy beds of shrubs and flowers with terraces of orchards and gardens below, the hospital loomed above them. Built of Tibetan-style rammed earth, the hospital was a U-shaped building three stories high with an interior courtyard. A large Chinese sign hung from the upstairs balcony.

The hospital was a temple of Western medicine, the only medical facility for a region the size of California. The nearest comparable hospitals were in Ya'an and Kunming. The dispensary where the doctors and medical assistants gave medical care was on the first floor, an airy well-lighted room with long shelved cupboards holding dozens of bottles lined up by size. A shiny mixing table stood in front of the cabinet.[97] Operating rooms were on the second floor above the courtyard, with glass windows facing out to a walkway so family and interested locals could observe the surgeries. The third floor held the isolation wards where withdrawing opium addicts often paced the floor. There were beds for more than fifty patients, though the hospital averaged thirty patients a day. The fee for services was ten cents, with a third to a half of the patients receiving free care. Chinese soldiers constituted the bulk of the hospital's patients. The payments from the Chinese government for the medical care were a substantial portion of the TCM revenues generated in China, about twenty dollars a month when the Chinese officer had money.[98] The patients received both medical care and evangelization, as the missionaries dispensed tracts to outpatients and preached the gospel in the wards for those who were bedridden or confined.[99]

The hospital was the culmination of fourteen years of missionary work on the Tibetan border and three years of furlough promotion, during which Dr. Shelton raised a good part of the hospital funds.[100] Initially, the missionaries planned to name the hospital after their fallen hero, Dr. Z. S. Loftis, but in the eternal way of fund-raising, the hospital eventually came to be named in honor of one of the major donors, Sue M. Diltz.[101] Casting a wide net, Shelton also applied for funds to the China Medical Board, John D. Rockefeller, Jr.'s ambitious charity that supported institutions all across China. In his application, Shelton stated that the hospital provided "Surgical of all kinds for an area 500 miles square," noting Batang's proposed designation as "the capital of the new province."[102] Albeit interrupted by revolution, war, and disrupted mission finances, the hospital construction stretched back almost five years to Albert Shelton's initial woodcutting and brick making.

The hospital opened in July 1917 with a gala celebration. Three hundred men attended the first day, including a small coterie of thirty monks—Flora attributed the light ecclesiastical showing to the local abbot's sudden headache. Five hundred women attended the next day, many with babies. The missionaries gave a large banquet for the local Chinese authorities. Dr. Shelton wrote, "The military and several officials, as well as several others, brought scrolls with complimentary sentiments written in white and gold on three large boards, extolling the virtues of the hospital and what it was able to do." An old man fell off the second floor balcony and broke his legs, allowing them to admit their first patient.[103]

Medical missionaries in China labored in a hard field. Studies of the China medical missionaries by benefactors such as Rockefeller were not positive. In general, observers characterized missionary doctors as overworked, underequipped, and woefully outdated in their techniques. One missionary, Randolph T. Shields, testified at a conference of China medical missionaries, "Given the

Figure 10.2   Built with donations from American mission supporters, the Batang hospital was a bastion of Western values deep in central Asia. It served a region the size of California. Albert Shelton photograph, courtesy the Collection of The Newark Museum. Reprinted with permission.

insufficiently equipped hospital & up to 100 patients a day. . . . It is remarkable how our medical men held up under [the] burden and kept up practically to date and done some first class work." Though he conceded, "many men have fallen into rut and have not kept up to date."[104]

At least the TCM doctors faced predictable ailments of chronic diseases and violence-related traumas. Sword cuts and bullet wounds predominated in the first month of hospital operation. In November, treatments for withdrawing opium addicts were the most common events.[105]

Teacher James Ogden reported, "Under adverse conditions due to war and unfavorable public opinion, the school has yet made advances." Fifty students attended the facility, taking courses in Tibetan, Chinese, English, and Bible Study. Most paid their tuition with various types of work, such as sewing, tutoring, and writing.

The TCM evangelists continued to labor, finding whatever success they did among the Chinese in Batang. Harold Baker left for the China coast to escort a new evangelist, Roderick MacLeod, to Batang. In his absence, Li Gway Gwang did most of the preaching to the locals, both in the mission chapel and in their homes. The converts the mission attracted included a leper who came because he had heard the biblical story of Jesus healing the afflicted such as he. A blind man and his wife joined the church after he had a momentous dream of his rock stove falling down and another rising in its place, interpreting it to mean religion. "One-legged Joe" became a trusted Christian rug-maker after Shelton amputated his frostbitten lower leg.[106]

The Protestant missionaries made inroads among the Tibetans in the post-Revolution years by distancing themselves from the worst depredations of Republican-era Chinese subjugation of Kham. In the heady days after Chao's invasion, the Christian missionaries thought they could use the Chinese power to reduce the monasteries and the control of the lamas. In the years following the revolution the worst sort of freebooters and carpetbaggers arrived in Kham as Chinese officers and officials. As they warily watched the corrupt officials, the Protestant missionaries began to forge relationships with the Tibetan leaders.

Nonetheless they still couldn't make converts among the Tibetans. In general, the TCM missionaries couldn't even convert their own servants and long-time associates, such as Gezong Ongdu and the Jo Lama. But Shelton put the best face on it, informing his mission supporters that the Jo Lama had no faith in his own necromancy. Shelton later wrote to his church audiences that both the Jo Lama and Gezong Ongdu were Christian believers but could not publicly convert because they feared persecutions.[107] The TCM failure wasn't unusual, as mission employees across China willingly accepted their salaries while deftly side-stepping conversion.[108]

Mission finances became tighter through 1917 as World War I cut the exchange rate of the dollar to the Chinese rupee in half. Finances began to dominate the mission meetings. The mission compound required substantial amounts of money to maintain, and the hospital cost substantially more to run than the dispensary. Without a market for its products, the Rug Industrial continued to founder financially. The missionaries had taken a 10 percent salary cut in 1916 to help with the budget. By October 1917, they were all on half-salary, as fighting prevented any transport of currency to Batang.[109]

A Rigorous Domesticity

After their return from furlough, Flora Shelton's work revolved around housekeeping and gardening, educating her children, holidays, and social relations with the other missionaries and townspeople her husband knew. She filled her daily diary with notations about supervising wallpapering, new matting in the halls, cleaning, laundry, and other domestic tasks. Her husband's itinerations often triggered major cleaning projects, sometimes undertaken consciously to assuage her fear and loneliness. She managed their large landscaped grounds that served as both a haven for her family and a showplace of Western order for the locals.[110]

As was the case with many colonials, her travails often included servant problems, albeit ones specific to China. "Cook & coolie will both have to go I guess. As the cook eats all the opium he can find and the coolie is buying & selling it," she wrote, adding a few days later, "The new cook comes tomorrow if he doesn't get scared at the tales the old ones tell of how hard the work is at that place."[111]

With few exceptions, the foreign missionaries to China began to educate their children at the age of six or seven. Acutely aware of the potential handicap their children faced in being so removed from Western education and culture, the missionaries made education a priority.[112] In the large urban centers, the missionary sent their children to boarding schools. Missionaries isolated in interior stations often used the home instruction materials provided by the Calvert School in Baltimore, Maryland, an upper-crust day school that began

Figure 10.3   Perched on Japoding Hill above Batang, the Sheltons' house also served as the girls' schoolhouse, where Flora Shelton acted as their schoolmaster. Photograph courtesy the Collection of The Newark Museum. Reprinted with permission.

providing home-schooling materials in 1906 to expatriate families scattered around the globe.[113]

With her background as a schoolmarm, Flora Shelton taught her own daughters, instructing them in the academic basics with curricula she obtained from stateside schools. The home schooling began in Tachienlu after their return from furlough. She reported a few years later, "School going nicely again & the girls had a good test this time."[114] The regime continued to work well, as Flora noted in her journal the year following: "Girls working hard. Dorothy learning violin. Dorris organ. . . . I had the tests sent from home & they both passed very well."[115]

When Dr. Shelton was in Batang, after a leisurely breakfast he would leave to check on the inpatients while Flora conferred with the Chinese cook and the Tibetan cleaning lady and gardener. The two girls went to their desks at opposite corners of the room to study for an hour until their mother arrived for the day's lessons. When Dr. Shelton returned from his hour or so of rounds, he taught Dorris Latin and math. After the family lunch at noon, the girls were free to play with their Tibetan friends, who included the two daughters of Gezong Ongdu. In the periods when he served as the dispensary physician, Dr. Shelton returned to the hospital in the afternoon and hoisted the American flag, signaling to the valley that he would see patients. After lunch Flora retired to rest until the arrival of Gezong Ongdu, who assisted her with translations until four o'clock teatime.[116]

The Shelton girls straddled two worlds in Batang, mediating between both.[117] "I think Dorothy and I helped the people of Batang overcome their fear of foreigners," Dorris wrote. "We enjoyed speaking their language and showed them that we wanted to be friends and we didn't even think of them as being different from ourselves." The children loved Tibetan food such as *tsampa* and yak-butter tea, to the dismay of their mother.[118] After Dr. Shelton learned the Tibetans preferred foreigners to dress in their own fashion, the girls wore American clothes purchased from the Montgomery Ward catalogue or sent in the "missionary barrels" that came across Kham by yak from the supporting churches back in America.[119] During the Tibetan holidays, the Shelton daughters sported Tibetan costumes to cavort with their friends. At one point, Dorris attempted to dye her blond hair with black ink to blend in with her friends.[120]

Holidays, including minor ones like Washington's Birthday, were a joyous time for the family, and the Sheltons celebrated them with a passion. With its religious significance, Christmas was a particularly fêted day. Flora wrote of their first Christmas back in Batang: "The man went up on the mountain for the tree & it was a very nice little one. Then we got it set up & and it was ready to trim. Such lots of fun we had trimming it with bells & ropes & flags & little birds. . . .

We put the candles on but didn't light them as we were afraid of the fire but lit the lamp. It looked very pretty."[121]

The TCM mission in Batang provided a comfortable retreat for the missionaries, with visits, tea parties, and dinners constantly exchanged. The mission compound's croquet and tennis courts sat amidst the gardens, allowing recreation to be interwoven with responsibilities. Hunting was a favorite pastime of the men.[122]

Beyond holidays and informal mission get-togethers, entertainment held little allure for Flora, even feasts with Chinese dignitaries at the *yamen:* "O my, such a lot of slugs & eels & pork & liver etc."[123] Albert socialized with a broad range of people in Kham, and his wife shared the responsibility. It was essential to both his mission and collecting work that Albert Shelton maintain strong connections to the Tibetan community, particularly as China's power waned in the Tibetan marches. As the military and political situation changed, the missionaries increasingly needed the Tibetans to continue their work. Bound by mutual respect, affection, and necessity, the missionaries interacted with the Tibetans in a way that was wholly different from their fearful early days in Kham. Albert averred, "The Tibetans are a kindly, generous hospitable people when you know them, but sometimes dangerous when you do not."[124]

Far more than he did during his first Batang posting, he reached out to the Tibetans, inviting them to mission dinners and offering gifts. Shelton thanked his contact at the *National Geographic* for the extra copies of the society's Lhasa issue, as he had given his copy to the Ba Lama. "He says it is like a return trip to Lhasa where he spent some 10 years for his education."[125]

Changing Ways: The Missionaries and the Tibetans

The Tibetans returned the hospitality: "Bert & the children went to see the Lamas & dance at the 'Yaba' temple," Flora recorded.[126] Shelton became a familiar face at Tibetan temple festivals, chatting with the lamas and laymen, snapping photographs, nurturing new contacts. Roderick MacLeod wrote of their visit to the Batang Monastery's New Year's festival, where the lamas pitched a tent for the missionaries' comfort for them to watch the religious dances the monks performed.[127]

Afterward, the lamas led the two Christian missionaries into the dimly lit temple where hundreds of monks gathered for scripture and chanting. "As we entered, we heard a low rolling sound like that of a gigantic electric-fan," MacLeod wrote describing the monks' low sonorous chanting. He went on to tell of the service, the temple, the accoutrements of the ritual, the recitations and music, all conveyed in neutral expressive language, without the pejoratives such as "Devil Dances," or "Satanism" that the missionaries had previously used, perhaps reflecting a growing respect between the Tibetans and the Tibetan Christian Mission. Describing the Buddhist ceremony, MacLeod wrote, "The Tibetans entered heartily into the spirit of the occasion, as they do in all the works of Lamaism," going on to discuss the Western ideas that the missionaries could offer the Tibetans to improve their lives. "Education, then is what the Tibetans need," MacLeod wrote without reference to Christianity. "They need to be taught to think clearly and consistently in regard to themselves and the world about them."[128] With her increased contact and familiarity, even Flora began to soften toward the Tibetans.

For well over a decade, the missionaries depended on Tibetans for instruction, assistance, and some comprehension of a strange land. Tibetan nannies tended their children; their playmates were Tibetan children. In the process of her translation work, Flora Shelton formed a deep bond with Gezong Ongdu, the man she referred to as "Teacher" in her diary. They worked together almost every day he was in Batang. She noted his mother's illnesses; his daughters' travails and triumphs.

Figure 10.4   Ethnologic work became Shelton's passion. Gezong Ongdu, to Shelton's left, served as his invaluable informant and assistant. Photograph courtesy the Still Family Archive. Reprinted with permission.

One winter when "Teacher" was gone on an itineration, she queried in her diary, "I wonder if he is as happy as I wish him to be."[129]

Flora and Albert began Tibetan language study soon after their return to Batang, again utilizing Gezong Ongdu as their teacher. While Albert's other interests and responsibilities kept him from the classroom, he spoke both Chinese and Tibetan well, with a clear understanding of idiom and nuance. He learned, he wrote, "By hiring a native to teach him so many hours every day and by constant daily association with the people."[130]

Albert Shelton never did learn to read Tibetan or Chinese script. "Too old to learn reading—no literature suitable for beginners," he wrote a mission supporter. This was in spite of owning a number of Tibetan primers published by missionary societies.[131] Albert's inability to read or write Tibetan caused little difficulty with the mass of the illiterate Tibetan population, but it was a barrier with educated Tibetan clerics and nobility, who placed scriptural and religious writing in high esteem.[132]

Soon after beginning her language study in Batang, Flora Shelton found her life's work. Early in her study, she harbored few aspirations, but she later began to formulate some modest translation goals. "Am at work in Tibetan & hope to do something. Perhaps a primer & a first reader for the use of the churches."[133] Within the year, her Tibetan language study and translation dominated the hours she could wrest from her domestic responsibilities. "This Tibetan study is so intensely interesting," she wrote. "I wish my eyes & nerves would let me study it 5 to 6 hours a day instead of only 1 or two besides the 'other things.'"[134] Her journals filled with notations of her satisfaction with the work.[135] Though mission-bound, Flora was able to ruminate on Tibetan culture and character through her translation of Tibetan religious books. "These Tibetan hymns are full of their belief & customs. It would be easy to be a Buddhist as there is little responsibility for sin."[136]

Beyond tasks of home and family, Flora began to chafe at any deflection from her translation and study.[137] In time, even the enforced idleness of Sundays became a burden. "Work again and glad to be at it again," she characteristically wrote on Mondays. "Sunday always seems to be a hard day."[138] Translation became Flora's obsession, and she began to formulate plans to write three books in Tibetan. In the period after her return from furlough, she prepared Tibetan translations of a songbook of one hundred and fifty hymns, a primer of geography and astronomy, a child's book of thirty-two stories, kindergarten songs, as well as extensive translations of biblical phrases into Tibetan. Given the importance the Disciples and other foreign missionary societies placed on providing literature in the vernacular language, she found support for the translation work.

Flora learned to read and write Tibetan well, though being isolated from day-to-day life outside the mission, she lacked her husband's glib facility in the spoken language. While continuing to find fulfillment in domestic management, parenting, and the reflected glory of her husband's celebrity, Flora Shelton sought recognition for her own independent translation work, a literary field in which her husband clearly demonstrated a lack of aptitude.

White Mind—Albert Shelton as Mediator

Dr. William Hardy's furlough required Dr. Shelton once again to become the mission doctor, perhaps unwillingly. Itineration and his dream of ministering in Lhasa remained his first priority. Shelton grumbled about his hospital work in his annual report to the FCMS: "The work is engrossing and tends to be confining."[139] While Shelton took over the responsibility for the hospital, he also began immediately training eight medical assistants to do treatments, in hopes of discovering a few promising candidates.

Dr. Albert Shelton began acting as a translator and intermediary between the Chinese officials and the Tibetans.[140] A translator in a war-torn, antagonistic region such as Kham was a crucial position, though open to manipulation and trickery. With the hard-won respect of both communities, missionaries like Shelton could serve as impartial interpreters.

Shelton came to his position after a local translator falsely translated to both sides to profit from his position. Very few Chinese officials learned Tibetan and instead relied on Chinese-Tibetan translators who attached themselves to every *yamen*.[141] In general, the translators had a bad reputation and the Tibetans held them responsible for many of the abuses of Chinese rule.[142] When the Chinese officials learned of the translator's duplicity, summary execution soon followed. Though somewhat insulated by his American citizenship, Albert Shelton took up the dangerous job.

The countryside around Batang was in complete chaos, and brigand tribes prowled the trade routes. In search of arms and ammunition, bandits attacked even the small outlying forts around Batang. "Human life was worth nothing at all," Albert wrote, "nor where the rights of property in any way respected."[143] Faced with their eroding power and the receding hope for reinforcement, the local Chinese officials decided to act in a conciliatory way toward the rebelling Tibetans.[144] Hoping to utilize Dr. Shelton's reputation for fairness, the Chinese official petitioned him to act as a middleman with the brigand tribes of the Sangen.

Shelton and his well-armed escort left in September 1916 in the midst of an exuberant Kham autumn.[145] Bert was characteristically giddy at getting on the road into new territory: "I longed to go into this place from which so many bands of brigands had come."[146] Two Sangen lamas who were interceding in Batang over the matter of a recent murder and robbery accompanied the caravan, providing some hope of safety. Three Chinese soldiers and a sergeant served as Shelton's Chinese escort. "In many ways it is embarrassing to travel under escort, but it was this or not go, and I would have put up with many more inconveniences rather than not go," he wrote.

The caravan entered the Sangen by passing through a beautiful valley, past a cliff where the Sangen brigands always paused before a raid to burn incense to the resident deity. That night the Shelton party camped with the black tent nomads. Shelton ingratiated himself with the Tibetan women by distributing small mirrors. For the balance of the trip, the news of his largesse preceded him, "and I was reminded by being told how nicely I had treated the ladies of the last place."

Shelton spent the next night at the small lamasery that was the home of the two lamas. After a period of reticence, the villagers emerged to inspect the first foreigner they had seen. An impromptu concert ensued. "The Tibetans have good voices," Shelton wrote, "and sing much better than the Chinese." Shelton spent two days in the lamasery, discussing with the abbot the problems of the Chinese depredations that had destroyed so many monasteries in eastern Tibet. He left on "quite friendly terms" with the Sangen people, who told him to return and hunt the "Great Blue Sheep" with them. The caravan was forced to take a detour because the Chinese had destroyed the next village in retribution for a recent Sangen raid. The people of the village came down from the mountain to tell Shelton angrily of their troubles. The headman demanded Shelton represent them with the Batang official or they would provide no *ula*. Shelton insisted that "it was none of my business." After a few days the headman relented, probably in part because Shelton had treated his ill son.

Shelton passed through a region of nomads and villagers, all of whom were inquisitive about the foreigner. "Of course our time was taken up mostly at each place with preaching to the curious crowds that would gather round. . . ." Shelton doctored as he went, making friends and allies in the process.

The road home was across the Yangtze in an alarmingly leaky boat. "My mule, poor fellow, thought his end had come and brayed pitifully as they shoved him off behind the boat for the last trip and he had to swim." From there Shelton traveled east through dramatic mountain ranges. After another ten days his party hit the well-traveled trail that led south to Batang. Shelton wrote, "On this trip I visited nearly fifty towns and villages never before visited by an American or European, but in all my travels I have never visited a district or people that appealed to me more than the robbers of the Badlands of Eastern Tibet."[147]

Though Shelton was unsuccessful in arranging a cessation in raids, at least he was free from attacks during his weeks of mediation. Eventually, he made three trips into the Sangen. The Tibetans responded to his attempts and even provided him with a safe passage letter: "We have understood the meaning of the letters which you have sent through this messenger," the Sangen letter read, telling Shelton to come "to see us in a short time with a 'white mind,'" meaning honesty. "Also we give you guarantees to a safe journey, not to have disturbance and robbery by our army."[148] Though the Chinese strategy of unilateral appeasement might have been flawed, Shelton's trips to the Sangen went well, and he solidified his position as a territorial leader and an impartial arbiter between the warring sides.

Albert Shelton was the first Westerner to travel in the Sangen.[149] As was most often the case in his journeys, Shelton doctored as he traveled, treating dozens of cases in the remote mountains and valleys. He relished the journeys in the high mountains and narrow defiles of Kham, marveling at the awesome landscapes and exotic lifestyles that he encountered. Shelton prided himself on his outdoor skills and shooting prowess. Returning down the Yangtze Valley during one Sangen trip, he shot a large Tibetan wolf. He recalled one of the escorts exclaiming, "Whenever he draws down on anything with that gun, the horse is in the barn."[150]

The Most Sacred Thing in the World

Though Albert Shelton had dramatically altered his view of the Tibetans, he still remained rooted in his Western world-views. He was a man in transit, slowly resolving his conflicted ideas. In his dealings with the Tibetans, he vacillated from compassionate tolerance to waspish ridicule.

Promulgating the power of Christianity and Western ways over Buddhism and traditional Tibetan culture remained the dominant theme of Shelton's work. While on a Sangen trip, a Batang acquaintance of Shelton's accompanied the expedition, hoping to recapture some horses taken by some Sangen rustlers. As it was a lawless region, the man was well armed and protected by his *ga'u*, a silver charm box around his neck that was filled with amulets and prayers. The second day out Shelton challenged the effectiveness of the expensive amulet box. The Tibetan insisted it had saved his life. "I've been shot at seven times and have never been hurt yet," Shelton remembered the man saying. "The bullets can't go in. They will sometimes penetrate my clothes or make a black and blue mark on my skin but they never go in." Shelton offered to test the charm box for the man: "You stand out there and let me shoot at you once and if I hit you, you name your own price, because if the thing works it is worth any amount of money." The Tibetan declined the opportunity to be a target, even though Shelton offered to doctor him for free if the charm box failed to deflect the bullet.

The two eventually decided to first test the charm box on a goat. If Shelton failed to shoot the goat, the Tibetan could have his pick of the shotgun or rifles Shelton carried.[151] Gezong Ongdu pulled Shelton aside, telling him the man was going to get his best rifle as he was never going to hit the goat. The Tibetan carefully picked the shotgun for Shelton to use in his attempt at shooting the enchanted goat, which baa-ed on the hillside wearing the charm box around his neck. "Well, it was only about ten seconds before he was gathering up the remains, for I had smashed the charm box as well as killed the goat. He was the most disconsolate man I ever saw," Shelton wrote. "He sat fingering over the different pills, pieces of cloth, etc., that had been contained in the charm box, the very picture of despair."[152]

The tale of Shelton's destruction of the charm box preceded him to Batang. Once home, a Tibetan friend, Adam, came to ask if the story was true. When Shelton assured him that he had shattered the charm box in the Sangen, the Batang man insisted that Shelton make the same wager with him. Shelton related the man said, "There was no chance of my hitting the goat with his charm box tied on him, and he proceeded to tell me the story of its wonderful power of protection." To make doubly certain, the man tied two silk *kata* scarves blessed by high lamas around his charm box before hanging it from the goat's neck. Shelton aimed at the charm-protected animal with an old Mauser the Tibetan loaned him, as he thought Shelton's armaments might have special powers.

Shelton wrote, "The goat had no more chance than the former one, and when the man was sorrowfully removing his charm box he was very discouraged and much bepuzzled." As the man's friends began to harass the Tibetan, Shelton walked over to console him. "Adam," Shelton said, "it is not with any intention of making fun of you or of ridiculing your religion, for a man's religion, no matter what it is, is to him the most sacred thing in the world. But you have some things in yours that are false, and your ought to get rid of them. These charm boxes are false."[153] After relating the story in her journal, Flora wrote, "It must be difficult, to have all your faith knocked out of you by a bullet & no new faith to which to cling. The backbone of the lamas' power is broken here."[154]

CHAPTER ELEVEN

THE NEXT LIVINGSTONE

Shelton in Kham, 1918–1919

To be an official is to lead a hard life.[1]

—Tibetan Proverb

The lamas proved to be more resilient than Flora Shelton anticipated. The Tibetans coped with the Westerners much as they did with the Chinese, merely persisting in their culture until the colonials absorbed their Himalayan ways. Flora wrote: "The Tibetan race Tibetanizes the Chinaman who makes Tibet his home. He learns to think, and feel, and act, and live as a Tibetan. This is a tribute to the persistence and individuality of the Tibetan."[2]

After a decade in the Tibetan highlands, the Sheltons began to make the same shifts. They lived in a Tibetan-style house and worked with Tibetans. Their children dressed in Tibetan clothes for Buddhist holidays, and played and gossiped with young Tibetan friends. Esther MacLeod wrote that the Shelton daughters "are real Tibetan girls, so far as the good qualities of Tibetan girls are concerned."[3] The Shelton girls ate Tibetan food when they could manage to get it. Albert Shelton became wholly accustomed to the local fare and relished his *tsampa* as much as the next Khampa resident. He traveled like a Tibetan and lived, for the most part, like Tibetans while on the road. He relied on Tibetan proverbs to make his points. Like most Tibetans, he yearned to visit Lhasa. Through trusting relationships with Gezong Ongdu and other Khampas, even Flora began to make her peace with the Tibetans.

On the battlefields of western Kham the Tibetans asserted a more aggressive kind of power. As the authority of Republican China continued to wane, the Lhasa government prospered in their new freedoms. British military support began to have a telling effect in the China-Tibet borderlands. A minor incident near Riwoche in western Kham eventually precipitated renewed warfare between Chinese and Tibetan troops. In the fall of 1917, a Chinese detachment was cutting grass in a disputed border area of red rock and high grassland. When two Tibetan soldiers arrived to complain, the Chinese carried them off to Chamdo.

The Kalon Lama attempted to avoid military action, sending letters to Chinese General P'eng Jih-sheng demanding the soldiers' release. P'eng failed to acknowledge the first letter, and his reply to the second was filled with dung. P'eng answered the Kalon Lama's third letter with an announcement the Chinese were advancing on Lhasa.[4]

Released from their pledge by the Chinese invasion, the Kalon Lama launched a Tibetan counterattack. P'eng anticipated a replay of the easy victories of Chao's day. Instead, he encountered a formidable Tibetan army. With the British assistance, the Dalai Lama had substantially reorganized and strengthened the Tibetan army in the four years since the initial Chinese Republican offensives into Kham. The Tibetans routed the Chinese advance. The Tibetans quickly captured Draya, along with two mountain guns and several hundred Chinese soldiers and their rifles. When they took two strategic passes on the northern Derge road, they completely surrounded the Chinese garrison town of Chamdo and laid siege to the thousand Chinese soldiers trapped inside. Clearly in control of the field, the Tibetans advanced into the southern Kham region of Markham west of Batang and drove out all of the Chinese troops. When the Chinese troops retreated, the Tibetans advanced to the historical frontier line on the Bum La, within easy marching distance of Batang.

The Only Thing to Do: Shelton as Mediator

The threat of invasion by the Tibetan army terrified most of the inhabitants of Batang. Remembering the horror of Chao Erh-feng's retributions in 1905 and long accustomed to Chinese rule, the Tibetans in Batang were less inclined than the rest of Kham to erupt in rebellion. They figured they would be the ultimate sufferers.[5] The Chinese commandant in Batang, General Liu Tsan-ting, the *Tingling,* was concerned, as he expected his unpaid and ill-fed soldiers to rebel if the Tibetans attacked.[6] He had further problems because he was getting rich by selling off land Chao Erh-feng had seized from the Tibetan noble families and the lamas in 1905.

Liu met with Dr. Shelton to discuss his inability to protect Batang and the missionaries. After the missionaries decided to stay, Shelton agreed to intercede with the Tibetan forces.[7] Albert Shelton was always ready to travel, however precarious the circumstances. However, until a replacement could be found for Dr. Hardy, he was tied to the Batang mission. He clearly chaffed at his mission fetters. He felt time was growing short for his dream of Lhasa. Shelton wrote, "I'm getting old and a few more years will put me out of the business for the long trips of mule-back mountain work."[8]

In late January 1918, he wrote an impassioned personal letter to Archibald McLean, pleading to be allowed to itinerate to central Tibet with Lhasa as the goal—"I want now to be set free."[9] Given the political realities of the frontier and his few remaining years on the border, he thought the time was right for his great foray into Tibet.

In another letter to FCMS's Doan a week later, he made the same forceful points. Albert Shelton wished for another doctor to be assigned to Batang so that he could reach Lhasa. He assured Doan he would be careful and not risk his life. "I glory in it and rest assured I'll never I'll never needlessly throw mine away."[10]

The same day he wrote a formal letter to the Executive Committee, requesting permission for his family to return home in the fall of 1919. "I regret this step and so does Mrs. S. but there seems to be no other way that is just—the children must go home to school. They will be 16 and 13 respectively when they reach home." With Dorris and Dorothy now reaching maturity, it was time for them to return to the United States for schooling. Most missionaries hastened to send their children back to the home countries before their teen years, fearing the taint of exotic romance and lack of new ideas.[11] Shelton also requested to itinerate exclusively until his own furlough was due.[12]

The hostile Tibetan forces waiting across the Yangtze in March 1918 clearly presented less threat to Albert Shelton than his fear of inaction and futility. At the behest of Chinese General Liu Tsan-ting, Albert, accompanied by the Ba and Jo lamas and Gezong Ongdu, crossed the Yangtze on a journey of mediation. In the bright sun of early Kham spring, they climbed past the boundary stone on the 13,500-foot Bum La pass into Markham. They stopped at a small village three days from Batang where there was a detachment of twenty-five frightened Chinese soldiers. There they stopped to send letters to the Tibetan governor asking if they might come. One of Shelton's men reconnoitered west and discovered the Tibetans had killed many Chinese and taken a large number prisoner. The scout reported that a band of Tibetan soldiers had been seen that day at the top of the pass and were expected at any moment. The news sent the Chinese into a panic, and they begged Shelton to arrange animals for a hasty retreat back toward Batang. By 4:30 the next morning, the terrified Chinese soldiers and their families were scurrying back to Batang on the animals Shelton had found.[13]

Figure 11.1   Adolescent Shelton daughters with Tibetan friends. Raised by Tibetan nurses, the girls spoke fluent Tibetan. Here they are dressed in Tibetan clothes for a Buddhist holiday.

The next afternoon, the governor sent a curt note telling Shelton and his party to come on to Gartok (Jangka).[14] "We were not greatly encouraged by the tone of the letter," Shelton wrote, "but made preparations to go on the following morning." They continued west into Tibet after a quick recall to Batang, traveling for two days across more passes toward the seat of the governor at Gartok.

As Shelton's peace caravan plodded toward Gartok, they had no sense of the reception they would receive. Arriving in Gartok, they found a near-medieval encampment of the Tibetan army milling in the flat grassy valley that lay at about 12,500 feet. Smartly dressed and well-armed Lhasa soldiers marched to uniformed bagpipers, the regular troops reinforced by "a great horde of the unkempt and dirty nomads in the sheepskin clothes and all carrying the old firelocks of the country," as Shelton wrote. A decade of fighting left most of previously bustling Gartok burned. Little remained but a modest monastery and the *dzong*, the Teji Markham's official residence where Shelton and his interpreter Ongdu were to meet the governor.

The governor of lower Kham, the Teji Markham, Zas Zhim pa, was a tall, dignified Tibetan official with a long, hangdog face. Except for the Kalon Lama, the Teji Markham was the most important personage in Kham.[15] "We went over and were received in a very frigid manner," Shelton wrote. "He was, however, scrupulously polite to me." Shelton's mission was simply to arrange a parley between the two commanders. He told the Tibetan governor that General Liu had sent him to see if they could arrange an armistice until the Chinese-Tibetan affairs could be settled by diplomacy. Shelton also told the Teji he deplored the loss of life on both sides, "and for the sake of humanity I would like very much if it could be arranged so that there need be no more fighting."[16]

The Teji Markham responded by saying the Chinese could simply surrender all of their arms and ammunition and the Tibetans would spare their lives and give them safe passage to Lhasa. Looking only for a parlay, Shelton told the governor a surrender on those terms would endanger General Liu's life. If a parley couldn't be arranged, he would return to Batang in the morning. The Tibetans were as anxious to arrange a truce as the Chinese were. Shelton related, "'Oh,' he said, 'don't be in a hurry; let's talk some more about it.'" Discussions lasted until midnight, when the Teji Markham proposed that Shelton send a letter requesting an armistice to the Kalon Lama encamped a month further west at Chamdo. The governor indicated he would abide by the Kalon Lama's decision, though Shelton needed to wait for it in Gartok. The Teji Markham pledged to hold off an attack on Batang in the interim, and he also agreed to Shelton's request to spare the mission, the lamasery, and the homes of the common people if an attack did occur.

The next morning a Tibetan courier cantered off with the express mail, and barely twelve days later the reply raced back into Gartok. Shelton wrote, "The answer was very gratifying, the Galon Lama saying that he was glad to know that I was interested in seeing the fighting stopped and that now whatever I should say would go."[17] However, Shelton, simply trying to facilitate the meeting, lacked the authority to negotiate.

Accustomed and emboldened by more than half a century of confrontation with Chinese political authority, foreign missionaries like Shelton were well prepared to act as mediators. As an American, Shelton had the further advantage of being perceived by the Chinese as more respectful and less aggressive compared to other foreigners.[18] Given that American foreign policy toward Tibet was overwhelmingly passive, private individuals in Tibet such as Shelton served an outsized diplomatic role between the two countries, increasing his prestige with the Tibetans.[19] However, the U.S. State Department had categorically stated that American citizens residing abroad should refrain from interfering in the internal affairs or political issues of an international character.[20]

Shelton sent the good news to Batang and told General Liu to come to Gartok for discussions.[21] Liu was reticent to travel into Tibetan-held territory. Beyond his fear of falling into Tibetan hands, Liu had no authority to negotiate with the Tibetans as he was cut off from his superiors in Chengdu and Beijing.

Albert sent increasingly impatient letters to Liu, which Flora couriered to the *yamen*. "I don't like diplomatic affairs at all," she opined in her diary.[22]

Liu continued to linger in Batang. Over several weeks the Ba and Jo lamas badgered him, and even Flora began haranguing the commandant to get a move on. She noted, "He had a hard time with me as I was as unreasonable as a woman knew how to be & of course being a woman made it worse."[23] Dr. Shelton finally sent an ultimatum: either Liu arrive by a certain day or he was returning to Batang. "This had the desired effect and a few days later he arrived and was very generously received with all honors by the Governor."[24]

During the several weeks of negotiations, Dr. Shelton remained in Gartok and doctored the wounded. While he was there, the Tibetans continued to mete out the rough justice of the frontier. Large firing squads blasted men into bits with volleys of musket balls. Swordsmen lopped off the hands of convicted traitors, whose friends waited with bowls of boiling butter to cauterize the bloody stumps. Severed hands festooned the front of the governor's residence. "I was kept busy all day caring for these people," Shelton wrote, noting that he approached the Teji Markham first to see if he had any objections to the doctor treating them. "'He said, 'Not at all. When I get through with them you can do as you like.'"[25]

While in the camp, Shelton met one of the leaders of the large robber bands operating in Kham, a raffish Tibetan self-named General Lozang. Lozang had traveled to Gartok to ask permission to sack Batang. With Shelton's intercession, the governor declined Lozang's request, indicating he would take Batang himself when the time was ripe. Shelton and Lozang became friends during their hiatus in Gartok, exchanging visits and companionship. One day Lozang proposed that he and Shelton become brothers through the custom of the country, by pledging themselves to mutual aid with a written contract. Shelton said no—"you kill people and you rob, and you drink whiskey and do a great many things against our religion." The bandit chief stormed off in a huff. A few days later he returned, asking what Shelton's religion would allow, and Shelton gave him "our conception of Christ's teaching."[26]

After another few days of contemplation, Lozang returned with an agreement written by a lama, which indicated that he would join Dr. Shelton in taking an oath to not kill, rob, or drink whiskey and that henceforth they would be brothers. The contract closed with the caveat, "Furthermore, this is to give notice that if any of you ever molest Dr. Shelton I'll bring a thousand men to wipe you off the face of the earth." It was "a pretty good passport in that country," Shelton wrote.[27]

During his two months in Gartok, Shelton grew close with the Teji Markham. They made a distinctive pair: Shelton in his Stetson and wool suit, the governor with his silk jacket's long Tibetan-style sleeves hanging below his waist.

The Teji Markham learned of Shelton's desire to build a teaching hospital in Lhasa and his years of frustration at being unable to find anyone to carry his request to the Dalai Lama. The Teji Markham told Shelton to write it and he would forward it with his endorsement.

A few days after the arrival of General Liu, Albert Shelton trotted out of Gartok on his way home. After he had witnessed four years of Republican Chinese freebooting on the frontier, Shelton's sympathies clearly lay with the Tibetans.[28] With General Liu still in Gartok and the threat of invasion hanging over Batang, the streets of the town were quiet and tense. On May 3, 1918, Shelton returned from his long sojourn.[29]

Shelton began writing letters in a bold, excited script to the society officials, a far cry from his grumpy mission-bound reports earlier in the year: "I had a great time with the Lassa people. I spent two days later with the Lassa General to the west of here and he is anxious that we open a hospital in Lassa and he forwarded my request to be permitted to do so to the Dalai Lama with his endorsement."[30]

The Worst Proposition: The Battle of Chamdo

Ten days after Albert Shelton's arrival back in Batang, a letter from the Teji Markham brought news that the Chamdo Chinese garrison had capitulated to the Tibetans after a siege of several months. With half of the Chinese garrison killed by illness and the Tibetans, General P'eng surrendered the surviving soldiers, fourteen hundred rifles, and two mountain guns to the Kalon Lama in April 1918.

Following P'eng's defeat, the remnants of China's once-vaunted frontier force consisted of a few worn-out battalions, a ragtag garrison at Batang, a few detachments along the Jung Lam, and a brigade at Tachienlu. Torn by civil war internally and demoralized by the Japanese externally, the Republican central government was in no condition to assist its forces in the borderlands.[31] Indeed, the war in Kham was almost exclusively a Sichuanese-Tibetan affair.

However localized and provincial the war appeared to be, the British rightly assessed it as a potentially explosive event that could ruin the border strategies they had promulgated at the Simla conferences. They dispatched their west China consular officer, Eric Teichman, to Chamdo to try to defuse the situation. A tireless, taciturn man with a kindhearted nature, Teichman was a veteran of the Chinese-Tibetan borderlands. His toneless Chinese was infamous in the Foreign Service, though better than his Tibetan, which was nonexistent.[32]

Teichman rode through a war-devastated region, where huge vultures gorged on dead horses, yaks, and men. He arrived in Chamdo in May 19, 1918, finding a low mud town perched on a spit of land where two rivers joined to become the Mekong—a strategic intersection of five main roads and two long cantilevered bridges that connected Tibet to Sichuan and Yunnan. The town bustled with immense caravans carrying army supplies from central Tibet.

Teichman met with the Kalon Lama, Champa Tendar, in his Chamdo residence.[33] It was a small wood and mud structure topped with a fluttering yellow flag of Tibet that carried the sun, moon, and a white snow lion. Teichman wrote, "The Kalon Lama himself, who has been at the head of the Tibetan army on the frontier for the past five or six years, is a middle-aged monk of commanding appearance and stature, with features showing great intelligence and refinement."[34]

Teichman's mission was to stop the Tibetan advance toward Tachienlu: "If we are unsuccessful in doing so, years of bitter border warfare will ensue; for the Chinese will never agree to surrender their claims to these districts, which they profess to regard as part of Szechuan; while the Lhasa Tibetans, once they have seized all the country up to Tachienlu, will never retire willingly from regions which they hold to be part of Tibet." He hoped to stop the fighting at the western edge of Kham, near the historical boundary that ran between the Yangtze and Mekong. The British thought that there was a reasonable chance both sides might accept the de facto situation and that they could continue their policy of using Tibet as a buffer state for their Himalayan Indian territories while placating China by not supporting Tibetan independence.[35]

The Tibetans argued that they were independent from China because their tributary relationship terminated when the Manchu Dynasty fell.[36] It took much persuasion on Teichman's part for the Kalon Lama to agree to discuss an armistice. However, it was difficult to determine who could negotiate for the Chinese. The Chinese administration of Kham, such as it was, consisted of a number of mutually independent, suspicious, and even hostile military rulers. Beijing had little influence of the border regions and was primarily indifferent to events there.

In the meantime, Chamdo overflowed with injured soldiers, many suffering suppurating bullet wounds from massive soft-lead Mauser slugs.[37] Teichman suggested that the Kalon Lama invite Dr. Albert Shelton to treat the wounded. Shelton's work at Draya and Gartok was well known, and the Kalon Lama readily agreed to the idea. Teichman quickly forwarded a letter to Batang.

Though critical of Christian evangelism, Teichman had great respect for the missionaries' humanitarian work. He singled out the Batang Tibetan Christian Mission for praise: "To evangelize the people in their present state is merely to add to the load of superstition with which their lives are already burdened. The Protestant missionaries at Batang appear to realize this, and educational and medical work stands in the forefront of their program."[38] He lauded the Batang missionaries for their humanitarian work: "They are surpassed by no mission in all China in respect of the amount of good they do and the sensible manner in which they do it."[39]

In search of a Chinese official who was willing to talk peace in Lower Kham, Teichman left for Batang on May 22, 1918, leading Chinese civilian refugees back to China.[40] The journey to Batang was a laborious one as the Chinese refugees slowly made their way with families and baggage stretching down the trail for miles—"beginning to resemble the exodus from Egypt," Teichman wrote.[41] After almost two weeks on the trail, the caravan arrived in Gartok in early June, where Teichman was surprised to find the Chinese General Liu. Teichman took advantage of the presence of the two principals to convince the Teji and the Chinese commander to sign an agreement to refrain from hostilities for a month. In the interim, Teichman hoped to contact the Sichuan authorities via telegraph to arrange a more permanent peace.

Teichman left Gartok with his steadily growing band of refugees. The Teji Markham allowed the former magistrate and other civilians to join the exodus. Teichman crossed the Bum La into the Batang region. They were in the neighborhood of Kungtzeding when they encountered Dr. Albert Shelton hurrying for Chamdo.

Shelton received Teichman's request on June 5, 1918.[42] The threat hanging over Batang strained the townspeople since Shelton's return, so the request for his assistance was a relief. By the next day Shelton was on the trail to Chamdo. "We got them packed & fed & off by one o'clock. Surely things did buzz," Flora jotted.[43]

Shelton spent his forty-third birthday on the trail. He passed through Gartok, where the Governor insisted he stop for a feast. The next day Shelton's caravan proceeded north toward Chamdo. A man assigned by the Governor acted as an advance man to secure lodgings and food for the travelers. "It was the only time for years," Shelton wrote, "that I had been permitted to travel unaccompanied by an escort."[44] The absence of an armed escort was testimony to the relative security of the Tibetan-ruled country compared to the anarchy of the Chinese-ruled regions. It was also a reflection of the relative safety enjoyed by the foreign missionaries in the interior of post-Revolution China. The foreign missionaries' position and security improved dramatically in the period following the Republican revolution. As Teichman stated, "since the Revolution of 1911, while no Chinese but brigands, soldiers, or the poorest of coolies can travel on the roads of Northern Shensi without great danger to property and life, a missionary or other foreigner can circulate where he pleases with comparatively little danger of being attacked."[45]

Unbeknownst to Albert, he also had some secret allies watching his back in Batang. With the Chinese administration essentially powerless to protect the city from Hsiang-ch'eng raiders, mutinous soldiers, or local bandits, Batang men formed the Twan Shang secret society. "This was sort of combined secret society, town meeting, and home guard," U.S. Major John Magruder wrote. The members took a blood oath by drinking chicken blood, and they armed themselves with old weapons and the extra rifles that General Liu sold them on the sly. The British consul in Yunnanfu reported that the Twan Shang had secretly elected Dr. Albert Shelton into their society without his knowledge. Shelton received this honor because he had saved society members' lives who were wounded in a fight.[46]

As Dr. Shelton raced for Chamdo, Teichman was busy in Batang. When he arrived in Batang, the Sichuan telegraph he expected to find was in its normal inoperative state. The Jung Lam swarmed with brigands, rendering it impassable. He had no alternative but to draft a treaty in Batang and use General Liu as a representative of China. With no Tibetan language skills, Teichman turned to missionaries for assistance with writing the agreement.[47] The timing was beginning to look crucial. The Chinese soldiers guarding a nearby village post disappeared, and the Batang garrison erupted in another mutiny over food. The missionaries once again paid enough money to keep the soldiers fed. Gezong Ongdu and James Ogden finishing drafting the treaty for Teichman a few days later.

On June 30, 1918, Teichman and Colonel Liu left for Chamdo with the proposed treaty. While Liu was in no way empowered to negotiate a treaty on behalf of the Chinese Republican government (or even the Sichuan one), he was all Teichman had at the moment. Flora felt it was too late: "The Tibetans have gone too far & have too much power in their hands now."[48]

When he arrived in Chamdo, Dr. Albert Shelton found a nightmare. He rode into town through a gauntlet of wounded Chinese prisoners: "Such of them as were able to drag themselves out had come and lined themselves at the side of the road to show their respect." After securing a stove for hot water and tables and benches for surgery from the Kalon Lama, Shelton set to work. He dealt with wounds not less than two months old—"rotten, stinking," he called them. "It was one of the worst propositions that I have ever had to undertake. We began with the worst and for ten days, beginning between seven and eight in the morning, I operated as long as I was able to stand up, being assisted by the three men who were with me."[49] During his time in Chamdo, Shelton performed forty major surgeries and many small operations of all kinds, besides training Chinese and Tibetan doctors how to dress the wounds Western-style.[50]

Shelton continued to mingle with the luminaries of the eastern Tibetan world. The Kalon Lama invited him for dinner each afternoon when Shelton finished his surgeries, and he spent the balance of the afternoon in conversation with him.[51] Once again Albert Shelton had an opportunity to revise his estimation of the Tibetans. Shelton averred, "I was never better treated anywhere—the Tibetan attitude has entirely changed towards the foreigners in two years."[52]

Well-educated and sophisticated Tibetans filled Chamdo and the fighting front. Many of them had studied in India, carried Kodaks and field glasses, slept on camp beds, and wore foreign clothes. Eric Teichman was startled to encounter one Tibetan commander dressed like an Anglo-Indian sportsman in riding breeches, tweed coat, and pith helmet. "Tibet is now an independent nation, and is developing with remarkable if not astonishing rapidity," Shelton enthused. "The Tibetans want foreign goods and foreign civilization."[53]

Shelton made the best of his time in Chamdo, teaching, distributing tracts, and working to build relationships to further his mission. "I was mobbed in a friendly manner while distributing tracts because I couldn't hand them out fast enough."[54] At the conclusion of his medical work, the Kalon Lama gave each of Shelton's assistants fifty rupees and Shelton three hundred rupees and a pair of finely wrought Derge vessels ornamented with gold and silver.[55] He also asked Shelton to consider opening a hospital in Chamdo.[56] Shelton wrote McLean: "My opinion is that Lhasa is open for mission work, right now. This recent progress and friendliness is radiating from Lhasa. It is a call to go up and possess the land."[57]

The Truce of Rongbatsa

The departure of Teichman and Liu for Chamdo in late June did little to ease the tension in Batang. While the Teji Lama promised to hold off hostilities for a month, time was running out and his Tibetan forces massed near the old Bum La frontier line prepared to overrun Batang. Another Tibetan column advanced south from Derge with Batang in its sights. The restive Hsiang-ch'eng tribesmen threatened from the east.

With the normal trade routes cut off and its larders diminished by extraordinary numbers of Chinese soldiers and refugees, Batang faced starvation. The situation for the Chinese was little better in northern and eastern Kham. The Tibetans held Chamdo, Draya, Markham, Gonjo, and Derge and were moving east and south toward Kanze and Batang. The rapid advance of the Tibetans finally roused General Ch'en Hsia-ling, the Chinese frontier commissioner in Tachienlu, from his inactivity. Realizing he had best make a strong move toward the west or the Tibetan army would soon be knocking on Tachienlu's door, he commanded his brigade of two to three thousand men to proceed west immediately to engage the Tibetans. But the Chinese reliance on *ula* undid the offensive. The Khampa tribesmen in the Yilung grasslands that sat astride the route west of Kanze emptied the country of transport animals from Kanze to the Yangtze River. The withdrawal mired the Chinese at the village of Rongbatsa, one long march west of Kanze in the green and well-watered Yalung River valley.[58]

The Chinese were sitting on a powder keg. Teichman wrote, "While they were sitting in Rongbatsa, comfortably billeted in the houses of the village, and contemplating the inhospitable wastes ahead, they awoke one morning to find the Lhasa Tibetans, who had advanced rapidly after the fall of Chamdo, streaming down the two valleys along the roads from Dzenko and Yilung."[59] Sharp skirmishing ensued. The more mobile Tibetan forces began encircling the Chinese forces from the rear to threaten their communications and supply lines back to Tachienlu. Teichman wrote, "Another month or two would possibly have seen several thousand more Chinese prisoners in Tibetan hands, and the Lhasa forces in possession of all the country up to Tachienlu."[60]

A day's march from Chamdo, Teichman and Liu were relieved to receive a letter from the Kalon Lama halting hostilities all across the front. He would wait until they arrived in Chamdo. Liu immediately sent copies to all of the Chinese frontier officials and officers.[61] They arrived on July 15 to a formal reception. "All Chamdo had turned out to see us," Teichman wrote, "including a number of the Chinese wounded, legless, armless, and otherwise mutilated; these latter representing the handiwork of, and owed their lives to, Dr. Shelton, who had come and gone during our absence in Batang."[62]

After two weeks of Tibetan diplomatic soirees, Teichman and Liu finally received instructions from the Chinese authorities. The governor of Sichuan and the frontier commissioner agreed to a truce, with the Yangtze as the proposed frontier line. The Kalon Lama agreed to start discussions on the first auspicious day. In spite of the cessation of hostilities, the two armies remained poised at Rongbatsa, ready to begin fighting at the least provocation.

The next day Teichman and Liu received a panic-stricken communiqué from the Chinese official still in Batang, imploring the Tibetans to allow them to evacuate the city and retreat to Litang or Tachienlu. Isolated from any news except by courier, the Batang missionaries were also concerned. A week later a letter arrived from Teichman telling them negotiations were progressing, though Liu was still awaiting instructions.[63]

On September 1, 1918, Liu and the Kalon Lama came to an agreement whereby each side maintained the territory it held at the time of the truce. In spite of the agreement, the two armies at Rongbatsa were still at loggerheads.

The Tibetans nearly surrounded the Chinese, and their barricades faced one another across a small shallow stream barely a stone's throw apart.[64]

With the agreement in danger of being destroyed by precipitate actions, diplomats at Chamdo tried to arrange for a mutual withdrawal a day's march apart. But it only increased the tension as each side accused the other of initiating combat. Teichman wrote, "The Chinese will insist on treating the Tibetans as naughty children; while the Tibetans, who consider that they have taken the measure of the Chinese, at any rate for the time being, are itching to renew the conflict."[65] The antagonists finally withdrew as autumn settled in. Local farmers scrambled to bring in the harvest as the two armies warily awaited further instructions from distant superiors.

The king of Chala arrived in Chamdo with news for the Kalon Lama and Teichman of the situation in Rongbatsa. The king proved to be a vital element in the negotiations. While he represented the Chinese case, he was a Tibetan himself and understood the Tibetan mentality. The Chinese negotiator was far more prone to alternately berate or patronize the "barbarians."

On October 10, 1918, the couriers returned bearing approvals. Traveling to Rongbatsa, the Kalon Lama and the Sichuan frontier authorities met in the conference tent erected between the two lines. After the treaty ceremony, all retired to a big tent the king of Chala had ordered set up beside the stream and spent three hours feasting on the jolliest of terms. The Rongbatsa truce ended the organized fighting between the Tibetan and Chinese armies.[66]

The truce laid out the provisional boundary lines giving control of the area generally east of the Yangtze, including Batang, to the Chinese, while the Tibetans controlled the region to the west of the river. This necessitated the withdrawal of the Tibetan forces from their forward lines in Kanze and Nyarong. The Chinese agreed not to station troops in Hsiang-ch'eng or Nyarong. If the tribesmen failed to restrain themselves, the Tibetan government agreed to not interfere with any Chinese actions against them. The Chinese agreed that Dalai Lama had control of all matters relating to monasteries and the "Buddhistic religion" in the Chinese-governed regions of Kham, including the right of appointing "all high lamas and other monastic functionaries." Section Six permitted traders and travelers to cross the border without interference. The truce gave amnesty to both forces and agreed to empower the British consul to mediate future disputes.[67]

On the Chinese side of the cease-fire line, the brigandage continued unabated. The cessation of organized warfare between the Chinese and the Tibetan army exacerbated the Khampas' antagonism toward the Lhasa government. While the Khampas welcomed the Tibetan army as brothers-in-arms, they resented the condescending attitude of the central Tibetans, who viewed them as uncouth country bumpkins.[68]

As Batang continued to suffer in terrifying isolation and privation, townspeople considered evacuation. Flora wrote on December 9, 1918, "Rumors of all kinds that the Shangchen people are coming & that the Tibetans have to furnish 5 months grain for the Chinese soldiers here which they say can't be done at all & all will starve to death."[69]

Mission Life, 1918–1919

In spite of the chaos that surrounded them in 1918–1919, the Tibetan Christian Mission operated from its strongest position yet. Protected behind its eight-foot-high walls, the TCM mission compound was a model of Western order, the hospital a beacon of scientific healing. In spite of laws prohibiting it, the missionaries continued to add to their land holdings.[70] Their influence on Sino-Tibetan politics was at its peak, with Shelton, Ogden, and Gezong Ongdu mediating and crafting diplomatic documents. The teachers taught a curriculum to a growing group of students. With the support of the mission, Flora carried on with her translation projects. The rug factory floundered on amidst growing controversy among the missionaries. Increasing numbers of orphans found their way to the care of the missionaries.

Converts continued to be a scarce commodity after a decade in Batang, in spite of techniques designed to appeal to Tibetans, such as painting bible-story banners in the style of Tibetan *tangka* paintings.[71] The few native Christians who did convert were Chinese or Chinese-Tibetans, though crowds of Tibetan beggars still clustered for Christmas dinner and Tibetan children gathered for the entertainment and food at Sunday school. Despairing of progress among the adults, the missionaries redoubled their efforts with orphans.[72]

The TCM wasn't alone in its frustration. After twenty-three years on the Tibetan border and the distribution of 115,000 tracts in Tibetan, CIM missionary and Tibetan scholar Theodore Sorensen counted ten Tibetan converts in Tachienlu.[73] The tracts the missionaries struggled to send into forbidden Tibet were often used by the Tibetans in ways not intended by the Christians. Travelers wrote of seeing them commingled with Buddhist prayer flags on bridges and trees, the Tibetans figuring that one more prayer fluttering in the air surely couldn't hurt. James Edgar huffed, "I have seen the pages containing Matt 1:1–18 posted on rods and erected on the housetops, where they were supposed to act as spiritual disinfectant."[74]

Though laboring in Ladakh since the mid-nineteenth century, the Moravian mission also struggled with a paltry congregation. The missionaries contended that the intense social pressure of the Tibetan culture and religion prevented would-be converts from joining the flock. In the Moravians' field on the western Tibetan border, Christians were held to be ritually unclean, preventing their entry into a Buddhist household where the household god might object.[75] The Khampas even found the missionaries' pale eyes and big noses to be terrifyingly alien, prompting the children to run in panic.[76] At best, the Tibetans maintained a wary distance from the missionaries, save for instances in which they could be useful to them politically or financially. Being staunchly Buddhist, they viewed Christianity as an alien religion that threatened their very existence as spiritual beings.

In January 1918 evangelist Roderick MacLeod and his wife Esther arrived in Batang to join the TCM. He was a Scotsman from Prince Edward Island who graduated from Butler University in Indianapolis and received his divinity degree from Yale. Esther MacLeod was a daughter of the heartland, born in Lawrenceville, Illinois. She graduated from an Illinois college and then earned her masters in mathematics from the University of Illinois.[77] Back in America, the TCM's parent society underwent a major change in 1919 when the two Disciples of Christ missionary societies, the Foreign Christian Missionary Society and the Christian Woman's Board of Missions, merged into the United Christian Missionary Society (UCMS).[78] Headquartered in St. Louis, the new entity strengthened the mission societies that were struggling with America's post–World War I materialism and the increasing volume of the Jazz Age.

With Dr. Shelton spending much of 1918 on the trail, his Batang medical assistants handled large patient loads.[79] While Shelton was in Gartok, Johnny and his three assistants reported that they served 1,027 patients in Batang. In September, a smallpox epidemic hit Batang. There were two hundred deaths in the city, and almost twelve hundred patients were treated. After making his own smallpox vaccines with cowpox, Shelton and his men vaccinated all who would take it, though many chose to forgo the treatment after the lamas counseled against it. Some Tibetans resorted to casting lots to see who should take the inoculation. The aftermath was clear. "All those who cast lots are dead while those who were vaccinated are alive."[80]

By early 1919, a cholera epidemic added to the caseload. When the Spanish influenza arrived in March 1919 via the mail courier from Atunze, fifty local people died. The Ogdens, the MacLeods, and Albert Shelton came down with the illness. Shelton also suffered pneumonia—"bad sick," the TCM reported. By the summer of 1919 the dispensary had settled down. August was "quiet medically," with only 519 cases. "It is rather fortunate," Shelton wrote, "that there is no more sickness as in many lines the hospital is entirely out of medicines—not a pound having arrived in 2 years."[81]

Dreams of Lhasa

In the meantime, Shelton waited impatiently for the Dalai Lama to reply to his Lhasa request. Lhasa was Albert Shelton's all-consuming dream, the mythic city guarded by the iron gates. He had devoted his life to the quest, having followed the Chinese army, learned Tibetan, forged alliances, and used Christian doctrine and Western scientific doctrine as rationales to get there. From the time he heard Dr. Susie Rijnhart speak of the place "high and lifted up" when he was a young man, Lhasa was his great goal.[82]

His fellow TCM missionaries shared his obsession. Nervous about another denomination beating them to the prize, Roderick MacLeod wrote to McLean a few weeks after Shelton's return from Chamdo: "It is heartbreaking to stand at a door which has been recently opened. . . . the Pentecostal Mission is waiting for a chance to enter. A wealthy Englishman is financing the mission. Should this mission enter before we do, our work will be much more difficult. They are a particularly emotional people who speak with tongues, and cast out devils."[83]

In August the good news came via courier. The Dalai Lama sent a letter with his distinctive red seal. Albert Shelton wrote, "It is as far as I know the only letter ever written by the Dalai Lama to a missionary. It runs somewhat after this fashion: 'I know of your work and that you have come a long way to do good, and so far as I am concerned, I will put no straw in your way, providing there are no foreign treaties to prevent your coming.'"[84]

While the Dalai Lama's letter was a standard Tibetan diplomatic missive, it was an exceptional document. The Dalai Lama had never extended an equivalent invitation to a Protestant missionary, in spite of a hundred and fifty years of entreaties.[85] Other missionaries were skeptical of the letter, thinking the compliments formulaic and the invitation fatally compromised by the reference to existing treaties.[86] Dr. William Hardy wrote about the letter, "My Tibetan Teacher says that the Tibetans when writing say so many nice things that it is almost the same as lying."[87] Fire-breathing CIM missionary James Edgar denigrated the invitation to open the Lhasa hospital, writing, "It might be pointed out that medical missionaries had been invited to Lhasa by the Dalai Lama. 'Yes'; and so would engineers of any race if they would introduce cheap dynamos to turn praying machinery."[88]

As Shelton reveled in his new hopes for Lhasa, the UCMS's McLean responded to Shelton's earlier request to itinerate by writing, "the committee is quite willing that you should spend a year or two itinerating through Tibet, and reaching Lassa if that be possible. It will be a great thing if you can enter that pagan stronghold with the gospel message and with modern medicine. . . . Like Livingstone, you are ready for any movement, provided it is a forward movement."

Dr. Albert Shelton's itineration to Lhasa hinged on whether an existing treaty prohibited a Christian missionary from entering central Tibet and Lhasa. It was a question of some delicacy. While there may have not been treaty language barring missionaries, the British, through their support of the Dalai Lama's government and armed forces, had an enormous say in which Westerners were allowed access to Lhasa. They were determined to bar foreigners who might upset the status quo, such as missionaries.

Tibet's isolation had changed little since the 1840s. Some contended that the Tibetans didn't care if visitors came, but the Chinese demanded that they prohibit entry to most foreigners. Fifty years later, missionary William Carey saw the Chinese and Tibetans conspiring to maintain the isolation: "Two persons watch the border with sleepless eyes. One is a Chinaman, and the other a lama. The lama guards his monopoly in religion, and Chinaman his monopoly in trade."[89]

British explorer William Gill argued that the Tibetans were wary of the missionaries because they feared they were part of the West's imperial ambitions and "they naturally fear for the supremacy of their faith."[90] British India officials of the Great Game era debated whether China or Tibet served the true arbiters of Tibet's isolation.[91] While the Chinese policy of Tibetan isolation was centuries old, the Tibetans themselves had an unalloyed reluctance to admit foreigners. The Dalai Lama's government rejected American consular official and explorer W. W. Rockhill's request for a passport three times, despite the entreaties of Chinese officials.[92]

The rise of British influence in Tibet following the Republican revolution certainly didn't lower any of the Tibetan barriers to Christian missionaries. As they wanted to maintain Tibet as a quiescent buffer state, the British discouraged missionaries from entering Tibet. As early as 1896, the British officials barred Theodore Sorensen from entering Tibet via Sikkim.

Into the twentieth century, the British Foreign Office authorities in London cast a baleful eye toward unrestricted travel on the Himalayan plateau. They even fretted about their diplomatic "frontier men," concerned their overzealous consular officers might stir up trouble. Accordingly, the London officials prohibited border crossings by any Europeans into Tibet except exploratory expeditions by well-vetted military men. In 1905 the British issued a standing order that barred travel into Tibet by British subjects without prior permission.[93]

In the precarious diplomatic balancing act of the post-Chinese revolution, when quasi-independent Tibet and warlord-torn Republican China vied for diplomatic attention, missionary exclusion became the British government policy. In an internal discussion note in 1922, the Government of India's foreign secretary, Sir Denys Bray, stated that passports into Tibet should be given freely, "except to sportsmen, missionaries, and undesirables." Anticipating a firestorm from British church leaders, Bray proposed that the British consult with Lhasa authorities when missionaries applied for entrance into Tibet, shifting the responsibility for denial onto the Tibetans. The Tibetans, on the other hand, were attempting to steer a course between two powerful neighbors. Hence, both the British and the Tibetans found it politically expedient to blame the other for the shared policy that excluded Protestant missionaries from central Tibet.[94]

The Dalai Lama's invitation to Dr. Albert Shelton with its caveat regarding foreign treaties begged the question: Did any treaty bar Shelton from entry into Lhasa? While Younghusband's convention that Great Britain and Tibet signed at Lhasa in September 1904 had long since been overshadowed by events in Lhasa and Beijing, one section stated that no foreign power would be allowed to intervene in Tibetan affairs, and "no representatives or Agents of any Foreign Power shall be admitted to Tibet. . . ."[95] Given the role the TCM missionaries played in U.S. military and diplomatic intelligence and British-led negotiations, it could be argued Shelton was an agent of the Western governments. Subsequent conventions were no better in defining whether Shelton would or would not be allowed entry.

The missionaries hung their hopes for central Tibetan itineration on the Rongbatsa Agreement, however discredited and rejected it became. Section Six stated that "Peaceful traders and travellers shall be permitted to cross the border without interfernence [sic]."[96] Since the Kalon Lama and the British Consul both signed it, the missionaries thought it gave them some potential for hope.

So as Albert Shelton and the United Christian Missionary Society celebrated the Dalai Lama's invitation to Lhasa, the thorny issue remained: How were the officials in Lhasa and Britain going to interpret the phase, "providing there are no foreign treaties to prevent your coming." The UCMS contended there was no problem. "So far as the officers of the Foreign Society know," a *World Call* article stated, "there is no treaty that would stand in the way of an American missionary traveling anywhere in Tibet. This being true, the last obstacle in the way of entering Lhassa is removed."[97]

The question stood: The Dalai Lama's letter may have been nothing more than a polite acknowledgement of Shelton's work and a diplomatic though nonbinding response to his request to come to Lhasa. The only way Dr. Albert Shelton was going to find out the Dalai Lama's intent and his power to execute it was to ride west to Lhasa. Ever optimistic, Shelton felt that the growing power of the Tibetans offered a grand opportunity for his mission to reach for Lhasa. Albert Shelton quoted Li Gway Gwang: "The devil must be having palpitation of the heart these days."[98]

The devil wasn't the only one suffering health problems in Batang. Flora's physical condition was rapidly deteriorating. Her eyes and facial neuralgia tormented her. Her limp continued to keep her generally mission-bound. Almost forty-eight years old, Flora Shelton was carrying a lot of weight, particularly in Batang's oxygen-deprived nine-thousand-foot altitude. She was five feet, seven inches tall and weighed 235 pounds.[99] Her cardiac problems began to concern her husband and impede her translation work: "When my heart misbehaves it is difficult to work & do clear thinking. But hope to complete what I have begun."[100] In early 1919, her husband wrote Corey, "Mrs. Shelton has been having a great deal of trouble with her heart this fall. Whether it is the altitude or her time of life I am unable to state, but a month ago I was greatly alarmed."[101]

The Greatest Menace: Dr. Shelton and the Opium Campaign

Along with his medical, political, and ethnologic work, Albert Shelton remained focused on the long-time issues of the Western missionaries. "Last spring," he wrote in 1919, "there came to Batang, in the planting of opium, what appeared to us to be the greatest menace that had ever come our way."[102] When Shelton encountered a man planting opium and learned that a group of men planned on growing a large crop, he burst into activity. He convinced the local Chinese official who condoned the cultivation to order the poppy crop destroyed. With Shelton's continuing insistence, the growers uprooted all of the fields, except for two owned by the local banker and a prominent merchant. When they asked Shelton if there was some way he could be persuaded to let them harvest the opium, he replied, "I told them there was just one way, that was to hire some one who was interested to shoot me."

Sichuan was a primary opium-growing region of China in the nineteenth century.[103] It became an alternative crop for the Sichuanese farmers after the arrival of Standard Oil's kerosene reduced the demand for Sichuan's traditional export of candle wax and imported chemical dyes impacted the vegetable dye production. Many foreign observers estimated (undoubtedly with some degree of exaggeration) that 80 percent of the Sichuan population smoked opium.[104]

In 1896 missionaries helped organize an anti-opium league to investigate the problem and agitate for anti-opium measures. In 1907, a nationwide campaign against opium began after the emperor issued an imperial edict eliminating the growing of opium poppies within three years. The anarchy of the post-Revolution warlord period again spurred the cultivation of opium poppies in western China. By 1913, poppy cultivation in Yunnan was four-fifths of pre-suppression levels. Remote Sichuan soon followed, as opium became a major revenue source for local and provincial warlords as well as a source of shakedown money. The officials would encourage peasants to grow the poppies and then arrive when the flowers were in full bloom to demand fines and part of the crop.

By 1919, opium was rampant in the hinterlands of Sichuan.[105] As the remaining Batang poppies continued to grow, Shelton issued an ultimatum to the Chinese official to order the destruction of the crop or Shelton would report him. Goaded into action, the magistrate ordered the banker and merchant put in chains and marched down the main street to jail. The opium fields were burned. Shelton reported, "The total result this year is that there will be no opium grown here and that I have made forty or fifty good enemies."[106] Shelton said he expected to be "plugged" for his campaign against opium.[107]

The Next Great Hero

By early 1919, the UCMS publicity machine began touting Shelton as the next great missionary hero. "The Way Open to Lhassa!" a headline read in the February *World Call*, the article touting the Dalai Lama's invitation and the planned offensive into Tibet. The magazine called for missionary volunteers to join Dr. Shelton in his great endeavor. "Surely the Holy Spirit is urging even now some of our finest and biggest men to leave places of prominence and leadership and answer this call of Tibet."

In June, *World Call* published a long feature on "Shelton of Batang," with a large photo of him astride his famous mule, Abe. It celebrated Shelton's family, his compound ("He has a good croquet ground in his yard and also a tennis court"), medical practice, itinerations, and evangelizations—even his harmonica and left-handed violin playing. The article portrayed him as a hybrid species of frontiersman-saint, a well-armed Paul stalking the borderlands of Tibet with a gracious panache. The article ended by linking Shelton with the missionaries' great exemplar: "To him 'the regions beyond' mean Derge, Chambdo, Leh, Gartok, Tankar, Shigates, and even Lhassa. Lhassa is as much a passion to him as was the heart of Africa to David Livingstone."[108]

The UCMS wasn't alone in heralding Shelton's invitation to Lhasa. A Kansas newspaper headline of the time blared "KANSAN INVADES TIBET; FORBIDDEN LAND OF THE EAST." The article spun the heroic Shelton of Tibet tales along with a picture of him posing on Abe.[109] Shelton's supporter in Chicago, O. A. Rosboro, also informed the *National Geographic* in April 1919. In May, the *National Geographic* offered Dr. Albert Shelton an assignment to write a four- or five-thousand-word article on eastern Tibet, to be published with his photographs. The editor additionally requested Shelton to purchase Tibetan daggers, swords, and knives to add to his personal weapons collection. The *National Geographic* provided Shelton a prestigious promotional opportunity. With its distinctive yellow-framed cover and massive circulation, the publication reached the good churchgoing, middle-class citizens of America as well as its most wealthy and influential people. In October Shelton accepted the assignment, "should everything go as well as I trust it will."[110]

Going Home

After a stint in the army during World War I, Dr. William Hardy finally decided to return to Batang. In early April, Doan cabled an urgent message to Shelton: "Hardy and another doctor sailing August."[111] Dr. Albert Shelton was free to itinerate in Tibet. The news also eased Albert Shelton's concern about his ailing wife, knowing she soon would soon be returning to America. He reported to Doan in the summer that her heart got better with the warm weather and she would be gone from Batang before the hard winter weather.[112] In any case, the UCMS began raising funds for Shelton's Lhasa expedition.[113]

Though July, Shelton organized the caravan to the China coast and planned his expedition to Lhasa, worrying that his time was running out: "a man's ability to ride a mule over 17000 ft mountains declines rapidly after he is 50 yrs old. But I thank God the man and the opportunities come together."[114]

In February 1919, Albert traveled south to Atunze to attempt to get cash for the mission. In the autumn he traveled with his daughters and Roderick MacLeod to Gartok at the invitation of the Teji Markham. It was yet another five-day journey by Yangtze boat and mountain mule to the little Tibetan garrison town. Dorris was fifteen at the time and Dorothy twelve. Just as they began their last day's journey, a messenger from the Teji Markham arrived to advise them that the stars were not auspicious for their arrival. He begged them to not to come to Gartok until the stars were more favorable.[115] When they arrived at the outskirts of Gartok two days later, they found an honor guard of two hundred soldiers drawn up in formation on a vast bleak plain to meet them.[116] The soldiers accompanied the missionary party into Gartok, loosing three volleys in welcome, an honor reserved for high officials. The troops stood at attention beside the entrance to the Teji's residence as the missionary party entered.

Soon after their arrival, a long line of men began to bring the Teji's gifts to his friend Shelton, including thirty pounds of yak butter, twenty pounds of tea, a quarter of beef, a mutton carcass, a keg of honey, and even barley for the mules and pack animals. Between elaborate feasts, the girls visited with the Teji's wife, swapping stories of Lhasa and America, speaking in the Shelton girls' preferred Tibetan. Dorris wrote, "One day we asked her if she had ever jumped rope. She'd never even heard of such a thing, so we got a rope and taught her; we all had lots of fun. It wasn't easy for her to do because she wore long skirts down to her ankles, and often would get caught on the rope."[117]

Dorris ran to get her rope one day and overheard a wealthy Tibetan asking her father's consent for his son to marry her. Her father thanked the Tibetan for the marriage offer, as it was a great compliment from a powerful family: "It is not our custom for to decide who our daughters are to marry. And you, Sir, know how important your customs are, so you will understand. Please respect my need to refuse this great honor."[118]

After many festive banquets enlivened with bagpipe music, the Teji Markham sent them on their way with great pomp and three horseloads of gifts—mutton, rice, butter, and honey. He asked them to write to him monthly, so that he might be kept apprised of conditions in Batang. Once again the authorities looked to the missionaries for intelligence reports, only this time the missionaries were thrilled that the officials were Tibetan.

While Kham was free of organized armies in battle, the peace was shaky. The Rongbatsa truce started to unravel as Chinese provincial and national officials began to question the document. When the frontier commissioner repudiated the truce, General Liu was forced to flee Batang to Atunze to escape arrest for signing the Rongbatsa truce, taking the town's civil authority with him. The Twan Shang secret society was the only real authority remaining in Batang. The society had evolved from a home guard into more of an anti-Chinese organization—though one happy to work with restive soldiers. One of Batang's Chinese officers began to conspire with the Twan Shang through the Ba Lama, who was influential in the society and the de facto administration of the town.[119] When no higher authority would sign it, the Rongbatsa truce became a dead letter on a formal diplomatic level, though it continued to act as a working agreement to halt hostilities along an agreed line.[120]

In China, further anti-foreign agitation such as the May Fourth Movement presaged the end of the special privileges and protections enjoyed by foreigners that dated back to the unequal treaties of the nineteenth century. Their foreign passports gave the missionaries a certain protection in western China by dint of the Republicans' embrace of Western institutions and the Western governments' continued military superiority over China. The Tibetans involvement with the British further gave the missionaries some immunity. However, the power of the Western cannons did little good in the backcountry of western China, where mutiny and brigandage was rampant. The U.S. State Department issued dispatches to the west China missionaries in 1919, warning them the Sichuan border was "fraught with danger for foreigners."[121]

The Sheltons planned to leave for the China coast in December 1919. The way home through Tachienlu was still deemed too dangerous as bandits were rife. As Hardy and the Bakers had done, the Sheltons planned on traveling south through Yunnan Province to the French railroad at Yunnanfu. Though southern Kham and Yunnan bristled with bandits, it was considered more orderly than the wild Jung Lam.

As was customary, the departing Sheltons sold and gave away their household goods, much going to the relative newcomers, the MacLeods. It was an awkward leave-taking, with Flora and the girls setting off for America permanently and Albert returning to Batang for his great lunge toward Lhasa. "It was 1919," Flora remembered, "almost time for another furlough, but we didn't want to leave. This last term of service, in spite of the unsettled state of the country, had been such a happy one; we loved the people, and they loved us; they had ceased to fear and come to trust us."[122] The Shelton girls resisted the move homeward with all their powers. Dr. Shelton reported, "It is a far greater trial to Mrs. Shelton and the girls to leave than most realize, and the girls have put forward all sorts of propositions and schemes to delay or prevent the leaving to go home."[123]

The Finest Collection

Beyond escorting his family to the China coast, Albert Shelton also intended to transport his trove of Tibetan treasures for the Newark Museum. Following his return from furlough in 1914, he acquired Tibetan artifacts with a passion, both in Batang and in the areas where he itinerated. While awaiting an opportunity to ship his artifacts, he packed his growing collection in wooden shipping crates from America, storing them in a shed on the mission property. He acquired a diverse collection, several hundred objects both sacred and secular. While doctoring at the burned and ruined Draya monastery, Shelton collected several pieces, including a *dorje* (celestial thunderbolt) and piece of a statue frieze that Chinese soldiers had looted.[124] In Gartok, Shelton acquired a religious costume from the head lama of Batang—"I took it in payment of a debt owing me from him."[125] The sacked Chamdo monastery was another rich source of artifacts where Shelton collected the monastery's Chinese vases.[126]

In Batang, Shelton again purchased artifacts from the Jo Lama, the Ba Lama, and Gezong Ongdu.[127] The turmoil of fifteen years of warfare in Kham loosened sacred and precious objects from their moorings, and made them available to be purchased by the Sheltons. "The lamas dug up their silver vessels, that they had had buried somewhere on the mountains, and sold them to buy back the land that had been taken away from them by the Chinese. . . ." At night, the lamas would slip in the mission gate to sell the objects to Albert Shelton.

As with the Batang scrolls he sent to the Newark Museum in 1916, Shelton purchased a number of objects from Gwei Tsen Chi of Batang's noble family.[128]

Beyond the ancient scroll the young man sold Shelton, he brought the Sheltons ornate tea bowls, "used by very wealthy Tibetans," a royal gown spun from gold and silver, and other family heirlooms that Shelton termed "treasures."[129]

In August 1918, just after his return from Chamdo, Shelton wrote an expansive letter to the Newark Museum. "I have the finest collection of Tibetan things," he wrote in a large bold script that could barely fit on the page. He donated the Batang scrolls he shipped in 1916, and stated the material he collected would add immeasurably to the museum's Tibetan holdings, "I'd like to see it the finest Tibetan collection in America." Shelton noted that his wife was returning to America in late 1919 and that he could ship the artifacts when she traveled.[130]

As with the first purchase, Shelton and the Newark Museum delicately maneuvered for bargaining position. Dana asked for a list of materials and queried if two thousand dollars would cover it.[131] Shelton countered with "not less than $2,500."[132]

To raise the boil at the Newark a bit, Albert Shelton concluded his letter by writing, "I would like to see all of it go with what I brought home before, otherwise I would sell everything in China, as oil men and British and French are very keen for these things and I have constant inquiries for them."[133] The Newark soon responded, "it is entirely possible that the museum will want to purchase all or least a good part of Dr. Shelton's new collection . . ."[134]

In November 1919, the Sheltons' journey to the coast was imminent, and the Tibetan Christian Mission began a flurry of activity. After organizing the Batang Christian Church to be run by local Christians, they formally ordained Li Gway Gwang into the ministry. With a crowd of bareheaded Chinese and Westerners in pith helmets and fedoras witnessing, he baptized the Shelton girls and twenty-nine other new Christians in the murky waters of a mission pond.[135]

The mission made a resolution: "Moved that This Mission wish to express their sincere appreciation of the faithful service the Sheltons have rendered the Cause of Christ in Eastern Tibet. Dr. Shelton for his Medical, Mission, and public services; Mrs. Shelton for her Literary, Musical, and Translation work, and Dorris and Dorothy for their tender and loving help and example as workers for Jesus in Social and Sunday School circles. May God's richest blessings go with them, and may the many ties not cease to bind them to this land of eternal snows, and to our loving hearts for Jesus Sake."[136]

CHAPTER TWELVE

THE DEVIL'S OWN CAULDRON

Yunnan, 1919—1920

I am nearly finished.[1]

—Dr. Albert Shelton

Escorted by Chinese soldiers, the Sheltons' caravan crept out of Batang early one November morning in 1919. Since Flora Shelton hated teary goodbyes, she had spent the day before offering her friends what she pretended was a preliminary farewell. Instead, the Sheltons quietly prepared the caravan to leave before dawn.

In spite of the Sheltons' plotting, that night their friends discovered their ruse and traveled to various places along the trail.[2] Instead of avoiding farewells at the city gate and down the road a bit, Flora Shelton ran an emotional gauntlet for twenty miles that lasted the entire day. It was a particularly difficult parting for the two Shelton girls and their Tibetan friends. "The girls were almost ill from sorrow. It was very touching to see Dorris and Dorothy with Tibetan girls leaning on their shoulders and weeping sad farewells," Roderick MacLeod wrote.[3]

The Sheltons' large caravan included a number of Chinese returning to China, including Dr. Shelton's long-time assistant Chang Shao-yu, whom they called Johnny. Tibetans carried Flora in her sedan chair and Dorris and Dorothy rode mules.[4] Packed on the jostling herd of yaks and mules were a dozen and a half wooden boxes containing Albert Shelton's collection of Tibetan artifacts bound for Newark, and six hundred dollars worth of mission rugs to be sold in Yunnanfu.[5]

As he guided the enormous caravan south to Yunnan, Dr. Albert Shelton was an important man, in control of his environment and destiny. Recognized as a central Asian leader, his reputation extended from Lhasa to Beijing. Diplomats in London, New Delhi, and Washington knew his name. His sprawling Batang mission was one of the largest non-Buddhist compounds in the borderlands. His fame as the designated successor to Livingstone had spread from America's mission supporters to a broad audience across the country. Journalists, ministers, and lecturers lauded his Christian spirit and American forthrightness. To many, Albert Shelton embodied a new kind of pioneer.[6]

The Sheltons' caravan proceeded south along the Yunnan Road trail that connected Chamdo and Atunze—the familiar path to Gartok for Albert Shelton and his daughters. The Sheltons intended to travel south through brigand-infested Yunnan to the provincial capital of Yunnanfu (Kunming). In the post-Revolution era, it was the least precarious route out of western Kham.

While the trail through Yunnan was perilous, it was clearly less dangerous than the route across the Jung Lam, which was perennially menaced by the rebels from the Hsiang-ch'eng. Even if the caravan managed to avoid misfortune on the Jung Lam, the Yangtze Valley was a raging channel of anarchy that few travelers chanced. Warlords vied for control, and unpaid troops formed bands of well-armed mutineers who preyed on the river traffic, particularly steamers flying foreign flags.[7]

After a month and a half of arduous muleback and sedan-chair travel, the Sheltons could look forward to a comparatively painless forty-hour train ride through the mountains from Yunnanfu to the French Indochinese seaport at Haiphong.[8] After the French wrested mining concessions in Yunnan from China late in the 1890s, they began construction on a narrow-gauge railroad that ran 473 miles through the mountains. Finished in 1910, the line was a marvel of engineering, snaking through tunnels across territory previously thought impassable.

The caravan climbed out of the upper Yangtze Valley into the highlands. On the sixth day, they began to crawl along the snow-covered trails, climbing T'sala Mountain's ice-covered sixteen-thousand-foot pass. One of the mules tumbled off the trail toward the river eight hundred feet below. While the mule managed to stop, the boxes it was carrying hurtled all the way down to the water.[9]

The Sheltons' journeyed south through the Tibetan regions of southern Kham that stretched across southwestern Sichuan and northwestern Yunnan. Many nights the family slept in remote tribesmen's cabins or under the stars, sheltered by oilskins when the skies opened. Flora wrote, "There were little rivers winding here and there, temples stuck up on the mountain sides, lamaseries of Tibetan monks hidden away, always wildly beautiful, very quiet, and intensely interesting."[10]

When the Sheltons arrived at Lijiang in northern Yunnan, they found hundreds of patients there awaiting treatment. "Some people who had heard of our coming had come some two or three days' journey in order to be there as we went through, wanting operations," Dr. Shelton wrote. "I was not able to do these at the time, but promised to stop on my way back in attend to as many as possible in a week or ten days."[11]

Yunnan in the Warlord Era

A high rumpled tableland between British Burma and French Tonkin, Yunnan was populated primarily by various mountain tribes. The Chinese considered it their most backward province.[12] As the Sheltons traveled further south into Yunnan, they began encountering Han Chinese towns mixed with the tribal villages.[13] In the period after the Republican revolution, the province was relatively calm, though travelers wrote of the appalling rural poverty, noting half-clothed women, naked young girls, and endemic starvation. As late as 1914, Yunnan was still relatively free of banditry, but as the revolution devolved into militarized provincialism, warlord battles and brigand raids roiled the region. Heads hung in the trees, and tales of mass butcheries filled the air.[14] If Sichuan was the devil's cave, by 1919 Yunnan was the devil's own cauldron.

The west China hinterland had become the warlords' main battleground. In spite of enormous numbers of soldiers, brigand bands swarmed Yunnan. Dozens of brigand bands with hundreds of bandits commanded the countryside around rich centers such as Yunnanfu.[15] The boundary between brigand and soldier was a highly permeable one, as most brigands were former soldiers, and vice versa.[16] "Brigand by night is soldier of morning," the Chinese said.[17] Unless spurred by the foreign consuls, the warlords seldom bothered with bandits, preferring not to risk their troops.

As the Sheltons made their way south through Yunnan, they were dependent on the fragile order held together by the military governor and warlord of Yunnan, T'ang Chi-yao. T'ang was an imperious ruler who boasted a genealogy that extended back to the T'ang or Ming Dynasty. In the turbulent warlord era, T'ang managed to maintain his power with alliances formed and broken with Machiavellian genius.[18] By 1919, T'ang was involved in numerous struggles for power. Yunnanese "guest armies" were embroiled in conflicts with neighboring provinces, straining T'ang's ability to maintain order. An officers' rebellion challenged T'ang's overall command. The province's finances were in shambles, and T'ang was increasingly dependent on the opium trade for funds. With the treasury near empty and much of T'ang's army outside of the province, Yunnan teetered on the edge of anarchy.

A Heavy Heart

Five days south of Lijiang on December 21, 1919, the Shelton caravan encountered Dr. William Hardy and his family in the ancient walled town of Dali. The Hardys were traveling north to Batang with an immense caravan of goods for the mission. They were returning after an absence of over two years, part of which Hardy spent as a U.S. medical officer. The missionaries visited for a day, the Hardys' sharing the good news of a raise for the Batang missionaries. When it came time to move on, Albert hired three sedan chairs for the Shelton women.[19]

The Sheltons turned east toward Yunnanfu along the old caravan route that extended west into Burma. On January 3, 1920, their fortieth day of travel, the Sheltons were three days from Yunnanfu when they stopped for a midday meal in the village of Lao Yoa Gwan. The local military official received Dr. Shelton's travel papers and arranged for their escort. When the caravan prepared to leave, four desultory soldiers sauntered out as their sole guard. Flora asked her husband if that was their entire escort. Insouciant from his many journeys through unsettled country, Albert assured her that their escort was the magistrate's business and the number of guards was his concern.

As they descended a pass beyond the village, the Sheltons' caravan stretched for more than half a mile down the mountainside trail, the three sedan chairs leading the way.[20] Riding Abe, Albert followed fifty yards behind with the four soldiers. The baggage animals carrying the Tibetan artifacts brought up at the rear of the caravan.

Someone suddenly screamed, "Robbers! The robbers are coming." Shots rang out from three sides. As bullets began to hit the chairs, the chair coolies dropped their poles and fled. One bullet passed through Flora's chair, smashing a thermos under her seat. Flora and the girls quickly jumped from their chairs and crawled into a little ditch.

Albert wrote, "One of the four soldiers that were with us jumped in front of my mule, stuck his gun in the air and pulled the trigger. Bang! He jumped behind my mule again, and away the four of them went just as fast as they could go."[21] Shelton pulled his rifle from the scabbard but, realizing he was alone and the bandits many, decided not to resist. After returning the gun to its scabbard, Shelton jumped off his mule and ran for the chairs. Robbers poured down from the mountain bluff to the left of the trail, quickly surrounding him. "One man who had tried to make himself look as scary as possible by putting a big smear of black across his face, stuck a big pistol in my stomach," Shelton wrote. "He looked so grotesque that I laughed."[22]

Carrying his rifle and saddlebags, the bandits herded Albert Shelton toward his family. "Ho ja Ho ja (quit shouting)," he told the robbers. The bandits began rifling their bags and pockets, stripping the rings from Dorothy's fingers before Dorris demanded they return them. "We were surrounded & everything grabbed," Flora wrote, "but the head robber said for them not to take our things & they put them down." A half-mile back, the robbers broke into a couple of the Tibetan artifact boxes. They smashed the box with a rare and precious volume of the sacred Buddhist scripture, the *Kanjur*, but abandoned the crates after a perfunctory browse.[23]

The bandits insisted that Albert Shelton accompany them to their leader. Flora Shelton wrote, "They said to Bert 'Come on & and send the soldiers back and we will give the boxes safe passage.' Bert started & I said—'O don't leave us.' He said, 'It's all right, you don't need to be afraid.' & was gone."[24]

As he walked back up the mountain with them, one of the brigands demanded Shelton show him how to work the camera that he'd just stolen. At the top of the pass, the brigand leader, Yang Tien-fu, waited with twenty of his men, fingering Shelton's Winchester shotgun. He likewise insisted Shelton teach him how to use his new gun.

As Shelton showed him how to work the gun, a shot whizzed from the valley below. Roused by the four guards, government soldiers rushed from Lao Yao Gwan. Yang told his men to withdraw up the mountain, taking their hostage with them. Yang quietly informed Shelton that he was being held for ransom. "This was somewhat of a surprise as I had expected to be allowed to return to my family," Shelton wrote.[25] "My mule and two of the animals of servants having been brought up, I mounted and we started. It was with a heavy heart."[26]

Albert Shelton could see the chairs on the valley road below. One of the men called for the chairs and women to be brought along. One commentator wrote, "Mrs. Shelton says the robbers also tried to hustle her up the side of the bluff but she is a large woman and it was impossible for her to climb the hill. Then they put her in her chair and commanded the chairmen to carry her up but they too said it was an impossible task to climb the steep mountain side with such a load."[27]

The bandits and Shelton hurried up the mountain with bullets flying overhead. As they climbed miles into the mountains, the sound of shots became fewer and fewer and finally died out completely. After dark, the band regrouped. "I counted seventy-one there at the resting place," Shelton wrote.[28]

At ten o'clock that night they began to move again, traveling for five hours to reach a small village. At daylight they were up again, but it was raining with a heavy wind so the bandits decided to linger for breakfast. Shelton tried to care for his mule, Abe, but the bandits insisted he be left saddled. Nor would they allow the fastidious Shelton to remove his clothes to wash himself.

After the robbers rifled his bags, Shelton was left with little but his horse blankets, a few clothes, his watch they inexplicably missed, and three books—

188 / PIONEER IN TIBET

the New Testament, a copy of Robert Service's *Rhymes of a Red Cross Man,* and Ian MacLaren's *Beside the Bonnie Briar Bush,* a lachrymose tale with chapters such as "The Doctor's Last Journey." With little chance of escape and his family safe, Albert Shelton sat down in an old shed among the bandits and began to write a diary in the margins and blank spaces of MacLaren's small volume.

Dr. Albert Shelton began his journal of capture and kidnap: "4 January, Have no idea how things will turn out and does not matter much just about me. Glad loads were not taken and Flo and girls allowed to go."[29] Yang Tien-fu told Shelton he hoped to use Shelton to get his family out of jail in Yunnanfu and to get a ransom of fifty thousand dollars of arms and ammunition from Yunnan governor T'ang Chi-yao. After Shelton told him he wouldn't be party to such a high ransom as it would put every missionary in Yunnan in danger, Yang softened his requirements to one hundred and twenty guns and control of the road from Yunnanfu to Dali.

Yang led a successful band of six hundred brigands that consisted primarily of mutinied soldiers and starving peasants.[30] Yang was a tall former army officer under Governor T'ang—"a born leader," one missionary said. After a defeat, T'ang cashiered Yang, who began his brigand ways. Shelton noted in his diary: "Dark pleasant face when in good humor and smiling, but smile turns to wolfish snarl when he is angry. . . . Utterly bad in a most plausible way."[31]

Yang and his men eventually wearied of their life on the run. Months earlier Yang appealed to a local French priest, Father Claude Bailly, to intercede with Governor T'ang for pardon and reinstatement of him and his men. After T'ang refused, Yang hit on the idea of seizing a foreigner to use as a bargaining chip. Yang told Dr. Shelton that he was kept informed of the caravan's progress across Yunnan, as he had targeted Shelton as the man to be captured.[32]

After Shelton's abduction, the brigands began to travel day and night through the steep mountains to avoid the pursuing soldiers.[33] Near the village of Mi Tsao, the bandits took one of Shelton's cards to the Catholic mission and returned with a card reading "Claude Bailly." They told Shelton the priest had left for the nearby town of Lao Yao Gwan to take the Shelton family to Yunnanfu and would return in five days. During the robber band's headlong flight the first night with Albert Shelton, they passed within a mile of his family in the village.[34]

The next day dysentery struck Shelton, making the incessant flight an ordeal. His exhaustion and feelings of desolation alternated with his determined attempts at Christian example. In his makeshift journal, Shelton scribbled, "awful spell of blues this A.M. wrote Flo to go on home to amer. But doubt if they will."[35] In spite of his anger and frustration, Shelton began to pray for grace to try to help his captors, adding, "There are several whom I am beginning to like."

The wild fugitive life of Yang's band continued, and on January 10, Shelton wrote, "I am nearly finished." His despair was complete. "Wish I could die without committing suicide." In spite of his depression, Shelton began to doctor those around him, primarily wounded brigands along with a few villagers.[36]

On January 12, the bandits received a letter from the Yunnan government telling them could submit a list of demands. "They want six things granted over the government seal before releasing me. (1) Pardon for all past offenses. (2) Restoration to citizenship. (3) Reinstatement of soldiers. (4) Release of head man's family. (5) Two hundred rifles. (6) Twenty thousand cartridges."[37] Buoyed by the news, the bandits accorded Shelton a newfound regard, and he began to evangelize and teach the brigands, including the leader Yang. "Many of them when they come around me want to show off and sing Do re mi and Jesus loves me and many other hymns." By January 15, Shelton thought the entreaties of the French consul and Father Bailly to Governor T'ang were working, and he would soon be released. "They promised me last night to let me go as soon as Yang's family is turned over to them."[38]

During the day the bandits could sometimes hear faint bugles, part of the two thousand Yunnan troops who chased them. Traveling under the cover of darkness, the band continued its endless flight, moving south through the steep mountains and narrow valleys of central Yunnan. Rather than expose themselves on the valley trails, the brigands often climbed straight up over the ridges. Some were so steep Shelton could only slide down on the heavy leather cowboy pants he was lucky to be wearing when abducted.

After a few weeks on the run, Shelton noticed a small tumor starting to grow in his neck. The long marches, poor food, and sleeping out in cold and rainy weather began to aggravate his condition. Even his mule Abe was worse for wear. "My poor mule is all in. He may pay for my being caught, but I can do no more."[39]

Shelton clung to his faith for solace. "We've been camping here since ten this morning," he recorded on January 18, "and I've been rereading as a whole all of Paul's letters. They were giants in those days. What a wonderful man, and what stimulation to emulation!" A few days later, he found inspiration in the eighth chapter of Romans: "For I am persuaded, that neither death, nor life, nor angels, nor principalities, nor powers, nor things present not things to come. Nor height nor depth, nor any other creature, shall be able to separate us from the love of God, which is in Christ Jesus our Lord."[40] "Amen," Albert Shelton wrote in his journal.

The brigands traveled through a countryside that was sometimes hospitable and sometimes hostile. A notably successful politician, Yang curried favor among the mountain people, which allowed the band to find supplies and shelter in many villages. When the village was uncooperative, the brigands rampaged. "The captain came through the village with a Colt Automatic in one hand and Mauser Automatic in the other. The people ran like rabbits before a pack of hounds." Shelton noted the pitiable sight of Chinese women wobbling off on tiny bound feet carrying their babies. Dead men littered the route. The bandits hustled trussed merchants along with them, threatening execution unless they acceded to their ransom demands.

The Lord is My Shepherd

Late on the night of January 21, Father Claude Bailly, the French priest who mediated between Yang and T'ang and escorted Shelton's family to Yunnanfu, came to the hidden mountainside temple where the band was holed up. A thirty-year veteran of the Yunnan missions, Bailly was as respected among the Yunnanese as Shelton was among the Khampas. Shelton described him: "He is rather a short man, round and fat, with a long white beard, a kindly smile, a twinkling eye, and a bald head."[41] Bailly stayed until 1:30 in the morning discussing terms with the brigands. He told them that T'ang had released Yang's family and they should reach the bandits by the following day.[42]

Letters moved back and forth between the Sheltons almost from the beginning of the kidnapping. The day after his capture, a letter from his wife arrived telling him the Newark shipment was essentially safe and Dorothy, who had been ill, was better. Flora Shelton thought he might be free within a week.[43] Later in the day, letters from both Dorris and Dorothy arrived, "which I was very glad to get," Shelton wrote. A postcard to his wife went back: "Hadn't you and babies go on home as there is no telling when I'll get out."[44] He wrote Flora on January 18: "Half a month gone and no sign of anything so far as I can see for the first week we traveled on average 12 to 15 hrs in the 24. . . . Plans for yr spoiled. . . . I'm helpless—I can't expedite matters in any way."[45]

Through January, Father Bailly attempted to mediate between the two prevaricating sides.[46] Governor T'ang continued to dispatch soldiers after the brigands in spite of his pledge not to do so, while Yang reneged on his promise to release Shelton after T'ang released his family. "They are like all Chinese," Shelton jotted, "don't want to keep their part of the bargain."

As Shelton sat nearby, the bandits discussed tactics one day. Should they kill him? Yang, who hoped to be governor eventually, decided against it, as he thought it would turn the vital foreign consuls against his rule. Should they capture the French consul and demand ten thousand guns as ransom? "They are desperate. Will go to any extreme. Flo and the babies are safe, so the worst they can do is to kill me."[47]

Just before February a hundred mutinied soldiers joined Yang's group. The reinforcements and the seemingly imminent deal may have softened Yang, as he requested Shelton to educate his son. Shelton agreed. "If I were a young man I would like more than anything else to go with these men and be their pastor. It would be a great opportunity to do the Lord's work. Oh, why wasn't I born a twin or a triplet?"[48]

But Shelton's spirits were at a low ebb. On February 3 he wrote a "last letter" to his family, saying the running over the mountains had done him in. "My business affairs so far as I know are in perfect order—I owe nothing on anything."[49]

It was a sickening fall for Albert Shelton, from his pasha-like situation in Kham to a point at which he was little more than a powerless pawn. Instead of having servants to do his bidding, he had to follow the orders of men who repeatedly displayed their powers of life and death over him. It was a devastating experience that eroded the very foundations of his faith and will to survive. But Father Bailly encouraged Shelton, telling him the negotiations were almost complete. Within a few days, however, the deal fell apart when the government refused the terms.

Pursued by soldiers, the bandits traveled for two days straight. The next day, exhausted and dispirited, Shelton talked to Yang. "Asked captain to shoot me this morning and quit running around. Told him this was day for me to go back or be killed." Yang assured Shelton they were traveling to Wuting to turn him over to an official friend before resuming their headlong flight. "Seems Government is after them with lot of soldiers."[50]

The next day Shelton attempted to incite the band to rebellion. "I spoke to the whole two hundred. A very seditious speech. Asked the captain to stand all of us who wanted to go back against the wall and shoot us." Shelton figured at least fifty of the men wanted to leave the bandit life and return home. His two-week bout with dysentery was worsening, and the tumor in his neck was growing alarmingly. With the growth pressing on a major nerve, Shelton was in considerable pain. "If something doesn't come off soon I'll fight Yang for leadership of the band. I can command small half now."[51]

Albert Shelton wrote a long rambling letter to his family on February 12: "Dear Ma, Pa, and all of you, I've been a prisoner now for 40 days and the prospect of my release is not as good as it was a month ago, so it is quite likely that I'll not get out." He told them of his gratitude that his family escaped, and for the French consul's fruitless work. Shelton railed against the American government lack of action. "It is a notorious fact, known all over the world, that the U.S. will do less for its citizens in foreign countries than any country on Earth. . . . This should be changed." He stated that the reason the bandits kidnapped him was because the Yunnan government had failed to pay its soldiers. "So I am a prisoner of China and the officials are responsible."[52]

The Grave Situation

Shelton was correct to be concerned about Washington's lack of urgent action. Washington first received notice on January 8, five days after his abduction. Two weeks later the Beijing chargé d' affairs notified the State Department that T'ang was negotiating with the brigands on the basis of amnesty.[53] On January 27, as Shelton continued to be a prisoner, the charge d' affairs wired Colonel W. S. Drysdale, the military attaché in Saigon, to go to his assistance. Drysdale sent preliminary report to the State Department. "Shelton well. Assistance is not required. Negotiations, release progressing slowly. In my judgement there is not much cause for anxiety."[54]

Instead of rushing to Yunnanfu, Drysdale traveled to Guangzhou to consult with the American consul. On January 24 he wired Governor T'ang in Yunnanfu, who assured the consul he had everything under control. "Every means had been used to convince them with the result that they now have been subjugated and [the captive] may be out of danger in a few days."[55] T'ang's forecasts flew in the face of the inept military and duplicitous diplomatic realities.

As Albert Shelton suffered his trials in the Yunnan mountains, a groundswell of concern back in America raised the profile of his kidnapping at the State Department. Reports of Shelton's plight began appearing in newspapers around the world soon after his capture. The Associated Press had it on the wire by January 7. On January 13 the *New York Times* reported, "Chinese Bandits Hold American Missionary."[56] Reuters also found the Shelton capture newsworthy enough to put out on the worldwide wire. By mid-January the *Times of London* reported in its "Imperial and Foreign News Items" column: "An American missionary, Dr. Shelton, was captured on January 3 near Laoyakuan, two days from Yunnan Fu, by brigands."[57]

Shelton's missionary supporters rallied to his cause. *World Call* alerted its readers in its February 1920 issue with an article carrying the Associated Press story. A January 17 telegram from Corey explaining the State Department efforts accompanied the article, which concluded by stating, "All indications point to Dr. Shelton's ample protection."[58] It was the first story in the magazine's monthly coverage of the kidnapping, with each succeeding month's article growing in size.

Concerned letters poured into UCMS headquarters from missionary supporters across the country. One penny postcard from John Nelson in Wooster, Ohio, was representative. "We are anxious but hopeful," it read. "Tibet is my favorite mission field. May God preserve him whom we have loved and honored."[59] Letters of inquiry from senators, congressmen, and governors to Acting Secretary of State Frank Polk began arriving at the State Department.[60]

It was not surprising that missionaries closest to the scene of Shelton's ordeals evinced more ambivalent sentiments. A Yunnanfu correspondent to the *West China Missionary News* wrote, "The more the authorities give in to the robbers, the more value will be set upon the capture of a foreigner. Not to make any commotion about capturing a foreigner would decrease his value of his capture, but would be most unfortunate for those who are in their hands."[61]

With a competent foreign correspondent in Shanghai, the *Chicago Tribune* jumped on the kidnapping. By February, journalist Frederick A. Smith was hot on the Shelton kidnapping. He and East China missionary Dr. E. I. Osgood sailed from Shanghai on a coastal steamer to Hong Kong en route to Yunnan. After a quick stop at Guangzhou to consult with the American consul, the two men intended to sail to Haiphong where they would get the train to Yunnanfu and proceed via "chair or donkeys to meet the bandits." Osgood and Smith intended to try to ransom Shelton with funds advanced by the Disciples of Christ, "which the Christian church will then try to collect from the Chinese government."[62]

Smith and Osgood made interesting traveling companions. With his dapper fedora, cigar, and hard-boiled demeanor, Fred Smith was almost a caricature of an adventuresome foreign correspondent. Dr. E. I. Osgood was a tall, lean man topped by a dark crest of hair. When Flora Shelton frantically searched for help after the collapse of negotiations, she wired the East China mission. The missionary officials deemed Osgood as the man best suited for the assignment, as he had successfully negotiated with Chinese troops to save the city of Chuchow during the revolution.[63]

Colonel W. S. Drysdale didn't arrive in Yunnanfu until the evening of February 23. He then began making the rounds, meeting with the French and British consuls, Flora, Father Bailly, "various members of the American community," and a number of Chinese officials and influential men. Both consuls recommended harsh military action against Yang's troop, lest its success at ransom embolden other brigands to attempt additional attacks against foreigners. Drysdale concurred, contending that acceding to the bandits' demands would have "resulted in strengthening this band of outlaws and giving them control of what is known as the Western District in the Province."[64]

After weighing T'ang's distinct lack of success apprehending Yang or affecting Shelton's release, Drysdale decided to negotiate with the bandits directly. To get the governor's cooperation, Drysdale sagely recommended that T'ang permit Yang and his men to migrate to Sichuan. Four days after his arrival in Yunnanfu, Drysdale proposed his draft settlement to Governor T'ang. He recommended T'ang cease troop movements against Yang's brigands, and offer them a complete pardon, free passage to Sichuan, money for resettlement, and a position of battalion commander for Yang, who would be allowed to organize his brigands into a troop. T'ang agreed to the terms and Drysdale's proposal to deal with Yang directly.

Carry On, My Soul

Life was not getting any better for Albert Shelton. Weeks after he had confronted Yang and plotted to seize control of the band, Shelton was still in captivity, living like a wild animal in the mountains. "I know I ought not to feel so," Shelton wrote in his diary, "but how I long for death!"[65] Time and again the governor promised conciliation, only to send attacking soldiers instead. One government ambush pinned Yang and his band in a building where soldiers besieged them for several hours, killing several of the brigands. Yang ordered a bodyguard of twelve men for Shelton, who moved him to an upstairs hall for safety. In spite of the pitched battle raging around him, Shelton was so tired he lay down in the hall and went to sleep. Sometime around four in the morning, the shooting almost ceased. Yang discovered the government soldiers couldn't restrain themselves from dividing the captured loot and had withdrawn about a mile away to divvy up the plunder. Yang quickly took advantage of the opportunity, and the surviving band slipped into the night with Shelton.

By now government soldiers continually shadowed the band, making travel a series of running battles. When not in the saddle, Shelton spent much of his time doctoring the sick and wounded. Even when not moving, the pain in his neck prevented sleep. One entire side of his head was numb, and pain shot down into his shoulder. By February 25 even his faith deserted him. "I am in the depths today. God seems to be gone. My God, my God, why hast Thou forsaken me?"[66]

That night the pain was so great he cried like a baby before falling asleep in a dark hole he shared with a dozen bandits. The morning and the promise of two days' rest brought hope and renewed faith. But the band was not to have a relief. At nine o'clock that night word came the soldiers were tramping toward them, and once again they raced into the darkness. "The Governor is an awful double-faced fellow," Shelton huffed before leaving."[67]

Shelton was declining rapidly, no longer able to sit on his mule. When the brigands lifted him onto Abe, Shelton just crumpled up and rolled off the saddle. The bandits hauled him through the mountains for five days on a crude litter called a *whagen*. Even Yang took a few shifts bearing Shelton. After almost two months of captivity, Shelton was sick, exhausted, and enveloped in suffering. "The pain was so great that I took a dose of opium last night. Opium dreams."[68]

As darkness fell word came that more than two thousand soldiers surrounded them and were closing the noose. During the night Yang's men slipped into the mountains with Shelton on his *whagen*. That evening they reached Tanao, a small Laka tribal village five days' journey from Yunnanfu.[69]

Early the next morning Yang and his men started on their way again, but not before locking Shelton in a low-ceilinged barn loft behind mounds of hay. Three tribesmen looked after him.[70] For five days Shelton lived in the loft that was barely high enough for him to sit upright. He began to think his neck growth was quickly becoming an inoperable cancer. The only light came from a hole where his keepers loosed a brick. At least the fresh straw made a comfortable bed.[71]

As Shelton slowly recovered some of his strength, Yang's men kidnapped George E. Metcalf and C. G. Gowman, two CIM missionaries from Taku, about a dozen miles from Shelton's barn at Tanao.[72] During the night, Gowman succeeded in escaping when his exhausted guards fell asleep. According to Gowman, when Shelton's health declined so dramatically, Yang sent his men to abduct the two CIM missionaries to be substitute hostages should Shelton die.[73]

A Refracted Limelight

On March 3, Dorris and Dorothy went to the city gate with their Tibetan servant, Andru, to see the rescue caravan off. The girls instinctively chose gruff Fred Smith as their champion, and Andru insisted that they translate his instruction that they quickly bring Shelton back. Dr. Osgood remembered, "I couldn't have answered if I had had to. My throat got full of something. 'Just tell Andru we'll bring back his master' was all Fred Smith said."[74]

The caravan bristled with special troops from the governor's own bodyguard. Chinese writers, servants, and swift runners accompanied the mission. Knowing the perfidy that plagued Father Bailly's negotiations, Drysdale remained in Yunnanfu to thwart betrayal by T'ang if indeed the negotiators arranged a deal with Yang. A private phone line snaked across Yunnan with them, connecting Drysdale and the mobile conciliators.

As the relief caravan wound across Yunnan, the *Chicago Tribune* printed a lengthy summary of the kidnapping, accompanied by large photographs of the Shelton family. Entitled, "Missionary Prisoner of Chinese Bandits," the story ballyhooed Shelton as the great Christian emissary to Lhasa, "the first white man ever invited to the city."[75] Additional reports included, "Hear Shelton is Ill" and "Tribune Man on Way."

Shelton's celebrity began growing as scores of major U.S. newspapers and hundreds of small ones began picking up Smith's stories on Shelton's saga from the *Tribune's* foreign news service.[76] The service widely distributed Smith's story of the kidnap diary that Shelton succeeded in sending to his wife. By Smith's account, the diary told a highly colored tale of grit, heroism, and Christian courage. "The diary alternately inspires tears and laughter, telling how the bandits kindly gave him $7 to spend as he pleased, and he bought crude sugar for his faithful mule," Smith wrote. He depicted Shelton as some latter-day Paul, teaching his tormentors the ABC's and Christian hymns while racing through the mountains. Like a good publicist, Smith neatly excised Shelton's rage with the American government and his wrenching crises of spirit.[77]

Papers in the heartland of missionary support followed the abduction closely. In Cincinnati, where the FCMS headquarters had long been, readers found a flamboyant article accompanied by a six-panel cartoon portraying Shelton in heroic light that began, "Like a chapter from a novel or an episode from a thrilling movie. . . ."[78] With Shelton's celebrity from the Newark Museum exhibit and New Jersey's Standard Oil connection, the *Newark News* covered the case extensively. One story headlined "Acts to Free Dr. Shelton" highlighted the rescue efforts of J. P. Thornton, Standard Oil's man in Yunnanfu.[79]

Thy Will Be Done

Back in China, the rescue column headed for Wuting, three days to the north of Yunnanfu and closer to Yang's territory. When the entourage reached Wuting, the authorities immediately dispatched more than twenty runners to try to contact Yang.

In Tanao, Yang posted a guard to prevent escape. As Shelton recovered some of his strength, his guard left to tell Yang his captive could travel again, leaving Shelton in the care of some village men. Shelton's weakened physical condition limited his options. He could barely stand for more than five minutes without shaking like a leaf. Months of bad food and arduous travel had emaciated him into a gaunt, pain-ridden man, forty pounds lighter than when he left Batang.[80] After a short respite, the sharp pain in his neck returned with a vengeance. "The pain last night was worse than it ever has been. I'm awfully sorry, but had to take opium again as a consequence."

Spent with pain and exhaustion, Shelton began to reconcile himself to his new fate and search for the meaning in it. "It appears that God did not want me to go inside to Lassa. It looks as if the end of my work was at hand. I hoped to accomplish so much, only to wind up in a hole like this. Thy ways, O God, are past all finding out, but help me to say, 'Nor my will but Thine be done.'"[81]

On March 9, the old man who served as Shelton's caretaker came crying into the loft. Soldiers were coming, he said. Terrified of the soldiers' reprisals, all the villagers scampered off into the brush, taking what belongings they could. But no soldiers arrived. Instead, a minor government official and his servant sent to investigate the kidnappings stood blinking at the sight of the long-sought Shelton. "He was greatly astonished at finding that I was there. The authorities had been using every effort for more than two months to secure my release, and here I now was in his hands."[82]

Still in grave danger from Yang who prowled nearby, the official told Shelton to immediately move on to the mission station at Taku. Unable to find any transportation, the men in the neighboring village twisted together a rope and towed and tugged a tethered Shelton up a steep mountain for three hours before he collapsed. "Being unable to walk and having no method of conveyance. Two of the huskiest men came, one on each side, and with their shoulders together, lifted me up, and I was able to wiggle my legs and away we went."[83] He arrived in Taku after midnight, only to find the mission nearly deserted. Fearing bandits or soldiers in Shelton's great torch-lit processional, all the villagers fled except one ancient couple. After determining the bewhiskered "Bolsheviki" was not a Russian, but rather the famous Dr. Shelton, the villagers returned to help. Shelton slept for an hour and a half before setting out with two tiny ponies. He alternated riding each pony, with one man leading it and another keeping him propped in the saddle. Other men scouted the trail ahead and behind, watching for Yang who by now knew of the escape. There was no telling when Yang might leap from the darkness to recapture his prize.

After twenty continuous hours of flight covering forty miles, Shelton reached the relative safety of a magistrate commanding a small garrison at Yenmo.[84] There he encountered Gowman, one of the kidnapped CIM missionaries who had escaped. "Thank God! Thank God!" was all that Gowman could say.[85] Shelton replied, "Well, this is the first word of English I have heard for sixty-six days."[86]

But the threat from Yang remained. If anything, the few soldiers guarding Shelton represented an opportunity for Yang to gather additional arms and ammunition along with his captive. A few days prior, Yang had fought a pitched battle with the local militia on a plain near Yenmo, and the garrison thought he might return to capture the place. Indeed, Yang's fight was probably the reason he failed to return to Tanao to retake Shelton. The telegraph at Yenmo quickly transmitted the news to Flora in Yunnanfu, and she alerted the governor.

Fearful of losing Shelton, Governor T'ang immediately dispatched additional troops to guard the group as they moved four days closer to the capital. By the time Shelton met Dr. Osgood on March 11, there were about eight hundred soldiers guarding the open chair with the shrunken, bearded doctor.

In a hard rain, Shelton traveled on to Wuting, where he used the phone to speak with his wife. After almost two and a half months of near-fatal captivity, Bert Shelton was at last able to talk to Flora again.

Early the next morning the column guarding Shelton moved on, and two days later Albert Shelton reached Yunnanfu.[87] "About four o'clock in the afternoon we topped the last pass and could look down into the great plain and in the distance see the great lake, on whose shore Yunnanfu is situated."[88] At the outskirts of town, he met his daughter Dorris. The first thing she said was, "Papa, God does answer prayer, doesn't he?" Haggard and near collapse, Shelton quietly replied, "Of course he does."[89]

Thanks to Smith, the State Department, Standard Oil, and the telegraph, news of Shelton's escape flew around the world. On March 10, the State Department wired the UCMS the heartening news, "State Department received telegram from military attaché saying it was reported Shelton was released and he expected confirmation of report soon."[90] Newspapers and magazines across the country echoed the news. The *Chicago Tribune* carried a lengthy story from Smith, "Chinese Troops Find Dr. Shelton in Bleak Stable," which covered Smith's heroics as much as Shelton's release. The *New York Times* reported, "Bandits Free Dr. Shelton."[91] The *Times of London* headlined, "Outrages by Chinese Bandits."[92]

Back in Yunnanfu, the French consul assigned a small hospital to the family, which Flora Shelton prepared for her husband's arrival. A half-hour after entering the city gates, the coolies carried Shelton into the hospital where Flora waited. She wrote, "He was with us once again, but so broken, in such pain."[93]

The next morning a French doctor, assisted by Dr. Osgood and another physician, removed part of the tumor in Shelton's neck. But it was only a temporary remedy. Shelton continued to suffer terrible pain, sleep coming only with morphine. After the surgery, Shelton fumed to Stephen Corey in a letter he dictated to his wife: "But now have a tumor on the side of my neck which seems to be quite serious. But there does not seem to a doctor in this place that has the grit to take it out. It gives me a great deal of pain and everyone is insisting that I go home. I am somewhat run down and under the circumstances, it seems the only thing to do."[94] While Shelton's doctors found no sign of cancer in the tumor, Dr. Albert Shelton was certainly not going to Lhasa. He was going home to America.

CHAPTER THIRTEEN

THE HERO RETURNS

Furlough, 1920–1921

Dr. Shelton is not posing as a hero or martyr, but his story is so gripping and intensely interesting that his services are in great demand.[1]

—*South Bend Tribune*

As Father Claude Bailly again passed through Yunnanfu's city gates, the good luck bells tinkled in the upturned eaves. This time he came to visit Albert Shelton rather than intercede for his life. Nursed by Flora, Shelton was slowly recuperating in the French hospital. Within a day or two of his arrival, well-wishers began dropping by—Chinese officials, the French consul, Colonel Drysdale, Frederick Smith, J. P. Thornton, and assorted merchants and missionaries. Each mealtime, the Shelton girls trooped in to visit their father. Dr. E. I. Osgood was a frequent companion, keeping constant pressure on Shelton to return to America for treatment. Osgood wrote that Shelton suffered from "a serious nervous condition because of the awful strain of his experience."[2] One day, when Shelton insisted he was instead going to Lhasa, Osgood rebuked him: "You don't seem to think that the Lord can manage things as well as you can."[3] It worked, as Shelton resigned himself to a medical furlough.

Nine days after being carried half-dead through the gates of the city, Albert Shelton was ready to travel home. Dr. Osgood accompanied the family, shepherding them so solicitously that Dorris nicknamed him, "Patience and Long-suffering." Coolies carried the party from the French hospital to the railway station, where the little narrow-gauge train took them to Haiphong.[4] There they caught a coastal steamer to Hong Kong, where Osgood left them to return to Chuchow.

They departed Shanghai on the *Empress of Asia* on April 10, 1920, the same day seventeen cases of Tibetan artifacts left Hong Kong bound via the Panama Canal for the Newark Museum.[5] Albert Shelton wrote the museum from the ship: "I trust there will be no great delay in the matter as I am in need of the money the collection represents. I have been in the hands of bandits for 2 1/2 months and at great expense I am proceeding at once to Mayo's for an operation.[6]

The Roaring Twenties were in their nascent days. America had changed in the war years, and a brash new attitude suffused the land. To the horror of missionaries, flappers brazenly smoked cigarettes in short dresses. As the missionaries gathered for shipboard Sunday service, the hedonists swam and played shuffleboard. For missionaries sequestered for years in the interior of China, it was a bewildering experience.

After a voyage of sixteen days, the family visited Flora's mother in Glendale, Oregon, before Flora and Albert traveled to the Mayo Clinic in Rochester, Minnesota.[7] Like Battle Creek, the Mayo Clinic was a paragon of modern medicine that catered to a well-heeled clientele.[8] The Mayo surgeons removed the tumor from deep in Albert Shelton's neck and, to relieve the pain, severed a major nerve.[9] Flora wrote the Newark Museum about the operation, "It was a hard and dangerous one & very deep on the neck, but it was not cancer, for which we give grateful thanks & hope to give the devil one more battle for Tibet before we are out of the running."[10]

In late May, the Sheltons traveled to Enid, Oklahoma, to stay with Albert's parents. While their daughters remained with the grandparents in June, Albert and Flora again took to the hustings.[11] They traveled to Chicago to stay with Albert's literary and photographic agent, O. E. Rosboro.[12] From there they traveled to Washington, D.C., where Albert met with Associate Editor John O. LaGorce at the National Geographic Society.[13] LaGorce contracted with Shelton to write his article on eastern Tibet and deliver two lectures at the society in December for four hundred dollars.[14]

A Very Remarkable Group of Things: Newark and Pomona

By late June, Shelton was working with Abe Cory in New York on his book, *Pioneering in Tibet*. When his collection arrived in Newark in early July, the museum staff began organizing the material. Shelton arrived a few weeks later to help. In mid-July J. C. Dana wrote the Newark trustees to urge the acquisition of Shelton's new collection: "the Association must acquire this collection. It is a very remarkable group of things."[15]

The Newark Museum administrators continued cataloguing the material and discussing the cost as Albert Shelton traveled across the country seeking treatment from doctors in Pomona, Los Angeles, and Detroit.[16] In late July Shelton underwent osteopathic treatment in Detroit. Though his shoulder was getting better, his neck continued to trouble him and he worried that the growth was coming back.[17]

Through the summer the museum trustees again sought verification of the value of Shelton's collection. Berthold Laufer at the Field Museum assured them, "As the first collection purchased by you years ago of Dr. Shelton was satisfactory, I see no reason why the second installment should not be equally good."[18] The Newark Museum paid Shelton $3,000 for the six hundred Tibetan objects, adding another $91 for his photographs.[19] Dana was soon crowing that the Newark Museum's Tibetan holdings constituted "the largest collection in the country."[20]

It was a substantial amount of money. In 1920 the average minister in America made about fifteen hundred dollars a year, a public school teacher less than a thousand. Back in Kham, $3,100 was a staggering fortune. In 1917 the Batang mission budgeted $60 for a year of coolie labor at a rate of 20 cents a day. Gezong Ongdu earned $120 for his year's translation and teaching work.[21]

The money received from their Tibetan collection and photography supplemented the Sheltons' approximately $1,500 annual salary.[22] Though the missionary society paid the Sheltons' salary, housing, medical expenses, and transportation, as well as the bulk of Albert's itineration expenses, the Sheltons, like most missionaries, also relied on donations from missionary supporters, particularly "Living Link" churches that pledged ongoing financial commitments.[23]

Albert and Flora spent most of August at his parents' home. On August 21, they left for California where Flora was scheduled to speak. By the end of August, the Sheltons were settled in Pomona, California, a leafy town of thirteen thousand in the orange groves near Los Angeles, then a small provincial city of a little better than half a million.[24] During the summer the Sheltons purchased an imposing three-story Shingle-style house with a wide wraparound porch. Located at 381 N. Gibbs, the fine turn-of-the-century house was within walking distance of the Disciples of Christ church and the railway station.[25]

Through the summer Albert continued working on his book, which the respected missionary publisher F. H. Revell contracted to publish. Albert Shelton wrote a book in the style of many missionary accounts. With a plethora of colorful, danger-filled stories, Shelton portrayed himself as a courageous, self-sacrificing Christian hero. Tales of adventure, plucky Christians, ignorant benighted heathens, and the glimmering hope of the gospel and Western ways filled the book. It was resolutely positive.

In spite of his commitment to his ethnologic work, Shelton made almost no note of it in his book. He noted only his explorations as itinerations for evangelical and medical work. There was no mention of his work for the National Geographic Society or his explorer society memberships, though his pride in his explorer life was evident.[26]

However famous he felt, his new California style of living was causing some financial discomfort. In September 1920, Shelton contacted the Newark Museum about some other objects to consider: part of his wife and daughters' Tibetan jewelry collection. Shelton sent thirty-nine pieces of gold, silver, pearl, ruby, coral, and turquoise jewelry. "One piece is especially valuable," he wrote, referring to a gold and pearl bracelet set with eight hundred pieces of turquoise. Asking a thousand dollars, he wrote, "Would really prefer not to sell as it represents the combined heartaches of the female portion of the family. Only the difficulties of buying a home induces me to sent [sic] it at all."[27] Citing lack of funds, the Newark Museum declined to purchase the jewelry.

Every Village and Hamlet: The Celebrity of Albert Shelton

In mid-September 1920, Flora scribbled a note to Archibald McLean that ran akimbo across the page: "You are certainly working Dr. Shelton too hard. He spoke twice yesterday & came near fainting in the street today. Don't you think it is too much to keep him busy the next two months with no rest. . . ."

Evidently McLean didn't, as Albert spent most of the fall speaking for churches and service clubs from California to the lower Midwest. He started at the Long Beach Convention of the Christian Churches, where two thousand people gave him a "great ovation."[28] He spoke at the Christian Church in Emporia, Kansas, where he had graduated from Kansas State Normal School. The college paper reported that he told the audience about his kidnapping, his destruction of the Tibetan charm box, and his passport to "Thassa [sic], the Thibetan religious stronghold where no white man had ever entered."[29]

After his kidnapping ordeal, Albert Shelton obsessed about his willingness to give his life to Christianity, echoing both the Disciples' and China missionaries' long tradition of glorifying martyrdom.[30] When Albert Shelton spoke in Emporia, someone in the audience asked him if he was going to return to Tibet. He replied, "I shall return to Tibet if it costs me my life that men might live. Why shouldn't I?"[31]

In October, he thrilled the crowds at the Disciples of Christ annual convention in St. Louis with his stories of adventure.[32] His talk completed a circle that began when he and Flora first heard Dr. Susie Rijnhart speak of far-off Tibet at a Disciples' convention. The St. Louis papers gave the Sheltons big play.[33] The *Post-Dispatch* trumpeted the upcoming speech with a long story and a recent photo that showed the effects of Shelton's ordeal. The article ballyhooed his drive to return to Lhasa: "He said, 'I should be here in Lhasa now, and here I am, 12,000 miles away from my work.'"[34]

The *St. Louis Times* gave the story even more ink, running three stories in as many days. The paper carried a report of an interview with Shelton held in his room at the Marquette Hotel. The reporter gushed, "The famed physician-missionary arrived yesterday and was seen by a reporter for The Times, to whom he gave a thrilling story of the sufferings he endured in his difficult mission field for 17 years and of the hardships he underwent while with the robber band for two months."[35]

Shelton's fame grew with every speech and press release; every breathless newspaper story and magazine article. Flora wrote, "When he returned to America the last time he was a celebrity. The newspaper reporters sought him out and gave him wide publicity of the 'front page' character. His pictures were featured in the great dailies of America. He was hailed a hero."[36]

Motion picture companies began to inquire about putting the Sheltons on the big screen. Corey at the missionary society worried that the film companies would ignore the "spiritual side of things" and "simply set forth adventure."[37] However, Corey went on to make the case for transforming Dr. Albert Shelton into a movie star: "I know how you hesitate about publicity but the whole matter has been featured in the Associated Press throughout the country until every village and hamlet knows something of your experience. It will mean much to the cause of Christ and for poor, old Tibet."[38]

To an increasingly urban, industrial America, Shelton represented a throwback to burly frontiersmen who shouldered civilization into the wilderness with their families in tow.[39] Dr. Albert Shelton was an American hero, a sharpshooting missionary-doctor who took Jesus to the heathens; an adventurer who coaxed and cajoled Tibetans out of their curios for America's elucidation and entertainment. He was a family man who kept his daughters' hair ribbons crisp on the frontier, a good Christian who had a stalwart church organ pumping in the wilderness. Albert Shelton was Teddy Roosevelt, a modern-day Paul, and Tarzan rolled into one.[40]

In spite of its operant myth of isolated agrarian life, post-frontier America was rapidly becoming a country of urban-dwellers in an era when the very essence of American manliness was questioned. Men of Shelton's generation missed the great bloodletting of the Civil War that framed their fathers' masculinity. As Albert Shelton experienced, the Spanish-American War scarcely lasted long enough to test a nation's manly courage. Growing women's rights and corporate power that eroded individualism further threatened the masculine mystique.

Shelton's life in the wilds of Tibet assuaged America's threatened masculine identity.[41] Part of the American public turned to missionary heroes for its models of virile, civilized masculinity in the wild. Like Dr. Livingstone and Britain's Cambridge Seven before him, the media catapulted Albert Shelton into the pantheon of heavily publicized religious celebrities.[42]

The Highlanders: Albert Shelton and the Tibetans

As he made his way around America, Albert Shelton still railed against Tibetan "devil-worship." But after fifteen years in Kham he spoke differently about the role of Christianity and the West in Tibet. "Come on!" he still exhorted his audiences, but now he talked of helping the Tibetans solve their problems rather than conquering Satan's last great redoubt.[43] Shelton's newfound respect for the Tibetans is obvious in his essay, "The Highlanders," in which he went so far as to link the Tibetans to the Scotch-English borderland Covenanters who begat the Disciples of Christ: "The Highlanders of Tibet, like all Highlanders, are poor; but will never ask for your pity. They dared to be poor with stout hearts, choosing the grim, stern, inhospitable refuge of the mountains rather than surrender to the conqueror of the plain. Loyal to lost cause, they stand like Elijah on Mt. Carmel, the Albergenses on the Alps, the Huegunots [sic] on the Pyrenees, and the Covenanters of Scotland. Save your pity for the beggars of the plains; the Highlanders deserve your admiration. . . . Tibet only surrendered to the spiritual power of the Buddha. Our task in Tibet is a spiritual task."[44]

After his long Himalayan experience, he had a nuanced perspective on the Tibetans. Describing the polygamy, polyandry, and naked children of Batang, Shelton termed the town "un-moral, not immoral."[45] He had learned subtle differences among cultures and peoples, noting, for instance, that the Tibetans felt clothes represented social position, not modesty.[46] Abstractions had become real people; vile customs made sense as comprehensible adaptations.

In the course of fifteen years, his political relationship with the Tibetans had also changed. When Shelton arrived in the Tibetan marches, he saw the Chinese as the phalanx to follow to Lhasa. By 1920, his position was wholly different. Now he was an independent agent who served as an intermediary between the Chinese and the Tibetans. Indeed, the Tibetans increasingly used the Americans in concert with the British to parry diplomatically with the Chinese. If he was going to Lhasa, it was with the help of the Tibetans, not behind the bayonets of the Chinese.

Shelton's initial contempt for the Tibetans and their culture was transmuted into respect. His desire to uproot Tibetan Buddhism had tempered into a grudging admiration for the resilience and steadfastness of Tibetans' faith. Rather than expecting to sweep Buddhism from the high plateau in his lifetime, by 1920 Albert Shelton hoped to offer modern medicine to the Tibetans—perhaps as a seed of Christianity.[47]

The Sacred and the Profane: Tibetan Art in America

There were more than six hundred Tibetan objects itemized in Shelton's second collection of Tibetan artifacts. Because of Batang's position on a major central Asian trade route and the extensive clerical travel between Kham and central Tibet, Shelton's collection included an extraordinary range of Tibetan art. Tibetan Buddhist art's primary function was to act as a religious meditation tool for the Tibetans' esoteric Vajrayana Buddhism. This apocalyptic strain of Buddhism sought to bridge the gulf between the fleeting world of the senses and the higher absolute truths. Vajrayana Buddhism was a ritually complex form, using meditation devices such as mandalas and *tangkas* to help human beings facilitate the discovery of their Buddha natures, most often with the help of a *guru* or teacher. In Tibet, where Buddhism overlaid various indigenous religions, the imagery exploded into a wild proliferation of deities that sprang from the rubrics of Buddhism, Hinduism, Himalayan folk traditions, and the other religions that filtered ideas over the central Asian trade routes.

The Tibetans developed a unique style that confidently mingled the various artistic elements of its component influences.[48] Ritual images, implements, and portrayals of mythical and historical figures dominated art production. Tibetans often revered the portraits as icons, considering the deities' spirits to reside in the object, particularly when an association, such as a learned lama's handprints, were affixed. When sanctified, the portraits served as potent meditation tools.

The collection of Tibetan art that Albert Shelton transported to America included forty-four portable cloth *tangka* paintings: religious depictions of Buddhas, lamas, fearsome deities, complex heavens, and fortune-telling charts. While the checklist of Shelton's acquisitions generally included dry descriptions, the cataloguer occasionally lapsed into whimsy, describing Item 33 as "Satan (in his Sunday clothes.) Demonic majesty riding a horse, which tramples human beings. Various mounted attendants and demons surround him."[49]

In the Tibetan view, once consecrated, the divine spirits depicted on the *tangkas* occupied the art, making the paintings nesting places for the spiritual energies. The artist, most often a commissioned layperson, crafted the painting to serve as an intermediary between the mortal and divine world. In order for the sacred objects' spirits to remain alive, it was vital for them to have an ongoing relationship with practitioners.[50]

Mandalas, whether two-dimensional wall paintings, sand paintings, painting-on-fabric *tangkas*, metal sculptures or even the monastery complexes themselves, represented the entire sacred cosmos to the Tibetans, objects in the Tibetan view that were actualized three-dimensional realities. They all acted as teaching tools to guide initiates through religious ritual and practice. The repetition and symmetry of form served to impart a vision of the ordered universe to the guided practitioner. One of Albert Shelton's *tangkas* depicted the ancient central Tibetan monastery of Samye. It was far more than a souvenir of a lama's alma mater. It was a depiction of the monastery's mandala-derived architectural plan, which in turn reflected the mythic land of Shamabhala, the Pure Land where the enlightened apocalyptic future lay, to be discovered in the present only by those free of anger and illusion. Both the two-dimensional painting and the three-dimensional monastery served as a portal into meditative reality of the universe.[51]

The Shelton collection included a dozen textiles, from saddle blankets and liturgical coats to a wealthy lama's brocade door curtains. A New Year's costume of fur-trimmed satin brocade and silk was another family heirloom that was well over a century old. Tantric skull bowls and a lama's ceremonial apron made of human bone commingled in the collection with decorative arts crafted from jade and a small assembly of guns, arrows, and equestrian gear, including a rare nineteenth-century saddle richly wrought with tooled silver, dragons, and floral motifs.

Fifty-five books included medical texts and a wooden printing block, as well as a precious sacred Buddhist text, the *Prajnaparamita*, the most popular volume of the 100- to 108-volume *Kanjur*, the Buddhist scriptural canon. Collected from the noble family of Batang, the *Prajnaparamita*'s words were written in raised gold and studded with turquoise and pearls.[52] Shelton spent a year trying to see the book and then another two to acquire it. "I've been in the Tibetan country 15 years and it is the finest thing we've seen," he wrote the Newark Museum.[53]

Shelton collected forty-two silver objects, including butter lamps, holy water bowls, trumpets, and tea holders and pots. Approximately a hundred works in metal ranged from brass bowls, daggers, pen cases, and inkpots to prayer wheels, cymbals, and charm boxes. Tibetans made extensive use of ritual objects such as *phurpas*, triangular-bladed daggers to assault demons magically and delineate sacred ground, as well as bells (associated with female energies) and *dorjes* (male-associated thunderbolts). When used together in Tibetan Buddhist ritual, the bell and *dorje* represented the paired opposites of female wisdom and male compassion, both essential forces for spiritual enlightenment.

Shelton had acquired sixteen valuable Tibetan Buddhist bronze statues.[54] They included statues of high lamas, protectors, and Buddha in various manifestations. One two-foot-tall sculpture of Tara, the *bodhisattva* who helped devotees overcome obstacles to enlightenment, proved to be over seven hundred years old. The lithe figure was wrought of gilded copper and embellished with silver wire and jeweled inlay.

In spite of the disapproving references to the "obscene" art of the Tibetan monasteries in both his and his wife's writings, Shelton collected a gilt-covered seventeenth-century *yab-yum* (*yab-yum,* literally "father-mother," depicted pairs of male and female deities in sexual union) statue of Padmasambhava embracing his mystical consort in ecstatic sexual congress. Shelton's notes delicately described the statue as "Gold plated, seated figure on elaborate rectangular base, holding second figure on lap, right hand raised, left hand holding small rodent."[55] The paired figures expressed a fundamental Buddhist concept of the essential need to join female-associated wisdom with male-associated compassion. The Tibetans believed the ancient tantric teachings provided a practical system for manipulating the human libido to focus on a transcendent object. The overtly sexual imagery of the *yab-yum* served as a linkage to intense unconscious drives that in turn delineated and sublimated the conscious and unconscious instincts into a powerful visual metaphor.[56]

With Shelton such a big success as a field agent, Dana cast a wider net for missionary collectors. In May 1921 he sent a circular letter to foreign missionaries appealing for artifacts. Dana told a newspaper reporter, "Through our missionaries we have secured good things, especially good in many cases because missionaries live close to the common people and are familiar with the things which make up the substance of the their lives, not merely curious things."[57]

High and Mighty Worthies

Albert Shelton arrived at the Newark in early December with "some high and mighty worthies," as the curator Louise Connolly called them. When Shelton requested she notify his friend in New York when the exhibit was ready, Connolly asked for the name. "The name he gave me was Mrs. J. D. Rockefeller Jr.!" she reported to J. C. Dana. "I told him he should have no doubt whatever that we would notify her."[58]

The previous night Shelton had dined with John D. Rockefeller Jr. and his family at their palatial nine-story Manhattan mansion at 10 West 54th Street. Rockefeller was a voracious collector and had crammed his house with rare European furniture, French tapestries, Renaissance paintings, antique Persian rugs, and his collection of seventeenth-century K'ang porcelain. Albert spent the evening in the sumptuous home regaling the Rockefellers with his tales of the Himalayan borderlands. Before the evening was out, he managed to drop the fact that he had some Tibetan jewelry for sale.[59]

Rockefeller was deeply involved with the Interchurch World Movement, his attempt to unify all missionary and benevolent efforts of the major Protestant denominational and church-related groups into a single unified organization—a kind of evangelical cartel that would operate with businesslike efficiency, economy, and scientific administration. Rockefeller had tapped veteran mission promoter Abraham E. Cory, the namesake of Shelton's mule, as the business manager of the campaign. Cory had arranged Shelton's dinner engagement by touting Shelton as an illustrious missionary hero who survived capture by Chinese bandits, served as the most remote missionary on earth, and had the singular honor of being invited to Lhasa by the Dalai Lama. "I will be glad to meet Dr. Shelton," Rockefeller wrote, "because you want me to as well as because of what he is and what he has done."[60]

A few days after the dinner, Dr. Shelton sent a polite letter from Pomona to Rockefeller thanking him for the evening. Shelton also noted, "RE: the Tibetan jewelry for Mrs. R. last evening. The charge will be $700."

Rockefeller quickly replied, "While you mention $700. as the price of the various articles which Mrs. Rockefeller selected, we are glad to enclose herewith check for $1,000, which we hope you will accept with the assurance of our best wishes for the success of your work."[61] Rockefeller's wife, Abby, also sent a note: "The beautiful Tibetan painting arrived safely yesterday. I have never seen one in such perfect condition."[62] Albert sent a second exuberant thank-you note, concluding: "I greatly appreciated the opportunity of meeting yourself and good wife and especially the boys.—I've never succeeded in growing up myself."[63]

The Newark Museum's Tibetan exhibit opened on December 6, 1921. Albert Shelton chose three hundred objects that he felt best represented Tibetan life. It included a range of ecclesiastic, political, and everyday artifacts, from prayer wheels and Kanjurs to swords and magic charms. Shelton included his great treasures of the silver Wheel of Law and the prince of Batang's yellow satin eighteenth-century Tibetan scroll.

The museum exhibit catalogue stated two reasons for the Tibetan exhibit: understanding and control. Firstly, following J. C. Dana's philosophy of popular education, the exhibit intended to help Newark citizens to understand life in Tibet. "These people are our cousins," the catalogue read. Secondly, the museum expected the exhibit to help Americans understand the challenge they faced as they spread their doctrines wide. "And these people are, on the other hand, closely allied to the oriental races whom we must understand if we are to keep a hand upon the reins which shall guide the Great Civilization that is to be."[64]

Shelton's collection of Tibetan material and the Newark Museum's subsequent exhibition reflected a shift in aesthetics that dated back to the turn of the century. Prior to 1900, museums and art connoisseurs most often viewed non-

Western objects such as Shelton's Tibetan artifacts as "curiosities." With the rise of modernist social sciences in the twentieth century, the material was seen as "ethnographic specimens," and avant-garde such as Pablo Picasso began incorporating the non-Western aesthetics into their art. Exotic curiosities began their journey into "primitive art," later given context and valorized by Western cultural institutions.[65]

The objects Shelton collected conferred an authenticity and authority that embellished his status as a Christian missionary. Shelton could use the objects to penetrate the upper strata of society he aspired to emulate, but his success as a fêted explorer-collector presented him with a conundrum: How could he balance his ideal of sacrifice with his upper middle-class individualist aspirations? It was a quandary he never resolved, ultimately leaving him a man caught in the borderland between a secure social position and an adventurous independent life.

A Universal Chord: The National Geographic Society

After his triumphant Newark exhibit and dinner with the Rockefellers, Shelton moved on to Washington for his lectures at the National Geographic Society. His talk was a smashing success. A *World Call* correspondent wrote: "I must tell you what a success Dr. Shelton's lecture was. . . ."[66] The *Washington Post* reporter winnowed some odd tidbits from the lecture, writing of the Tibetans' bagpipes and habit of boiling captured enemies alive. "Tibet, whose people are modern enough to use Enfield rifles but benighted enough to believe charms will protect them from enemy bullets, was the subject of a lecture before the National Geographic Society by Dr. A. L. Shelton," the story read.[67]

Aside from the lecture, Shelton had been writing his *National Geographic* article with Rosboro's help. Shelton's piece depicted a wild and exotic Kham, a land of robust nomads, rapacious lamas, happy polyandrists, and unyielding warriors. Shelton opened his article: "Where East meets West on the border line between China and Tibet, the broad roles that have come to be understood by those brief terms are completely reversed. There it is the East, personified by China, that has represented the greater progress; and Tibet, which stretches far to the west, that has preferred to exist for centuries behind the world's greatest rampart of mountains, inhospitable to the knocking of ideas more modern than its own." Thirty-five large photos accompanied the article, beginning with a reproduction of Shelton's invitation from the Dalai Lama to visit Lhasa, a "unique distinction," the caption stated.

Shelton portrayed everyday Khampa life with hair-raising photos of precarious cantilevered wooden trails crudely hammered into cliffsides and a one-rope slide bridge across the Mekong with a man and a tethered donkey hurtling across in a sling. A band of Tibetan archers, two convicts with lopped-off limbs, and the brass tea cauldron the Chinese used in Draya to cook Tibetans depicted Kham's brutal, bellicose conditions. The cauldron caption read, "Lovers of peace, haters of war and militarism, the Chinese are capable of extraordinary barbarities, which seem as natural to them as holding a chisel with their toes."

In his text Shelton described the lawless conditions, banditry, and endemic warfare. He portrayed little of his admiration for the people or the friends he made. Gezong Ongdu was identified as "the old man who taught me the Tibetan language." For his U.S. audience, Albert Shelton recycled several of his mission-promotion stories such as his conversion of the bandit leader in Gartok and the mutual vow he and the Kalon Lama took to "work together for the good of our brother men."[68] Shelton touted his upcoming publication in the highly respected *National Geographic* in his lectures and writings. "It struck a universal chord," he wrote LaGorce.[69]

In August 1921 LaGorce returned Shelton's photographs and acknowledged the receipt of the edited eastern Tibet story. He wished Shelton bon voyage. "With all good wishes and the hope that when you make the your Lhasa trip you will write the story for The Geographic." Tucked among the advertisements for American Express, Victrolas, and Old Dutch Cleanser, Shelton's thirty-one-page piece, "Life Among the People of Eastern Tibet," came out in September 1921, one of only two articles in the issue. Seven hundred fifty thousand issues of one of America's most prestigious publications made its way to homes and offices across the country. Albert Shelton was a household name.[70]

The Hero's Journey

As Albert Shelton recovered from his surgery, he reveled that he could make his life-defining journey to Lhasa—in spite of his wife's entreaties. "I tried in every way, but he could only see the ideal in the completion of his life's work," Flora wrote.[71] By December 1920 Shelton was feeling much better, though the severing of the nerve made his arm almost useless. He felt confident the growth in his neck was not going to return.[72] In April 1921 he reported, "I am doing fine. I can work all day and night and enjoy it."[73] In spite of the nation's acclaim and adulation, Albert Shelton never lost his drive to return to Tibet. A minister recalled Shelton saying in a fancy Detroit hotel: "I'm dead tired of it all; I'm aching to get back to Tibet. I am needed more there than I am here. I can't say I am at home here; I know I am there."[74]

As the Disciples realized their hero was continuing his great quest, his supporters became even more enthusiastic. Among the multitude of donations and honors, Gotner College in Nebraska conferred a Doctor of Law; the South Dakota Christian Missionary Society donated an electric generating plant; Sue M. Diltz contributed five thousand dollars; Fred Haslam & Co. of Brooklyn offered government surplus medical instruments; and a Kokomo, Indiana church proudly sent surgical instruments made of noncorrosive Stellite, "a Kokomo product."[75]

In early June 1921, the Sheltons attended the College of Missions' commencement in Indianapolis. The college was graduating one of its largest classes: fifty-one new missionaries. A Lhasa-themed pageant dedicated to Dr. Shelton highlighted the conference afterward. Inspired by his adventure and example, two missionary couples pledged to follow him back to Tibet: J. Russell and Gertrude Morse, and Marion and Louise Duncan. In a post-commencement speech, Albert Shelton promised, "Every Christian force in the last century that has gone against the rock of Tibet has crumbled. The Disciples of Christ are not going to crumble. When we go by the board, if you don't send out somebody else, we will come back and ha'nt you."[76]

The Crows' Cry: Chaos in Batang

Albert Shelton was returning to a Batang ravaged by warfare. In January 1920, when Yunnan brigands captured Shelton, a new Chinese military commander, Yang Teh Shih, arrived in Batang, replacing General Liu, who had fled to Yunnan in disgrace after Republican officials repudiated his signature on the Rongbatsa treaty. General Yang quickly attempted to institute order by disarming and disbanding the town's Twan Shang secret society, which had become the de facto government.

Yang, however, miscalculated the depth of historical hostility simmering in Batang. With one of his ongoing land deals, General Liu had sold the town *yamen* (city hall) back to the widow of the Prince of Batang. Confiscated earlier by Chao Erh-feng, the *yamen* previously was the Prince's palace. The Prince's widow arrived in May 1920 to reclaim her palace, but Yang refused to vacate.

The leader of the Twan Shang, A'tso, wrote to Yang telling him to move out of the palace within three days or the society would drive him out. Yang had only twenty loyal men among his restive two hundred soldiers, with one particularly suspect contingent commanded by Major Wen Han Chin. In spite of his uncertain forces, Yang responded to A'tso's threats by sending men to arrest him. A'tso and his men in turn fired on the soldiers.

An attempt by the Ba Lama and the Catholic priest to mediate a compromise only allowed A'tso and his followers to escape. In the early hours of June 19, A'tso's men attacked Batang, breaching the town walls near a barracks.[77] The Tibetans spread through the town with house-to-house combat, killing the Chinese civilian official. When looting broke out, Wen's soldiers joined in the pillage. Soon the Tibetans attacked the *yamen* and invaded the TCM mission compound. While the missionaries cowered behind the thick walls of their houses, the Tibetans commandeered the mission school to fire salvos on the town.

Yang tipped the balance by deploying a small artillery piece on the roof of the *yamen* to fire into the attackers. From time to time, the Chinese sallied forth to set fire to the Batang houses sheltering the Tibetans. Their cover destroyed, the Tibetans began to withdraw. Seeing the tide had shifted, Major Wen and his vacillating troops joined the fight and slaughtered many of the retreating Tibetans. When the smoke cleared, half of the town was burned down. The Ba Lama fled town and the Chinese once again confiscated the monastery property. Grisly reprisals and beheadings wracked Batang. The heads of A'tso and another leader soon hung on the town gatepost.

After a decent interval, the Ba Lama returned with amnesty, and the Chinese reinstated his properties. Most of A'tso's men refused the offer of amnesty and became bandits. One observer wrote, "The roads leading to Batang, never quite safe, became even more dangerous."[78]

Major Wen again mutinied in July, marching south to Yunnan to join up with the former General Liu. Soon Liu was stirring up trouble with the Hsiang-ch'eng peoples.

The roads around Batang became increasingly treacherous. When General Yang sent seventy soldiers on the Jung Lam to escort an official back from Tachienlu in October, Hsiang-ch'eng raiders ambushed the returning column. Forty soldiers died before the Hsiang-ch'eng men allowed the balance to escape in exchange for rifles. Esther MacLeod wrote Flora: "O Wi Gi ge just poked his head in here, showing himself greatly disturbed, to remark that the crows are all making the sort of cry that means trouble is coming. I guess it is safe to prophesy trouble for Batang, whatever the crows say."[79]

The countryside around Batang was in anarchy. Nina Hardy wrote Flora in February, "One week there were three robberies and one murder committed within shouting distance of Batang . . . and never a soldier stirred outside of town."[80] Even the Tibetan officials suffered. A servant of the Teji Markham came to town for supplies for the Kalon Lama. At the top of Khuyuk La pass on the way to the Yangtze crossing, robbers attacked and killed the servant and the *ula* drover. Two days later, two servants were robbed at the same place. Nina Hardy wrote, "Things have been bad in Batang but never this bad since we have been here—since the trouble last summer no one seems to discern between right and wrong."[81] The Chinese authorities dared not confront the rebels, withdrawing into secure bastions in Yerkolo and Batang. An American consular officer cited the "more or less chronic state of unrest which exists along the Thibetan border," stating that restive Tibetans were gathering west of Batang preparing to attack.[82]

Allied with the Hsiang-ch'eng, tribesmen from Sangen region took advantage of the disorder to drive stolen cattle audaciously past the northern walls of Batang, with the Chinese garrison refusing to challenge the rustlers. On April 19, Tibetan battle shrieks rent the night as shots rang out. The Tibetans called for the surrender of the Chinese garrison. The battle sent bullets buzzing past the TCM mission buildings as one group fired from near the Ogden house on one side of the river and a second group shot from across town near the Hardys' home in Jaranong.

Prior to an attack, Hsiang-ch'eng men tried to lure James Ogden into a kidnapping, but when it began, the raiders protected the mission. As they continued to enjoy some immunity, the missionaries once again escaped injury.[83] The Teji Markham even sent them notice that the attack was coming, reassuring them they would be protected as best he could manage.[84] Minnie Ogden wrote Flora, "The Shang Chen soldiers were here & were so nice as could be. They knew we would be afraid of them, so told us not to fear they wouldn't touch us or our stuff."

By August 1921, the conflict subsided enough for trade caravans again to make their way north from Atunze. One TCM intelligence agent reported to the U.S. War Department, "In general the country is more quiet than it has been for several years. Salt caravans from Yangen [Yerkolo], opium and general caravans from Atunze, and tea, rice and soldiers goods from Tachienlu, all have been moving for a month."[85]

During the TCM annual meeting, the missionaries debated opening a mission station in Chamdo. The missionaries had apprised the British government of their intent but worried that the Tibetans would fail to protect the station and they would lose their lives like Petrus Rijnhart. William Hardy said, "We have looked upon Batang as a strategic center for preparing workers for other places in Tibet when the time comes that these other places can be opened. As such, Batang is a miserable failure."[86]

Back in America, Albert responded to the discussion by writing to Abe Cory that the TCM was somewhat "discouraged." Shelton felt they were struggling with the endemic border uncertainties and the residual effects of the internal disputes. The missionaries were additionally frustrated when the TCM rejected a long-awaited Batang missionary doctor who was found to be an alcoholic. In spite of the grumbling, Shelton was resolute in his drive to go forward to Lhasa.[87] In September the Batang mission learned Shelton was returning with the two new missionary families. James Ogden prepared to go on furlough. Dr.

William Hardy reported in his typical acerbic manner, "The work here is about as rotten as it ever was. We have not set the world on fire."[88]

Taxi to Tibet

Dr. Albert Shelton was a complex creature: a man who craved both adventure and social esteem; a doctor who practiced medicine intermittently; a missionary who seldom preached; a devout family man who endangered himself and his family in a perilous post. He was a martial man with numerous guns who espoused a gospel of love, a zealous Christian who came to admire the spirituality of the Tibetans.

Flora was herself a complicated mixture, a conservative Christian wife and mother, yet a hardheaded woman who pursued her chosen career of translation with a willfulness and determination unusual for her time. While deferring to her husband's fame and career, she never lost her own drive to excel and be recognized for her contributions. Her work as a de facto diplomat and general goad during her husband's kidnapping and diplomatic mission in Gartok displayed her grit and competence. Her interpretation work with the Tibetan artifacts her husband collected considerably enhanced their value. Though Albert was the primary collector, she occasionally acted as a dealer herself.[89]

But it was her translation work that fired Flora Shelton with the greatest zeal. Confident of the worth of her seven-year-long Tibetan translation project, she never faltered in her desire to publish her books. The best place to print the books was in Calcutta at the Baptist Mission Press, which had the requisite Tibetan type fonts. Her intent was to travel there to supervise the publication.[90]

In May 1921, Flora Shelton pleaded with the missionary society to allow her to accompany her husband to China when he returned to go to Tibet. From the China coast she would continue on to Calcutta to supervise the printing of the books, "as they were needed so badly on the border."[91] Although the missionary board turned her down, Flora Shelton found a woman in Pomona who agreed to donate $2,000 for her trip and the publication of her manuscripts.[92]

As Flora and Albert prepared to return to Asia, they organized domestic arrangements for their daughters, who would be staying in America to attend high school. Albert's parents arrived in Pomona to care for the girls while Flora was in Asia. After her Tibetan books were completed, Flora planned to come back to Pomona and wait a few years for her husband's triumphant return from Lhasa. A well-earned retirement in sunny southern California would be their future.

The Shelton girls had made a smooth entry into Pomona, immediately becoming involved in the local church and Pomona High School. But as their father prepared to return to Batang, they felt an understandable longing. "I wanted to go back to Tibet with my father," his daughter Dorris wrote. "When my parents' taxi started to leave, I hung on to the window and made one last plea to go with him." Albert Shelton gently loosed his daughter's hands and told her she needed to stay and study, in order to be of more use to her friends in Tibet. "You know I love you," he said as the taxi pulled away.[93]

CHAPTER FOURTEEN

BACK TO BATANG, 1921

It was a great journey. All difficulties melted at our approach.[1]

—Dr. Albert Shelton

Flora and Albert's journey across the Pacific reminded them of their first voyage. "A honeymoon it was," Flora wrote, "far happier than the first one in 1903, for I was not homesick—he was my home."[2] When the Sheltons landed on the Shanghai wharf, they only had a couple of minutes to say goodbye before he had to return to his ship. They clasped one another, and Albert shuddered with a great sob.[3] "God be with you," were his parting words.[4]

As Flora sailed on to Calcutta, Albert shepherded the four new missionaries across French Indochina and western China. J. Russell and Gertrude Morse were from Oklahoma. Russell was a slender, dark-eyed city kid from Tulsa who was inspired by Albert Shelton while still a teenager. Round-faced Gertrude was a frontier girl who was given to shy smiles. They were traveling with their sturdy baby, Eugene, who often commanded the group's attention. Marion Duncan was a tall, intense orphaned boy from rural Ohio and Louise was a German farm girl from near Niagara, New York. Considered an ideal candidate for Batang, Marion Duncan had testified at his commencement, "When God is in Tibet, all will be right with the world."

Leaving Shanghai, the missionaries sailed for fifteen hours through a tropical typhoon to reach Hong Kong. They made a final provisioning foray before boarding a steamer loaded with cement for a choppy ride to Haiphong.[5] Arriving on September 4, 1921, they stayed for almost a week at the Grand Hotel Du Commerce while French customs officials examined their baggage endlessly. The tons of baggage included enormous quantities of medicine as well as Shelton's meticulously chosen barter and tribute goods that included pocketknives, mirrors, and cheap watches, and the jewels he packed for high lamas and Tibetan officials.[6]

After an additional delay for landslides to be cleared from the tracks, the party boarded the French narrow-gauge railroad for Yunnanfu. By day the missionaries trundled west, first through the palms and rice paddies of Indochina, then up into the Yunnan mountains. Each night they stayed in the comfortable French hotels that dotted the line. Compared to the laborious journey up the Yangtze that the Sheltons had faced in their first journeys to Kham, the new missionaries had a relatively easy passage. However, they still faced the cultural jolts that told them they were in the Orient.[7]

Batang by Christmas

On September 23, 1921, the little wood-burning locomotive pulled into the Yunnanfu station."[8] Shelton began the laborious negotiations and arrangements to outfit the caravan for the long journey to Batang. Sedan chair makers constructed two *jou dzi* for the foreign women, structures made of thin wood and woven bamboo, topped by stiff black rainproof material. Two twelve-foot-long poles extended from each chair for the four coolies to carry. Gertrude Morse had a small basket made to fit over the armrests to keep baby Eugene close at hand. There was some concern as Louise Duncan was several months pregnant. The journey was a race with the stork, as the baby was due almost to the day of their scheduled arrival in Batang. For crossing the Himalayan passes in winter, the women purchased full-length lambskin coats, with the fluffy white wool facing out, which gave them the appearance of an exotic species of upright sheep.

Albert Shelton found a surprise when he arrived in Yunnanfu. His faithful old black mule, Abe, was waiting for him. When his kidnappers hid Shelton in the barn, they broke his heart by taking Abe. Flora recalled, "he felt he would have died if he had not the dear old mule to love and sleep against."[9] After Shelton left for America, bandit leader Yang Tien Fu wrote the magistrate, "I do not know where the doctor had gone, but I am sending his mule to you and trust you will see that it gets to him." Once in Yunnanfu, Governor T'ang had made sure the mule was well tended.[10] Albert wrote Dorothy, "My old mule is fine, and it does seem good to get on him once more—I haven't a new one." A few weeks later he wrote an update: "I'm going to get a new mule tomorrow. His name will be Abe."[11]

In late October Shelton wrote S. J. Corey, "The rains are over now and we have before us fifty-five days of the best weather of the year in which to reach Batang by Christmas."[12] The caravan left Yunnanfu at sunrise on October 31, 1921. As a curious crowd looked on, five missionaries, one baby, fourteen coolies, over one hundred pack and saddle horses, and unburdened and doted-upon old Abe headed west toward Dali. Dr. Shelton led the caravan on his new red Abe. After Shelton's earlier peril, Governor T'ang took no chances, dispatching an escort of malnourished but well-armed soldiers to accompany the group. The escort varied from fifty to over a hundred men.

Shelton worried about Yang Tien-fu recapturing him. In the fall of 1920, Father Bailly wrote to Shelton telling him that Yang was waiting for his return.[13] Shelton wrote to Archibald McLean, "Seems as though Yang Tien Fu is waiting for me to came back and resume my stay with him."[14] But in June 1921 Shelton learned that Yang could no longer be his tormentor, nor could Shelton be his redeemer. He was dead, executed by Governor T'ang.[15] But danger remained on the trail ahead. The same gang of brigands continued to operate where they previously kidnapped Shelton, and rumor had it they planned on capturing him again.[16] Shelton was startled one day to see his captors. He wrote Dorris, "I saw two of them in Yunnanfu; they saw me too, but hurried away."[17]

The missionaries plodded through the Yunnan hills in drenching rain and mist for ten days. The route was a muddy path through flooded rice terraces that rose as many as five fields high above the trail.[18] On the second night they encountered James and Minnie Ogden and their two children, who were returning to America on their second furlough. The Ogdens were suffering road weariness and James Ogden was near nervous collapse.[19] Gezong Ongdu accompanied them, giving the new missionaries their first glimpse of a Tibetan in typical Khampa dress.[20] Each day Shelton and his party traveled ten to thirty miles closer to their goal. As they neared the ravine where the brigands had abducted Albert Shelton, the missionaries' trepidation increased. Worried about another capture, T'ang ordered an additional sixty soldiers to join the caravan. Perhaps scared off by the show of force by the Chinese officials, the bandits never appeared.

At the village of Ch'u Hsiumg, as Shelton sat writing a letter to Dorris, his little terrier, Jack, climbed into his lap. The old mule Abe ambled over and also put his head in Shelton's lap. Not wanting to be displaced, the terrier climbed on the mule's head. After feeding the two of them sugar, Shelton told Dorris his new Abe was working out well.

"If he carried me till I have doctored and preached to as many people as the old one has, I'll pension him too. I suspect, though, that he will last longer than I will."[21]

After two weeks of travel, the caravan reached Dali, where they turned north through fields of indigo toward Lijiang in the lower reaches of the Himalayas. Villages along the trail were tinted a ubiquitous blue by the rotting plants. "Blue everywhere," Duncan wrote. "I almost expected to see a race of blue people creep out of the besmirched one-story shacks!"[22]

The trail crept upward into increasingly mountainous terrain. Glaciers sparkled in the high mountains. Misty peaks rose in the far horizon. The caravan reached the white walls of Lijiang on November 19. The new missionaries availed themselves of a Pentecostal missionary's hospitality, while Dr. Shelton took shelter with the Lees, a wealthy Yunnanese family, where he treated patients, often long into the night.[23]

The Lees made Shelton a guest of honor at a family wedding. The following banquet consisted of dozens of courses, including some that made the fresh-from-the-Midwest missionaries squirm—whipped chicken brains, cow's stomach, shark fin, and snake among them.[24] After four days in Lijiang the caravan moved west toward the Yangtze. The missionaries cached one hundred and fifty boxes of their baggage to lighten their load, as Louise Duncan's pregnancy required them to move at a faster pace.[25]

The trail led on through the Chinese town of Weishi, where the missionaries intended to hire twenty-five animals. Unfortunately, the local magistrate was opium-addled, forcing Shelton to send his caravan leader twice a day to remind him before the mules finally arrived. The expedition relied wholly on Shelton's hard-learned pastiche of borderland skills that he used to bargain, cajole, flatter, and mildly threaten to accomplish his tasks. Duncan wrote, "All along the road there were evidences of the high respect and warm feeling with which the people regarded him. A quick trip would have been impossible with the power established by this friendly feeling."[26]

The caravan was at the southern reaches of Kham now, moving north toward Atunze. On the last day of November they followed a small stream down to the canyon of the Mekong, along which they traveled for two weeks.[27] Albert wrote his wife in India, "My Beloved, We arrived here yesterday, after having traveled along the Mekong for fifteen days in from Wei Shi without having lost a single box or any serious accident whatever. The Lord surely looked out for us."[28]

By now Shelton was pushing the caravan with fair dispatch. Louise Duncan's due date was rapidly approaching, and he wanted her to be in Batang when the baby came. After arranging transport in Atunze, the caravan clambered up a steep grade out of the town's north gate and climbed a high stony pass into a rocky valley. Suddenly, Albert Shelton was back in Tibet. Yaks gamboled in the high pastures. Bright blue skies opened above him. Snow-capped peaks sparkled in the clear light. Buddhist monasteries and giant piles of thousands of Mani stones inscribed with sacred texts were common sights. Spinning their prayer wheels, chanting pilgrims passed the caravan, heading for Lhasa and other holy sites.

Six days later the caravan was in the salt-mining town of Yenjin, where throngs of happy people greeted Dr. Shelton with outstretched palms. His medical skill and gregarious nature had won the Khampas over.[29] The mayor of Yenjin honored Shelton with another lavish banquet, twenty courses of food still exotic to the new missionaries. Marion Duncan recalled, "The walnuts and pears were welcome but the sour, hairy cheese, the limburger butter, the leathery dirt-encrusted pancakes were passed over to the servants, although Dr. Shelton, who had become accustomed to such food would often help eat these last four articles."[30]

After a short break at Yenjin, the caravan pushed on, rising from the river plain into a deep canyon. It was December 17, and they were on their last leg to Batang, seven days' march north. The next day, the caravan climbed to the top of a 15,600-foot-high pass, the highest on the trip. As the missionaries gasped for air on the barren pass, the Tibetans celebrated with yells to the mountain gods and stones to the mani piles.

Within a few days they began seeing burned hulks of houses along the trails and mountainsides, stark reminders of the unending violence in Chinese-controlled Kham. Warfare and bandits had depopulated much of the high region.[31] A few days later Dr. Shelton treated a woman whose toes were sloughing off after bandits had thrust her feet into boiling water.

At Cluysalung, the missionaries ferried across the Yangtze on what was the largest craft on a thousand miles of the Yangtze: a giant flat-bottomed johnboat that was over fifty feet long and nine feet wide. Six men manhandled three immense oars, using the rapid current to hurl the boat across the river. The missionaries trooped into the village of Lipa that evening. It was to be their last night on the road. They were only a few hours' trek from Batang.

They awoke to a beautiful day, though intensely cold. The women walked the high mountain trail to warm themselves. When the intense Himalayan sun rose in the blue sky at midday, they shed their coats and swept, jubilant, along the trail.

They climbed the steep trail to Khuyuk La pass, the infamous "Robber Hill."[32] As they picked their way down the other side, they encountered William Hardy and Roderick MacLeod riding out to meet them. The TCM women arrived soon after with their children, who rode donkeys led by their Chinese servants. A crowd of Chinese and Tibetans followed—mission orphans, soldiers, and townspeople of all descriptions.

That night in the TCM mission the travelers took baths in their folding tubs and ate strawberry ice cream made from snow Tibetan servants hauled down from the mountains.[33] The Duncans and Morses slept in the mission's clean beds, and marveled at the contrast with their long dangerous journey through west China. In just fifty-four days Albert Shelton had shepherded his group from Yunnanfu to Batang, the quickest trip ever.[34] He reported to S. J. Corey,

"It was a great journey. All difficulties melted at our approach."[35] On December 29, Herbert Franklin Duncan was born. "The stork had lost the race by six days," proud father Marion Duncan wrote.[36]

The new missionaries found Batang to be a town of over a thousand including a growing number of lamas and declining number of Chinese soldiers. The ongoing lawlessness continued to erode the Tibet-China trade that passed through Kham. "Batang is awfully poor now and robbers all around," Shelton wrote his daughter.[37] In the thirteen years since Shelton first moved to Batang, the Tibetans and Chinese had developed it into an agricultural paradise, with terraced fields and orchards covering the valley. The fifty-acre Tibetan Christian Mission constituted one of the most formidable institutions in eastern Tibet. The TCM missionaries resided in their walled compound on Japoding Hill and in other mission houses in the walnut-shaded northern suburb of Jaranong.[38] The mission hospital was a dominant structure in Batang, rivaling the Buddhist Monastery, the Chinese *yamen,* and the remains of Chao Erh-feng's crumbling palace. The TCM orphanage sheltered almost forty children, and a hundred and twenty students attended the mission school.[39] With the new missionaries, there were fourteen American missionaries posted to Batang, and another eight stationed in Tachienlu, mainly with the CIM mission there.[40] But Christian conversion among the Tibetans remained as elusive a goal as ever. After thirteen years in Batang, there were only twenty-five converts in the TCM congregation, and few of those were Tibetans.[41]

The Saddest Day: Shelton in Batang

With the MacLeods now living in the big house in the compound, Albert stayed in the mill house that had been his family's first home in Batang, a dark, dank dungeon of a place beside the river.[42] On December 26, 1921, he wrote his daughters from his room as his servant Drashi cleaned a gun for him: "Christmas at the church had about four hundred people, but they couldn't handle them very well. Dorris and Dorothy, nearly all the girls cried when they saw your pictures, and they asked how long it would be before you come back. I cried, too, I am so so lonesome for you all. I kept looking around for you and Mammy all day." He told them about the attack on Batang and his planned trip to see the Teji Markham after the New Year. He closed his letter mournfully, "It's awfully lonesome being here all alone and I must keep moving to keep from getting homesick. I can't stand it. I think yesterday was about the saddest day of my life. I love you so much. Pappy."[43]

Dr. William Hardy wrote, "A month ago yesterday Dr. Shelton hit Batang on the run. He had been running hard over since he got his freight in Yunnanfu."[44]

Shelton toured the Batang Valley to visit with old friends, who came running with smiles and gifts. He prepared a report for the TCM annual meeting in January. Shelton dealt with the mission affairs as elder statesman. He had come back from America a certified hero, well financed for his upcoming leap into the pantheon of Christian heroes. At the meeting, Dr. Shelton contended that the mission could not determine the feasibility of opening a station in Chamdo until the mission understood the conditions inside Tibet. After some discussion, the missionaries decided to postpone further talks on the Chamdo station until Shelton returned from his meeting with the Teji Markham. Shelton told his colleagues that he arranged the Gartok trip, but further travel in Lhasa-controlled Tibet was dependent on additional permissions from the Dalai Lama.[45]

The missionaries continued to worry that the British might arrange to have them barred from Tibet. The British diplomatic corps kept a close eye on the west China approaches to Tibet, with a particular focus on itinerating missionaries. The British worried that the Teji Markham's protection of the mission against the Hsiang-ch'eng raiders represented a major expansion of the Americans' power in eastern Tibet. The British diplomats were also concerned that the Batang missionaries were publicizing "the road through Gartok, Draya, Chamdo, and Derge, all under the Lhasa Government, is open to travel and missionary work." Concerned about events that might follow, Tachienlu consul Louis King kept close tabs on Shelton's progress as he made his way through west China. "Now, it is well known that Dr Shelton proposes to try and proceed to Lhasa shortly after his return to Batang. Further, Mr. Sorenson here is also desirous of proceeding to Lhasa and will no doubt follow Dr Shelton if the latter succeeds in getting through." King urged his superiors to permit him to travel at will in Lhasa-controlled Tibet for "the Consular officer's personal mediation," in the expected event of a crisis caused by evangelizing Christian missionaries or other destabilizing foreigners.[46]

To the Gleaming

As Albert prepared for his Gartok journey, Flora worked on her books near Calcutta. After separating from her husband in Shanghai, Flora spent a month touring eastern China, traveling first through a region devastated by drought, flood, and starvation to Nanjing. Following a stay in Nanjing, she took the train to Beijing.[47]

On October 1 she was back in Shanghai to sail on the *Empress of Russia* bound for Manila and Hong Kong. Flora disembarked with the other passengers. She found Manila to be a noisy American city with a few old Spanish structures and a business class dominated by Chinese merchants. At midnight the ship traveled on to Hong Kong.[48]

En route to Calcutta, Flora stopped in the Malay city of Penang. The formerly timid traveler now explored the city fearlessly, searching out fellow missionaries, fruitlessly searching for traditional Malay handicrafts in a town of British goods, and, escorted by other missionary ladies, seeing the Penang sights, including "the local den of heathenism, a snake temple."[49] By the next day the ship was plowing though the South Seas toward the Bay of Bengal and Calcutta.

Calcutta was the ultimate Indian city, a densely populated tangle of urbanity on the Hooghly River. Capital of the British Raj for a century and a half, the city had evolved a highly educated class of civil servants to handle the sahibs' needs and attracted a churning mass of the desperately poor to scrabble for the remaining scraps. Flora's destination was the hill station of Darjeeling, located in the foothills of the Himalayas. Affluent foreigners most often took the overnight Darjeeling Mail, the fastest train in India, which rocketed along at fifty miles an hour. In the early morning hours, Darjeeling passengers disembarked in Siliguri to catch the tiny Darjeeling Himalayan Railway train that climbed the fifty-five miles to Darjeeling along a serpentine route of loops, switchbacks, S-curves, and chasm-spanning bridges.

Founded in the nineteenth century to provide a cool respite from the heat of India, the town grew to be, like China's Kuling, another calming island of Westernism in an ocean of exoticism. Founded in a Tibetan Buddhist region, Darjeeling's name derived from *dorje,* the iconic thunderbolt of Vajrayana Buddhism. The town was filled with Christian mission activity, particularly schools that educated the children of middle-class colonial expatriates and upper-class Indians and Bhutanese. Flora Shelton worked on her three books at the Baptist Mission Press, which began in 1818 to produce publications for the missionary market.[50] The press was one of the few Western publishers that possessed Tibetan type fonts.

As Flora transformed her many years of translation into books for the Tibetan field, her lonely husband in Batang sent forlorn letters to friends and family in America. In February as he prepared for his journey to Gartok, Albert Shelton wrote a letter to a Pomona minister. "I have not dared tell how lonesome I have been, and if I ever meet with Mrs. Shelton again we will never be separated until we come to the gleaming."[51]

CHAPTER FIFTEEN

THE THORN BUSH, 1922

The life of all living things is like bubbles of water.[1]

—Tibetan Proverb

On the afternoon of February 16, 1922, Albert Shelton led his caravan back up the cliffside trail toward Batang. Instead of returning to the mission, he expected to be on his way to Gartok. There he hoped to finalize his Lhasa expedition with the Teji Markham. Though he felt immune to borderland banditry, Shelton scanned the mountainsides for highwaymen.

The previous morning Shelton had saddled up in Batang for his journey. Before leaving, he rode over to the mission to say goodbye. He played with the Hardy children for a bit and then walked to the MacLeods. While he was gone, the children ran out and tied a Valentine on his saddle. When he found his card, he came up to "kiss the one who did it," but the children were off playing Cupid. So Albert Shelton mounted up for his trip to Gartok.[2]

Nina Hardy noticed how healthy he looked: "When Dr. Shelton first came back, he seemed tired and not very well. But in the seven weeks or so, there was such a change. He was feeling fine or least he seemed to be. He looked well, and he was so jolly, and, as always, the life of all our gatherings together."[3]

A Peach Tree Over There

Conditions around Batang were wildly unstable as renegade tribesmen prowled the trails looking for booty. The local military commander gave Shelton a pro forma warning that the roads were unsafe, but Shelton assured him he traveled armed and he knew the people of the region. In spite of Shelton's certainty, the commander ordered an escort for Shelton's caravan.[4]

After the promised escort of Chinese soldiers failed to arrive, the caravan left Batang around 8:30 that morning. Many of Shelton's old friends and servants were with him, including Gezong Ongdu, Gwei Tsen Chi, and Shelton's retainer Demnbajangtsen, who served as cook.[5] His trusted Tibetan servants Samden and Andru helped care for the eight baggage mules that scuffled behind, some carrying his gifts of jewels and goods for the Tibetan officials. Shelton wore his big Stetson, a long, khaki sheepskin-lined Tibetan coat, and his worn brown yak-leather riding pants.[6] Ruddy from the sun and easy riding, at a glance he looked indistinguishable from his Chinese-Tibetan colleagues.[7]

About half a mile down the trail, two unarmed soldiers trotted after them, the escort dispatched by the *yamen* officials. Dr. Shelton protested their lack of weapons but, after loaning one a gun, traveled on. With some nervousness, the caravan began climbing the notorious Robber Hill at Khuyuk La pass, scanning the rocks and bushes scattered among the ubiquitous bowl-shaped Resurrection plants for bandits.[8] The 9,500-foot-high pass was part of a defile the rushing Batang River cut through the shoulder of a mountain as it raged its way to the Yangtze.[9] The narrow trail made it a favorite ambush point. Tibetan bandits typically stationed men about five hundred yards apart to lie in wait for the tinkle of caravan bells. As the leaders passed, the brigands would suddenly ambush the men and drive the caravan animals up the mountain. Though the region still bristled with brigands from the Hsiang-ch'eng and the Sangen's Seven Tribes, Shelton's caravan passed without incident.

They descended to the ferry at Drubalong, arriving a little before dusk. A messenger from the Teji Markham waited for them with a letter, which Gezong Ongdu translated for Shelton. The Teji Markham indicated it was not appropriate for Shelton to travel into Tibet at that time. The Kalon Lama had ordered him to refuse travel permits to foreigners without his permission. The Teji wrote, "Please write the Galon Lama and get his permission. Please do not come until you do."

The messenger indicated that the Kalon Lama's order came from the Dalai Lama, which in turn came from the British authorities in India. If Shelton entered Tibet, the Teji Markham might be beheaded. Shelton was in an uncertain position. While he had the Dalai Lama's invitation to Lhasa, it was unclear whether it actually guaranteed entry. Was the Dalai Lama just being diplomatic when he issued the letter? Had the British stymied the American advance into Tibet? The only way Shelton could find out was to try to travel to Tibet.[10]

But Shelton never went where he wasn't permitted. He sent a message back to the Teji Markham, telling him he intended to pay his respects at Tibetan New Year's. Since this was not allowed, he would return to Batang.

The next morning the caravan made its way east toward Batang. By mid-afternoon they were about six miles from Batang where the trail wound through the horseshoe-shaped Paimokou Valley and then climbed abruptly along the cliff face toward Khuyuk La pass.[11] Albert Shelton led the party with a Chinese soldier behind him. In single file, Gwei Tsen Chi, Demnbajangtsen, and then Gezong Ongdu followed. Shelton led the party through the high mountain valley and began to urge his mule up the steep grade toward the pass. The road was narrow and quickly made a sharp turn to the east. Shelton rode out of sight around the side of the mountain.

Three shots rang out. At first the party thought Shelton had fired at a rabbit or game bird, but this was not the case. A bandit crouched in a thorn bush ten feet above the trail had threatened Albert Shelton with a gun. Shelton called out his name and told the robber not to shoot. The Tibetan placed the barrel of his gun about a foot from Dr. Shelton and pulled the trigger. The blast knocked Shelton off his mule, and he sprawled in the road with his arm almost torn off.

Riding forward, Demnbajangtsen found him lying in the road. Thinking the mule had slipped, he ran toward him. But Shelton angrily told him to go back. Demnbajangtsen recounted, "I ran toward him but he commanded me to go back. I couldn't understand what was the matter. I thought he was angry with me that day because I was late." When Demnbajangtsen saw the blood on Shelton and felt bullets spit past his ears he knew the reason for Shelton's warning. "Then I began to sense the danger—we met robbers," he said.[12] As Shelton lay in the road, the rest of the party leapt to shelter on the lower side of the trail and began exchanging gunfire with the band of twenty brigands. Armed with guns given them by Shelton and Gezong Ongdu, the two Chinese soldiers added their fire. Shelton groaned and called to Demnbajangtsen to bring water, but the cook slid down the hill toward the Batang River roiling far below. Finding a path, Demnbajangtsen ran to a village to borrow a mule and then raced off to Batang.

Hidden in the brush on the cliff above, the brigands kept the caravan pinned down with close shooting. Other bandits drove off Shelton's baggage mules that were trailing a quarter-mile to the rear. When their riders dismounted, the caravan's riding animals galloped up the mountain trail. With bullets whizzing around him, Gwei Tsen Chi grabbed Shelton's rifle from its scabbard as Shelton's mule scrabbled by. Further up the trail, the robbers slowed the stampeding steeds and stole the remaining firearms from the saddles. Their mission complete, the brigands retreated.[13]

As his party crowded around him, Albert Shelton tried to rise from the road but fell back. The bullet had shattered his right elbow and entered his abdomen at a downward angle. The entrance wound in his elbow was the size of a nickel, but the bullet had smashed the bone, leaving a gaping exit wound. There was a massive hole in Shelton's abdomen where the deflected bullet entered. With the help of his compatriots, Shelton began to doctor himself. He compressed the wounds and swabbed them with iodine. After improvising a tourniquet made of a handkerchief tightened with his riding crop, he gave himself a shot of morphine and strychnine.[14] Shelton assured the men he was not badly hurt, but was afraid he couldn't ride all the way to Batang.

Gwei Tsen Chi raced off on his fast horse to alert Batang as the rest of the group tried to make the doctor comfortable with a bed made of saddle blankets. A little after four o'clock, Gwei Tsen Chi reached Batang and raised the alarm. Dr. William Hardy grabbed some dressings and rubber bandages and galloped off on Gwei Tsen Chi's horse. Roderick MacLeod followed on foot with a hospital bed and some bearers.

An hour later, when Hardy reached the group on the far side of Khuyuk La pass, Shelton was unconscious with no radial pulse. His friends were attempting to rig Shelton's cot into a stretcher. Hardy re-dressed the wounds and replaced the handkerchief tourniquet with a rubber one. Demnbajangtsen remembered, "It was found necessary to amputate Doctor's arm, which had been badly wounded. They stuffed in the guts which came out. I was extremely sad, a man who loved me as his own son, now I had to carry his amputated arm on the back of my horse."[15]

They loaded Shelton on the cot at about 6:00 o'clock and began the trek back to Batang. Now and again Shelton swam into consciousness, telling them he was feeling all right, then complaining of the pain and thirst. Near the top of the pass Shelton complained that the stretcher poles hurt his hips, so they rigged stout bamboo poles under the hospital bed and carried him into Batang. "Before we reached Batang," Hardy wrote, "more than 50 (probably 100) people met us, to help carry the stretcher or to light the way with pine torches." The procession reached Batang at 10:10 P.M. and proceeded to the Hardy house, where they placed Shelton in Hardy's ground-floor study.

Given Shelton's condition, Hardy could do nothing more than wash the wounds and change the dressings. Nina Hardy came down from the upstairs and asked Shelton if she could get him anything. He said, "No, Missus, you can't do anything."[16] About midnight the missionaries and Gezong Ongdu went upstairs, leaving Shelton in the care of the two medical assistants. Hardy told them to call him if Shelton moved. Not long after, Hardy heard Shelton telling the assistant to help him sit up: "I told him he must not think about sitting up. After a minute, he pointed to the stove in the corner of the room and asked if that was a peach tree over there. After that, he said no more and was dead in less than five minutes."[17]

Dr. Albert Shelton died at 12:48 A.M. on February 17, 1922.[18] Hardy reported in his postmortem that the musket ball had ranged across the abdomen and downward, perforating an intestine. He believed an internal hemorrhage of a large vessel of the liver caused Shelton's death.[19] A general practitioner, Dr. Hardy simply didn't have the surgical training or skills to perform an operation of that nature.

After Shelton died, Gezong Ongdu and one of his servants took their bedrolls and slept on the floor beside his deathbed until morning. Dr. Albert Shelton's friends kept repeating a Tibetan proverb, "A good man dies at the top of the pass with his boots on."[20]

The next day a crowd of Americans, British, French, Chinese, and Tibetans gathered in the mission yard for the funeral service. First, the foreigners held a service, and then the Chinese and Tibetans were allowed to join for another. Seven men took part in the ceremony, including Americans and Chinese, and a lone Tibetan, Gezong Ongdu, who read Tibetan scripture.

The missionaries buried Dr. Albert Shelton in the mission cemetery on the caravan trail leading west to Tibet. In a barren stretch of ground at the far edge of China, Albert Shelton lay next to his fallen comrade Dr. Zenas Loftis, both of them facing Lhasa.[21] In time, the missionaries found suitable stones at a ruined lamasery, and with the help of the Chinese military commander, brought them back to Batang. The missionaries arranged for the markers to be inscribed in English, Chinese, and Tibetan. Albert L. Shelton's name curved around the arched top that featured a Masonic symbol. The inscription read, "June 9, 1875- Feb. 17, 1922. Not to be ministered unto but to minister." Inscriptions in Chinese and Tibetan followed.[22]

Alone: Albert Shelton and His Family

On March 4, 1922, the United Christian Missionary Society headquarters in St. Louis received a postal telegram from Lijiang. Fifteen days south of Batang, it was the closest telegraph station. The telegram read, "ROBBERS KILLED SHELTON NEAR BATANG FEBY SEVENTEENTH NOTIFY GIRLS. HARDY."[23] Ever alert to the power of breaking news, the UCMS notified the United Press and Reuters, which sent the story out on the wire. In Pomona, word ricocheted around the town. The wire story was even posted on a bulletin board. However, the mission society failed to notify the Shelton family before beginning the media campaign.[24]

Learning of Shelton's death from a subsequent UCMS cable, four men from the Disciples church strode up the front walk of the Shelton house. When the family saw the men they thought there was something wrong with their mother.

Quickly they discovered the news. "Just a few curt lines on a cablegram sufficed to plunge a home into deepest mourning here yesterday," the *Pomona Progress* reported. The girls were inconsolable at first, especially Dorothy.[25] The church people did the best they could to soothe the family with rubs, hot drinks, and baths. Besides the distraught daughters, Albert Shelton's father was in precarious health. "Most of the time he shakes as in a nervous chill and can scarcely get food to his mouth," a Pomona Disciple worried.[26]

Flora was unaware of her husband's death for almost three weeks. Until she heard the news, she blithely wrote letters to him from Darjeeling as Albert Shelton lay cold in his grave.[27] Flora had persevered in her translation work in spite of her declining health and the inevitable frustrations of industrial work in a pre-industrial land. By late February she felt that the project was under control and she could go. She planned to leave Darjeeling on March 6. Her daughters worried she might miss the news of her husband's death before she sailed. But she was still in Darjeeling when the news came.

On April 8, 1922, Flora Shelton sailed from Bombay on the SS *Caledonia*, bound for England via the Suez Canal and the Mediterranean. S. J. Corey wrote to a colleague, "The missionaries from India write that Mrs. Shelton was stunned for many days after the news came and has been rather helpless."[28] The missionary society arranged for British missionaries to meet her in Britain and shepherd her to the next ship. On May 3 she left England on the SS *Olympic*, arriving a week later in New York, where UCMS officials met her ship. On May 17, 1922, three months after her husband's murder, Flora's daughters and friends met her at the railway station in Pomona. The Pomona *Bulletin* reported, "The meeting of Mrs. Shelton and her two daughters when they met the Santa Fe train was as affecting as the last time they had parted the husband and father had been with them and the joy of the mother's return was shadowed by the renewed grief at the thought of that other who is never to return."[29] Flora told her daughters, "I always knew that Dr. Shelton would give his life for Tibet but I never meant that he should be alone."[30]

The Most Useful of Men: Shelton's Murder and the Press

Fueled by the missionary society publicity, Shelton's murder ignited a flare of media attention. He was the UCMS poster boy, but if he wasn't going to get to Lhasa, he was still useful to the cause. The mission society trumpeted his martyrdom and asked for support to memorialize him. With purple prose that would have done Edgar Rice Burroughs proud, one press release sensationalized his drive to return to Tibet. "He was urged to tarry longer in America and secure more complete rest before returning, but the missionary fires burned deeply in his soul and he felt he must go back to his people and his task. He was always talking about his Tibetans and was restless to be among them again."[31]

The New York papers immediately picked up the story. The *New York Times* carried an article on the front page March 6, 1922, blaring, "Dr. Shelton Slain by Chinese Bandits." The story related Shelton's kidnapping and his work in west China. The subtitle read, "American Was First Christian Missionary to Be Allowed to Enter Tibet."[32] The *New York American, New York Tribune,* and *New York World* ran stories as well, with the *World* waxing melodramatic: "The mountain passes of Thibet, where death has come to many missionaries and scientists, were the scene of another such tragedy on February 17, when Dr. Albert Le Roy Shelton, an American medical missionary, was slain by robbers, according to advices received here yesterday." The article noted, "In addition to being one of the best known men in the foreign missionary service, it was said, Dr. Shelton was also a collector of art and curios, and pieces gathered by him are to be seen at the American Museum of Natural History in this city and elsewhere."[33]

As testimony to the UCMS's efficiency, the *China Press* also had the story on March 5. Another China newspaper, the *Evening Star,* noted, "He was entertained at the home of John D. Rockefeller Jr., in New York, and later addressed the National Geographic Society in Washington."[34]

Locales familiar with Dr. Albert Shelton soon picked up the story, each claiming him as a native son. Terming him to be an "Indianapolis missionary," the *Indianapolis Star* ran a story and photograph on the front page, with other related stories on the inside.[35] The *Anthony Republican* headlined the story, noting, "Dr. Shelton had had many narrow escapes in his missionary work in China and had often stated that he expected to 'leave his bones in China.'"[36] Kansas State Normal's State *Normal Bulletin* and Kentucky University's *Crimson Rambler* both covered his life and murder. Covering the story as a local tragedy, the Pomona papers headlined the news in bold black type.

With easy access to the UCMS files and press agents, the *St. Louis Post-Dispatch* ran a story that sprawled across the front page and into interior pages with a collage of adventure-soaked Shelton photos. The story led, "The epic of Dr. Albert Leroy Shelton whose adventurous career as a medical missionary in Tibet has been likened to Dr. David Livingstone in Central Africa a half a century ago, has ended as he was preparing to write its glowing climax."[37]

The *West China Missionary News* confirmed Shelton's death, writing, "He was well known all through the border land as a man of energy, courage, resource and strong believer in practical religion."[38] The *Illustrated London News* added to Shelton's international fame when it ran lengthy features on Shelton and his photography for two weeks in September.[39]

The Newark newspapers headlined Shelton's museum connection when they reported his death. The *Call* subhead read, "Newark Museum Thibetan Exhibit Collector Slain While on Trip to L'hasa."[40] A second *New York World* article focused on the Newark's Tibetan collection: "Newark will probably grieve more than any other community over the death of Dr. Alfred Le Roy Shelton. . . . It was through his interest that the Newark Museum Association acquired a collection of Thibetan objects that is probably more representative of the customs and culture of that land than was ever brought together elsewhere and the value of which is enhanced by the descriptions and explanations of the objects."[41]

With Flora Shelton still in Darjeeling, Shelton's American agent O. A. Rosboro received many condolences. J. O. LaGorce at the National Geographic Society wrote, "I have never met or known a man for whom I had more respect and admiration, or one who I thought in his chosen field was doing a finer and more disinterested work for humanity." F. L. Fisher of the *National Geographic* wrote, "In my opinion, Dr. Shelton was one of the most useful of men. . . . He is as much a hero as any soldier who died on the battlefield."[42]

Shelton's legacy was the coin of the realm in terms of publicity and reflected power for both men and institutions associated with Shelton. Rosboro wrote LaGorce in early May, "As a result of Dr. Shelton's untimely death in Tibet, there is a very widespread interest in missionary work among our particular denomination, and also among others interested in missionary work generally." O. A. Rosboro was overwhelmed with orders for Shelton's photographs.[43] Frederick Smith, the Chicago newspaperman who had chronicled Shelton's kidnapping, announced his intent to write a book on Shelton. The UCMS looked askance at the idea after Rosboro complained he was strictly mercenary and "has the newspaper correspondent's ailment of distorting facts."[44]

Letters, cables, and contributions began pouring in to the UCMS, and tribute services began almost immediately.[45] Abe Cory led services in New York's Central Christian Church on Thirty-first Street on Sunday, March 6. In St. Louis, the Union Avenue Christian Church featured UCMS president F. W. Burnham as a speaker. Reverend S. G. Buckner dispensed with his normal sermon at the First Christian Church in Pomona to honor Dr. Albert Shelton.[46] Disciples of Christ organizations around the world began passing resolutions lauding the sacrifice of Dr. Shelton, from the Campbell Club of Yale University to congregations in Athens, Alabama and Unley, South Australia. The missionary society immediately proposed churches honor Shelton with a massive fundraising effort. Telegrams to the churches poured out of UCMS headquarters announcing the nationwide campaign.

The response was gratifying. As Flora was still trying to make her way home to Pomona, thousands of Christians filed into their pews across America and opened their pocketbooks. In St. Louis, the Reverend C. C. Crawford thundered from the pulpit,

"I do not consider Dr. Shelton second to works of Dr. Livingstone. I think he was the equal of Livingstone. What Livingstone did for darkest Africa, Shelton did for Tibet."[47]

A Sincere Solicitude: American and Chinese Investigations

U.S. Minister to China Schurman relayed the report of Shelton's death to Washington on March 4, and warned of diplomatic repercussions relating to "the possible failure of provincial authorities to afford proper protection to foreign residents until facts and delinquencies of local officials are more clearly ascertained." Chinese officials in Sichuan scuttled for cover. Ch'en Tung Chi, the commissioner for foreign affairs in Chongqing, cited a 1919 memo to the American consulate that instructed the foreign consuls to stop issuing passports to the Sichuan borderlands. Ch'en blustered:

> With regard to the recent murder of Dr. A. L. Shelton by bandits, this office has no way to find out whether he had obtained permission from the Chinese officials, whether a huchao [travel permit] was issued to him and whether he had requested some soldiers to escort him upon his departure. In case he was urged to refrain from proceeding to that region and no permission was obtained beforehand then the Chinese officials cannot, of course, bear the responsibility, but in compliance with your request, I will ask the Generalissimo to issue a telegraphic instruction to the local officials to investigate into this matter.[48]

The vice-consul in Chongqing, N. F. Allman, did not "absolve the Chinese Authorities from the responsibility for the protection of the lives of American citizens from robbers in Szechuan."[49] Allman petitioned the American Legation in Beijing for permission to travel to Batang to investigate, but Schurman refused to allow passage.[50]

On March 18, 1922, Minister Schurman wired to the State Department the Chinese report from the Sichuan military commander-in-chief and the frontier commissioner, "Troops sent to locality to offer rewards and take most stringent measures apprehension of murderers for punishment."[51] Conveying "a sincere solicitude for the lives of foreign persons," Chinese Minister of Foreign Affairs W. W. Yen reiterated that the Sichuan border regions were dangerous and travel by foreigners was suspended.[52] "This is on record," Yen wrote. He went on to state, "At the present time the bandit activities in that region are still dangerous and foreigners traveling in Szechuan unavoidably incur danger." Liu requested that the foreign ministers prohibit further travel by their nationals in the frontier regions.[53]

Schurman responded to W. W. Yen on June 17, 1922, noting that there were twenty-two American missionaries in Kham: "The missionaries are residing at these places in accordance with rights conferred by treaty . . . I must therefore insist that the authorities of the region assume full responsibility to the protection of the American lives and property involved."[54] Four days later Yen replied tersely: "As regards those missionaries who already reside there it is, of course, necessary that the local authorities should exert their utmost efforts to protect them according to treaty."[55] International newspapers quickly picked up the diplomatic snit. The *Times of London* reported that the Chinese authorities stated that Shelton declined to "follow the advice of the local authorities against proceeding into the disturbed area," as did the *New York Times.* [56]

To a certain extent, the Chinese were correct. Even two years before during Shelton's kidnapping, Colonel Drysdale stated that the Chinese commissioner for foreign affairs in Chengdu requested the American consul suspend issuance of passports to the borderlands of Tibet, "owing to the large no. of bandits."[57] The disorder was not without implications for foreigners. Several Americans and other foreigners were held up and robbed by bandits during 1921, and it was a frequent occurrence for foreign cargoes to be robbed. Armed robbers entered a number of foreign houses across the province.

When news of the diplomatic exchanges following Shelton's death reached America, James Ogden spoke to a reporter, who wrote: "Ogden doubts that the Chinese commander of Batang gave Dr. Shelton any special warning against the journey. The conditions were no different along the route than those that have persisted for the last 15 years." Ogden contended that the Chinese escorts may actually have attracted the attack as the bandits often sought the arms and ammunition carried by the soldiers. He scoffed at the idea that the Chinese would pursue the killers: "The Chinese soldiery does not venture often beyond the walls of their garrisons. They spend their efforts resisting attacks from without. If the murderers are caught, it will be by other bands of robbers, many of whom have been faithful friends of the mission."[58]

Who Killed Dr. Shelton?

Who killed Albert Shelton, and why? A number of theories sprang up in the mission field and the borderlands. As Shelton was the only casualty in the attack, many initially suspected the shooting was premeditated and the robbery merely a cover-up. "It still seems strange that he alone was the target, and no one else harmed in the least," Explorer-professor J. W. Gregory wrote after inquiring into the murder during an expedition to the marches just after Shelton's death.[59]

Some missionaries thought the killing related to the opium suppression campaign Shelton had waged prior to his furlough, and the killing was an assassination done at the order of corrupt Chinese officials.[60] Other observers contended that eastern Tibetan lamas, angered by the links Shelton was forging with the Dalai Lama, were behind the murder. The Pomona *Bulletin* lambasted the Khampa monks: "What strange rites of priestcraft are performed or barbarous practices are also mysteries. Its lamas are noted for their fierceness and intolerance, and hence it is within the bounds of possibility that Dr. Shelton was slain by them."[61]

Dorris had several theories. She contended the killing had to have taken place more than ten days' journey from Batang, "since in the surrounding country he is well known." As did the *Chinese Recorder*, Dorris Shelton stated that members of Yang's old gang from Yunnan might have done it, or her father may have died defending a village from brigands.[62]

In Indianapolis, where he was teaching Tibetan language, James Ogden was interviewed: "'I am positive,' said Mr. Ogden, 'that Dr. Shelton was not slain deliberately. The people loved him too much for that. Even the bandits loved him, some of them had sworn to protect him. Not one of them would harm him intentionally. He must have been killed accidentally in a fight between soldiers and robbers.'"[63] Virulent anti-Tibetan CIM missionary James Edgar blamed the Hsiang-ch'eng tribesmen for the murder. Edgar claimed it was be suicidal for Western missionaries to work in the Hsiang-ch'eng-controlled territory, as the tribesmen were unrelenting in their hostility.[64]

A number of missionaries focused their greatest suspicions on the British, contending they were behind the shooting to eliminate an interloper in their arena. Flora, in particular, blamed the British for her husband's death, publicly writing, "The mystery is the order to turn back from the governor of Kham, a man who has been his friend over a period of years and such an order had never been heard before."[65] In private correspondence, she was more forthright in her assertions that the British were behind her husband's murder.[66] She wrote Berthold Laufer, blaming the British, "They did not like the friendship, love & medical work that was going from America & so this was the manner to stop it."[67]

Once back in Pomona and working on her new book, *Shelton of Tibet*, Flora baldly stated her opinion that the British had arranged for the assassination of her husband by Tibetan proxies. It caused considerable stir and throat-clearing among the publishers and the missionary society. After reviewing the galley proofs of Flora's book in March 1923, Corey wrote to James Ogden at the College of Missions. "I am especially anxious about the reference she makes to British interference. Perhaps she has to put it in a way that will not cause embarrassment but I doubt it."[68]

In spite of the editors' efforts, Flora's theories of the killing crept into *Shelton of Tibet:* "Tibet is kept sealed for diplomatic reasons. . . . China opened the door on the eastern side and gave the opportunity. Dr. Shelton saw it and took it. Is the door closed again?" She concluded her description of her husband's death by writing suggestively, "What happened was not the Tibetans' fault entirely, nor wholly the fault of the Chinese, that I well know."[69]

The British in India clearly pursued a policy of barring missionaries from Tibet. Indeed, from the earliest days of the East India Company, the British officials feared the upheaval among the local Hindus and Muslims from proselytizing missionaries. "The sending out of missionaries into our Eastern possessions is the maddest, most extravagant, most costly, most indefensible project that has ever been suggested by a moonstruck fanatic," one British East India official blustered.[70] While the missionaries insinuated and muscled their way into India, the British India authorities attempted, through the Great Game era and beyond, to keep missionaries out of the sensitive Tibetan regions.[71]

The British authorities in India and China also hastened to investigate Shelton's death. Louis King heard about the murder on March 9 when a runner sent by MacLeod arrived in Tachienlu. King summarized MacLeod's and Hardy's reports for his superiors in Beijing and New Delhi and noted that Hardy blamed the Chinese officials for failing to provide adequate security. After observing that he and the previous Tachienlu Consuls, Coales and Teichman, had reported the unsafe conditions around Batang, King stated, "The Chinese authorities have of course all along been perfectly aware of the dangerous state of affairs obtaining in that region for years past, and their responsibility for the present tragedy cannot be gainsaid."[72]

In late April 1922, British Legation Minister Alston in Beijing wrote to Lord Curzon in India about Shelton's murder and the larger question of Christian missionaries journeying into Tibet. Begging a response to his earlier inquiries about missionary entry into Tibet, Alston enclosed King's report. Alston wrote: "It will be noted that Dr. Shelton, the American missionary doctor at Batang, was in the course of preparations for a journey to Lhasa by direct negotiation with the Tibetan frontier authorities when he met his death. While the murderers were in all probability brigands of Tibetan race, it must be understood that the murder took place in Chinese controlled territory within a few miles of the principal Chinese centre on the frontier, and that the responsibility for the tragedy must rest entirely with the Chinese authorities and the Chinese Government."[73]

British Major F. M. Bailey, the political officer in Sikkim, asked the prime minister of Tibet, Lonchen Shokang, to find out the circumstances of Shelton's death. The Prime Minister in turn ordered the Kalon Lama to inquire into the killing. Before he could investigate, the Kalon Lama died, but the acting commissioner of Eastern Tibet, Kenchung, obtained information from the Tibetan leaders in the Markham district of southern Kham. Kenchung's report read: " . . . it was admitted unquestionably that Dr. Shelton was murdered by brigands from De-ge, Mo-shog and Batang, which are in Chinese territory. . . . Originally the murderers would have been Tibetans and the place of occurrence would have been in Tibet, but the Chinese have taken possession of these places by force and they are no longer under the control of the Tibetans."[74]

While the British continued their long-standing policy of discouraging missionary travel to Tibet, there was no evidence that the British sponsored or encouraged the assassination of Dr. Albert Shelton, or any other missionary, to prevent the evangelization of Tibet. For the most part, there was no need. The British had excellent intelligence on the Indian side of Tibet and easily discouraged entry of unauthorized travelers. On the Chinese side, the Tibetans were happy to prevent troublesome visits by itinerating Christian missionaries, blaming the British if the situation required. If for no other reason, the British authorities would not have assassinated Shelton because the uproar from mission supporters in Britain would have destabilized the home government.

The Batang missionaries eventually decided a band of brigands from the wild Seven Tribes of the Sangen region were responsible for Shelton's murder. Shelton was just another unfortunate victim of the most robber-plagued stretch of trail between Batang and Yunnanfu.[75] Gertrude Morse wrote that the bandits were members of a small tribe of Kemo people, a group the missionaries sometimes hired as guards, both to strengthen the caravans and preempt the tribesmen as brigands. After an earlier alliance, the Kemo had offended the powerful Hsiang-ch'eng tribe in some way, provoking its men into independent brigandage.[76] According to reports, the tribesmen had seen Shelton pass through the day prior and recognized him as a protected foreigner. When he unexpectedly rode back east the next day, the bandits thought it was another caravan.[77] By 1924 even Flora appeared to have discarded her conspiracy theory, telling colleagues the murder was simply due to a random shot in ordinary brigandage.[78]

Following the diplomatic unpleasantness between China and the United States, the new Chinese military commander in Batang made a concerted effort to stamp out banditry along the dangerous trail where Shelton was ambushed. S. J. Corey wrote Flora Shelton, "During the last several months about a half dozen Tibetans reputed to be robbers have been executed, and he seems to be really trying to get the man who killed Dr. Shelton." The commander talked of building a fort on Khuyuk La pass.

China Bones and Tibetan Wonder

With his adventurer heart and missionary soul, Albert Shelton operated on the cusp between confidence and hubris. He knew the risks of the trail to Gartok. He knew the Chinese authorities could not and would not protect him. Did Albert Shelton have a death wish? A deep-seated longing to sanctify his life by "leaving his bones in China"? Though he repeatedly glorified martyrdom, the truth can never be known. Did he wholly and deeply yearn to profess the Gospel in Lhasa? That, at least, was certain.

But now that he was dead, who was going to carry on the work into Tibet? Nina Hardy wrote, "There is no one as we see, to take Dr. Shelton's place in the mission, and the carrying the Gospel into Tibet must wait, (God must not be ready to open Tibet.) Three times Dr. Shelton tried to get into the interior and couldn't. The first time he got as far as Derge, when he was called back by Mrs. Baker's illness. The second time he was captured by the Chinese bandits, and the third time Tibetan robbers took his life."[79]

Shelton's death demoralized even the UCMS officials, who felt that his murder thwarted their great push to Lhasa. S. J. Corey wrote Rosboro six months after Shelton's death, "The British are in control in Lhasa in quite a strong way and there would probably be opposition to starting a hospital there."[80] The next spring Corey dispiritedly wrote to Flora Shelton. "How long," he wrote, "before missionaries will be allowed there we wonder."[81]

THE LEGACY OF
DR. ALBERT SHELTON

Our place in life has been determined beforehand, but our clean deeds are the product of our own hands.[1]

—Tibetan Proverb

In the fall of 1999, I was on a rattletrap Chinese bus jouncing down the Jung Lam toward Batang. Like most journeys through Kham, my research trip was punctuated with landslides, horrendous roads, tetchy Chinese officials, breakdowns of a dozen stripes, and a constant threat of bandits. The Khampa passengers crammed on board were getting nervous as we approached an area notorious for ambushes. I was, too, as my research notes and film were in my grungy backpack. I asked my Khampa guide, Kalsang Anyetsang, if I could negotiate with the robbers to keep my research material.

He glanced at me and turned to speak in Tibetan to our bus mates. Soon they were all rollicking with laughter. "No!" Kalsang laughed. "We get robbed, bandits take everything—our bags, clothes, everything." At least my naiveté broke the tension.

But we never did get robbed, and eventually rolled down the mountain switchbacks into the Batang valley, where I hoped to discover the Tibetan legacy of Dr. Shelton.

Shelton's legacy in the United States was secure, though a touch dimmed with the passing of time. In the aftermath of his death, the Disciples of Christ elevated him to near mythic status. "He belongs to a kingdom without frontiers," one Disciples official said.[2] Impassioned contributors made the Shelton Memorial

Fund one of the denomination's largest endowments, a status it held for most of the twentieth century.[3] Inspired by Shelton, scores of young people volunteered for life service in the missions—twenty-eight in Enid, Oklahoma alone. The congregation in his old hometown of Ulysses, Kansas dedicated their church to "the memory of the divine Christian, Dr. Shelton."[4] The denomination invoked him as a model for Sunday school classes, and lauded his "Christ-like ministry" in their appeals.[5] A play about Shelton was published and performed, and his adventures depicted in *Missionary Hero Stores*.[6] Through the decades, the denomination continued to hold Shelton in high regard, and sermonizing ministers still evoke his memory.

The unexpected connection between Indiana and Tibet that began with the Disciples of Christ missionaries and the College of Missions has flourished.[7] A World War II need for central Asian language specialists precipitated the emergence of Indiana University's now-famous Tibetan Studies Department at the Bloomington campus. Thubten Norbu, incarnate lama and the former abbot of Tibet's largest monastery, Kumbum, arrived to teach in 1965. Norbu (also known as Takster Rimpoche) was also the oldest brother of the Dalai Lama. His presence in the town attracted a steady stream of Tibetans. Today Bloomington is home to a sprawling Tibetan Cultural Center, two Tibetan Buddhist monasteries, three Tibetan restaurants, a number of Hoosier-Tibetan families, and an enthusiastic group of Tibet supporters. The Dalai Lama's autumn 2003 visit to Indiana was his fourth trip, underscoring a wholly counter-intuitive relationship that is more than a century old.[8]

The chance encounter between Shelton and the Newark Museum's Edward C. Crane on a Pacific liner in 1910 eventually contributed to Shelton's enduring renown. Thanks to his collection at the Newark Museum, Dr. Albert Shelton remained a well-known name among scholars and academics specializing in Tibet. The museum had augmented Shelton's acquisitions with additional collections from missionaries to eastern Tibet and a wide range of explorers and collectors to form the world's most comprehensive collection of Tibetan sacred and secular material. During the decades after the Communist Revolution, when China and Tibet were closed, the Newark Museum's extraordinary Tibetan Collection remained accessible to scholars. By enlisting scholars from the Tibetan community in exile, the institution also became a leader in culturally sensitive museum practice. Beginning in the 1970s, revered incarnate lamas, such as the fourteenth Dalai Lama and the head of the Kagyu order, the sixteenth Gyalwa Karmapa, came to Newark to view the collection, perform ceremonies, and deliver addresses.[9]

The Newark Museum also maintained a long relationship with the Shelton family. Flora Shelton lived in Pomona for many years, where she raised her two daughters. She lived a modestly comfortable life, helped with insurance money, pensions, royalties, and the property the couple had acquired. However, her decades-long efforts to claim an indemnity from the Chinese government for her husband's murder came to nothing.

Flora never flagged in her work on Tibet. Decades after Albert's death she was still at it, seeking publishers for her Tibetan stories; submitting hundreds of pages of English-Tibetan translations to biblical phrases to the Disciples of Christ; querying author James Hilton about the origins of his "Shangri-La" tale; railing about the Chinese Communist takeover of Tibet.[10] "How grieved I am that the abominable Reds are going to take over that little country, how cruel they will be to them & loot them of all their treasures."[11] Later in life, Flora joined her daughter, Dorris, in Scottsdale, Arizona, where she continued to lecture on Tibet. Flora Shelton died on April 5, 1966, at the ripe old age of 94.

Dorris and Dorothy quickly segued into American life after their return from Tibet, sporting bobbed and permed hairdos for their Pomona High School yearbook photos. They attended the First Christian Church, and Dorris was a frequent speaker on Tibet at church conventions. Mission supporters paid for their college educations.

Long after they married, both Shelton daughters maintained connections to their Tibetan childhoods. Dorris wrote two books on her Tibetan experiences, and edited a book of Tibetan chants that her mother had translated. In the 1970s Dorris traveled to Dharamsala, India with her doctor husband, where they met with the fourteenth Dalai Lama.

Dorothy became a high school teacher. Though more reticent than her sister about her Tibetan past, Dorothy was in attendance at the Newark Museum's "Night in Old Lhasa" celebration in 1987, where she hobnobbed with celebrities such as Richard Gere and Brooke Shields. Dorothy died on May 4, 1991, while residing at a retirement home for foreign missionaries near Pomona. She was eighty-four. Dorris Shelton Still died on April 29, 1997 at ninety-three years of age.

It was dense black night when Kalsang and I finally rolled into the town of Batang. A kindly Khampa father and son named Lobsang befriended us on the bus and invited us to stay at their home in Batang. Kalsang had told them of my quest to find Dr. Shelton's heritage in Tibet. I had heard there was little left of the Batang mission, and even Shelton's gravestone had disappeared in the chaos of the Cultural Revolution. They promised to try to find someone to help.

The Tibetan Christian Mission fell on hard times in the years after Dr. Shelton's murder. Warfare continued to wrack Batang, as the Chinese and Tibetans fought for control of the town. For four years Hsiang-ch'ang forces led by the rebel Rana Lama ravaged the countryside around Batang, and launched attacks against the town. Banditry was rife. While the Tibetans gave the missionaries a degree of immunity, the anarchy isolated the missionaries in their compound.[12]

The missionaries were further isolated by the death of a number of Tibetans who had been allies of the mission. In the summer prior to Shelton's death, the king of Chala died while trying to escape Chinese captivity. The Kalon Lama unexpectedly died the summer following.[13] In 1923, the Jo Lama died from drinking too much Chinese wine.[14]

Internal discord rent the mission. A large group of new missionaries had arrived in 1923. From the beginning there was intense disharmony. Without Shelton as the mutually agreed-upon leader, the mission dissolved into acrimony. By 1926, a number of the restive missionaries had resigned to either return to America or form independent missions elsewhere. The group was further roiled by allegations of immorality, as a married missionary had an illegitimate baby with a missionary daughter. At least one Tibetan-American baby was born.[15] In spite of the conflicts and continuing warfare, the missionaries soldiered on through the rest of the 1920s. They lost two good friends in 1929, when Gezong Ongdu died in Batang and James Ogden died in Hollywood, California.[16] The cause of Ogden's death was listed as "chronic malaria & mental & physical breakdown, suicide."[17]

By 1931, the mission's situation was desperate. The Great Depression had devastated mission fundraising in America, and as part of a dramatic retrenchment, the United Christian Missionary Society decided to close the remote, troubled Batang mission. The Tibetan Christian Mission missionaries mounted a vociferous defense, but the reality was clear—they needed to prepare for their departure.[18] They decided to turn the mission property over to the local congregation when they left. But as the missionaries packed for their retreat, war invaded Batang.

On the night of May 21, 1932, the Tibetans attacked. The Chinese stationed men in the mission hospital and school, and the Tibetans fired from the washhouse and garden walls through most of the next day. Late in the day, the Chinese made an attack on the Tibetan positions and routed them. But on June 12, the Tibetans returned in force, occupying the mission orphanage and the missionary residences, including the Sheltons' old house. From there, they bombarded the Chinese-occupied hospital. With the fighting going on in the midst of the mission compound, the TCM workers moved across the river to the old mill house, where they barricaded themselves in the bricked-up basement with an American flag fluttering on the roof. When the Tibetans finally withdrew, the compound was in shambles—trees dead, houses pillaged and destroyed. Minnie

Ogden wrote, "the poor old hospital was found a standing wreck, even worse than the dwellings."[19] The mission was finished.

On August 22, 1932, after twenty-eight years of evangelism on the Tibetan frontier, the TCM turned the mission over to the small Batang congregation of sixteen, led by Li Gway Gwang.[20] The missionaries plodded home. Some went south through Yunnan, others traveled east along the Jung Lam, negotiating their way through Nationalist and Communist lines in Sichuan during a Long March battle.

The morning after we arrived in Batang, I came down to the sunny Lobsang kitchen for breakfast. The place was astir with the extended family churning yak-butter tea and making morning *momos,* the filled dumplings that are a Tibetan specialty. A squadron of unidentified people filed in and out of the kitchen to inspect the new folks. A solid man with a finely woven straw fedora and a pale purple jacket sat at one of the benches, drinking tea and quietly talking to Kalsang. After what seemed to be an eternity of yak-butter tea-drinking, I asked if we might see about finding that person who could show us the mission site. Kalsang pointed to the man across from me.

He was a local historian who had rescued Shelton's gravestone after it was destroyed during the upheaval of the Red Guards in the 1980s. "You are lucky man. Gravestone is at my home," Kalsang translated for him. It was leaning against the side of his house. "I thought people would come some day," he said. In fear of repercussions, he refused to give his name, but did agree to show me the site of Shelton's old mission.

We puttered though the terra cotta- and pumpkin-colored adobe town in a three-wheeled motorcycle taxi. Batang was a clean town, a far cry from many of the seedy border towns that Kalsang and I went through in our circuitous route through Kham. The old mission site overlooked the town. The historian pointed to a cornfield where the hospital once stood. One earthen wall in the front yard of a worker compound was all that remained of the Sheltons' house. I noticed the orchards of old apple trees that covered the hillside, and asked the historian if the missionaries planted them. "Yeshu" [Jesus] apples, he called them. Thanks in part to the missionaries' Midwestern trees, Batang was Tibet's fruit center.

We were standing at the main intersection of Batang when it struck me that I could interview Shelton's old friend, the Ba Lama. Now, given that Shelton died in 1922, this would make the Ba Lama about 117 years old. I figured I couldn't talk to that Ba Lama, but I could interview his *reincarnation* about Dr. Shelton. When I asked if there was a Ba Lama in town, the historian walked over to a young moon-faced lama who was on the opposite corner. It was Danduna, the secretary to the Ba Lama. The historian explained my quest to him, pointing to the mission hill. As the historian talked, I heard the word, "Yeshu." Danduna looked at me and smiled, "Oh," he said, "Dok-tor Shel-tan. Ba Lama and Dok-tor Shel-tan," and he linked a finger of each hand.

The Ba Lama was an old old man, with a thick underslung lower lip and large ears that lay close to his grizzled shaven head. He was big-boned with thick hands. His shoulders were still muscular above his saffron and red Buddhist robes. Considered the reincarnation of a great Buddhist teacher, a *rimpoche,* he sat in a lotus position on a platform above us, the very picture of ancient concentrated wisdom. A small Lhasa Apso dog lay tucked beside him.

Danduna told us that the Ba Lama had gone with the guerrillas into the mountains when the Khampas had revolted against the Chinese Communist rule in the 1950s. The Chinese eventually wounded and captured him, and he spent many years in labor camps and on penal road crews.[21] Through the intermediaries of Danduna and Kalsang, the Ba Lama recounted the terror of Chao Erh-feng early in the twentieth century. "Many monks killed," he said with chopping motion to neck. "Many soldiers come. Monasteries burned. Monks no head. Monasteries all destroyed."

Then I asked the question I had come around the world to ask: What did he think of Dr. Shelton and his work? The question passed from Kalsang to Danduna and on to the Ba Lama. I waited. Then Kalsang translated the answer. "Rimpoche thinks he was a good man. Helped poor people, helped children. Feed, clothes, teach English. Helped. He was good man."[22]

NOTES

Prologue

1. Dorris Shelton Still, *Beyond the Devils in the Wind* (Tempe, Arizona: Synergy Books, 1989), 7.
2. This account of Dr. Shelton's ride between Batang and the Tibetan border utilizes material from the following sources: Still, *Beyond the Devils in the Wind,* 108–110; Flora B. Shelton, *Shelton of Tibet* (New York: George Doran, 1923), 256; Valrae Reynolds and Barbara Reynolds, *The Museum New Series* (Newark, New Jersey: Newark Museum, 1972), 42–48; February 17, 1922 William Hardy letter to Stephen J. Corey, Albert Shelton Files, 1918–1928 Missionary Correspondence, Disciples of Christ Historical Society, Nashville, Tennessee.
3. Eric Teichman, *Travels of a Consular Officer in Eastern Tibet* (Cambridge, England: Cambridge University Press, 1921), v.
4. Albert L. Shelton, *Pioneering in Tibet: A Personal Record of Life and Experience in Mission Fields* (New York: F. H. Revell Company, 1921). Albert L. Shelton, "Life Among the People of Eastern Tibet," *National Geographic* (Sept. 1921): 293–326.

Chapter 1

1. Jeanette Covert Nolan, *Hoosier City: The Story of Indianapolis* (New York: Messner, 1943), 213. Hoosier poet James Whitcomb Riley was writing in 1879.
2. "Who's Who in Our Missionaries," questionnaire, filled out by Dr. Albert Shelton, files of Disciples of Christ Overseas Ministries Office, Indianapolis, Indiana; Summary of Indianapolis City Directories at the Indiana State Library and the Indiana Historical Society noted a J. O. Shelton, carpenter, at 172 Eddy in 1873; a Joseph O., laborer, at 573 S. Illinois, in 1874; no Joseph or J. O. Shelton in 1875; two J. O. Sheltons, carpenters, in 1876, one at 43 Bates St., one at the northeast corner of Wilkens and Maple; none in 1877 or 1878; and a J. O. Shelton, laborer, at 113 Elm in 1879. The 1880 and 1881 Indianapolis City Directories listed no Joseph or J. O. Shelton in 1880 or 1881. All addresses are in the southside working class districts. The directories listed information collected in the year prior to publication, so the 1875 directory, for example, is listing residence in 1874.

    Joseph O. Shelton's listing as both carpenter and laborer indicated a set of skills that were not that of a fine carpenter or cabinetmaker, but rather that of a common construction carpenter, suitable for simple construction. Robert G. Barrows noted the 1870s distinctions between skilled and unskilled labor in Robert G. Barrows, *A Demographic Analysis of Indianapolis, 1870–1920* (Bloomington, Indiana: Unpublished dissertation, Indiana University, 1977), 305, and discussed on page 245 migrations up and down the occupational ladder.
3. Barrows, *A Demographic Analysis of Indianapolis, 1870–1920,* 49, noted population increased 55.6 percent in the decade from 1870 to 1880. David Bodenhamer, *Encyclopedia*

of Indianapolis (Bloomington, Indiana: Indiana University Press, 1994) noted the 1880 census' 1880 enumeration of 75,000 people in Indianapolis made it the twenty-fourth largest city in the country. William J. Doherty, *Indianapolis in the 1870s: Hard Times in the Gilded Age* (Bloomington, Indiana: Unpublished Dissertation, Indiana University, 1981), 196, estimates an 1877 population of nearly 67,000. *Illustrated Historical Atlas of the State of Indiana* (Chicago: Baskin, Forster, & Company, 1876, reprinted Indianapolis, Indiana: Indiana Historical Society, 1968); and a map found in H. R. Holloway, *Indianapolis: Railroad City* (Indianapolis, Indiana: Indianapolis Journal Print, 1870), provided housing and development overviews. The population of the United States in 1875 was 45,073,000 according to U.S. Bureau of Census, *The Historical Statistics of the United States*, 2 vols. (Washington, D.C.: U.S. Department of Commerce, Bureau of Census, 1975), vol. 1.

4. James Greene, *The Personal Diary of James Greene: A Record of Life in Indianapolis, Indiana during 1875* (Manuscripts Collection, Indiana Division, Indiana State Library, Indianapolis, Indiana).

5. Doherty, *Indianapolis in the 1870s*, 36.

6. Eli Lilly, ed., *Schliemann in Indianapolis* (Indianapolis, Indiana: Indiana Historical Society, 1961), 6, 25. Lilly termed Schliemann's wife, "a stubborn, ferociously frigid person who never gave him any affection and scant attention." Indiana at the time had the most liberal divorce laws in the Union, or the Western world, for that matter. Indiana courts could award a divorce for any cause "the court shall deem proper." An Indianapolis *Journal* editor complained in 1858 that "we are overrun by a flock of illused, and illusing, petulant, libidinous, extravagant, illfitting husbands and wives as a sink is overrun with the foul water of a whole house." Quoted in Doherty, *Indianapolis in the 1870s*, 46.

7. James H. Madison, *The Indiana Way: A State History* (Bloomington, Indiana: Indiana University Press, 1986), 151, 157. Madison noted, "Nothing destroyed pioneer life so thoroughly as the railroad; nothing more deserved recognition as the symbol of late nineteenth century progress and change."

8. *Encyclopedia of Indianapolis*, 368; Doherty, *Indianapolis in the 1870s*, 102.

9. James Bartlow Martin, *Indiana, An Interpretation* (New York: Alfred A. Knopf, 1947), 67; Emma Lou Thornbrough, *Indiana in the Civil War Era, 1850–1880* (Indianapolis, Indiana: Indiana Historical Bureau), 314, noted that through the Grange embattled farmers petitioned the state legislature from 1875 to 1877 to fix the legal rate of interest at 6 percent, as they were being charged 10 and 12 percent, which was "absolutely eating up the laboring and business men, and paralyzing every branch of industry through the land." For the first time, farmers ceased to be the most numerous occupational category, outnumbered by other workers in manufacturing, trade, transportation, and services. The modern rise of the urban proletarian working class began here. See Miller, Nugent, and Morgan, *1876*, 38.

10. James J. Divita, *Ethnic Settlement Patterns in Indianapolis* (Indianapolis, Indiana: Marian College, 1988), 20–25. In 1880, a generation after most of the German immigration, foreign-born Germans still outnumbered Kentucky-born residents such as J. O. Shelton: 14 percent German to 8 percent Kentuckian. *Encyclopedia of Indianapolis*, 53. Barrows, *A Demographic Analysis of Indianapolis, 1870–1920*, 139, noted 59 percent of the Germans were petty proprietors or skilled laborers in 1871, rising to 68 percent in 1880, while 38 percent of the Irish were in these two categories in 1871, rising to 41 percent by 1889.

11. Eva Draegert, *Indianapolis: The Culture of an Inland City* (Bloomington, Indiana: Unpublished Dissertation, Indiana University, 1952), 48.

12. Doherty, *Indianapolis in the 1870s*, 61–100; *Encyclopedia of Indianapolis*, 104, 203, 219, 352, 368, 392, 394, 888, 894, 1095.

13. *WPA Index to Morgan County Marriage Records, 1850–1920.* The 1880 census for Pawnee Township, Bourbon County, Kansas lists thirty-two-year-old Joseph O. Shelton, born in Kentucky; twenty-four-year-old Emma R. Shelton, born in Indiana. Barrows, *A Demographic Analysis of Indianapolis, 1870–1920,* 109, discussed the population surge to the cities rivaled the migration to the West. "Rural-urban migration increased as towns replaced 160 acres as symbols of a better future. City to city migration was also a common phenomenon."

14. The 1860 Morgan County, Indiana Census listed a forty-eight-year-old H. J. Shelton, born in Kentucky, married to Martha Shelton, forty years old, born in Kentucky, with an eleven-year-old boy named Joseph, also born in Kentucky. Migration in 1857 was noted in Still Family Archives, Scottsdale, Arizona

15. Charles Blanchard, ed., *Counties of Morgan, Monroe, and Brown, Indiana: Historical and Biographical* (Mt. Vernon, Indiana: Windmill Publications, 1884), 98, 149, 167.

16. Commodore Wesley Cauble, *Disciples of Christ in Indiana* (Indianapolis, Indiana: Meigs Publishing Company, 1930), 57; Portrait of Stone, Henry Shaw, *Hoosier Disciples* (Indianapolis, Indiana: Bethany Press for the Association of the Christian Churches in Indiana, 1966), photos after page 192; portrait of Campbell in Cauble, *Disciples of Christ in Indiana,* after p. 96.

17. David Hackett Fischer, *Albion's Seed: Four British Folkways in America* (New York: Oxford University Press, 1989), 605–623.

18. Ibid., 638–639.

19. Ibid., 680, 687–690, 736. Fischer wrote, "Whenever a culture exists for many generations in conditions of chronic insecurity, it develops an ethic that exalts war above work, force above reason, and men above women. The pattern developed on the borders of north Britain, and was carried to the American backcountry, where it was reinforced by a hostile environment and tempered by evangelical Christianity. The result was a distinctive system of gender roles that continues to flourish even in our own time."

20. Ibid., 629–631.

21. Ibid., 700–707. Fischer noted camp meetings followed the pattern set in the British borderlands' "field meetings" and "Holy Fairs." The enthusiasm for camp meetings spread over the Alleghenies with the Revolution and developed into the "Kentucky style," which included close interdenominational cooperation, careful advance preparation, fire-and-brimstone preachers, anxious seats, and fellowship meetings. The traditional "Love Feast" of the British Isles was transmuted into the sumptuous church suppers that accompanied the upper South church meetings and revivals.

22. L. C. Rudolph, *Hoosier Faiths: A History of Indiana Churches and Religious Groups* (Bloomington, Indiana: Indiana University Press, 1995), 107n, summarizing Richard T. Hughes, "The Apocalyptic Origins of the Churches of Christ and the Triumph of Modernism," *Religion and American Culture* (Summer 1992): 181–214.

23. Tibetan Buddhist has a distinctly apocalyptic strain, as manifested in the Shambhala belief structure and Tantric ceremonies such as the Kalachakra ceremony. Donald Lopez, *Prisoners of Shangri-La* (Chicago: University of Chicago Press, 1998), 207.

24. Marcia Ann Wheeler, *A Journey of Faith in the Hoosier Heartland: A History of the First Christian Church* (Noblesville, Indiana: First Christian Church, 1999), 25.

25. Rudolph, *Hoosier Faiths,* 76.

26. Kent Calder, "Growing Up in the Christian Church," *Encounter* (Spring 1999), lucidly explored the Disciples movement as it applies to ecumenism. Calder cited Disciples historians Lester G. McAllister and William E. Tucker, who wrote in *Journey in Faith* (St. Louis, Missouri: Bethany Press, 1975), "Disciples, in short, prize freedom and are not of a mind to feel guilty about their diversity."

27. *125 Significant Years: The Story of the Central Christian Church,* 1833–1953 (Indianapolis, Indiana: Central Christian Church, 1958), 9.

28. Henry K. Shaw, *Hoosier Disciples* (St. Louis, Missouri: Bethany Press for the Association of the Christian Churches in Indiana), 239.

29. Doherty, *Indianapolis in the 1870s,* 122. Beecher's vision of middle-class propriety was a remarkably prescient depiction of the Shelton family home in Batang, western China, forty years later.

30. The depression of the 1870s proved to be the second-longest and most severe in American history according to economist Asher Achinstein, "Economic Fluctuations," in Seymour E. Harris, ed., *American Economic History* (New York: McGraw-Hill Book Company, 1961), 163–168.

31. Doherty, *Indianapolis in the 1870s,* 112–116. Another economic historian, using a different set of statistics, concluded that national money wages fell every year through the 1870s from a cyclical peak of $486 in 1872 to a drought in 1879 of $373, thus showing a decline in both money and real wages in the 1870s; see Doherty, *Indianapolis in the 1870s,* 141–157.

32. Lawrence M. Lipin, *Producers, Proletarians, and Politicians: Workers and Party Politics in Evansville and New Albany, Indiana, 1850–1887* (Urbana, Illinois: University of Illinois Press, 1994), 94–95. Lipin noted, "Though the ranks of propertyless workers swelled only slightly during the 1860s for 54.1% to 59.6%, later developments suggest that this increase was a long-term trend."

33. Ibid., 95–96.

34. The 1880 census for Pawnee Township, Bourbon County, Kansas lists thirty-two-year-old Joseph O., born in Kentucky; twenty-four-year-old Emma R., born in Indiana; four-year-old Albert L., born in Indiana; and one-year-old Fredrick R., born in Indiana.

35. Draegert, *Indianapolis,* 33. The Indianapolis *Journal* editorial was typical when it wrote, "Let the rich and poor, who alike enjoy the blessings of freedom, rejoice together."

36. Indianapolis *News,* July 5, 7, 8, 1876. Evan S. Connell, *Son of the Morning Star* (New York: Harper & Row, 1984), 383, indicated the final death count of American soldiers was 265.

37. Draegert, *Indianapolis,* 52.

38. Ibid.

39. Doherty, *Indianapolis in the 1870s,* 154. Given that there was no Joseph O. Shelton listed in the city directory for 1877 or 1878, it can be conjectured that the Sheltons may have returned to live with one of their families in these hard years.

40. Dunn, *Greater Indianapolis,* vol. 1, 261.

41. Edward A. Leary, *Indianapolis: A Pictorial History* (Virginia Beach, Virginia: Donning, 1980), 57; Doherty, *Indianapolis in the 1870s,* 136–138.

42. The 1873–1879 Depression proved to be the longest depression in U.S. history and the seventh greatest in amplitude from trough to peak. Using a joint criteria of duration and amplitude, 1873–1879 ranks only behind that of the 1929–1933. Harris, *American Economic History,* 166–167.

43. Lillian B. Miller, T. K. Walter, H. Nugent, and Wayne Morgan, *1876: The Centennial Year: Indiana Historical Society Lectures* (Indianapolis, Indiana: Indiana Historical Bureau), 39. Barrows, *A Demographic Analysis of Indianapolis, 1870–1920,* 108, notes semi-skilled, unpropertied workers formed the most transient element of the Indianapolis population in the 1870–1920 period.

44. Brad S. Lomazzi, *Railroad Timetables, Travel Brochures and Posters* (Spencertown, New York: Golden Hill Press, Inc., 1995), 93.

45. Kenneth S. Davis, *Kansas, A History* (New York: Norton, 1984), 112; Federal Writers' Project of the Works Project Administration for the State of Kansas, *Kansas, Guide to the*

Sunflower State (New York: Viking Press, 1939), 56; Leola Howard Blanchard, *Conquest of Southwest Kansas* (Wichita, Kansas: 1931), 57.

46. The German Mennonites on the Russian steppes were but one group recruited by land companies anxious to settle their land with good farmers.

47. Don Banwart, *Rails, Rivalry, and Romance* (Fort Scott, Kansas: Historical Preservation Organization of Bourbon County, Inc., 1982), 90.

48. Recorder of Deeds, Bourbon, County, Kansas records a purchase by Joseph O. Shelton from Kansas City, Fort Scott, and Gulf Railroad of 80 acres of "east half of southeast quarter of Section 28 in Township 26 south of Range 24 east of the 6th principal meridian."

49. Albert Shelton, *Pioneering in Tibet; A Personal Record of Life and Experience in the Mission Fields* (New York: H. Revell, 1921), 11.

Chapter 2

1. Grace Service (John S. Service, ed.), *Golden Inches: The China Memoir of Grace Service* (Berkeley, California: University of California Press, 1989), frontispiece.

2. Craig H. Miner, *West of Wichita: Settling the High Plains of Kansas: 1865–1890* (Lawrence, Kansas: University Press of Kansas, 1986), 3; John Ise, *Sod and Stubble* (Lawrence, Kansas: University Press of Kansas, 1996), 147, noted that it was 22 degrees below zero the winter of 1880 in northern Kansas.

3. Virginia Brown, Bourbon County, Kansas Genealogical Library, Jan. 17, 2000 phone interview.

4. "Small Towns of Bourbon County" (Fort Scott, Kansas: Old Fort Genealogical Society of Southeastern Kansas, Inc.); A. T. Andreas, *History of the State of Kansas* (Chicago: A. T. Andreas, 1883, reprint Walsworth, 1978), 1092.

5. Don Banwart, *Rails, Rivalry, and Romance* (Fort Scott, Kansas: Historical Preservation Organization of Bourbon County, Inc. 1982), 79.

6. Miner, *West of Wichita,* 26–39. Miner likens the railroads, with their linear bands of urban enculturation, to a "Steel Nile."

7. "Who's Who in Our Missionaries," questionnaire, filled out by Dr. Albert Shelton, files of Disciples of Christ Overseas Ministries Office, Indianapolis, Indiana.

8. 1880 Bourbon County, Kansas Federal Census Pawnee Township. The railroads advertised heavily in the Midwest, and over half of the immigrants to southeast Kansas were born in Illinois, Indiana, and Ohio. James R. Shortridge, *Peopling the Plains: Who Settled Where in Frontier Kansas* (Lawrence, Kansas: University Press of Kansas, 1995), 49.

9. Bourbon County, Kansas, Recorder of Deeds records. The parcel that Shelton purchased from the railroad is the east half of southeast quarter of Section 28 in Township 26, south of Range 24, east of sixth principal meridian.

10. Miner, *West of Wichita,* 10–12.

11. Ibid., 19.

12. Ibid., 109–118; Smith quote, 118.

13. John F. Stover, *American Railroads* (Chicago: University of Chicago Press [1961] 1997), 93–94.

14. Nyle H. Miller and Joseph W. Snell, *Great Gunfighters of the Kansas Cowtowns* (Lincoln, Nebraska: University of Nebraska Press, 1963), 3–4.

15. Stanley was the hot foreign correspondent of his era, pursuing the most adventurous locales of his day—the Indian Wars of the plains and later the deep penetration of foreign lands by Christian missionaries.

16. Miner, *West of Wichita,* 119.

17. Miller and Snell, *Great Gunfighters of the Kansas,* pictures after page 214.

18. Ibid., 94.

19. Federal Writers' Project of the Works Project Administration for the State of Kansas, *Kansas, Guide to the Sunflower State* (New York: Viking Press, 1939), 181, 518.

20. Glenda Riley, *The Female Frontier: A Comparative View of Women on the Prairie and the Plains* (Lawrence, Kansas: University Press of Kansas, 1988), 77.

21. Leola Blanchard, *Conquest of Southwest Kansas* (Wichita, Kansas: Wichita Eagle Press, 1931), 72.

22. Robert Richmond, *Kansas: Land of Contrasts* (Wheeling, Illinois: Harland Davidson, 1999), 141.

23. Sandra L. Myres, *Westering Women and the Frontier Experience, 1800–1915* (Albuquerque, New Mexico: University of New Mexico Press, 1982), 186. Regarding women as pioneer educators, Myres notes that thirty-four of fifty-nine Colorado counties had female superintendents in 1906.

24. Harper County, Kansas Recorder of Deeds records. The legal description of the Shelton homestead is Spring Township, Township 34–35, south range 8 west. With their veterans' preference, there was a preponderance of Union veterans among the Kansas homesteaders. In 1877, one writer estimated Kansas had over a hundred thousand ex-soldiers in residence, one factor that contributed to the violence of the post–Civil War Kansas frontier. Shortridge, *Peopling the Plains,* 77.

25. Gwendoline and Paul Sanders, *The Harper County Story* (West Newton, Kansas: The Mennonite Press, 1968), 137.

26. *Historical Atlas of Harper County, Kansas* (Chicago: Davy Map and Atlas Co, 1886).

27. A. T. Andreas, *History of the State of Kansas* (Chicago: 1883), 364. The school attendance of less than half of the potential schoolage children reflects the reality of the days before compulsory education. Wayne E. Fuller, *The Old Country School* (Chicago: University of Chicago Press, 1982), 41, notes that Kansas instituted free public education in 1861. The rudimentary educational system must have been successful because the Kansas illiteracy rate dropped from 9.2 percent in 1870 to below percent in 1900, below the Midwest average of 4.2 percent. Ibid., 191.

28. Albert L. Shelton, *Pioneering in Tibet: A Personal Record of Life and Experience in the Mission Field* (New York: F. H. Revell, 1921), 12.

29. Robert E. Morsberger, *Lew Wallace, Militant Revolutionary* (New York: McGraw-Hill, 1980), 312, 447.

30. Flora B. Shelton, *Shelton of Tibet* (New York: George Doran, 1923), 25, wrote that *Ben Hur* gave Albert Shelton his first idea of being a missionary. See also *Dictionary of American Biography* entry on Shelton in National Geographic Shelton archives. Lew Wallace was himself reared a Disciples of Christ by his formidable mother, Zerelda, with weekly attendance at Sunday service, though he stated in his autobiography, "I fear the services failed to impress me as she desired." Lew Wallace, *Lew Wallace, An Autobiography* (New York: Harper & Brothers Publishers, 1906), 48. Wallace remained a Christian, though not organized.

31. Julian Pettifer and Richard Bradley, *Missionaries* (London: BBC Books, 1990), 23.

32. Ibid., 37.

33. Ibid., 23.

34. Paul A. Varg, *Missionaries, Chinese, and Diplomats* (Princeton, New Jersey: Princeton University Press, 1958), vii. Some modern commentators have compared the idealism of volunteer organizations such as the Peace Corps to the missionary movement, though it is easy to forget most missionaries to China, Roman Catholic priests particularly, made lifetime commitments to the faraway places to which the societies posted them. In the case

of the French priests, they never saw home again, pledging to remain in China for the rest of their lives.

35. *A Historical Collection of Harper County Churches* (Anthony, Kansas: Harper County Religious Heritage Committee, 1961), 32; Andreas, *History of the State of Kansas,* 367.

36. Albert L. Shelton, *Pioneering in Tibet,* 12.

37. The shortcut on the Santa Fe Trail passed through a particularly arid region that became Grant County. The Lower Cimarron Springs (later known as Wagon Bed Springs) outside of Ulysses was a major watering hole on this stretch of the trail. It is where mountain man Jedediah Smith met his death at the hands of a band of Comanches in 1831. "Lower Cimarron Springs" flyer, archives of Historic Adobe Museum, Ulysses, Kansas.

38. Miner, *West of Wichita,* 242.

39. Albert L. Shelton, *Pioneering in Tibet,* 11–12.

40. John Mack Faragher, ed., *Rereading Frederick Jackson Turner: The Significance of the Frontier in American History and Other Essays* (New York: H. Holt, 1994), 39.

41. Rowland Berthoff, *Unsettled People: Social Order and Disorder in American History* (New York: Harper and Row, 1971), 303.

42. Miner, *West of Wichita,* 132.

43. The location of the Shelton homestead is Northeast quarter 160 Section 20, 28, 35. Grant County, Kansas Recorder of Deeds records. The Sheltons filed a patent on November 23, 1891, theoretically five years after they made a homestead claim.

44. Miner, *West of Wichita,* 172–173. In June 1887, Bradstreet's national real estate survey listed Kansas City as second only to New York City for real estate transactions, Wichita was third, and Topeka tenth. The 1887 population growth of New York City was 30 percent. With 500 percent growth, Wichita was the fastest growing city in the country.

45. Archives of Historic Adobe Museum, Ulysses, Kansas.

46. *Grant County Republican,* Aug. 27, 1887.

47. *Grant County Republican,* Feb. 5, 1887. The county organized in 1888, prior to that time it was part of Hamilton County.

48. John Ise, *Sod and Stubble* (Lawrence, Kansas: University Press of Kansas, 1996), 214.

49. The Grant County petition is in the Kansas State Historical Society archives.

50. Ibid.

51. Albert L. Shelton, *Pioneering in Tibet,* 13.

52. Archives of Historic Adobe Museum, Ulysses, Kansas.

53. Blanchard, *Conquest of Southwest Kansas,* 67.

54. Miner, *West of Wichita,* 51.

55. Albert L. Shelton, *Pioneering in Tibet,* 13.

56. Miner, *West of Wichita,* 150. The settlers' snakebite remedy in those days was an application of turpentine and wet soda, followed by someone sucking out the venom after washing out his or her mouth with salt.

57. Miner, *West of Wichita,* 13.

58. Book 4, page 299, Harper County, Kansas Recorder of Deeds records.

59. "Our History," Archives of Historic Adobe Museum, Ulysses, Kansas.

60. Ibid.

61. William Allen White wrote: "Kansas, like Gaul, was divided into three parts. Eastern Kansas has proven herself good for agriculture; central Kansas is proving herself worthy; western Kansas is a dead failure in everything but the herd." Shortridge, *Peopling the Plains,* 143, 186. Shortridge noted the interplay of late industrialization in the upper South contributing to its peoples pursuit of traditional agricultural frontiers. Their conservative cultural ways spelled economic disaster when they encountered an ecology that would not support their lifestyle.

62. Fuller, 10–11.
63. Teachers Certificates, 1891 and 1892, Still Family Archives, Scottsdale, Arizona. Shelton took the exam again in August 1897 after he had been in college. His average was 94½.
64. First Presbyterian to Christian Endeavor, July 28, 1892, Still Family Archives, Scottsdale, Arizona.
65. "Old Church" flyer, Archives of Historic Adobe Museum, Ulysses, Kansas.
66. "Hiram Warner Newby," *Christian Standard,* June 25, 1932, 23. Mary Newby Miller to Flora Shelton, undated, Still Family Archives, Scottsdale, Arizona. The daughter of the evangelist Eric Newby indicated there were 115 baptized in Ulysses during the revival period when Shelton was baptized. According to her, it was at a time when there were only 250 voters in the county.
67. Lena Tarbet, "History of Shelton Memorial Christian Church," Ulysses, Kansas: Shelton Christian Church, 1965. In archives of Historic Adobe Museum, Ulysses, Kansas; "Who's Who in Our Missionaries," questionnaire, filled out by Dr. Albert Shelton, files of Disciples of Christ Overseas Ministries Office, Indianapolis, Indiana.
68. Still Family Archives, Scottsdale, Arizona.
69. Fuller, *The Old Country School,* 159–162; Leslie C. Swanson, *Rural One-Room Schools of Mid-America* (Moline, Illinois: Self-published, 1976, revised 1984), 11.
70. Fuller, *The Old Country School,* 14.
71. Swanson, *Rural One-Room Schools of Mid-America,* 7.
72. Albert L. Shelton, *Pioneering in Tibet,* 15.
73. Archives of Historic Adobe Museum, Ulysses, Kansas. Undated and unidentified newspaper clips circa 1922 on vintage bulletin board from Ulysses Christian Church.
74. Albert L. Shelton, *Pioneering in Tibet,* 15.

Chapter 3

1. Albert Shelton to Flora Beal, Aug. 30, 1898, Still Family Archives, Scottsdale, Arizona.
2. *The Kodak,* published by Kansas State Normal College, Emporia, 1898, 18–19. Shelton was part of another surge to the cities. By 1900, 30 percent of the population on the Kansas plains was urban; Glenda Riley, *The Female Frontier: A Comparative View of Women on the Prairie and the Plains* (Lawrence, Kansas: University of Kansas Press, 1988), 93.
3. Paul Theobald, *Call School: Rural Education in the Midwest to 1981* (Carbondale, Illinois: Southern Illinois University Press, 1995), 221n; Edward L. Dejnozka and David E. Kapel, *American Educators' Encyclopedia* (New York: Greenwood Press, 1991), 392; Paul Monroe, ed., *A Cyclopedia of Education* (New York: The Macmillan Company, 1913), 481, stated the institution evolved from the Ecole Normale beginning in 1794. By 1834, the British established a national "normal school" so that "the candidates for the poorer classes may acquire the knowledge necessary to the practice of the their future profession, and may be practiced in the most approved methods of religious and moral training and instruction."
4. *The Kodak,* 18–19.
5. "Memorial Service for Dr. A. L. Shelton," *The Emporia Daily,* Apr. 10, 1922.
6. Robert W. Richmond, *Kansas: A Land of Contrasts* (Wheeling, Illinois: Harland Davidson, 1999), 100.
7. "The State Normal School," Brochure, Academic year 1895–1896, in files, Emporia State University Library, Emporia, Kansas. The school changed its name in 1923 to Kansas State Teachers College, and in 1974 to Emporia Kansas State College, and again in 1977 to Emporia State University.

8. Albert L. Shelton, *Pioneering in Tibet: A Personal Record of Life and Experience in Mission Fields* (New York: F. H. Revell Company, 1921), 15.
9. "Dr. A. L. Shelton K. S. N. Graduate Killed in Tibet," *State Normal Bulletin,* Mar. 16, 1922.
10. "Memorial Service for Dr. A. L. Shelton," *The Emporia Daily,* Apr. 10, 1922.
11. "Who's Who in Our Overseas Missionaries," questionnaire, filled out by Flora Beal Shelton, files of Disciples of Christ Overseas Ministries Office, Indianapolis, Indiana.
12. University of Kansas, Kansas Collection/Wilcox Collection archives. J. O. Shelton and his wife may have forsaken Grant County to rejoin family members in Anthony. Albert Shelton listed Anthony as his home address in the company roster. In February 1898, J. O. Shelton bought five town lots in Anthony for $75, and mortgaged them for $50.
13. Albert Shelton to Flora Beal, May 10, 1898; Flora Beal to Albert Shelton; May 12–13, 1898, Flora Beal to Albert Shelton, May 14–15, 1898; Albert Shelton to Flora Beal, May 16, 1898, Still Family Archives, Scottsdale, Arizona.
14. Kirche Mecham, ed., *Annals of Kansas* (Topeka, Kansas: Kansas State Historical Society, 1954), vol. 1, 295.
15. Albert Shelton to Flora Beal, May 21, 1898, Still Family Archives, Scottsdale, Arizona.
16. Albert Shelton to Flora Beal, Aug. 30, 1898, Still Family Archives, Scottsdale, Arizona.
17. Albert Shelton to Flora Beal, June 2, 1898; Flora Beal to Albert Shelton, June 6–7, 9–10, 1898, Still Family Archives, Scottsdale, Arizona.
18. Albert Shelton to Flora Beal, June 27, 1898, Still Family Archives, Scottsdale, Arizona.
19. Albert Shelton to Flora Beal, Aug. 24, 1898, Still Family Archives, Scottsdale, Arizona.
20. University of Kansas, Kansas Collection/Wilcox Collection archives.
21. Albert Shelton to Flora Beal, Nov. 17, 1898, Still Family Archives, Scottsdale, Arizona.
22. Albert Shelton to Flora Beal, Apr. 29, 1899, Still Family Archives, Scottsdale, Arizona.
23. "Who's Who in Our Missionaries," questionnaire, filled out by Dr. Albert Shelton, files of Disciples of Christ Overseas Ministries Office, Indianapolis, Indiana.
24. Wedding Photo, Still Family Archives, Scottsdale, Arizona.
25. Albert L. Shelton, *Pioneering in Tibet,* 16.
26. Still Family Archives, Scottsdale, Arizona.
27. *Catalogue of Kentucky University, Session of 1902–1903* (Lexington, Kentucky: Transylvania Company, 1903).
28. Albert L. Shelton, *Pioneering in Tibet* 16.
29. Grace Service, John S. Service, ed., *Golden Inches The China Memoir of Grace Service* (Berkeley, California: University of California Press, 1989), 49.
30. Christopher Martin, *The Boxer Rebellion* (London: Abelard-Schuman, 1968), 43.
31. Richard O'Connor, *The Spirit Soldiers: A Historical Narrative of the Boxer Rebellion* (New York: G. P. Putnam's Sons, 1973), 339.
32. University of Louisville Kornhauser Health Sciences Library archives. There are no records of Shelton's grades from his junior year.
33. Flora Shelton had a Harper County, Kansas, teaching certificate dated Sept. 8, 1900, and a Labette County (her parents' home county) certificate dated Oct. 26, 1901. Presumably she lived with family and taught in Kansas while her husband was in his first years of medical school in Louisville. Still Family Archives, Scottsdale, Arizona.
34. Rijnhart dateline sheet in Rijnhart Files Disciples of Christ Historical Society, Nashville, Tennessee.
35. C. T. Paul, "Brown Churches of Christ," biography of Dr. Susie Rijnhart, Rijnhart Files, Disciples of Christ Historical Society, Nashville, Tennessee.
36. Susie. C. Rijnhart, *With the Tibetans in Tent and Temple* (Chicago: Fleming H. Revell Company, 1901), 310–311.

37. Dr. Susie Rijnhart, "Tibet," in *Missionary Tidings* (November 1902): 273–275.

38. Marian L. Duncan, *A Flame from the Fire* (Spring Hill, Tennessee: Marian Duncan, 1999), 15.

39. C. T. Paul, "Brown Churches of Christ," biography of Dr. Susie Rijnhart, in Rijnhart Files, Disciples of Christ Historical Society, Nashville, Tennessee.

40. Dr. Susie Rijnhart, "Prayer-Meetings in Tibet," *The Christian-Evangelist* (Feb. 19, 1903): 150.

41. C. T. Paul, "Missions to Tibet," *The Christian-Evangelist* (May 21, 1903): 410.

42. Albert Shelton to Flora Shelton, May 10, 1903, Still Family Archives, Scottsdale, Arizona.

43. Still Family Archives, Scottsdale, Arizona.

44. All Emporia and Louisville quotes, Albert L. Shelton, *Pioneering in Tibet,* 15–18.

45. Albert L. Shelton [ALS] to "Dear Friends Ed and Hattie," June 17, 1903, Archives of Historic Adobe Museum, Ulysses, Kansas.

Chapter 4

1. Flora B. Shelton, *Shelton of Tibet* (New York: George Doran, 1923), 34.

2. Albert L. Shelton, *Pioneering in Tibet: A Personal Life and Experience in the Mission Fields* (New York: F. H. Revell Company, 1921), 19–20; Rijnhart/Shelton Chronology, Shelton Files, 1918–1928 Missionary Correspondence Disciples of Christ Historical Society, Nashville, Tennessee.

3. Albert L. Shelton, *Pioneering in Tibet,* 19–20; Rijnhart/Shelton Chronology, Shelton Files, 1918–1928 Missionary Correspondence Disciples of Christ Historical Society, Nashville, Tennessee.

4. John K. Fairbank and Denis Twitchett, eds., *The Cambridge History of China* (Cambridge, England: Cambridge University Press, 1978), vol. 10, 574, estimates there were three hundred medical missionaries in China in 1905, a sharp rise from 1874 when there were only ten fully qualified medical missionaries; Kenneth S. Latourette, *A History of Christian Missions in China* (London: Society for Promoting Christian Knowledge, 1929), 652, states in 1905 there were 301 physicians, 207 men and 94 women, out of 3,445 missionaries. There were 166 hospitals and 241 dispensaries serving 35,301 in-patients and 1,044,948 out-patients.

   Along with Islam and Buddhism, Christianity is one of the world's great evangelical religions. Historians theorize Christianity evolved into a missionary religion because of its roots as a tiny persecuted Jewish sect. The religion had to grow to survive.

5. Fairbank and Twitchett, *The Cambridge History of China,* vol. 10, 547; Julian Pettifer and Richard Bradley, *Missionaries* (London: BBC Books, 1990), 165–175; Jessie Gregory Lutz, *Christian Missions in China: Evangelists of What?* (Boston, Massachusetts: Heath, 1965), v-xii.

6. Jonathan D. Spence, *The Great Chan's Great Continent: China in Western Minds* (New York: W. W. Norton, 1998), 12.

7. Christopher Martin, *The Boxer Rebellion* (London: Abelard-Schuman, 1968), 19.

8. Ibid.

9. Fairbank and Twitchett, *The Cambridge History of China,* vol. 10, 546–547.

10. Hunter Miller, ed., *Treaties and other International Acts of the United States of America* (Washington: U.S. Government Printing Office, 1942), vol. 7, 905.

11. Fairbank and Twitchett, *The Cambridge History of China,* vol. 10, 543; John K. Fairbank, *The Missionary Enterprise in China and America* (Cambridge, Massachusetts: Harvard University Press, 1974), 263; Sidney A. Forsythe, *An American Missionary Community in China, 1895–1905* (Cambridge, Massachusetts: East Asian Research Center, Harvard University, 1971), 62.

12. Fairbank, *The Missionary Enterprise in China and America*, 8.

13. Ibid., 346.

14. Paul A. Varg, *Open Door Diplomat: The Life of William W. Rockhill* (Urbana, Illinois: University of Illinois, 1952), 28.

15. Forsythe, *An American Missionary Community in China, 1895–1905*, 63.

16. Fairbank, *The Missionary Enterprise in China and America*, 356.

17. Thomas W. Blakiston, *Five Months on the Yang-Tsze, and Notices of the Present Rebellions in China* (London: J. Murray, 1862), 225. William R. Hutchison, *Errand to the World: American Protestant Thought and Foreign Missions* (Chicago: University of Chicago Press, 1987), 46.

18. Fairbank and Twitchett, *The Cambridge History of China*, vol. 10, 558–559; Lutz, *Christian Missions in China; Evangelists of What?*, vii.

19. Lutz, *Christian Missions in China; Evangelists of What?*, 16.

20. Fairbank, *The Missionary Enterprise in China and America*, 360–361.

21. Flora B. Shelton, *Sunshine and Shadow on the Tibetan Border* (Foreign Christian Missionary Society, 1912), 16.

22. Flora B. Shelton, *Sunshine and Shadow on the Tibetan Border*, 16.

23. Albert L. Shelton, *Pioneering in Tibet*, 19.

24. Dorris Shelton Still, *Beyond Devils in the Wind* (Tempe, Arizona: Synergy Books, 1989), 4–5.

25. Flora B. Shelton, *Sunshine and Shadow on the Tibetan Border*, 16. Albert Shelton wrote that they sailed on September 29. "In The Far East," *Anthony Republican*, March 11, 1904.

26. Flora B. Shelton, *Shelton of Tibet*, 27.

27. Flora B. Shelton, *Shelton of Tibet*, 27; Albert L. Shelton, *Pioneering in Tibet*, 21.

28. Albert L. Shelton, *Pioneering in Tibet*, 21.

29. "Missionary Journal," *The Chinese Recorder* (November 1903): 582.

30. Tolley, *Yangtze Patrol*, 54.

31. Ping-ti Ho, *Studies on the Population of China, 1368–1953* (Cambridge: Harvard University Press, 1959), indicated the population of China to be about 341 million in 1911 according to official census data. He judged Qing Dynasty population figures to be highly conjectural, the result of "government self-deception."

32. "In the Far East," *Anthony Republican*, March 11, 1904.

33. Stella Dong, *Shanghai: The Rise and Fall of a Decadent City* (New York: William Morrow, 2000), 1.

34. Richard McKenna, *The Sand Pebbles, a Novel* (New York: Harper & Row, 1962), 46.

35. The word "compound" comes from Malay meaning walled enclosure where foreigners lived. "Chinese compound" would have been an oxymoron.

36. Flora B. Shelton, *Shelton of Tibet*, 28.

37. Albert L. Shelton, *Pioneering in Tibet*, 22; Flora B. Shelton, *Shelton of Tibet*, 28; Still, *Beyond Devils in the Wind*, 7; Flora B. Shelton, *Sunshine and Shadow on the Tibetan Border*, 17.

38. Carl Crow, *The Traveller's Handbook for China* (Shanghai, China: Hwa-Mei Concern, 1913), 2.

39. Service, *Golden Inches*, 21.

40. Flora B. Shelton, *Shelton of Tibet*, 29.

41. Service, *Golden Inches*, 22n.

42. Isabella Bird, *The Yangtze Valley and Beyond: An Account of Journeys in China* (Boston: Beacon Press [1899] 1987), 136.

43. Flora B. Shelton, *Shelton of Tibet*, 31.

44. Bird, *The Yangtze Valley and Beyond*, 127.

45. Flora B. Shelton, *Shelton of Tibet*, 30–31.

46. Tolley, *Yangtze Patrol*, 117. Westerners dropped a scheme to install steam winches at the rapids in 1910 over concerns about the potential starvation of the trackers.

47. Crow, *The Traveller's Handbook for China*, 139–140.

48. Service, *Golden Inches*, 41.

49. Albert L. Shelton, *Pioneering in Tibet*, 25.

50. Flora B. Shelton, *Shelton of Tibet*, 32–33.

51. Albert L. Shelton, *Pioneering in Tibet*, 23–24.

52. Flora B. Shelton, *Shelton of Tibet*, 33.

53. Albert L. Shelton, *Pioneering in Tibet*, 25.

54. William John Gill, *The River of Golden Sand*, 2 vols. (London: John Murray, 1880), vol. 2, 278.

55. Ibid., vol. 2, 274–275.

56. Service, *Golden Inches*, 39–40.

57. Albert L. Shelton, *Pioneering in Tibet*, 24.

58. Flora B. Shelton, *Shelton of Tibet*, 33.

59. Flora B. Shelton, *Shelton of Tibet*, 33; *Sunshine and Shadow on the Tibetan Border*, 35.

60. Service, *Golden Inches*, 171n. Ping-ti Ho, *Studies on the Population of China, 1368–1953*, 146, 187, states that maize reached China in the mid-sixteenth century via Yunnan, allowing an agrarian revolution with the cultivation of dry hills and mountains and sandy soil unsuited for rice cultivation. Carried by Spanish missionaries, corn reached Sichuan by the seventeenth century. By the early nineteenth century, corn was the primary crop in the mountainous districts of southwest China.

61. Albert L. Shelton, *Pioneering in Tibet*, 25.

62. Gill, *The River of Golden Sand*, vol. 2 47.

63. Gill, *The River of Golden Sand*, vol. 2 108; Christopher Beckwith, "The Impact of the Horse and Silk Trade on the Economies of T'ang China and the Uighar Empire," in *Journal of the Economic and Social History of the Orient*, 34 (June 1991): 183–198.

64. W. W. Rockhill, *Land of the Lamas: Notes of a Journey through China, Mongolia and Tibet* (San Francisco: Chinese Materials Center, [1891] 1976), 281.

65. Gill, *The River of Golden Sand*, vol. 2, 87. American Army Major John Magruder stated after a 1921 trip, "Tea for Tibet is not a luxury, but due to the important part it plays in the daily diet, it is a necessity, and tremendous quantities are used." See "Report of a Trip Thru Yunnan, Eastern Tibet, and Szechwan by Major John Magruder, F.A., Asst. Military Attaché, Jan. 17-July 11, 1921 SERVICE REPORT," 11. Microfilm reel 2, U.S. War Department Military Intelligence Division China, 1918–1941.

66. T. T. Cooper, *Pioneer of Commerce* (New York: Arno Press, [1871]1967), 263.

67. Fairbank and Twitchett, *The Cambridge History of China*, vol. 10, 397.

68. Henry R. Davies, *Yünnan, the Link Between India and Yangtze* (Cambridge: Cambridge University, 1909), 293–294.

69. Andre Migot, *Tibetan Marches* (New York: Dutton, 1955), 72.

70. Ernest Henry Wilson, *A Naturalist in Western China* (London: Cadogan Books, [1913] 1986)

71. Gill, *River of Golden Sand*, vol. 2, 80, 323. T. T. Cooper used Mantzu as a synonym for Tibetan, Gill, *ibid.*, 174.

72. Elliot Sperling, "The Chinese Venture in K'am, 1904–1911, and the Role of Chao Erhfeng," *The Tibet Journal*, 2, no. 2 (April/June 1976): 10.

73. Ibid.

74. May Holdsworth, *Sichuan* (Lincolnwood, Illinois: Passport Books, 1993), 134. This strategic bridge, still in use, is famous in the lore of the Chinese Communists' Long

March. Hoping to trap the fleeing Red Army, the Nationalists removed half the planks to prevent the Red Army from crossing. Twenty-two Red Army volunteers swung hand over hand across the iron links while the Nationalists sprayed them with machine-gun fire from the opposite bank, Eventually the Red Army took the bridge and escaped the Nationalist trap. The Nationalists contend that the Communists bribed crucial bridge defenders to allow the conquest.

75. Peter Goullart, *Princes of the Black Bone: Life in the Tibetan Borderland* (London: J. Murray, 1959), 72.
76. Gill, *River of Golden Sand,* vol. 2, 86.
77. Marion H. Duncan, *Love Songs and Proverbs of Tibet* (London: Mitre Press, 1961), 236.
78. Flora B. Shelton, *Shelton of Tibet,* 34.
79. Ibid., 34.
80. Albert L. Shelton, *Pioneering in Tibet,* 26.
81. Ibid.
82. Flora B. Shelton, *Shelton of Tibet,* 38.

Chapter 5

1. Isabella Bird Bishop, *Among the Tibetans* (New York: Fleming H. Revell, 1894), 41.
2. "A Letter From Thibet," *Anthony Republican,* June 24, 1904.
3. Andre Migot, *Tibetan Marches* (New York: Dutton, 1955), 75.
4. "A Letter From Thibet," *Anthony Republican,* June 24, 1904.
5. Susie C. Rijnhart, *With the Tibetans in Tent and Temple* (Chicago: Fleming H. Revell Company, 1901), 275.
6. William Gill, *River of Golden Sand,* 2 vols. (London: John Murray, 1880), vol. 2, 60.
7. James H. Edgar, *The Marches of the Mantze* (London: Morgan & Scott, 1908), 25.
8. Flora B. Shelton, *Shelton of Tibet* (New York: George Doran, 1923), 78.
9. A. De Rosthorn, *On the Tea Cultivation in Western Ssuch'uan; and, the Tea Trade with Tibet viâ Tachienlu* (London: Luzac & Co., 1895), 14.
10. E. H. Wilson, *A Naturalist in Western China* (London: Cadogan Books, 1986), 95.
11. Gill, *River of Golden Sand,* vol. 2, 77.
12. W. W. Rockhill, *Land of the Lamas: Notes of a Journey through China, Mongolia and Tibet* (San Francisco: Chinese Materials Center, [1891] 1976), 282–283.
13. Z. S. Loftis, *A Message from Batang* (New York: Fleming H. Revell Company, 1911), 102.
14. Rockhill, *Land of the Lamas,* 278. Other foreign observers estimated the *gams* to weigh sixty to seventy pounds.
15. De Rosthorn, *On the Tea Cultivation in Western Ssuch'uan,* 39–40.
16. Peter Goullart, *Princes of the Black Bone: Life in the Tibetan Borderland* (London: J. Murray, 1959), 31.
17. "A Letter From Thibet," *Anthony Republican,* June 24, 1904.
18. William Carey, *Travel and Adventure in Tibet, Including the Diary of Miss Annie R. Taylor's Remarkable Journey from Tau-Chau to Ta-Chien-Lu through the Heart of the Forbidden Land.* (London: Hodder and Stoughton, 1902), 68.
19. Marion H. Duncan, *Mountain of Silver Snow* (Cincinnati, Ohio: Powell & White, 1929), 127.
20. Ibid., 128.
21. Henry R. Davies, *Yünnan, the Link Between India and the Yangtze* (Cambridge: Cambridge University Press, 1909), 292.
22. Andre Migot, *Tibetan Marches* (New York: Dutton, 1955), 83.
23. Goullart, *Princes of the Black Bone,* 14; Earnest Henry Wilson, *A Naturalist in Western China* (London: Cadogan Books, [1913] 1986), 205.

24. Wilson, *A Naturalist in Western China,* 206–207.
25. Goullart, *Princes of the Black Bone,* 14, wrote about a pass and a lake south of Tachienlu: "There was a great battle around it some centuries ago and a considerable number of soldiers had been pushed into the water and drowned. Now and then people manage to fish out shields, armour and chain mail."
26. Edgar, *The Marches of the Mantze,* 22–23.
27. Wilson, *A Naturalist in Western China,* 205.
28. Goullart, *Princes of the Black Bone,* 14.
29. "A Letter From Thibet," *Anthony Republican,* June 24, 1904; "Another Letter From Thibet," *Anthony Republican,* July 29, 1904.
30. "Another Letter From Thibet," *Anthony Republican,* July 29, 1904.
31. Ibid.
32. Carl Crow, *The Traveller's Handbook for China* (Shanghai, China: Hwa-Mei Concern, 1913), 2.
33. Archibald McLean, *The History of the Foreign Christian Missionary Society* (New York: Fleming H. Revell, 1919), 97–102
34. Grace Service (John S. Service, ed.), *Golden Inches: The China Memoir of Grace Service* (Berkeley, California: University of California Press, 1989), 46
35. Flora B. Shelton, *Shelton of Tibet* (New York: George Doran, 1923), 39.
36. Albert L. Shelton, *Pioneering in Tibet, A Personal Record of Life and Experience in Mission Fields* (New York: F. H. Revell Company, 1921), 26; Flora B. Shelton, *Shelton of Tibet,* 38–39; Dorris Shelton Still, *Beyond the Devils in the Wind* (Tempe, Arizona: Synergy Books, 1989), 9.
37. "Another Letter From Thibet," *Anthony Republican,* July 29, 1904.
38. Flora B. Shelton, *Shelton of Tibet,* 39–40.
39. Albert L. Shelton, *Pioneering in Tibet,* 30.
40. Wilson, *A Naturalist in Western China,* 206–207.
41. F. Kingdon Ward, *The Land of the Blue Poppy: Travels of a Naturalist in Eastern Tibet* (London: Cadogan Books, [1923] 1986), 53.
42. Robert Ekvall, *Fields on the Hoof: Nexus of Tibetan Pastoralism* (New York: Holt, Rinehart and Winston, 1968), 33.
43. Bishop, *Among the Tibetans,* 41.
44. Rockhill, *Diary of a Journey through Mongolia and Tibet in 1891 and 1892,* 248.
45. Geoffrey Samuel, *Civilized Shamans: Buddhism in Tibetan Societies* (Washington, D.C.: Smithsonian Institution Press, 1993), 49.
46. Elliot Sperling, "The Chinese Venture in K'am, 1904–1911, and the Role of Chao Erh-feng," *The Tibet Journal,* 2, no. 2 (April/June 1976): 11.
47. Marylin Rhie and Robert Thurman, *Wisdom and Compassion* (New York: Harry Abrams, 1996), 61.
48. Samuel, *Civilized Shamans,* 335.
49. Ibid.
50. Robert Ekvall, "Peace and War Among the Tibetan Nomads," *American Anthropologist* (1964): 1119–1148, delineated the nomads' early twentieth-century armaments, which included dagger, spear, saber, bow and arrows, and matchlock. Tibetan gunsmiths made the matchlocks with great skill and embellished them with leather, gold filigree, silversmithing, and semi-precious stones. The Tibetan gunsmiths leapt from bows and arrows directly to matchlocks, the intervening gun types of wheellock, flintlock, and breechlock never reaching the plateau. Some percussion cap rifles were kept in princely and monastic armories, probably British army discards. The antelope horn gun-rests folded forward from the Damascus steel barrels on pin-hinge when not in use, and Tibetan horse riders

carried the rifle carried across their backs with a leather strap, creating a distinctive silhouette that was often noted and recorded. When the Chinese army became equipped with modern German weapons in the post-Boxer period, captured Mausers became the rifle of choice for the Khampa warriors. 1130–1133.

51. Jamyang Norbu, *Warriors of Tibet: The Story of the Aten and the Khampas Fight for the Freedom of the Country* (London: Wisdom Publications, 1986), 32–33.

52. Robert Ekvall, "Nomadic Patterns of Living among the Tibetans as Preparation for War," *American Anthropologist* (1961): 1250–1265; Ekvall, "Peace and War Among the Tibetan Nomads," 1119–1148.

53. Migot, *Tibetan Marches*, 63–64.

54. James Huston Edgar, *The Land of Mystery, Tibet* (Melbourne: China Inland Mission, 1930), 9; Francis Kingdon Ward, *The Land of the Blue Poppy: Travels of a Naturalist in Eastern Tibet* (London: Cadogan Books, [1923] 1986), 255.

55. Lyman Van Slyke, *Yangtze: Nature, History, and the River* (Reading, Massachusetts: Addison-Wesley Publishing Co., 1988), 8.

56. J. W. Gregory, *To the Alps of Chinese Tibet* (London: Seely, Service & Company, 1923), 19.

57. Jared Diamond, *Guns, Germs, and Steel* (W. W. Norton & Co., New York, 1997), 183–186.

58. Peter Hopkirk, *The Great Game: The Struggle for Empire in Central Asia* (New York: Kodansha, 1992), 149.

59. Sperling, "The Chinese Venture in K'am, 1904–1911, and the Role of Chao Erh-feng," 16.

60. Susie C. Rijnhart, *With the Tibetans in Tent and Temple* (Fleming H. Revell, 1901), 322.

61. Eric Teichman, *Travels of a Consular Official in Eastern Tibet* (Cambridge, England: Cambridge University Press, 1921), 3.

62. Samuel, *Civilized Shamans*, 73.

63. John K. Fairbank, *The Missionary Enterprise in China and America* (Cambridge, Massachusetts: Harvard University Press, 1974), 197–206.

64. W. W. Rockhill, *Diary of a Journey through Mongolia and Tibet in 1891 and 1892* (Washington, D.C.: Smithsonian Institution, 1894), 227.

65. Ibid., 206–207.

66. Ibid., 357.

67. Samuel, *Civilized Shamans*, 136, quoted plant hunter Joseph Rock's interview with a Golok in 1956. The tribesman said, "Our tribe is the most respected in Tibet, and we rightly look down with contempt on both Chinaman and Tibetan."

68. Albert Shelton to Archibald McLean, Mar. 20, 1905 Shelton Files, 1918–1928 Missionary Correspondence, Disciples of Christ Historical Society, Nashville, Tennessee.

69. McLean, *The History of the Foreign Christian Missionary Society*, 121. Z. S. Loftis stated one rupee equaled 25 cents in Kham. After Chao's invasion, the Chinese introduced a silver Chinese rupee similar in weight and purity to try to supplant the Indian rupee in wide circulation in eastern Tibet. Z. S. Loftis, *A Message From Batang* (New York: Fleming H. Revell Company, 1911), 128.

70. Flora B. Shelton, *Shelton of Tibet*, 39.

71. Albert L. Shelton, *Pioneering in Tibet*, 27.

72. Ibid., 29–30.

73. McLean, *The History of the Foreign Christian Missionary Society*, 118.

74. Stephen Batchelor, *The Tibet Guide* (London: Wisdom Publications, 1987), 19, 371–372.

75. John MacGregor, *Tibet: A Chronicle of Exploration.* (New York: Praeger Publishers, 1970), 37.

76. G. W. Houston, ed., *The Cross and the Lotus: Christianity and Buddhism in Dialogue* (Delhi: Motilal Banaridass, 1985); Lama Anagrika Govinda, "A Lama Looks at Christianity," 124–125. Scholars disputed that Andrade made it all the way to Lhasa. Most

contend he was stopped short. MacGregor, *Tibet,* 68. Cornelius Wessels, *Early Jesuit Travellers in Central Asia 1603–1721* (The Hague: Martinus Nijhoff, 1924), 88. Captain Young found no trace of the Christian church in 1912, though he noted one Buddhist chorten stood forty feet above the others, topped by "a weather-beaten cross of wood."

77. Robert Barnett, ed., *Resistance and Reform in Modern Tibet* (Bloomington, Indiana: Indiana University Press, 1994), 2–3.

78. G. W. Houston, ed., *The Cross and the Lotus: Christianity and Buddhism in Dialogue* (Delhi: Motilal Banarsidass, 1985), 125.

79. MacGregor, *Tibet,* 103; Samuel Louis Graham Sandberg, *The Exploration of Tibet: Its History and Particulars, from 1623–1904* (Calcutta: Thacker, Spink & Co., 1904), 41.

80. MacGregor, *Tibet,* 107; Sandberg, *The Exploration of Tibet,* 90.

81. G. W. Houston, "Jesus and His Missionaries in Tibet," *The Tibet Journal* 16 (Winter 1991): 21.

82. David B. Woodward, *Aflame for God: Biography of Fredrik Franson* (Chicago, Illinois: Moody Press, 1966), 17; Edvard P. Torjesen, *Fredrik Franson: A Model for Worldwide Evangelism* (Pasadena, California: William Carey Library, 1983), 17.

83. Howard Van Dyck, *William Christie: Apostle to Tibet* (Harrisburg, Pennsylvania: Christian Publications, Inc., 1956), 34.

84. M. Geraldine Guinness, *The Story of the China Inland Mission,* 2 vols. (London: Morgan and Scott, 1894), vol. 2, 245, 250. Mike Guy, archivist, OMF International, Littleton, Colorado, to author, Nov. 2, 1999.

85. Bray, "Christian Missions and the Politics of Tibet, 1850–1950," 180, Wilfried Wagner, ed., *Kolonien und Missionen: Referate des 3. Internationalen Kolonialgeschichtlichen Symposiums 1993 in Bremen* (Munster; Hamburg: Bremer Asien-Pazifik Studien; 12), 180–195.

86. Howard Lamar and Leonard Thompson, *The Frontier in History: North America and Southern Africa Compared* (New Haven: Yale University Press, 1981), 268, noted the same pattern of religious integration between incorporative North American Indian cultures and the exclusivist Christian missionaries.

87. Edgar, *Marches of the Mantze, 56.*

88. "Another Letter From Thibet," *Anthony Republican,* July 29, 1904.

89. Flora B. Shelton, *Shelton of Tibet,* 69.

90. MacGregor, *Tibet,* 107; Sandberg, *The Exploration of Tibet,* 90.

91. Bray, "Christian Missions and the Politics of Tibet, 1850–1950," 184–185.

92. Bishop, *Among the Tibetans,* 155–156.

93. Bray, "Christian Missions and the Politics of Tibet, 1850–1950," 188.

94. Ibid.; Rockhill, *Land of the Lamas,* 273.

95. Bray, "Christian Missions and the Politics of Tibet, 1850–1950," 188.

96. Rockhill, *Diary of a Journey through Mongolia and Tibet in 1891 and 1892,* 221. Rockhill noted that the lamas' penalty for murder in northern Kham varied by the status of the deceased: "Among the Horba the murderer of a man of the upper class is fined 120 bricks of tea (equivalent to Rs. 120); for the murder of a middle-class man he is fined 80 bricks, for killing a woman 40 bricks, and so on down through the social scale, the murder of a beggar, or a wandering foreigner, as my informant laughingly added, being fined only a nominal amount, 3 or 4 bricks. In case the victim is a lama, the murderer has often to pay a much larger amount, 200 or 300 bricks."

Chapter 6

1. Marian L. Duncan, *A Flame of the Fire* (Spring Hill, Tennessee: Marian L. Duncan, 1999), 21.

2. J. W. Gregory, *To the Alps of Chinese Tibet* (London: Seely, Service & Company, 1923), 163.

3. Laurent Deshayes to author, Feb. 7, 2001; Robert Loup, *Martyr in Tibet: The Heroic Life of Father Maurice Tornay, St. Bernard Missionary to Tibet* (New York: D. McKay, Inc., 1956), 146.

4. Alastair Lamb, *The McMahon Line: A Study in the Relations Between India, China, and Tibet, 1904–1914*, 2 vols. (London: Routledge and Kegan Paul, 1966), vol. 1, 181–184.

5. Elliot Sperling, "The Chinese Venture in K'am, 1904–1911, and the Role of Chao Ehr-feng," *The Tibet Journal* 2, no. 2, 14–15; Lamb, *The McMahon Line*, 186–187.

6. Flora B. Shelton, *Shelton of Tibet, Shelton of Tibet* (New York: George Doran, 1923), 52.

7. "Diplomatical Archives of Nantes, Pekin 37, First petition presented to the Imperial Authorities by the Samkiengtsong of Bathang, dated 3rd moon of the 31st year of Guangxu appended to the report number 99 from M Bons d'Anty, French Consualte at Chengdu to M. DUBAIL, French Ambassador at Pekin, Chengdu, 25th/05/1905," Laurent Deshayes to author, Feb. 7, 2001.

8. Laurent Deshayes to author, Feb. 7, 2001.

9. Sir Hamilton Bower, *Diary of a Journey Across Tibet* (Kathmandu, Nepal: Ratna Pustak Bhandar, [1893] 1976), 225–226; Marku Tsering, *Sharing Christ in the Tibetan Buddhist World* (Upper Darby, Pennsylvania: Tibet Press, 1988), 86; Loup, *Martyr in Tibet*, 83, 146; Gregory, *To the Alps of Chinese Tibet*, 161–162. Marion H. Duncan, *The Mountain of Silver Snow* (Cincinnati, Ohio: Powell & White, 1929), 105.

10. James Mack Faragher, *Rereading Frederick Jackson Turner: The Significance of Frontier in American History, and Other Essays* (New York: H. Holt, 1994), 56. The Chinese imperial government shared a fear of nomadic peoples with other colonizing powers. As the Chinese feared the military threat of their tribal neighbors' mobility, the British feared their American colonists "going native." As this quote of Burke, which Frederick Jackson Turner incorporated into his frontier thesis, indicated, the British also feared the destabilizing impact of "English Tartars" loose over the Cumberlands: "Already they have topped the Appalachian mountains. From thence they behold before them an immense plain, one vast, rich, level meadow; a square of five hundred miles over this they would wander without possibility of restraint; they change their manners with their habits of life; would soon forget a government by which they were disowned; would become hordes of English Tartars; and, pouring down upon your unfortified frontiers a fierce and irresistible cavalry, become masters of your governors and your counselors, your collectors and comptrollers, and of all the slaves that adhered to them."

11. Peter Hopkirk, *The Great Game: The Struggle for Empire in Central Asia* (New York: Kodansha, 1992), 507.

12. Geoffrey Samuel, *Civilized Shamans: Buddhism in Tibetan Societies* (Washington, D.C.: Smithsonian Institution Press, 1993), 25, estimated 10 to 15 percent of the monks in the three major Geluk monasteries around Lhasa were *dobdo*, or "fighting monks." Samuel wrote, "These monks had a distinctive appearance (style of hair, manner of tying their robes) and belonged to clubs that held regular athletic competitions. They also typically engaged in ritualized combat with weapons according to a code of chivalry, and often acted as bodyguards for the monastery."

13. Hopkirk, *The Great Game*, 510.

14. Sperling, "The Chinese Venture in K'am, 1904–1911, and the Role of Chao Erh-feng," 11.

15. Lamb, *The McMahon Line*, vol. 1, 186.

16. Lamb, *The McMahon Line*, vol. 1, 188–189; Melvyn Goldstein, *A History of Modern Tibet, 1913–1951: The Demise of the Lamaist State* (Berkeley, California: University of California Press, 1989), 46.

17. "Diplomatical Archives of Nantes, Pekin 37, extract *Peking Gazette,* appended to the report number 99 from M. Bons d'Anty, French Consulate at Chengdu to M. DUBAIL, French Ambassador at Pekin, Chengdu, 25th/05/1905." Laurent Deshayes to author, Feb. 7, 2001.

18. Laurent Deshayes to author, Feb. 7, 2001.

19. Goldstein, *A History of Modern Tibet, 1913–1951,* 45.

20. Simon Winchester, *The River at the Center of the World* (New York: Henry Holt, 1996), 364–365.

21. Lamb, *The McMahon Line,* vol. 1, 183.

22. Goldstein, *History of Modern Tibet,* 46–47.

23. Lamb, *The McMahon Line,* vol. 1, 121.

24. Sperling, "The Chinese Venture in K'am, 1904–1911, and the Role of Chao Erh-feng," 11–13.

25. Laurent Deshayes to author, Feb. 7, 2001, "This man [Feng] was, as said the French Consular Bons d'Anty (in Chengdu) who knew him, very irritable and could suddenly become very furious."

26. Peter Fleming, *Bayonets to Lhasa: The First Full Account of the British Invasion of Tibet in 1904* (New York: Harper, 1961), 301.

27. Flora B. Shelton, *Shelton of Tibet,* 53.

28. Bower, *Diary of a Journey Across Tibet.* The Tibetan name for the Hsiang-ch'eng region was Chengtreng.

29. John Huston Edgar, *The Marches of the Mantze* (London: Morgan & Scott, 1908), 30.

30. Jamyang Norbu, *Warriors of Tibet: The Story of the Aten and the Khampas Fight for the Freedom of the Country* (London: Wisdom Publications, 1986), 28; A Shelton photo of a cauldron used to boil Tibetans in Draya was widely reprinted. Shelton Collection photo archives, Newark Museum, Newark, New Jersey. Edgar, *Marches of the Mantze,* 16, stated, "It was the intention of the Chinese General to first sack and then destroy the huge monastery of Tinglintsze, but the Lamas forestalled him by themselves burning the wonderful building and the bridge over the Chihtsuen River, and fleeing with the temple treasures to the inaccessible mountains of Sanai." It is the only recount of the monastery being self-destructed this author encountered, the balance of the accounts giving the responsibility to the Chinese.

31. Susie C. Rijnhart, "Word from Dr. Rijnhart," in *The Christian-Evangelist* (Nov. 30, 1905): 1560.

32. Flora B. Shelton, *Shelton of Tibet,* 43.

33. Albert L. Shelton, *Pioneering in Tibet* (New York: F. H. Revell Company, 1921), 39.

34. Flora B. Shelton, *Shelton of Tibet,* 43.

35. Undated E. H. Wilson letter, Still Family archives, Scottsdale, Arizona.

36. Albert L. Shelton, "A Letter From Tibet," *The Christian-Evangelist* (Feb. 8, 1906): 168–169.

37. Marian L. Duncan, *A Flame of the Fire,* 18.

38. Albert L. Shelton, "A Letter From Tibet," *The Christian-Evangelist* (Feb. 8, 1906): 168–169.

39. L. C. Rudolph, *Hoosier Faiths: A History of Indiana Churches & Religious Groups* (Bloomington, Indiana: Indiana University Press, 1995), 92–93; Henry K. Shaw, *Hoosier Disciples* (St. Louis, Missouri: Bethany Press for the Association of the Christian Churches in Indiana), 220.

40. F. M. Bailey, *China-Tibet-Assam: A Journey, 1911* (London: J. Cape, 1945), 64–65.

41. Edgar, *The Land of Mystery,* 19.

42. J. H. Edgar, "Hsiang Ch'eng or Du Halde's 'Land of the Lamas,'" *Journal of the West China Border Research Society,* 7: 13–22, quoted in Chris Elder, "The Man Who Found Shangri-La: James Edgar Huston [sic]," *New Zealand Journal of East Asian Studies* (1993): 21–48.

43. Sperling, "The Chinese Venture in K'am, 1904–1911, and the Role of Chao Ehr-feng"; Lamb, *The McMahon Line*, 188; Jacques Bacot, *Le Tibet Revolté* (Paris: Hachette et cie, 1912), 134–141; Teichman, *Travels of a Consular Official in Eastern Tibet*, 22. Teichman stated Chao had 3,000 troops.

44. Bailey, *China-Tibet-Assam: A Journey, 1911*, 64–65.

45. O. L. Kilborn, *Heal the Sick; An Appeal for Medical Missions in China* (Toronto: Missionary Society of the Methodist Church, 1910), 63. Chao was a man of his times. Medical missionary O. L. Kilborn wrote of another Chinese viceroy, Ts'en Chw'en Suen, who pacified the Kwangsi by allowing missionary activity to continue. Kilborn described him as an intelligent, progressive man. Ts'en Chw'en Suen executed the leader of a Kwangsi rebellion by beheading. "Immediately on the striking off of the head," Kilborn wrote, "a cup of blood was caught and drank by the latter [the viceroy], in order to give him courage!"

46. Bailey, *China-Tibet-Assam: A Journey, 1911*, 64–65. Bailey later discovered there was substantial hyperbole involved, as the man in question had stabbed himself on the way to the execution ground, which forced the executioner to hurry back with sword in hand to finish the job lest the man evade his sentence.

47. Lamb, *The McMahon Line*, vol. 1, 189.

48. Batang was considered to be a thirty-day journey from Tachienlu by caravan stages. Ogden wrote it was 460 miles between Tachienlu and Batang. See Marian L. Duncan, *A Flame of the Fire*, 19.

49. Albert Shelton, *Pioneering in Tibet*, 41, 43.

50. Marian L. Duncan, *A Flame of the Fire*, 20.

51. Ibid.

52. Albert L. Shelton, *Pioneering in Tibet*, 47.

53. Marian L. Duncan, *A Flame of the Fire*, 20.

54. Ibid.

55. Ibid., 20–21.

56. Ibid., 21.

57. Flora B. Shelton, *Shelton of Tibet*, 71.

58. Marian L. Duncan, *A Flame of the Fire*, 21.

59. Albert L. Shelton, *Pioneering in Tibet*, 38.

60. Flora B. Shelton, *Shelton of Tibet*, 64.

61. Albert L. Shelton, *Pioneering in Tibet*, 38. Rijnhart-Shelton Timeline, Shelton Files, Disciples of Christ Historical Society, Nashville, Tennessee, notes dates of August 1905 for Moyes' typhoid, and February 1906 for Flora Shelton's typhus attack.

62. Marian L. Duncan, *A Flame of the Fire*, 19; Rijnhart-Shelton Timeline, Shelton Files, Disciples of Christ Historical Society, Nashville, Tennessee.

63. Sperling, "The Chinese Venture in K'am, 1904–1911, and the Role of Chao Ehr-feng," 21. Sperling notes, "It has always been general practice for Chinese government authorities to refer to those who defy or oppose them as bandits and robbers, regardless of the political motivations involved."

64. Ibid.

65. Ibid. A *li*, a common Chinese standard of measurement, is approximately a third of a mile, though measurement varies dependent on the topography and the energy expended to cross it. A mountainous *li* is shorter than a level *li*.

66. Lamb, *The McMahon Line*, vol. 1, 172.

67. John Bray, "Christian Missions and the Politics of Tibet, 1850–1950," 180; Wilfried Wagner, ed., *Kolonien und Missionen: Referate des 3. Internationalen Kolonialgeschichtlichen Symposiums 1993 in Bremen* (Munster; Hamburg: Bremer Asien-Pazifik Studien; 12), 180–195. The missionaries hoped to follow the sword into Tibet. The message that R. H.

Clive of the British Legation in Beijing wrote to British Foreign Secretary Lord Curzon in 1920 also applied to the Protestant missionaries, "For fifty years the Catholics had been working on the borders of Eastern Tibet under the protection of Chinese bayonets, have identified their interests with those of the Chinese, and had aroused the bitter hostility of the Tibetans. As the Chinese wave in eastern Tibet goes forward, the Catholics follow in its wake; as it recedes they retire; and they consequently found their hopes of entering Tibet proper on the eventual conquest of that country by the Chinese."

68. Ibid., 19–20.
69. Albert Shelton questionnaire for Tibet Bulletin, 1911, Disciples of Christ Historical Society, Nashville, Tennessee, Shelton Files.
70. Rin-chen Lha-mo King, *We Tibetans*, 55. King wrote, "He [Chao Ehr-feng] first deposed *vi et armis* the territorial princes, lay and cleric of Eastern Tibet, recovering from them the seals they had been given by the Emperor Yung Cheng, and cutting up their territories into Chinese administration units or hsien, under Chinese officials."
71. Edgar, *The Marches of the Mantze*, 19.
72. Flora B. Shelton, *Shelton of Tibet*, 44–45. The parallels with the U.S. Cavalry and the war with the Sioux over the Black Hills gold rush are obvious.
73. As Shelton's fame grew, so did Abe's. One photo of Stetson-hatted Shelton on Abe was widely reprinted. Abe was not a small Tibetan pack mule. Most likely he was an expensive riding mule either from the Gansu border or Gonbo in southeastern Tibet. Teichman, *Travels of a Consular Official in Eastern Tibet*, 222.
74. "Who's Who Among Our Missionaries," Shelton Files, Disciples of Christ Historical Society, Nashville, Tennessee.
75. Flora B. Shelton, 41.
76. Flora Shelton Diary, July 5, 1907, Still Family Archive, Scottsdale, Arizona.
77. Flora Shelton Diary, August 18, 1907, Still Family Archive, Scottsdale, Arizona. The Sheltons gave each other Asian objects for their eighth anniversary. Bert Shelton gave his wife four leopard-skin rugs and a red Tibetan one. She gave him a tiger-claw watch charm mounted in silver. April 28, 1907 diary entry.
78. Flora B. Shelton, *Shelton of Tibet*, 67.
79. Marian L. Duncan, *A Flame in the Fire*, 17, quote from Shelton Collection Files, Newark Museum, Newark, New Jersey, "Daddy's little girl" is Dorris Shelton Still's phrase in describing her relationship with her father.
80. Paul C. P. Siu, "The Sojourner," *American Journal of Sociology* 58 (July 1952): 34 stated, "The essential characteristic of the sojourner is that he clings to the culture of his own ethnic group as in contrast to the bi-cultural complex of the marginal man. Psychologically he is unwilling to organize himself as a permanent resident of the country of his sojourn. . . . The sojourner is par excellence an ethnocentrist."
81. Howard Lamar and Leonard Thompson, eds., *The Frontier in History: North America and South Africa Compared* (New Haven: Yale University Press, 1981), 268, quote historian James Axtell: "On any frontier, acculturation is normally a two-way process, especially in the early stages of contact."

Chapter 7

1. Flora B. Shelton, *Shelton of Tibet* (New York: George Doran, 1923), 65.
2. John K. Fairbank, *The Missionary Enterprise in China and America* (Cambridge, Massachusetts: Harvard University Press, 1974), 357.
3. John Huston Edgar, *The Marches of the Mantze* (London: Morgan & Scott, 1908), 12–13. Edgar estimated a chair sedan journey would cost 42 taels.

4. Marian L. Duncan, *A Flame of the Fire* (Spring Hill, Tennessee: Marian L. Duncan, 1999), 21.

5. William Gill, *The River of Golden Sand*, 2 vols. (London: John Murray, 1880), vol. 2, 151.

6. Marion Duncan, *Mountain of Silver Snow* (Cincinnati, Ohio: Powell & White, 1929), 154.

7. Andre Migot, *Tibet Marches* (New York: Dutton, 1955), 72.

8. Gill, *The River of Golden Sand*, vol. 2, 58.

9. Z. S. Loftis, *A Message From Batang: The Diary of Z. S. Loftis, M.D.* (New York: Fleming H. Revell Company, 1911), 112–113.

10. J. H. Jeffrey, *Khams or Eastern Tibet* (Ilfracombe, Devon: Arthur H. Stockwell, Ltd., 1974), 55.

11. Migot, *Tibet Marches*, 104–105.

12. Oliver Coales, "Eastern Tibet," *Geographical Journal* (January-June, 1919): 236.

13. Albert L. Shelton, *Pioneering in Tibet* (New York: F. H. Revell Company, 1921), 53.

14. Edgar, *Marches of the Mantze*, 27–28.

15. Gill, *The River of Golden Sand*, vol. 2, 186–189

16. Edgar, *Marches of the Mantze*, 31.

17. T. T. *Travels of a Pioneer of Commerce* (New York: Arno Press, [1871] 1967), 255–256.

18. Flora B. Shelton, *Shelton of Tibet*, 80–81.

19. Marion H. Duncan, *Love Songs and Proverbs of Tibet* (London: Mitre Press, 1961), 28. Tibetan Buddhists ritually circumambulate sacred sites clockwise, keeping the sacred object to their right. Cedars circled the Batang monastery.

20. Rijnhart-Shelton Timeline, Shelton Files, Disciples of Christ Historical Society, Nashville, Tennessee; Albert L. Shelton, *Pioneering in Tibet*, 52.

21. Marion H. Duncan, *The Mountain of Silver Snow*, 81.

22. Loftis, *A Message From Batang*, 146; Jamyang Norbu, *Warriors of Tibet: The Story of the Aten and the Khampas Fight for the Freedom of the Country* (London: Wisdom Publications, 1986), 28.

23. Eric Teichman, *Travels of a Consular Officer in Eastern Tibet* (Cambridge, England: Cambridge University Press, 1921), 23.

24. Edgar, *Marches of the Mantze*, 29–30.

25. Loftis, *A Message From Batang*, 123; Alistair Lamb, *The McMahon Line: A Study in the Relations Between India, China, and Tibet, 1904–1914* (London: Routledge and Kegan Paul, 1966), 171.

26. Julian Pettifer and Richard Bradley, *Missionaries* (London: BBC Books, 1990), 49–50.

27. Mrs. Howard Taylor, *The Call of the China's Great North-West or, Kansu and Beyond* (London: China Inland Mission, 1926), 20. Missionary child John Espey recalled, "We heard wild stories from the other parts of China, stories of battles between the lesser breeds for the souls of a few wretched sinners." John Espey, *Minor Heresies, Major Departures: A China Mission Boyhood* (Berkeley, California: University of California Press, 1994), 25.

28. Albert L. Shelton, *Pioneering in Tibet*, 60.

29. November 1, 1919 Shelton Invoice to Newark Museum, 5, item 8, Shelton Files, Newark Museum, Newark, New Jersey noted Ongdu's previous position as the Prince's headman. Marion H. Duncan, *Mountain of Silver Snow*, 30, noted he was a "wealthy Tibetan."

30. Still, *Beyond the Devils in the Wind*, 11. Gezong Ongdu would be transliterated to Kalsang Wangdu in the modern system. Albert Shelton wrote the name as Gezong Ondu.

31. Albert L. Shelton, *Pioneering in Tibet*, 58–59.

32. Ibid., 56.

33. Ibid.

34. Ibid., 71. The great majority of Shelton's patients paid about five cents for treatment that ranged from stomachache medicine to leg amputation.

35. Geoffrey T. Bull, *When Iron Gates Yield* (Chicago: Moody Institute, 1955), 26, 41. The old missionary formula for many ailments was "An aspirin for all pains above the waist, and epsom salts for all below." Bull was fervent espouser of the Christian gospel in the borderlands until the Communist takeover. He wrote about encountering a Tibetan boy suffering from dysentery and dropsy. A lama was in attendance when Bull arrived. He told the boy's parents there were dire consequences to calling both a Christian missionary and a lama for medical treatment. "God would not allow His work to be attributed to demons," he wrote.

36. *Encyclopedia Britannica* (Cambridge, England: Cambridge University Press, 1910), vol. 12, 191–192, 247–249, 262–267, 508–509. Robert L. Ekvall, *Cultural Relations on the Kansu-Tibetan Border* (Chicago: University of Chicago Press, 1939), 37.

37. Flora B. Shelton, *Sunshine and Shadow on the Tibetan Border* (Cincinnati, Ohio: Foreign Christian Missionary Society, 1912), 56–57.

38. John MacGregor, *Tibet: A Chronicle of Exploration* (New York: Praeger Publishers, 1970), 55–56.

39. Evariste Regis Huc, *Lamas of the Western Heavens* (London: The Folio Society, [originally published 1851–1854 as Souvenirs d'un Voyage dans la Tartarie et le Thibet] 1982), 236.

40. Isabella Bird Bishop, *Among the Tibetans* (New York: Fleming H. Revell, 1894), 110–111.

41. Albert L. Shelton, *Pioneering in Tibet*, 34.

42. Flora B. Shelton, *Sunshine and Shadow on the Tibetan Border* (Cincinnati, Ohio: Foreign Christian Missionary Society, 1912), 44–45.

43. Albert L. Shelton, *Pioneering in Tibet*, 67.

44. Dr. Yeshi Dönden, *Health Through Balance: An Introduction to Tibetan Medicine* (Ithaca, New York: Snow Lion Publications, 1986), 183.

45. Ibid., 80, 86–87, 133 for overview of Tibetan medical practices and systems; Chinese pulses from Kilborn, *Heal the Sick*, 66.

46. Marion H. Duncan, *Love Songs and Proverbs of Tibet*, 183.

47. Albert L. Shelton, *Pioneering in Tibet*, 60.

48. W. W. Rockhill, *Diary of a Journey through Mongolia and Tibet in 1891 and 1892* (Washington, D.C.: Smithsonian Institution, 1894), 329.

49. Edgar, *Marches of the Mantze*, 43.

50. Photo I–15 M caption Shelton Photo Collection, Newark Museum, Newark, New Jersey.

51. Within the Tibetan tradition, great spiritual masters such as Padmasambhava and Milarepa have been laymen.

52. Albert L. Shelton, *Pioneering in Tibet*, 67–68.

53. Ibid., 61.

54. Valrae Reynolds and Barbara Lipton, *The Museum New Series* (Newark, New Jersey: Newark Museum, 1972), 22–23; Valrae Reynolds, *From the Sacred Realm: Treasures of Tibetan Art from the Newark Museum* (Munich: Prestel Verlag, 1999), 122.

Chapter 8

1. Flora B. Shelton, *Shelton of Tibet* (New York: George Doran, 1923), 147.

2. Z. S. Loftis, *A Message From Batang: The Diary of Z. S. Loftis, M.D.* (New York: Fleming H. Revell Company, 1911), 7–8, 142.

3. The Nepalese Tribute Mission had its roots in 1792 at the conclusion of the Chinese intervention in the Tibeto-Nepalese War. The Chinese saw the Nepalese as bearing the bona fide tribute of a subject nation. The Nepalese saw it as a five-year-long trading expedition. The 1907 Tribute Mission was the last of the quinquennial embassies, as the Nepalese

found they could no longer profit from the trade and found the humiliation of the subordinate status irksome.

4. Alastair Lamb, *The McMahon Line: A Study in the Relations Between India, China, and Tibet, 1904–1914,* 2 vols. (London: Routledge and Kegan Paul, 1966), vol. 2, 276.

5. Lamb, *The McMahon Line,* vol. 1, 190–191.

6. Eric Teichman, *Travels of a Consular Officer in Eastern Tibet* (Cambridge, England: Cambridge University Press, 1921), 67n.

7. Albert Marrin, *Sitting Bull and His World* (New York: Dutton Children's Books, 2000), 183, quotes General Phillip Sheridan's statement about the buffalo hunters, "They are destroying the Indians' commissary, and it is a well-known fact that an army losing its base of supplies is placed at a great disadvantage."

8. Owen Lattimore, *Studies in Frontier History; Collected Papers, 1928–1958* (London: Oxford University Press, 1962), 469, 471, noted: "If there is a great difference in social vigor and institutional strength the weaker community may simply be subsumed by the stronger; but if the difference in kind is great, while the difference in strength in not so great, the result will be a new community not only larger in numbers and occupying a greater territory, but differing in qualities from both of the communities by whose amalgamation it was created. . . . The region [frontier] is a body that does not have an edge, but shades off into a margin of uncertainty, a no-man's-land where other bands or communities may be encountered." Lattimore saw the northern frontier of China along the Great Wall as being a static zone of exclusion, while the southern frontier in Kham and Burma was one of inclusion and amalgamation.

9. Lamb, *The McMahon Line,* vol. 1, 121, 132.

10. Loftis, *A Message From Batang,* 146–155. Albert Shelton photo, Newark Museum Collection, #D 25-S and #M 42-S.

11. Teichman, *Travels of a Consular Officer in Eastern Tibet,* 27; Melvyn C. Goldstein, *A History of Modern Tibet, 1913–1951* (Berkeley, California: University of California Press, 1989), 51–52.

12. Peter Fleming, *Bayonets to Lhasa: The First Full Account of the British Invasion of Tibet in 1904* (New York: Harper, 1961), 302. Fleming recounted the trail-worn and weary Dalai Lama's arrival at the telegraph station in Sikkim manned by two British sergeants, Luff and Humphreys. Luff demanded of the fur-clad party of Tibetans: "Which one of you blighters is the Dalai Lama?"

13. Melvyn C. Goldstein, *A History of Modern Tibet, 1913–1951* (Berkeley, California: University of California Press, 1989), 52.

14. Fleming, *Bayonets to Lhasa,* 304; Goldstein, *A History of Modern Tibet, 1913–1951,* 57.

15. Lamb, *The McMahon Line,* vol. 1, 195.

16. Teichman, *Travels of a Consular Officer in Eastern Tibet,* 24.

17. F. M. Bailey, *China-Tibet-Assam: A Journey, 1911* (London: J. Cape, 1945), 74.

18. Marian L. Duncan, *A Flame of the Fire* (Spring Hill, Tennessee: Marian Duncan, 1999), 24; Rijnhart-Shelton Timeline, Shelton Files, Disciples of Christ Historical Society, Nashville, Tennessee.

19. Flora B. Shelton, *Sunshine and Shadow on the Tibetan Border* (Cincinnati, Ohio: Foreign Christian Missionary Society, 1912), 92–93.

20. Albert L. Shelton, "Batang, the New Station," *The Christian-Evangelist* (Feb. 11, 1909): 176.

21. Flora B. Shelton, *Sunshine and Shadow on the Tibetan Border,* 72.

22. 1911 questionnaire, Shelton Files, Disciple of Christ Historical Society, Nashville, Tennessee.

23. Nancy Tomes, *The Gospel of Germs: Men, Women, and the Microbe in American Life* (Cambridge, Massachusetts: Harvard University Press, 1998), 148; Peggy Pascoe, *Relations of*

Rescue: The Search for Female Moral Authority in the American West, 1874–1939 (New York: Oxford University Press, 1990).

24. Sandra L. Myres, *Westering Women and the Frontier Experience, 1800–1915* (Albuquerque, New Mexico: University of New Mexico, 1982), 6.

25. Ibid., 95.

26. Flora B. Shelton, *Sunshine and Shadow on the Tibetan Border,* following 84.

27. "Christmas Day in Tibet," *Anthony Republican,* [Kansas], Mar.18, 1910.

28. Ibid.

29. Berthold Laufer to George Dorsey, May 27, 1909, Blackstone Expedition Files, Field Museum Archives, Chicago, Illinois.

30. Flora B. Shelton, *Sunshine and Shadow on the Tibetan Border,* 86.

31. Hartmut Walravens, ed., *Kleinere Schriften von Berthold Laufer.* In *Sinologica Coloniensia* (Wiesbaden: Franz Steiner, 1976), vol 1, vii-viii, xv, xvi.

32. Berthold Laufer to George Dorsey, Sept. 23, 1910, Blackstone Expedition Files, Field Museum Archives, Chicago, Illinois. "List of Specimens collected in Sikkim, Darjeeling, Ghoom, and Kalimpong . . ." Blackstone Expedition Files, Field Museum Archives, Chicago, Illinois. In China, the standard money was the tael, which was not a coin but a fixed weight of lump silver, one Chinese ounce. However, each locale had a different standard weight, and there were various grades of silver. In Beijing alone, Laufer found seven different taels. False scales, wildly different conversions of silver to copper cash coins, and the recent introduction of silver dollars that included Hong Kong, Mexican, and Chinese provincial currency added to the complexity. In the back blocks of the empire, the situation was worse, as people were understandably suspicious of coinage in general and downright hostile to unfamiliar currency. Laufer indicated rupee conversions in 1908 in the Indian Himalayas was 100 Indian rupees = $32.77. Z. S. Loftis stated that one rupee equaled 25 cents in Kham. After Chao's invasion, the Chinese introduced a silver Chinese rupee similar in weight and purity to try to supplant the Indian rupee in wide circulation in eastern Tibet. Loftis, *A Message From Batang,* 128. Laufer's invoices indicated the exchange rate in July 1908 for the dominant currency in Chinese circulation, the Mexican dollar, was one Mexican dollar = $2.27 U.S. dollars.

33. Bennet Bronson, "Berthold Laufer at the Field Museum," unpublished manuscript. Laufer collected approximately four thousand secular and religious Tibetan objects, mostly from Kham and Beijing. The majority dated from the seventeenth to nineteenth centuries.

34. Flora B. Shelton, *Sunshine and Shadow on the Tibetan Border,* 63.

35. Flora B. Shelton, *Shelton of Tibet,* 147.

36. Flora B. Shelton, *Sunshine and Shadow on the Tibetan Border,* 60.

37. Ibid., 61.

38. Shelton Exhibit catalogue descriptions from *The Newark Museum* 2, 3 (July 1912): 16–48, Newark Museum Archives, Newark, New Jersey.

39. Ibid.

40. Albert Shelton to J. C. Dana, Mar. 11, 1912, Shelton File, Disciples of Christ Historical Society, Nashville, Tennessee.

41. William Gill, *The River of Golden Sand,* 2 vols. (London: John Murray, 1880), vol. 2, 253.

42. Ibid. vol. 2, 253.

43. Ibid., vol. 2, 112–113.

44. Ibid. Gill wrote of the material that arrived after they expressed interest in purchase. "Then all sorts of ornaments came pouring in for sale, for we had been inquiring about them—enormous finger rings, barbaric earrings, brooches and buckles, some of silver and

some of gold, and all set with huge lumps of coral and turquoise. The greatest curiosities, and best worth buying, were the charm boxes, made of gold or silver."

45. Tibet missionary Father C. H. Desgodins lamented the loss of the *"d'objects de curiosité provenant du Thibet"* the missionaries collected for the Verdun Museum when the Tibetans destroyed the Bonga mission station in 1864. They included manuscripts, arms, potteries, clothing, and natural history objects. C. H. Desgodins, *La Mission Du Thibet de 1855 à 1870* (Verdun: C. Laurent, 1872), 100.

46. Susie C. Rijnhart, *With the Tibetans in Tent and Temple* (Chicago: Fleming H. Revell Company, 1901), 258.

47. S. B. Sutton, *In China's Border Provinces* (New York: Hastings House, 1974), 218.

48. James H. Edgar, *The Land of Mystery, Tibet* (Melbourne: China Inland Mission, 1930), 18–20.

49. Grace Service (John S. Service, ed.), *Golden Inches: The China Memoir of Grace Service* (Berkeley, California: University of California Press, 1989), 254, wrote about Edgar, "He was a man of a thousand interests, who could talk well on many topics. Beyond his righteous zeal in God's work, he had a broad knowledge of ethnography, geography, philology, Asia, and his native Australia." Also see Chris Elder, "The Man Who Found Shangri-La: James Edgar Huston [sic]." *New Zealand Journal of East Asian Studies,* 1, no. 2 (1993).

50. A. G. Castleton, *Rough, Tough, and Far Away: James Edgar of Tibet* (New York: Friendship Press), 1948, 7.

51. Loftis, *A Message From Batang,* 152–153.

52. Per Kvaerne, *A Norwegian Traveler in Tibet: Theor Sörensen and the Tibetan Collection at the Oslo University Library* (New Delhi: Manjusri Publishing House, 1973), 29.

53. *Anthony Republican,* [Kansas], Mar. 4, 1910.

54. Ibid.

55. Albert L. Shelton, *Pioneering in Tibet,* 75.

56. *Anthony Republican,* [Kansas], Mar. 4, 1910.

57. *Anthony Republican,* [Kansas], Mar. 4, 1910; "From the Roof of the World," *Christian Standard* (Feb. 23, 1911): 1. The missionary newspaper stated the Sheltons needed to return home for the "long-overdue furlough," in part because the Shelton daughters "have never known the association of white children."

58. Marian L. Duncan, *A Flame of the Fire,* 24.

59. Dorris Shelton Still, *Beyond the Devils in the Wind* (Tempe, Arizona: Synergy Books, 1989), 14. Phillip (Hodabah) Ho and Marguerite Fairbrother, *Wandering Tibetan* (Long Beach, California: Christian Press, 1966), 33, stated the Wahee nomads who lived on the plateau above Batang specialized in providing animals for caravans from Batang to Tachienlu.

60. Albert L. Shelton, *Pioneering in Tibet,* 79.

61. Ibid., 79.

62. Ibid., 79–80.

63. Ibid., 80.

Chapter 9

1. Archibald McLean to Flora Shelton, Apr. 13, 1911, Still Family Archives, Scottsdale, Arizona.

2. Thomas R. Heinrich, *Ships for the Seven Seas: Philadelphia Shipbuilding in the Age of Industrial Capitalism* (Baltimore: Johns Hopkins University Press, 1997), 125.

3. Still Family Archives, Scottsdale, Arizona

4. Albert L. Shelton, *Pioneering in Tibet, A Personal Record of Life and Experience in the Mission Fields* (New York: F. H. Revell and Company, 1921), 80.

5. *Historical Statistics of the U.S.: Colonial Times to 1970* (Washington, D.C.: Bureau of the Census, 1975), A 1-A.

6. Page Smith, *America Enters the World* (New York: McGraw-Hill Book Company, 1985), 179–352; Paul Johnson, *A History of the American People* (New York: HarperCollins, 1997), 617–645.

7. Elizabeth Ewing, *History of Twentieth Century Fashion* (Totawa, New Jersey: Barnes and Noble, 1986), 1–67.

8. Sidney A. Forsythe, *An American Missionary Community in China, 1895–1905* (Cambridge, Massachusetts: East Asian Research Center, Harvard University, 1971), 19.

9. Ibid., 99. The Laymen's Mission Inquiry found that the periods of time between furloughs ranged most often from five to eight years.

10. Marian L. Duncan, *A Flame of the Fire* (Spring Hill, Tennessee: Marian Duncan, 1999), 27, wrote, "Furlough is much harder than being in the mission field because expectations are so high for speaking engagements."

11. Arlene Adams to Marion Duncan, Apr. 1, 1931, Tibetan Christian Mission File, Disciples of Christ Historical Society, Nashville, Tennessee, stated, "You no doubt know the Un-Ch-M-Soc receives many valuable courtesies from different railroads in America."

12. Marian L. Duncan, *A Flame of the Fire,* 27, 28.

13. "The Men and Millions Movement, History and Report, 1913–1919," United Christian Missionary Society Archives, Yale Divinity School Library Special Collections, New Haven, Connecticut.

14. Marian L. Duncan, *A Flame of the Fire,* 26.

15. Dr. Albert Shelton to Flora Shelton, Jan. 8, 1911, Still Family Archives, Scottsdale, Arizona.

16. Edward N. Crane to J. C. Dana, Feb. 18, 1911, Newark Museum Archives, Newark, New Jersey, Crane Files. Neither the Still Family Archives nor the archives of the Field Museum Archives contain any record of correspondence between the Sheltons and the Field Museum in this period. There is some record of interchange between the two after 1920.

17. Valrae Reynolds, *From the Sacred Realm: Treasures of Tibetan Art from the Newark Museum* (Munich: Prestel Verlag, 1999), 12.

18. J. C. Dana to Dr. Berthold Laufer, Mar. 29, 1911, Newark Museum Archives, Newark, New Jersey, Crane Files.

19. Edward N. Crane to J. C. Dana, Apr. 8, 1911, Crane Files, Newark Museum Archives, Newark, New Jersey.

20. Berthold Laufer to J. C. Dana, Apr. 5, 1911, Crane Files, Newark Museum Archives, Newark, New Jersey.

21. Edward N. Crane to J. C. Dana, May 6, 1911, Crane Files, Newark Museum Archives, Newark, New Jersey.

22. Edward N. Crane Memorial document, Oct. 16, 1911, Crane Files, Newark Museum Archives, Newark, New Jersey.

23. Reynolds, *From the Sacred Realm,* 13, 128, 157; Eleanor Olson, *Catalogue of the Tibetan Collection and other Lamaist Articles in The Newark Museum,* 5 volumes (Newark, New Jersey: The Newark Museum, 1950–1971), vol. 2, 30–31. In vol. 1, 46, the catalogue stated "Due to the destruction of the great monastery, quantities of valuable books, paintings and ritualistic articles were endangered. Many had been buried by the Tibetans during the years of fighting. Such sacred objects had seldom if ever been allowed to pass into foreign hands. Some were given to Dr. Shelton. Most were sold to him to obtain funds to buy back land from the Chinese."

24. Still Family Archives, Scottsdale, Arizona.

25. Marian L. Duncan, *A Flame of the Fire,* 28.

26. Gerald Carson, *Cornflake Crusade* (New York: Rinehart & Company, Inc., 1957), 12, 27, 55, 231, 233, 249

27. Harper County, Kansas, Recorder of Deeds records.

28. Flora B. Shelton, *Sunshine and Shadow on the Tibetan Border* (Cincinnati, Ohio: Foreign Christian Missionary Society, 1912), 138.

29. Ibid., 133.

30. Ibid., 135.

31. Marian L. Duncan, *A Flame of the Fire*, 27.

32. Flora B. Shelton, *Sunshine and Shadow on the Tibetan Border*, 138. This was probably part of Shelton's fund-raising speech during the Sheltons' first U.S. furlough.

33. "Burdettes Lecture," Still Family Archives, Scottsdale, Arizona.

34. "A Line A Day," Albert and Flora Shelton 1912–1918 diary, Jan. 1–12, 1912, Still Family Archives, Scottsdale, Arizona.

35. Flora B. Shelton, *Shelton of Tibet* (New York: George Doran, 1923), 83.

36. Still Family Archives, Scottsdale, Arizona.

37. Dr. Albert Shelton to Flora Shelton, Sept. 29, 1912, Still Family Archives, Scottsdale, Arizona.

38. Dr. Albert Shelton to J. C. Dana, Mar. 11, 1912, Shelton Files, 1918–1928 Missionary Correspondence, Disciples of Christ Historical Society, Nashville, Tennessee, Shelton File.

39. Clinton Holloway to author, Dec. 5, 2001, Disciples of Christ Historical Society Historical Society, Nashville, Tennessee.

40. Peggy Pascoe, *Relations of Rescue: The Search for Female Moral Authority in the American West, 1874–1939* (New York: Oxford University Press, 1990), xviii, xx.

41. Dr. Albert Shelton to Flora Shelton, Sept. 23, 1912, Still Family Archives, Scottsdale, Arizona.

42. Archibald McLean to Flora Shelton, Apr. 13, 1911, Still Family Archives, Scottsdale, Arizona.

43. Dr. Albert Shelton to Flora Shelton, Sept. 19, 1912, Still Family Archives, Scottsdale, Arizona.

44. David Templeman, "J. H. Edgar, an Australian Missionary in the Tibetan Marches," *Lungta* (Winter 1998): 31. CIM missionary J. H. Edgar noted, "Many, too, in the Mission Field have created an ideal China for the homeland . . . they . . . build up a composite edifice from which the ordinary elements are excluded . . . it is not reality."

45. Forsythe, *An American Missionary Community in China, 1895–1905*, 23.

46. Dr. Albert Shelton to Flora Shelton, Sept. 23, 1912, Still Family Archives, Scottsdale, Arizona.

47. Dr. Albert Shelton to Flora Shelton, Feb. 11, 1913, Still Family Archives, Scottsdale, Arizona.

48. Melvyn C. Goldstein, *A History of Modern Tibet, 1913–1951* (Berkeley, California: University of California Press, 1989), 52, 60–62.

49. "Report of a Trip Thru Eastern Tibet and Szechwan, by Major John Magruder, F.A., Asst. Military Attaché, Jan. 17-July 11, 1921 Service Report," Reel 2—U.S. War Department Military Intelligence Division, China, 1918–1941, Appendix 6 Chronology.

50. F. M. Bailey, *China-Tibet-Assam*, A Journey, 1911 (London: J. Cape, 194542, noted Chao stripped the king of Chala and thirty other local chiefs of most of their power in 1911, forcing them to hand over their seals. The 1911 revolution deprived the king of whatever power remained to him. The Chinese also changed the name of the town from Tachienlu to Kangding in 1911.

51. Eric Teichman, *Travels of a Consular Official in Eastern Tibet* (Cambridge, England: Cambridge University Press, 1921), 38.

52. Goldstein, *A History of Modern Tibet, 1913–1951,* 69.

53. Teichman, *Travels of a Consular Officer in Eastern Tibet,* 42.

54. Alastair Lamb, *The McMahon Line: A Study in the Relation Between India, China, and Tibet, 1904–1914,* 2 vols. (London: Routledge and Kegan Paul, 1966), vol. 1, 399–411; Goldstein, *A History of Modern Tibet, 1913–1951,* 65–66; Teichman, *Travels of a Consular Official in Eastern Tibet,* 38–40.

55. Marian L. Duncan, *A Flame of the Fire,* 30–31.

56. The rent on the perpetual lease on eight acres of Japoding Hill was sixty taels per year. Located across the river from the current town, Japoding Hill was the former site of Batang before an earthquake shook it down. Marian L. Duncan, *A Flame of the Fire,* 26; "Chronology, compiled by Marian (Duncan) Adams, 1992," Shelton Files, Disciples of Christ Historical Society Archives, Nashville, Tennessee.

57. Albert L. Shelton, *Pioneering in Tibet,* 81.

Chapter 10

1. Dr. Albert Shelton to J. C. Dana, May 20, 1916, Shelton Files, Disciples of Christ Historical Society Archives, Nashville, Tennessee.

2. Albert L. Shelton, *Pioneering in Tibet, A Personal Record of Life and Experience in the Mission Fields* (New York: F. H. Revell Company, 1921), 82–83.

3. Edith Eberle, rev. Lois Anna Ely, *They Went to China: Biographies of Missionaries of the Disciples of Christ* (Indianapolis, Indiana: Missionary Education Department, the United Christian Missionary Society, 1948), 34.

4. Marian L. Duncan, *A Flame of the Fire* (Spring Hill, Tennessee: Marian Duncan, 1999), 29, 32.

5. Albert L. Shelton, *Pioneering in Tibet,* 82.

6. Dr. William Hardy to Archibald McLean, Aug. 30, 1913 Hardy Files, Disciples of Christ Historical Society, Nashville, Tennessee.

7. Tibetan Christian Mission minutes, Aug. 25, 1913 Hardy Files, Disciples of Christ Historical Society, Nashville, Tennessee.

8. Marian L. Duncan, *A Flame of the Fire,* 30.

9. Ibid., 32.

10. Flora B. Shelton, *Shelton of Tibet* (New York: George Doran, 1923), 86.

11. Dr. Albert Shelton to Bro Henry, Jan. 18, 1914 Disciples of Christ Historical Society, Nashville, Tennessee, Shelton File.

12. Alastair Lamb, *The McMahon Line: A Study in the Relation Between India, China, and Tibet, 1904–1914,* 2 vols. (London: Routledge and Kegan Paul, 1966),vol. 2, 480.

13. Melvyn C. Goldstein, *A History of Modern Tibet, 1913–1951* (Berkeley, California: University of California Press, 1989), 74; Peter Fleming, *Bayonets to Lhasa: The First Full Account of the British Invasion of Tibet in 1904* (New York: Harper, 1961), 304; John Bray, "Christian Missions and the Politics of Tibet, 1850–1950," Wilfred Wagner, ed., *Kolonien & Missionen, Referate des. 3. Internationalen Kolonialgeschichten Symposiums 1993 in Bremen* (Bremen: Bremer Asien-Pazifik Studien, 1993), 191.

14. While the British finally attained their goal of breaking the Chinese tea monopoly in Tibet, their Assam product may have failed to capture the market. Writing of the Tibetans' love of yak-butter tea mixed with *tsampa,* Eric Teichman stated, "Indian tea, which does not stew very well, is not suitable for making a brew of this kind." Eric Teichman, *Travels of a Consular Officer in Eastern Tibet* (Cambridge, England: Cambridge University Press, 1921), 62. It may have been just as well, as the British imported village coolies to clear the virgin jungle in Assam with an onerous system of five-year contracts

of indentured servitude. A contemporary historian termed the tea-field workers in Assam to be laboring "under conditions that amounted to slavery." The peak years of production were 1911 to 1921. William Hardy McNeill, *The Great Frontier: Freedom and Hierarchy in Modern Times* (Princeton, New Jersey: Princeton University Press, 1983), 50.

15. Educating young Tibetans at Western institutions was not a new idea. Younghusband bandied the idea about, and the Dalai Lama explored the idea with British consular officer Clive Bell during his 1910–1912 exile in Darjeeling. When the Dalai Lama returned to Lhasa following the Chinese revolution, he implemented the idea. In early 1913, four Tibetan boys arrived at the British Trade Agency in Gyantse with a letter from the Dalai Lama requesting "four first class educations at Oxford College, London." The four youths, accompanied by a Tibetan official and two servants, reached England in April 1913. After English language lessons taught by the Berlitz School of Languages, the boys attended Rugby. Lamb, *The McMahon Line,* vol. 2, 599–603; Karl Ernest Meyer and Shareen Blair Brysac, *Tournament of Shadows: The Great Game and Race for Empire in Central Asia* (Washington, D.C.: Counterpoint, 1999), 434, 517.

16. "Report of a Trip Thru Yunnan, Eastern Tibet and Szechwan by Major John Magruder, F.A., Ass't. Military Attache, Jan. 17-July 11, 1921, Reel 2—U.S. War Dept. Military Intelligence Division China, 1918–1941.

17. Teichman, *Travels of a Consular Officer in Eastern Tibet,* 124.

18. "Report of a Trip Thru Yunnan, Eastern Tibet and Szechwan by Major John Magruder, F.A., Ass't. Military Attache, Jan. 17-July 11, 1921, Reel 2—U.S. War Dept. Military Intelligence Division China, 1918–1941, contained quoted reports from "an American missionary at Batang" on military conditions and maneuvers.

19. Norman Hall, "The U.S., Tibet, and China—A Study in American Involvement in Tibet," *Tibetan Review* (January 1978): 13, 15. Most of the foreign relations between the United States and Tibet took place between private unofficial individuals such as missionaries, explorers, and scientists. It was an intermittent exchange that consistently deferred to America's larger China policy. The United States' relations with Tibet were primarily passive. Hence, private individuals such as Albert Shelton took on an out-sized diplomatic role. Bray, "Christian Missions and the Politics of Tibet, 1850–1950," 190; Lucian Bodard, *The French Consul* (New York: Knopf, [1973] 1977), 58; Coales, "Eastern Tibet," *Geographical Journal* 53, no. 4 (January-June 1919); Louis King despatch to Sir Beilby Alston, 24 Aug. 1921 Oriental and India Office Collections, British Library, London; "Report of a Trip Thru Yunnan, Eastern Tibet, and Szechuan, by Major John Magruder, F.A., Ass't Military Attache, Jan. 17-July 11, 1921," 13, Reel 2—U.S. War Dept. Military Intelligence Division China, 1918–1941; United States War Department, Military Intelligence Division, *Correspondence of the Military Intelligence Division Relating to General, Political, Economic, and Military Conditions in China, 1918–1941* (reels 1–4, 1918–1923) (Washington, D.C., National Archives and Records Administration, 1986).

20. "Articles and Resolutions," 4, Disciples of Christ Historical Society, Nashville, Tennessee, Shelton Files. Albert L. Shelton, *Pioneering in Tibet,* 84, stated it was "some hundred or more coolies."

21. "A Line a Day," Flora and Albert Shelton diary 1912–1918, February 11–16, 1916, Still Family Archives, Scottsdale, Arizona.

22. Flora B. Shelton, *Shelton of Tibet,* 86.

23. P. D. Coates, *The China Consuls: British Consular Officers, 1843–1943* (Hong Kong: Oxford University Press, 1963), 417–423.

24. "A Line a Day," Flora and Albert Shelton diary 1912–1918, Feb. 23, 1914, Still Family Archives, Scottsdale, Arizona.

25. Tibetan Christian Mission minutes, June 15, 1914, Hardy Files, Disciples of Christ Historical Society, Nashville, Tennessee.

26. Albert L. Shelton, *Pioneering in Tibet,* 85.

27. "A Letter from Brother Ogden," *Christian-Evangelist* (Nov. 5, 1914): 1432.

28. "From America to Tibet—Batang at Last," *Christian-Evangelist* (Nov. 4, 1915): 1403.

29. Teichman, *Travels of a Consular Officer in Eastern Tibet,* 224.

30. "A Line a Day," Flora and Albert Shelton diary 1912–1918, Sept. 20–25, 1914, Still Family Archives, Scottsdale, Arizona.

31. Flora B. Shelton, *Shelton of Tibet,* 89–91; "A Line a Day," Flora and Albert Shelton diary 1912–1918, July 8, 1914, Still Family Archives, Scottsdale, Arizona. She wrote, "Came to a big lamasery & was frightened so badly at the hundreds of lamas on the roof I cried. Bert stayed behind & shot badgers or rather marmots, & I'm afraid of lamas anyway."

32. "From America to Tibet," *Christian-Evangelist* (July 22, 1915): 935; "From America to Tibet: A Perilous Journey," *Christian-Evangelist* (Oct. 14, 1915): 1308 for photo.

33. Flora B. Shelton, *Shelton of Tibet,* 87; "Articles and Resolutions," 4, Disciples of Christ Historical Society, Nashville, Tennessee, Shelton Files.

34. "A Line a Day," Flora and Albert Shelton diary 1912–1918, July 19–21, 1914, Still Family Archives, Scottsdale, Arizona.

35. Marian L. Duncan, *A Flame of the Fire,* 35.

36. Tibetan Christian Mission minutes, Nov. 2, 1914, Hardy Files, Disciples of Christ Historical Society, Nashville, Tennessee.

37. Teichman, *Travels of a Consular Officer in Eastern Tibet,* 43.

38. Draya was a town of about 150 families located in a plain where three rivers came together. Prior to the Chinese incursions, it was a lama state ruled by reincarnate lamas. Oliver Coales, "Eastern Tibet," 247.

39. Albert Shelton to J. O. LaGorce, Dec. 17, 1920, National Geographic Society Archives, Washington, D.C.

40. Albert L. Shelton, *Pioneering in Tibet,* 93–94.

41. Howard Van Dyck, *William Christie: Apostle to Tibet* (Harrisburg, Pennsylvania: Christian Publications, Inc. 1956), 83, 96–97; B. L. Putnam Weale, *The Fight for the Republic in China* (New York: Dodd, Mead and Company, 1917), 62; Teichman, *Travels of a Consular Officer in Eastern Tibet,* 47–49.

42. Goldstein, *A History of Modern Tibet, 1913–1951,* 78–79

43. "A Line a Day," Flora and Albert Shelton diary 1912–1918, Jan. 25–31, 1915, Still Family Archives, Scottsdale, Arizona.

44. Goldstein, *A History of Modern Tibet,* 78.

45. "A Line a Day," Flora and Albert Shelton diary 1912–1918, Jan. 1, 1915, Still Family Archives, Scottsdale, Arizona.

46. Given their affluent status in Kham, the TCM and CIM missionaries served as banks for merchants. Marion H. Duncan described the process whereby a Batang merchant would give the TCM cash and get a draft written in English. Once he traveled to Tachienlu, he would present it to the CIM mission there for cash, which he used to purchase his trade goods. A journey for cash such as Albert Shelton embarked upon normally brought back five to ten loads of silver, enough for a year for the mission. Naturally, it was a well-guarded caravan. Marion H. Duncan, *The Mountain of Silver Snow* (Cincinnati, Ohio, Powell & White, 1929), 97.

47. "A Line a Day," Flora and Albert Shelton diary 1912–1918, Dec. 30, 1914, Still Family Archives, Scottsdale, Arizona.

48. Albert L. Shelton, *Pioneering in Tibet,* 102.

49. Ibid., 104.

50. Marian L. Duncan, *A Flame of the Fire,* 36. Duncan stated 1,500 rupees was equivalent to $750. Sidney A. Forsythe, *An American Missionary Community in China, 1895–1905* (Cambridge, Massachusetts: East Asian Research Center, Harvard University, 1971), 35, noted the indifference of the missionaries toward status gradations within the Chinese gentry class. From his analysis of missionary writings, it appeared that missionaries lumped all gentry under the level of viceroy and governor into one class of civil servants. As was the case in Tachienlu and Batang, most interactions were at the district magistrate level.

51. "A Line a Day," Flora and Albert Shelton diary 1912–1918, Nov. 3, 1914, Still Family Archives, Scottsdale, Arizona.

52. "A Line a Day," Flora and Albert Shelton diary 1912–1918, Nov. 5, 1914, Still Family Archives, Scottsdale, Arizona.

53. Marion H. Duncan, *The Mountain of Silver Snow,* 82.

54. TCM meeting minutes, May 1, 1916, Disciples of Christ Historical Society Archives, Nashville, Tennessee, Hardy Files.

55. Marion H. Duncan, *The Mountain of Silver Snow,* 82.

56. "An interview with Dr. Hardy of Batang," Disciples of Christ Historical Society Archives, Nashville, Tennessee, Hardy Files. The mission used outdoor privies for toilet facilities during the Sheltons' posting there. Dorris Shelton Still and Dorothy Shelton Thomas discussed the issue in a series of filmed interviews in the 1980s. John Basmajian Film Archives, Los Angeles, California.

57. Marian L. Duncan, *A Flame of the Fire,* 35.

58. Ibid., 36.

59. Ibid.

60. Photograph, Miscellaneous Tibet Files, Disciples of Christ Historical Society, Nashville, Tennessee.

61. Marion H. Duncan, *The Mountain of Silver Snow,* 93.

62. Coates, *The China Consuls,* 417–423; Louis Magrath King, *China in Turmoil, Studies in Personality* (London: Heath, Cranton, Limited, 1927), 36–37.

63. Teichman, *Travels of a Consular Officer in Eastern Tibet,* 47.

64. "A Line a Day," Flora and Albert Shelton diary 1912–1918, Jan. 21–22, 1915, Still Family Archives, Scottsdale, Arizona.

65. "A Line a Day," Flora and Albert Shelton diary 1912–1918, Aug. 4, 1915, Still Family Archives, Scottsdale, Arizona.

66. Flora B. Shelton, *Shelton of Tibet,* 94.

67. "A Line a Day," Flora and Albert Shelton diary 1912–1918, Feb. 20, 1917, Still Family Archives, Scottsdale, Arizona.

68. "A Line a Day," Flora and Albert Shelton diary 1912–1918, June 9–29, 1915, Still Family Archives, Scottsdale, Arizona.

69. "A Line a Day," Flora and Albert Shelton diary 1912–1918, Aug. 2, 1915, Still Family Archives, Scottsdale, Arizona.

70. Archibald McLean, *History of the Foreign Christian Mission Society* (New York: Fleming H. Revell, 1919), 355.

71. Louise Connolly, "Tibet," 35, Newark Museum Archives, Newark, New Jersey.

72. Albert Shelton Monthly Report, July 31, 1917, Shelton Files, 1918–1928 Missionary Correspondence, Disciples of Christ Historical Society, Nashville, Tennessee.

73. "A Line a Day," Flora and Albert Shelton diary 1912–1918, Aug. 15–16, 1915, Still Family Archives, Scottsdale, Arizona.

74. "A Line a Day," Flora and Albert Shelton diary 1912–1918, Aug. 31, 1916, Still Family Archives, Scottsdale, Arizona.

75. "Report of a Trip Thru Yunnan, Eastern Tibet and Szechwan by Major John Magruder, F.A., Ass't. Military Attache, Jan. 17-July 11, 1921, Reel 2—U.S. War Dept. Military Intelligence Division China, 1918–1941.

76. Kemp Tolley, *Yangtze Patrol: The U.S. Navy in China* (Annapolis, Maryland: Naval Institute Press, 1971), 24. In 1915, Japan presented "Twenty-one Demands" to China that would have reduced China to the status of a Japanese colony. Internal order decayed to the point to which there was virtually no traffic on the Yangtze as armed bands shot at anything moving.

77. Robert A. Kapp, *Szechuan and the Chinese Republic: Provincial Militarism and Central Power, 1911–1938* (New Haven: Yale University Press, 1973), 69–70. Kapp noted from the late 1920s to the early 1930s, Sichuan seldom made it into statistical province-by-province abstracts of the Nationalist government. It was just out there.

78. Teichman, *Travels of a Consular Officer in Eastern Tibet*, 51.

79. "A Line a Day," Flora and Albert Shelton diary 1912–1918, July 8, 1916, Still Family Archives, Scottsdale, Arizona.

80. "A Line a Day," Flora and Albert Shelton diary 1912–1918, March 5, 1917, Still Family Archives, Scottsdale, Arizona.

81. "Report of a Trip Thru Yunnan, Eastern Tibet and Szechwan by Major John Magruder, F.A., Ass't. Military Attache, Jan. 17-July 11, 1921, Reel 2—U.S. War Dept. Military Intelligence Division China, 1918–1941 noted the existence of the Twan Shang secret society. The Seven Tribes of the Sangen plotted with the Hsiang-ch'eng; rebel lamas from south in Yunnan also allied themselves with the renegade groups. Mutinying Chinese officers sometimes joined forces with the tribesmen.

82. "An interview with Dr. Hardy of Batang," Hardy Files, Disciples of Christ Historical Society Archives, Nashville, Tennessee.

83. Beyond their first purchase, the Newark Museum purchased Tibetan material from Shelton in 1914, 1918, and a large collection in 1920. Shelton's diary of his trip to the Hsiang-ch'eng during his first Batang posting offered a glimpse into the role of collection in his itinerations. He noted some pricing detail at the Derge printing house when he itinerated there. "I made inquiries as to the cost of these and found that the cost of the Gangur, which is printed in red, is about twelve hundred rupees. . . ." Albert L. Shelton, *Pioneering in Tibet*, 109.

84. "A Line a Day," Flora and Albert Shelton diary 1912–1918, Sept. 7, 1916, Still Family Archives, Scottsdale, Arizona.

85. "A Line a Day," Flora and Albert Shelton diary 1912–1918, Apr. 30-May 1, 1916, Still Family Archives, Scottsdale, Arizona.

86. Flora B. Shelton, *Shelton of Tibet*, 186–187.

87. "A Line a Day," Flora and Albert Shelton diary 1912–1918, Aug. 24, 1915, Still Family Archives, Scottsdale, Arizona.

88. Dr. Albert Shelton to J. C. Dana, May 20, 1916, Shelton Files, Disciples of Christ Historical Society Archives, Nashville, Tennessee.

89. J. C. Dana to Albert Shelton, Jan. 18, 1915; Albert Shelton to J. C. Dana, return undated, Shelton Files, Newark Museum Archives, Newark New Jersey.

90. Newark Museum to Naomi Shelton, Apr. 13, 1918; Newark Museum to Naomi Shelton, Apr. 4, 1918, Shelton Files, Newark Museum Archives, Newark, New Jersey. Inventory: Valrae Reynolds, Curator of Asian Collections, to author, Dec. 3, 1999, Newark Museum, Newark, New Jersey. Purchase in 1914 is accession numbers 14.1074-.83; 1918 purchase is 18.141–2.

91. Valrae Reynolds, *From the Sacred Realm: Treasures of Tibetan Art from the Newark Museum* (Munich: Prestel Verlag, 1999), 128.

92. Eleanor Olson, *Catalogue of the Tibetan Collection and other Lamaist Articles in The Newark Museum,* 5 vols. (Newark, New Jersey: The Newark Museum, 1950–1971), vol. 3, 123–124. The prince's scion was another well-connected Khampa. Beyond his family's prominence in Batang, he was the nephew of the influential Tibetan government officials in the adjacent Lhasa-controlled region of Markham.

93. O. A. Rosboro to National Geographic Society, May 5, 1916; J. O. LaGorce to O. A. Rosboro, May 15, 1916; O. A. Rosboro to J. O. LaGorce, May 17, 1916; J. O. LaGorce to O. A. Rosboro, July 1916, National Geographic Archives, Washington, D.C. Marian L. Duncan, *A Flame of the Fire,* 37, 45. Duncan stated, "Developing film and printing pictures was an activity of all the missionaries, producing excellent records of the people and country."

94. Still Family Archives, Scottsdale, Arizona; Royal Geographical Society Archives, London.

95. Albert Shelton, "Certificate of Candidate for Election," Royal Geographical Society Archives, London.

96. Photograph of Shelton home, Miscellaneous Tibet Files, Disciples of Christ Historical Society Archives, Nashville, Tennessee.

97. Photo in Miscellaneous Tibet File, Disciples of Christ Historical Society, Nashville, Tennessee.

98. McLean, *The History of the Foreign Christian Missionary Society,* 355.

99. Marion H. Duncan, *The Mountain of Silver Snow,* 85–86.

100. A Hutchinson, Kansas newspaper noted, "R. A. Long, the Kansas City lumberman, gave Dr. Shelton $5,000 for a hospital at Batang." "Are Alone in Thibet," Undated and unidentified clipping [1914?], Historic Adobe Museum, Ulysses, Kansas.

101. S. J. Corey to Albert Shelton, Mar. 24, 1921, Shelton Files, 1918–1928 Missionary Correspondence, Disciples of Christ Historical Society, Nashville, Tennessee. The hospital was named Diltz Memorial Hospital in 1921, after she gave Albert Shelton another $5,000 toward the hospital.

102. The Rockefeller Archive Center, RG4 (China Medical Board), Box 21, folder 409 Foreign Christian Missionary Society, Hospital, Batang, Szechuan 1917, Rockefeller Archive Center, North Tarrytown, New York. Shelton indicated his salary was $1,200 a year, with the mission providing housing. Marian L. Duncan, *A Flame of the Fire,* 39. Beyond their FCMS salaries, the missionaries depended on Living Link churches that provided financial aid, prayer, and friendship. Some missionaries like the Sheltons also developed further financial support from wealthy donors.

103. Flora B. Shelton, *Shelton of Tibet,* 186.

104. Albert Schenkel, *The Rich Man and the Kingdom: John D. Rockefeller, Jr. and the Protestant Establishment* (Minneapolis, Minnesota: Fortress Press, 1995), 98.

105. TCM Reports, August, October, November 1917, Shelton Files, 1918–1928 Missionary Correspondence, Disciples of Christ Historical Society Archives, Nashville, Tennessee. Shelton reported 984 treatments with an income of 1,065 rupees. Expenses were 52 rupees, leaving 1,013 rupees to send to the TCM treasury.

106. Flora B. Shelton, *Shelton of Tibet,* 186.

107. Albert L. Shelton, *Pioneering in Tibet,* 66, 79. There is no record of either man's conversion. Gezong Ongdu read Buddhist scripture at Shelton's funeral.

108. Presbyterian missionary child John Espey described his own missionary parents' attempts to convert the domestic help in Shanghai as running in six-month cycles. The servants always parried the attempts with diplomatic rejoinders. The amah said she was, of course, ready to convert, but her husband wasn't. It wouldn't do to have married couple split, would it? The cook was always a half-step closer, though he still had a few doubts and concerns. John Espey, *Minor Heresies, Major Departures: A China Mission Boyhood* (Berkeley, California: University of California Press, 1994), 43–44.

109. Marian L. Duncan, *A Flame of the Fire,* 39.

110. "A Line a Day," Flora and Albert Shelton diary 1912–1918, Mar. 4, 1914, Mar. 18, 1915, Still Family Archives, Scottsdale, Arizona.

111. "A Line a Day," Flora and Albert Shelton diary 1912–1918, Mar. 26, 1915, Apr. 22, 1915, Still Family Archives, Scottsdale, Arizona.

112. A few days after his son Charlie's birth, Dr. Susie Rijnhart's husband, Petrus, vowed Charlie "must have the best training in English, French, and German, so that he may not feel that because he was a missionary's son he missed the joys that brighten other lives." Alvyn Austin, *Saving China: Canadian Missionaries in the Middle Kingdom, 1888–1959* (Toronto: University of Toronto Press, 1986), 331.

113. "I liked the excellently planned sheets sent for daily lesson use," Grace Service wrote about the Calvert School, "and found the textbooks all that could be desired." Grace Service (John S. Service, ed.), *Golden Inches: The China Memoir of Grace Service* (Berkeley, California: University of California Press, 1989), 184.

114. "A Line a Day," Flora and Albert Shelton diary 1912–1918, Feb. 4, 1915, Still Family Archives, Scottsdale, Arizona.

115. "A Line a Day," Flora and Albert Shelton diary 1912–1918, June 19, 1917, Still Family Archives, Scottsdale, Arizona.

116. Dorris Shelton Still, *Beyond the Devils in the Wind* (Tempe, Arizona: Synergy Books, 1989), 61–62.

117. The Shelton daughters' relationship with the local populace was characteristic of foreign missionary children's. John Espey wrote of his missionary childhood: "Even though we lived a transplanted middle-class American life when it came to food and clothing, we lived another part of our lives with the Chinese servants. We found ourselves in a trying position, knowing not only that we should honor our parents but that we should do nothing to disgrace the household or risk anything that would make our parents lose face in the eyes of the Chinese. Sometimes the roles overlapped; sometimes they seemed irreconcilable." Espey, *Minor Heresies, Major Departures,* 4.

118. Still, *Beyond the Devils in the Wind,* 39–44.

119. Espey, *Minor Heresies, Major Departures,* 46. Service, *Golden Inches,* 4n. Missionary child Robert Service wrote: "Monkey Ward gave a very useful discount to Y people and probably to other missionaries as well. Through our childhood, the more-or-less annual arrival of a shipment from Montgomery Ward was a joyously, exciting event. And the fat, brightly illustrated catalogue was a vivid and sometimes perplexing view of a remote, vaguely known home."

120. Still, *Beyond the Devils in the Wind,* 40.

121. "A Line a Day," Flora and Albert Shelton diary 1912–1918, Dec. 20, 1914, Still Family Archives, Scottsdale, Arizona.

122. Roderick MacLeod to Bert Wilson, MacLeod Files, Feb. 22, 1918, 1918–1928 Missionary Correspondence, Disciples of Christ Historical Society, Nashville, Tennessee.

123. "A Line a Day," Flora and Albert Shelton diary 1912–1918, Mar. 3, 1915, Still Family Archives, Scottsdale, Arizona.

124. "In the Bad Lands of Eastern Tibet," Shelton Files, Disciples of Christ Historical Society, Nashville, Tennessee.

125. Albert Shelton to J. O. LaGorce, Oct. 28, 1919, Shelton Files, National Geographic Society, Washington, D.C.

126. "A Line a Day," Flora and Albert Shelton diary 1912–1918, Feb. 13, 1915, Still Family Archives, Scottsdale, Arizona.

127. Roderick MacLeod account of Tibetan New Years to Archibald McLean, Mar. 28, 1918, MacLeod Files, Disciples of Christ Historical Society Archives, Nashville, Tennessee. Rit-

ual dance in Tibet, 'chams, have been performed since the seventeenth century. With roots in pre-Buddhist shamanistic practices, monk dancers performed the dances with monk orchestras for the Tibetan public. In essence morality plays, the dances were an opportunity for laymen to gain spiritual merit. Reynolds, *From the Sacred Realm*, 130–131.

128. Roderick MacLeod account of Tibetan New Years to Archibald McLean, Mar. 28, 1918, MacLeod Files, Disciples of Christ Historical Society Archives, Nashville, Tennessee.

129. "A Line a Day," Flora and Albert Shelton diary 1912–1918, Jan. 11, 1917, Still Family Archives, Scottsdale, Arizona.

130. Shelton Files, Disciples of Christ Historical Society Archives, Nashville, Tennessee.

131. In a letter to College of Missions Chinese instructor T. T. Liu, Albert Shelton asked for a translation of a letter from a Chinese general, "as I have no sufficient knowledge of the written Chinese to be able to make it out." Albert Shelton to T. T. Liu, Oct. 23, 1920, Shelton Files, Disciples of Christ Historical Society Archives, Nashville, Tennessee.

132. Shelton's Chinese and Tibetan illiteracy was discordant with the Disciples of Christ's strong scripture-based faith. Disciples' founder Alexander Campbell preached that all believers should have the ability to read the bible as if it were delivered direct to them without the intercession of clergy or other professionals. Indeed, the Disciples valued sacred literature and commentary so highly it was commonly said that the Disciples didn't have bishops, they had editors. L. C. Rudolph, *Hoosier Faiths: A History of Indiana Churches and Religious Groups* (Bloomington, Indiana: Indiana University Press, 1995), 76–77.

In 1919 Esther MacLeod estimated there were a million people in her reporting area of 126,000 square miles. Of those, 5 percent of the men were literate; 1 percent of the women. "Campaign Survey Interfaith World Movement of North America," Tibet Files, Disciples of Christ Historical Society, Nashville, Tennessee.

133. "A Line a Day," Flora and Albert Shelton diary 1912–1918, Jan. 15, 1915, Still Family Archives, Scottsdale, Arizona.

134. "A Line a Day," Flora and Albert Shelton diary 1912–1918, Sept. 16, 1915, Still Family Archives, Scottsdale, Arizona.

135. "A Line a Day," Flora and Albert Shelton diary 1912–1918, Mar. 3, 1916, Still Family Archives, Scottsdale, Arizona.

136. "A Line a Day," Flora and Albert Shelton diary 1912–1918, Feb. 16, 1916, Still Family Archives, Scottsdale, Arizona.

137. "A Line a Day," Flora and Albert Shelton diary 1912–1918, Apr. 15, 1915, Still Family Archives, Scottsdale, Arizona.

138. "A Line a Day," Flora and Albert Shelton diary 1912–1918, Jan. 28, 1917, Still Family Archives, Scottsdale, Arizona.

139. Marian L. Duncan, *A Flame of the Fire*, 39.

140. Flora B. Shelton, *Shelton of Tibet*, 131; Hall, "The U.S., Tibet, and China—A Study in American Involvement in Tibet," 14.

141. T. T. Cooper wrote: "Of all the rogues one encounters in Thibet and the frontier towns of China, the professional interpreters are the greatest, and should be carefully avoided. Their profession is a lucrative one, and their appearance, generally speaking is very respectable; indeed, without some previous knowledge of the class, one might take them for petty mandarins, whose air and manners they generally assume." T. T. Cooper, *Travels of a Pioneer of Commerce* (New York: Arno Press, 1967 (originally published in 1871), 235.

142. Flora B. Shelton, *Shelton of Tibet*, 190; Teichman, *Travels of a Consular Officer in Eastern Tibet*, 147.

143. Albert L. Shelton, *Pioneering in Tibet*, 124.

144. Ibid., 123–124.

145. "A Line a Day," Flora and Albert Shelton diary 1912–1918, Sept. 7, 1916, Still Family Archives, Scottsdale, Arizona.

146. "In the Bad Lands of Eastern Tibet," Shelton Files, Disciples of Christ Historical Society, Nashville, Tennessee.

147. Ibid.

148. Valrae Reynolds to Dorothy Thomas, Aug. 12, 1982, Newark Museum Archives, Newark, New Jersey, Shelton Files.

149. Teichman, *Travels of a Consular Officer in Eastern Tibet,* 142.

150. Albert L. Shelton, *Pioneering in Tibet,* 125

151. Albert L. Shelton, *Pioneering in Tibet,* 116–118; "Making a Goat of the Goat," *Christian-Evangelist* (Apr. 19, 1917): 475.

152. Albert L. Shelton, *Pioneering in Tibet,* 116–118. The story of the smashed charm box became one of Shelton's most oft-told tales, one that he recounted to Batang visitors, furlough audiences, and reporters for the rest of his life. In a small box in the Disciples of Christ Historical Society in Nashville, Tennessee, are the remains of a smashed-up Tibetan charm box without any explanation or provenance. It looks as though a bullet hit it.

153. Albert L. Shelton, *Pioneering in Tibet,* 116–118; "Making a Goat of the Goat," *Christian-Evangelist* (Apr. 19, 1917): 475–476.

154. "A Line a Day," Flora and Albert Shelton diary 1912–1918, Oct. 18, 1915, Still Family Archives, Scottsdale, Arizona; Flora B. Shelton, *Shelton of Tibet,* 133.

Chapter 11

1. Memoranda page, "A Line a Day," Flora and Albert Shelton 1912–1918 Diary, Still Family Archives, Scottsdale, Arizona.

2. Flora B. Shelton, *Shelton of Tibet* (Cincinnati, Ohio: Foreign Christian Missionary Society, 1923), 101. Eric Teichman, *Travels of a Consular Official in North-West China* (Cambridge, England: Cambridge University Press, 1922), 67, wrote of encountering in 1918 a remnant colony of Chinese farmers in northern Kham attached to a Catholic mission. As almost all of the Chinese agriculturists had long since fled Kham, he found it of interest. He attributed their presence to the fact they were northern border country semi-tribesmen rather than Sichuanese, who he felt were incapable of settling the uplands.

3. "Cast Thy Bread Upon the Waters," *World Call* (March 1920): 47.

4. Eric Teichman, *Travels of a Consular Officer in Eastern Tibet* (Cambridge, England: Cambridge University Press, 1921), 53.

5. Teichman, *Travels of a Consular Officer in Eastern Tibet,* 135. Teichman quoted a west China missionary's letter to the Shanghai English press, "To sum up what China is doing here in Eastern Tibet, the main things are collecting taxes, robbing, oppressing, confiscating, and allowing her representatives to burn and loot and steal."

6. The *Tingling* was the ranking military officer in Batang. *T'ing* were the subprefectures the Chinese established in the mountainous margins of the empire to rule the aboriginal people with a type of military district. These districts were in the west borderlands of Sichuan, Yunnan, Gansu, northern Shaanxi, and along the Mongolian and Chinese-Burmese borders. Both military and civilian officials shared the district administration. Teichman, *Travels of a Consular Official in North-West China,* 45. Batang served as the Chinese military headquarters for a region stretching from Litang west to Yenjin on the Mekong. The troops were the remnant of Chao's *Pien Chün* frontier force—"now so completely worn out, sodden with opium, and generally demoralized as to be nearly useless as a fighting force." Teichman, *Travels of a Consular Officer in Eastern Tibet,* 136–137.

7. "A Line a Day," Flora and Albert Shelton 1912–1918 Diary, Mar. 6–8, 1918, Still Family Archives, Scottsdale, Arizona. Shelton had previously traveled to Gartok in 1915 at the behest of the Batang Chinese commandant. Marian L. Duncan, *A Flame of the Fire* (Spring Hill, Tennessee: Marian Duncan, 1999), 34.

8. Dr. Albert Shelton to Brother Doan, Jan. 17, 1918, Shelton Files, 1918–1928 Missionary Correspondence, Disciples of Christ Historical Society, Nashville, Tennessee.

9. Dr. Albert Shelton to Archibald McLean, Jan. 28, 1918, Shelton Files, 1918–1928 Missionary Correspondence, Disciples of Christ Historical Society, Nashville, Tennessee.

10. Dr. Albert Shelton to Brother Doan, Jan. 28, 1918, Shelton Files, 1918–1928 Missionary Correspondence, Disciples of Christ Historical Society, Nashville, Tennessee.

11. Marion H. Duncan, *The Mountain of Silver Snow* (Cincinnati, Ohio: Powell & White, 1929), 100. "In the formative years of adolescence it may be very detrimental to the morality and ideals of the child if he is forced to live in an entirely Oriental environment," TCM missionary Marion Duncan wrote. "The missionary is compelled either to leave his children in America with strangers or stay with them at least until they are out of high school."

12. Dr. Albert Shelton to Archibald McLean and the Executive Committee, Feb. 5, 1918, Shelton Files, 1918–1928 Missionary Correspondence, Disciples of Christ Historical Society, Nashville, Tennessee.

13. Albert L. Shelton, *Pioneering in Tibet, A Personal Record of Life and Experience in the Mission Fields* (New York: F. H. Revell and Company, 1921), 128; Flora B. Shelton, *Shelton of Tibet*, 196. Albert Shelton termed the lamas "headmen," while Flora Shelton noted they were lamas. Their presence buttressed Shelton's position as an arbiter.

14. The town was often referred to as Markham Gartok to distinguish it from the Tibetan city of Gartok far to the west.

15. Tibet Photo #I 14-M, Newark Museum, Newark, New Jersey.

16. Albert L. Shelton, *Pioneering in Tibet*, 130.

17. Ibid., 131.

18. Julian Pettifer and Richard Bradley, *Missionaries* (London: BBC Books, 1990), 174; Kemp Tolley, *Yangtze Patrol: The U.S. Navy in China* (Annapolis, Maryland: Naval Institute Press, 1971), 41, quoted an 1861 memorial to the imperial emperor, "Of all the Western barbarians, the English are the most crafty, the French next; the Russians are stronger than either the English or French and are always struggling with them. The Americans are pure-minded and honest disposition and long recognized as respectful and compliant toward China."

19. Norman Hall, "The U.S., Tibet, and China—A Study in American Involvement in Tibet," *Tibetan Review* (January 1978): 13, 15.

20. Records of the Department of State Relating to Internal Affairs of China, 1910–1929 (Washington, D.C.: National Archives and Record Service, 1973), 809–810.

21. The Batang missionaries and Eric Teichman termed Liu a general, though U.S. Major John Magruder titled Liu a colonel.

22. "A Line a Day," Flora and Albert Shelton 1912–1918 Diary, Mar. 11–12, 1918, Still Family Archives, Scottsdale, Arizona.

23. April 13–14, 1918, Albert L. Shelton, *Pioneering in Tibet*, 131.

24. Albert L. Shelton, *Pioneering in Tibet*, 131–132. General Liu left for Gartok on April 20, 1918. "A Line a Day," Flora and Albert Shelton 1912–1918 Diary, Apr. 20, 1918, Still Family Archives, Scottsdale, Arizona.

25. Albert L. Shelton, *Pioneering in Tibet*, 132; Flora B. Shelton, *Shelton of Tibet*, 196.

26. Albert L. Shelton, *Pioneering in Tibet*, 133.

27. Ibid., 134.

28. *Ibid.*, 136.

29. "A Line a Day," Flora and Albert Shelton 1912–1918 Diary, May 3, 1918, Still Family Archives, Scottsdale, Arizona.

30. Dr. Albert Shelton to Archibald McLean, May 15, 1918; Dr. Albert Shelton to Doan, May 20, 1918, Shelton Files, 1918–1928 Missionary Correspondence, 1918–1928, Disciples of Christ Historical Society, Nashville, Tennessee.

31. Alastair Lamb, *The McMahon Line: A Study in the Relations Between India, China, and Tibet, 1904–1914,* 2 vols. (London: Routledge and Kegan Paul, 1966), vol. 2, 527–528.

32. P. D. Coates, *The China Consuls: British Consular Officers, 1843–1943* (Hong Kong: Oxford University Press, 1988), 417–423.

33. Jamyang Norbu, "The Tibetan Resistance Movement and the Role of the C.I.A.," Robert Barnett, ed., *Resistance and Reform in Tibet* (Bloomington, Indiana: Indiana University Press, 1994), 191.

34. Teichman, *Travels of a Consular Officer in Eastern Tibet,* 116–117.

35. *Ibid.*, 73.

36. *Ibid.*, 152n.

37. *Ibid.*, 120.

38. *Ibid.*, 229.

39. *Ibid.*, 137.

40. *Ibid.*, 229.

41. *Ibid.*, 128.

42. "A Line a Day," Flora and Albert Shelton 1912–1918 Diary, June 5, 1918, Still Family Archives, Scottsdale, Arizona.

43. "A Line a Day," Flora and Albert Shelton 1912–1918 Diary, June 6, 1918, Still Family Archives, Scottsdale, Arizona.

44. Albert L. Shelton, *Pioneering in Tibet,* 138.

45. Teichman, *Travels of a Consular Official in North-West China,* 59.

46. Despatch No. 205/137, H. A. Ottewill, Yunnanfu Consular Official to H.B.M. Minister, Peking, Apr. 6, 1922, British Library Oriental and India Collections, London.

47. "A Line a Day," Flora and Albert Shelton 1912–1918 Diary, June 14–16, 1918, Still Family Archives, Scottsdale, Arizona.

48. "A Line a Day," Flora and Albert Shelton 1912–1918 Diary, June 30, 1918, Still Family Archives, Scottsdale, Arizona.

49. Albert L. Shelton, *Pioneering in Tibet,* 139–140.

50. "A Line a Day," Flora and Albert Shelton 1912–1918 Diary, July 10, 1918, Still Family Archives, Scottsdale, Arizona.

51. Albert L. Shelton, *Pioneering in Tibet,* 142.

52. UCMS report, Aug. 1, 1918, Shelton Files, 1918–1928 Missionary Correspondence, Disciples of Christ Historical Society, Nashville, Tennessee.

53. Albert Shelton to A. McLean, June 15, 1918, Shelton Files, 1918–1928 Missionary Correspondence, Disciples of Christ Historical Society, Nashville, Tennessee.

54. "From the Roof of the World," *World Call* (February 1919): 19.

55. Archibald McLean, *History of the Foreign Christian Missionary Society* (New York: Fleming H. Revell, 1919), 355–356.

56. UCMS report, Shelton Files, Aug 1, 1918, 1918–1928 Missionary Correspondence, Disciples of Christ Historical Society, Nashville, Tennessee.

57. Albert Shelton to A. McLean, June 15, 1918, Shelton Files, 1918–1928 Missionary Correspondence, Disciples of Christ Historical Society, Nashville, Tennessee. In 1918, CIM missionary Theodore Sorensen was also in Chamdo. According to his biographer, he was the first Westerner in Chamdo, though he probably shared the honor with Berthold

Laufer. The same year he established the Tibetan Literature Depot to produce tracts for central Tibet.

58. James Edgar, *The Land of Mystery: Tibet* (Melbourne: China Inland Mission, 1930), 44–47.

59. Teichman, *Travels of a Consular Officer in Eastern Tibet,* 164. The proud Scot MacLeod wrote to McLean that while at Chamdo, Albert Shelton watched a regiment march off to attack a Chinese position behind a piper with a real Scottish bagpipe, "skirling out a tune; that put life and metal in their heels." Roderick MacLeod to S. J. Corey, July 21, 1918, MacLeod Files, 1918–1928 Missionary Correspondence, Disciples of Christ Historical Society, Nashville, Tennessee.

60. Teichman, *Travels of a Consular Officer in Eastern Tibet,* 57–58, 73.

61. Ibid., 145.

62. Ibid., 146

63. "A Line a Day," Flora and Albert Shelton 1912–1918 Diary, Aug. 1, 9, 1918, Still Family Archives, Scottsdale, Arizona.

64. Teichman, *Travels of a Consular Officer in Eastern Tibet,* 153.

65. Ibid., 153.

66. Ibid., 168.

67. "Copy of Agreement for the Restoration of the Peaceful Relations, and the Delimitation of a Provisional Frontier between China and Tibet," Miscellaneous Tibet File, Disciples of Christ Historical Society, Nashville, Tennessee.

68. Melvyn C. Goldstein, *The Modern History of Tibet, 1913–1951: The Demise of the Lamaist State* (Berkeley, California: University of California Press, 1989), 178. Goldstein noted the resentment the Khampas felt toward the central Tibetan traders' and officials' abuse of *ula* in Kham.

69. "A Line a Day," Flora and Albert Shelton 1912–1918 Diary, Dec. 9, 1918, Still Family Archives, Scottsdale, Arizona.

70. Ibid., 46–47, 83, noted Hardy bought a small native house across town from the mission. After a forcible loan by Chinese General Liu, James Ogden maneuvered to get possession of additional land surrounding the mission as collateral. Chinese who obtained it from Chao Erh-feng's confiscation of monastery and noblemen land held the land. As Sino-American treaties forbade American land-holding, Ogden and the TCM skirted the law by not registering the transactions with the American Consulate in Chungking until 1925.

71. Photos of posters and *tangka* paintings, Shelton Files, Newark Museum, Newark, New Jersey.

72. "Missionary News," *Chinese Recorder* (September 1918): 621.

73. Per Kvaerne, *A Norwegian Traveler in Tibet: Theor Sörensen and the Tibetan Collection at Oslo University Library* (New Delhi: Manjusri Publishing House, 1973), 6; *The Tibet Journal* (Winter 1991): 64. Sorensen changed the name of his Tibetan Religious Tract Society in 1918 to the Tibetan Religious Literature Depot. By 1922, the CIM distributed 160,400 tracts in the Tibetan regions, with titles such as "Buddhist and Christian Explanation of *MAN*" and "Buddhist and Christian Explanation of *SIN*."

74. James Edgar, *Land of Mystery, Tibet* (Melbourne: China Inland Mission, 1930), 53–54; Lt. Col. F. M. Bailey, *China-Tibet-Assam; A Journey, 1911* (London: J. Cape, 1945), 85. Eric Teichman stated, "Every year millions of copies of translated Scriptures are distributed in China by the native colporteurs of the great Bible societies, not more than ten or twenty per cent of which are ever read by any one. One often hears of statistics of the large numbers of copies disposed of, not given away, but sold; but it is nor stated in explanation that the books are disposed of so cheaply that they are sometimes bought for

the paper they contain and used in the manufacture of Chinese shoes (which, curiously enough, is also the use to which the Chinese are said to have put the sacred books of the lamas when campaigning amongst the monasteries of Eastern Tibet)." Teichman, *Travels of a Consular Official in North-West China,* 151.

75. Bray, "Christian Missions and the Politics of Tibet, 1850–1950," 4.

76. Rin-chen Lha-mo King, *We Tibetans: An Intimate Picture* (London: Seely Service & Company, Limited, 1926), 131–132, King wrote, "We consider your noses too big, often they stick out like kettle-spouts; your ears are too large, like pigs' ears, your eyes blue like children's marbles; your eyesockets too deep and eyebrows too prominent, too simian."

77. Marian L. Duncan, *Fire from the Flame,* 42–43.

78. The UCMS was composed of six national missionary boards: The American Missionary Society, Foreign Christian Missionary Society, Board of Church Extensions, Christian Woman's Board of Missions, Board of Ministerial Relief, and the National Benevolent Association.

79. The TCM reliance on local medical assistants for the bulk of medical treatment was hardly unique in China, nor were the long absences and short clinic hours kept by Shelton and Hardy. Hardy estimated he spent two to three hours a day in the dispensary, and Shelton's daughter Dorris described a similar schedule for her father. Another medical missionary, Dr. Francis F. Tucker of the Pang Chuang station in China proper, listed his daily routine. The day began with private devotions followed by breakfast. After breakfast he joined the other missionaries for morning prayers and a half-hour of bible reading and instruction in Chinese. The balance of the morning he studied Chinese. Lunch was followed by medical cases, but by late afternoon Dr. Tucker was engaged in miscellaneous duties and physical exercise. He devoted his evenings to writing and record keeping. A. Sidney Forsythe, *An American Missionary Community in China, 1895–1905* (Cambridge, Massachusetts: East Asian Research Center, Harvard, 1971), 18.

80. 1918–1928 Missionary Correspondence, Disciples of Christ Historical Society, Nashville, Tennessee.

81. Medical Reports April 1918-October 1919, Shelton Files, 1918–1928, Missionary Correspondence, Disciples of Christ Historical Society, Nashville, Tennessee. In 1925 Dr. Hardy reported 40 percent of the caseload as Tibetans, 42 percent as Sino-Tibetan, and 18 percent as Chinese.

82. "Shelton of Batang," *World Call* (June 1919): 10.

83. Shelton Files, 1918–1928 Missionary Correspondence, Disciples of Christ Historical Society, Nashville, Tennessee. A map in the same archive indicated Adensi (Atunze), southwest of Batang, was "occupied by Pentecostal Mission."

Teichman, *Travels of a Consular Official in North-West China,* 201, stated the Chinese used the immersion versus "sprinkle" Christian baptism to divide the Christian sects and denominations into the Great Wash, Little Wash, and No Wash groups of Christians. He described the "smaller and more irregular Protestant missions" such as the Seventh Day Adventists, the Tongues Movement Mission, and the Faith Mission thus: "some of which hold very strange beliefs, and may offer to instruct him in foreign languages by giving exhibitions of its foreign members rolling on the ground, or insist on attempting to cure cataracts by prayer instead of visiting the nearest foreign doctor."

84. Albert L. Shelton, *Pioneering in Tibet,* 135. James Ogden provided another, somewhat more florid translation that read in part: "Being informed as to your good purpose and your religious deeds to all mankind and your ministry of healing through the science of medicine. I would assure you that you should you undertake the tiresome journey to the city of the gods, your way will not be blocked by the Tibetan Government, provided there is no treaty to the contrary, and should you come you should be given every lawful assistance en route." *St. Louis Post-Dispatch,* Mar. 31,1922.

Professor Elliot Sperling of Indiana University translated a copy of the letter that was partially illegible. His translation read in part, "With the good intention of benefiting those who have been taken ill and of curing rampant fevers, and for the purpose of benefiting other people who practice the dharma, [the bearer of this letter] wishes to traverse the realm of Lhasa. In this regard, and with no contravention of agreements, in order that [the bearer of this letter] may travel back and forth between Tibet and other countries note well that all is to be done to accommodate him and no obstructions are permitted." June 6, 2000, Professor Elliot Sperling e-mail to author.

85. Dr. Albert Shelton to S. J. Corey, Sept. 3, 1918, Shelton Files, 1918–1928 Missionary Correspondence, Disciples of Christ Historical Society, Nashville, Tennessee.

86. Flora Shelton was less enthusiastic about her husband's potential Lhasa journey than about the objects that accompanied the news, writing, "that Bert might come to Lassa & the Tigi sent two books to him. The work is very beautiful on them." "A Line a Day," Flora and Albert Shelton 1912–1918 Diary, Aug. 25, 1918, Still Family Archives, Scottsdale, Arizona.

87. Dr. W. M. Hardy to J. W. Hardy, Nov. 8, 1922, Hardy Files, Disciples of Christ Historical Society, Nashville, Tennessee.

88. James H. Edgar, "The Great Open Lands," *Journal of the West China Border Society* (1930–1931): 20.

89. William Carey, *Travel and Adventure in Tibet, Including the Diary of Miss Annie R. Taylor's Remarkable Journey from Tau-Chau to Ta-Chien-lu through the Heart of the Forbidden Kingdom* (London: Hodder and Stoughton, 1902), 60.

90. William J. Gill, *River of Golden Sand,* 2 vols. ((London: John Murray, 1880), vol. 2, 268.

91. Carey, *Travel and Adventure in Tibet, Including the Diary of Miss Annie R. Taylor's Remarkable Journey from Tau-Chau to Ta-Chien-lu through the Heart of the Forbidden Kingdom,* 62, 64.

92. Perceval Landon, *Lhasa: An Account of the Country and People of Central Tibet, and of the Progress of the Mission Sent There by the English Government in the Year 1903–1904,* 2 vols. (London: Hurst and Blackett, 1905) vol. 1, 26–27.

93. Lamb, *The McMahon Line: A Study in the Relations Between India, China, and Tibet, 1904–1914,* vol. 1, 62.

94. John Bray, "Christian Missions and the Politics of Tibet, 1850–1950," Wilfred Wagner, ed., *Kolonien & Missionen, Referate des. 3. Internationalen Kolonialgeschichten Symposiums 1993 in Bremen* (Bremen: Bremer Asien-Pazifik Studien, 1993); Lamb, *The McMahon Line,* vol. 1, 57–67, vol. 2, 571–573; Kvaerne, *A Norwegian Traveler in Tibet,* 2. Being far more interested in Western commercial expansion compared to the Protestant religion, the British India officials had little sympathy for foreign missionaries from the earliest days. The first missionary of the London Missionary Society, Robert Morrison, was forced to begin his work in China rather than India because of the British resistance to his arrival. Missionary historian Kenneth S. Latourette wrote, "Because of the English East India Company's hostility to missions, he was obliged to go to the East on an American ship." Morrison arrived in Canton in 1807. Kenneth S. Latourette, *A History of the Christian Missions in China* (London: Society for Promoting Christian Knowledge, 1929), 212n.

95. Lamb, *The McMahon Line,* vol. 1, 244.

96. "Copy of Agreement for the Restoration of the Peaceful Relations, and the Delimitation of a Provisional Frontier between China and Tibet," Miscellaneous Tibet File, Disciples of Christ Historical Society, Nashville, Tennessee.

Oriental and India Collections include material relating to Shelton and Sorensen's proposed Tibetan travels: Louis King, Tachienlu to Beilby Alston, Peking, Aug. 24, 1921 (F

4594/59/10 Sorensen to Norwegian Minister, Peking, Sept. 2, 1921 (F 4594/59/10); Beilby Alston, Peking to Minister for Norway, Johan Michelet, Sept. 28, 1921 (F 4594/59/10); Beilby Alston, Peking to Curzon, Delhi, Oct. 27, 1921, No. 623 (7378/21) British Library Oriental and India Collections, London.

J. A. Simpson, Secret Political Department Minute Paper, "Subject: *Tibet* Request by a Norwegian missionary stationed at Tachienlu for permission to proceed through Tibet to India." Jan. 23, 1922. Stamped "Approved by Political Committee," Feb. 3, 1922. British Library Oriental and India Collections, London.

Viceroy of India to Secretary of State for India and Minister at Peking, Dec. 26, 1921 British Library Oriental and India Collections, London. Another Government of India telegram refusing British missionary Mr. Fraser's request for entrance into Tibet from the Indian side is mores succinct: "Government of India regret inability to grant permission. Foreign Secretary to the Government of India to Mr. Fraser, English Missionary, Darjeeling, Nov. 29, 1922, British Library Oriental and India Collections, London. An unsigned note relating to it stated, "I am therefore averse to allowing another missionary to visit Gyantse at the present time though I see no harm in ordinary travelers, whom the Tibetans quite understand, going to the Trade Marts."

97. "The Way Open to Lhassa!" *World Call* (February 1919): 18.

98. Dr. Albert Shelton to Doan, Shelton Files, July 28, 1919, 1918–1928 Missionary Correspondence, Disciples of Christ Historical Society, Nashville, Tennessee.

99. Physical dated February 1921. A 1914 "Biographical Sketches of Our Missionaries" entry on the Sheltons noted, "This good man and his wife weigh two hundred pounds each." Shelton Archives, Collection 53, Folder 2, University of Oregon Special Collections. In a 1925 UCMS Information Schedule, Shelton Files, 1918–1928 Missionary Correspondence, Disciples of Christ Historical Society, Nashville, Tennessee, Flora Shelton listed her physical condition as "Rather useless." In filmed interviews in the 1980s, Dorris and Dorothy found the number of sedan chair coolies needed to haul their mother across China a source of great levity. "We needed two coolies," they said, "Mama needed four." John Basmajian Film Archives, Los Angeles, California.

100. "A Line a Day," Flora and Albert Shelton 1912–1918 Diary, Nov. 29, 1918, Still Family Archives, Scottsdale, Arizona.

101. Dr. Albert Shelton to S. J. Corey, Jan. 8, 1919, Shelton Files, 1918–1928 Missionary Correspondence Disciples of Christ Historical Society, Nashville, Tennessee.

102. Albert L. Shelton, *Pioneering in Tibet,* 145.

103. Sir Alexander Hosie, who made a long tour of the major opium-growing regions in 1910–1911, wrote, "Szechuan was for many years the greatest opium-producing province in China, and the province whence the bulk of native opium consumed in the east south of the empire was derived." Kathleen L. Lodwick, *Crusaders against Opium: Chinese Missionaries in China, 1874–1917* (Lexington, Kentucky: University Press of Kentucky, 1996), 5, 12, 129, 136, 139, 155, 161, 173, 178; Robert A. Kapp, *Szechuan and the Chinese Republic* (New Haven: Yale University Press, 1973), 4, 37, 44. The United States equally faced an opium crisis in the last part of the nineteenth century. Many Civil War wounded veterans developed an addiction from the morphine given as a painkiller for amputees. Morphine-laced laudanum was a crutch for many middle- and upper-class women. The solons of the FCMS could see opium addicts on the streets of Cincinnati even as they railed against the problem in China. Reformer Lafcadio Hearn wrote about the drug problem in Cincinnati: "Walk along the streets any day and you will meet opium slaves by the score . . . they are slaves, abject slaves suffering exquisite torture. Once in the fetters of opium and morphine, they are, with few exceptions, fettered for life." Marc McCutcheon, *Everyday Life in the 1800s* (Cincinnati, Ohio: Writers Digest, 1993), 165.

104. Isabella L. Bird, *The Yangtze Valley and Beyond: An Account of Journeys in China* (Boston: Beacon Press, [1899] 1987), 496–502; Lodwick, *Crusaders against Opium,* 161.

105. Teichman, *Travels of a Consular Official in North-West China,* vi.

106. UCMS Monthly Report, June 30, 1919, Shelton Files, 1918–1928 Missionary Correspondence, Disciples of Christ Historical Society, Nashville, Tennessee.

107. H. A. Ottewill, Yunnanfu Consular Official to H.B.M. Minister, Peking, Apr. 6, 1922, Despatch No. 205/137, British Library Oriental and India Collections, London.

108. "Shelton of Batang," *World Call* (June 1919): 10–11. The article noted that the *Life of Livingstone* was one of Shelton's favorite books.

109. "Kansan Invades Tibet; Forbidden Land of the East," undated clipping, University of Oregon Special Collections, Shelton Archives. Collection 53, Folder 2.

110. O. A. Rosboro to J. H. LaGorce, April 16, 1919; J. H. LaGorce to O. A. Rosboro, Apr. 18, 1919; J. H. LaGorce to Dr. Albert Shelton, May 5, 1919; Dr. Albert Shelton to J. H. LaGorce, Oct. 28, 1919, Shelton Files, National Geographic Archives, Washington, D.C. O. A. Rosboro was an UCMS supporter and a church leader in his local bible school. He worked for Vapor Heat Railcars of Chicago. Additionally, Rosboro had a collection of fifteen hundred photographs of Tibet.

111. Doan to Dr. Albert Shelton, Apr. 2, 1919, Shelton Files, 1918–1928 Missionary Correspondence, Disciples of Christ Historical Society, Nashville, Tennessee.

112. Dr. Albert Shelton to Stephen J. Corey, July 27, 1919, Shelton Files, 1918–1928 Missionary Correspondence, Disciples of Christ Historical Society, Nashville, Tennessee.

113. Sheet marked "World Call June 1919," Shelton Files, 1918–1928 Missionary Correspondence, Disciples of Christ Historical Society, Nashville, Tennessee.

114. Dr. Albert Shelton to Doan, Mar. 24, 1919, July 22–28, 1919, Shelton Files, 1918–1928 Missionary Correspondence, Disciples of Christ Historical Society, Nashville, Tennessee.

115. "A Visit to Gartok," *World Call* (March 1920): 9.

116. Gartok photo, Miscellaneous Tibet File, Disciples of Christ Historical Society, Nashville, Tennessee.

117. Dorris Shelton Still, *Beyond the Devils in the Wind* (Tempe, Arizona: Synergy Books, 1989), 75. The Teji Markham's wife was a Gurkha-speaking noblewoman from the southern border of Tibet. Though a tiny woman about four and a half feet tall, she jealously guarded her status with the Governor. When a young damsel caught the Teji Markham's eye in a neighboring town, his wife traveled there and had the woman's ears and nose cut off. During her visit with the Shelton girls, she wore a full-length skirt covered with the long striped apron of a married woman. To add to her jump-rope handicap, she wore a complex Lhasa-style jewelry-encrusted hairdo, heavy earrings, and a charm-box choker. "A Visit to Gartok," *World Call* (March 1920): 9.

118. Still, *Beyond the Devils in the Wind,* 76.

119. "Report of a Trip Thru Yunnan, Eastern Tibet and Szechwan, by Major John Magruder, F.A., Asst. Military Attaché, Jan. 17-July 11, 1921 Service Report, Reel 2—U.S. War Dept. Military Intelligence Division China, 1918–1941.

120. Lamb, *The McMahon Line,* vol. 2, 569–570.

121. U. S. State Department memo 1919, Shelton Files, 1918–1928 Missionary Correspondence.

122. Flora B. Shelton, *Shelton of Tibet,* 205.

123. Shelton Report to UCMS, November 1919 Shelton Files, 1918–1928 Missionary Correspondence, Disciples of Christ Historical Society, Nashville, Tennessee.

124. Dr. Albert Shelton Invoice to Newark Museum, dated Nov. 1, 1919, Item 14 listed source as "Ruined lamasery of Draya." Item 15 read "Source—From Draya. Chinese loot." Newark Shelton Files noted Items 20.355A and 20.355B as two silver butter lamps collected by Shelton after the war when "local temple was looted by the Chinese soldiers in 1916."

125. Dr. Albert Shelton to S. J. Corey, July 28, 1921, Shelton Files, 1918–1928 Missionary Correspondence, Disciples of Christ Historical Society, Nashville, Tennessee.

126. Dr. Albert Shelton Invoice to Newark Museum, dated Nov. 1, 1919, Item 6, page 4.

127. Dr. Albert Shelton Invoice to Newark Museum, dated Nov. 1, 1919, Item 8, page 5. Noted Gezong Ongdu as "formerly one of the Prince's head men."

128. Flora B. Shelton, *Shelton of Tibet*, 187.

129. Dr. Albert Shelton Invoice to Newark Museum, dated Nov. 1, 1919, Item 3, page 20.

130. Dr. Albert Shelton to J. C. Dana, Aug. 18, 1918, Shelton Files, Newark Museum, Newark, New Jersey.

131. J. C. Dana to Dr. Albert Shelton, Mar. 5, 1919, Shelton Files, Newark Museum, Newark, New Jersey.

132. Dr. Albert Shelton Invoice to Newark Museum, dated Nov. 1, 1919, Notes, pages 1–2. The prince's scion was related to the Teji Markham and was hence an important link for the Sheltons to the Lhasa authorities. The Sheltons tried to reform the man's opium and alcohol addictions, to no avail. Dr. Shelton attempted to teach him medicine in the dispensary, "but washing a beggar's sores was not the work for an eastern prince," as Flora Shelton wrote. Flora B. Shelton, *Shelton of Tibet*, 187.

133. Dr. Albert Shelton to J. C. Dana, June 4, 1919, Shelton Files, Newark Museum, Newark, New Jersey.

134. Newark Museum Association initialed AWK to J. C. Dana, Sept. 19, 1919, Shelton Files, Newark Museum, Newark, New Jersey.

135. "Cast Thy Bread Upon the Waters," *World Call* (March 1920): 47. The organization of native churches was controversial in the foreign missionary community, rife with attendant issues of cultural imperialism and paternalism. Though the Batang missionaries had begun to ameliorate their views of the Tibetans and their culture, the UCMS was still leery of placing much trust with the indigenous Christian congregations. In general, the missionary society still reflected the cultural superiority that characterized most of the foreign mission movement from the nineteenth century on. The terms "pagan" and "heathen" were the most common phrases used to describe non-Western people in the society publications and were still used in the Disciples of Christ writings until 1953. D. Newell Williams, *A Case Study of Mainstream Protestantism*, 226–228, 228n110.

The Christian Church in Batang run by the local people was less than a stunning success. In February 1921, Nina Hardy wrote, "The Chinese Church has just about gone to the dogs, Gwei Gwang is a good preacher but he hasn't got the back bone enough for a pastor, he is afraid of the natives and he knows his wife's rottenness therefore can't say anything to the church members." [His wife stole Gezong Ongdu's property and sold it on the street, and she had a reputation as a harpy.] "The time has not come when these Christians can manage their own affairs and a foreigner will have to be at the had of the native churches for years to come. We've tried and Gway Gwang and he is certainly not equal to the task." February 4, 1921 Nina Hardy to Flora Shelton, Still Family Archives, Scottsdale, Arizona.

136. TCM Resolution, 1919, Miscellaneous Tibet File, Disciples of Christ Historical Society, Nashville, Tennessee; Marian L. Duncan, *A Flame for the Fire*, 46, 51.

Chapter 12

1. Flora B. Shelton, *Shelton of Tibet* (Cincinnati, Ohio: Foreign Christian Missionary Society, 1923), 218–219.

2. Albert L. Shelton, *Pioneering in Tibet, A Personal Record of Life and Experience in the Mission Fields* (New York: Fleming H. Revell Company, 1921), 152.

3. Roderick MacLeod to Archibald McLean, Nov. 21, 1919, MacLeod Files, 1918–1928 Missionary Correspondence, Disciples of Christ Historical Society, Nashville, Tennessee.

4. Albert L. Shelton, *Pioneering in Tibet,* 152–153. When Dr. William Hardy and his family left in 1917, the caravan included twelve Chinese servants and chairmen, and sixteen pack animals. As was the custom, they utilized *ula* to travel through Kham. Presumably the Sheltons' caravan was much larger as it included their hundreds of artifacts for the Newark Museum and the baggage of the fleeing Chinese. The Hardy's escort varied from two to thirty soldiers. Hardy carried a "horse gun," a handgun, a revolver, and a rifle, and his coolie carried a sword. "An Interview with Dr. Hardy of Batang," Hardy Files, Disciples of Christ Historical Society, Nashville, Tennessee.

5. Marian L. Duncan, *A Flame of the Fire* (Spring Hill, Tennessee: Marian Duncan, 1999), 53; J. C. Dana to Mr. Crane, July 8, 1920, Shelton Files, Newark Museum, Newark, New Jersey, noted the arrival of "17 boxes of curios." A few boxes were lost on the journey, and a few were broken open by bandits. A note in the Newark Museum files on the 1920 Shelton purchases noted, "Two of the boxes were lost on the way, falling over a cliff 800 feet high." Shelton Files, 1920 Purchase, Newark Museum, Newark, New Jersey.

6. John Mack Faragher, ed., *Rereading Frederick Jackson Turner: The Significance of the Frontier in American History and Other Essays* (New York: H. Holt, 1994), 59.

7. Kemp Tolley, *Yangtze Patrol: The U.S. Navy in China* (Annapolis, Maryland: Naval Institute Press, 1971), 79–80, 84, 101. In 1921, bandits attacked a missionary family on the Yangtze with "huge knives," only to be saved by the British gunboat, H. M. S. *Widgeon.*

8. "An Interview with Dr. Hardy of Batang," map, Hardy Files, Disciples of Christ Historical Society, Nashville, Tennessee.

9. Albert L. Shelton, *Pioneering in Tibet,* 155.

10. Flora B. Shelton, *Shelton of Tibet,* 209.

11. Albert L. Shelton, *Pioneering in Tibet,* 157.

12. M. M. Dymond, *Yunnan* (London: Marshall Brothers, 1929), 9.

13. Flora B. Shelton, *Shelton of Tibet,* 209

14. Donald S. Sutton, *Provincial Militarism and the Chinese Republic: The Yunnan Army 1905–1925* (Ann Arbor, Michigan: University of Michigan Press, 1980), 30, 142. Sutton stated that by 1916, 70 percent of the Yunnan provincial budget was military related.

15. S. E. Finer, *The Man on Horseback: The Role of the Military in Politics* (New York: Praeger, 1962), 92–93, 205–208, contrasted the politicized professionally trained soldier with the aristocratic military man or the soldier of fortune. Jerome Ch'en, "Defining Chinese Warlords and Their Factions," *Bulletin of the School of Oriental and African Studies* (1968): 563–600, noted 30 percent of the 1300 warlords in the 1912–1928 warlord period had Japanese training with the balance illiterate or semi-illiterate. While the rank and file moved from bandit to soldier status repeatedly, only 23 warlords came from bandit leader origins. In the 1912–1928 warlord period alone there were 140 provincial and inter-provincial wars.

16. Louis Magrath King, *China in Turmoil, Studies in Personality* (London: Heath, Cranton, Limited, 1927), 168–169.

17. Sutton, *Provincial Militarism and the Chinese Republic,* 1–2. Robert A. Kapp, *Szechuan and Chinese Republic: Provincial Militarism and Central Power, 1911–1938* (New Haven: Yale University Press), 54–55, stated bandit activity increased with military conflict, acting as an indices of the attendant social disruption.

18. Ch'en, "Defining Chinese Warlords and Their Factions," 581, 591, 599–600.

19. Albert L. Shelton, *Pioneering in Tibet,* 158. Dorris Shelton Still, *Beyond the Devils in the Wind* (Tempe, Arizona: Synergy Books, 1989), 86–87. The record is contradictory regarding the Shelton daughters' mode of transport when attacked by bandits. Albert Shelton

wrote that they were on mules. Flora Shelton and Dorris Shelton Still wrote that the women were all in sedan chairs. A photograph showed three sedan chairs in the caravan. Shelton stated that his daughters rode on muleback on leaving Batang. Presumably they rode mules through Kham and switched to sedan chairs in Yunnan, where they were the common mode of transport.

20. "Copy of Statement Sent to 'World Call.' By E. I. Osgood." Shelton Files, 1918–1928 Missionary Correspondence, Disciples of Christ Historical Society, Nashville, Tennessee.
21. Albert L. Shelton, *Pioneering in Tibet,* 159.
22. Ibid., 160.
23. Note in 1920 Shelton Purchase File, Newark Museum, Newark, New Jersey.
24. Marian L. Duncan, *A Flame of the Fire,* 53.
25. Albert L. Shelton, *Pioneering in Tibet,* 160.
26. Ibid., 160.
27. "Copy of Statement Sent to 'World Call.' By E. I. Osgood." Shelton Files, 1918–1928 Missionary Correspondence, Disciples of Christ Historical Society, Nashville, Tennessee.
28. Albert L. Shelton, *Pioneering in Tibet,* 161.
29. Flora B. Shelton, *Shelton of Tibet,* 214.
30. *Papers Relating to the Foreign Relations of the United States, 1921,* 3 vols. (Washington, D.C.: United States Printing Office, 1935), vol. 1, 800–801.
31. Flora B. Shelton, *Shelton of Tibet,* 242. Shelton's description of Yang's illiteracy casts doubts on the newspaper accounts of Yang as a graduate of a Japanese military academy.
32. "Copy of Statement Sent to 'World Call.' By E. I. Osgood." Shelton Files, 1918–1928 Missionary Correspondence, Disciples of Christ Historical Society, Nashville, Tennessee.
33. Flora B. Shelton, *Shelton of Tibet,* 215.
34. Flora Shelton and her daughters took shelter with the CIM mission in Yunnanfu during Shelton's kidnapping.
35. "Photograph of pages of 'Beside the Bonnie Briar Bush," Shelton Files, 1918–1928 Missionary Correspondence, Disciples of Christ Historical Society, Nashville, Tennessee.
36. Flora B. Shelton, *Shelton of Tibet,* 218–219.
37. Ibid., 219.
38. Ibid., 221.
39. Ibid., 222.
40. *Holy Bible* (Ashland, Ohio: Landoll's, Inc., 1994), New Testament, 74.
41. Albert L. Shelton, *Pioneering in Tibet,* 174.
42. Flora B. Shelton, *Shelton of Tibet,* 225.
43. The importance of the Newark Mueum shipment to the Sheltons was evident in Flora's letter to J. C. Dana on February 24, apologizing for the delay of the shipment as she suffered with the ongoing travail of her husband. Flora Shelton wrote, "I'm sorry you have been disappointed in the arrival of the boxes from Tibet. Dr. Shelton was taken captive by Chinese brigands Jan 3, just 2 days from this place." Flora Shelton to J. C. Dana, Feb. 24, 1920, Shelton Files, 1921–1922 Correspondence, Newark Museum Archives, Newark, New Jersey.
44. Albert Shelton postcard to "Mrs. Shelton c/o J. Graham, Yunnan," Still Family Archives, Tempe, Arizona.
45. Albert Shelton to Flo and Girls, Jan. 18, 1920, Still Family Archives, Nashville, Tennessee.
46. Ibid., 227–228.
47. Flora B. Shelton, *Shelton of Tibet,* 230.
48. Albert Shelton to Flora Shelton and daughters, Feb. 3, 1920, Still Family Archives, Scottsdale, Arizona.
49. Flora B. Shelton, *Shelton of Tibet,* 233

50. Ibid., 234.
51. Dr. Albert Shelton to "Ma, Pa, and all of you," Feb. 12, 1920, Shelton Files, 1918–1928, Missionary Correspondence, Disciples of Christ Historical Society, Nashville, Tennessee; Blackburn Collection, Kansas State Historical Society, Topeka, Kansas.
52. U.S. State Department to UCMS, Jan. 22, 1920, Shelton Files, 1918–1928 Missionary Correspondence, Disciples of Christ Historical Society, Nashville, Tennessee.
53. State Department telegram to FCMS, Jan. 28, 1920, Shelton Files, 1918–1928 Missionary Correspondence, Disciples of Christ Historical Society, Nashville, Tennessee. Flora Shelton concurred, wiring the missionary society, "Doctor Shelton well. Negotiations slow. Hope release shortly." January 29, 1920, Flora Shelton telegram to FCMS, Shelton Files, 1918–1928 Missionary Correspondence, Disciples of Christ Historical Society, Nashville, Tennessee.
54. *Papers Relating to Foreign Relations of the United States, 1920*, vol. 1, 797.
55. "Chinese Bandits Hold American Missionary," *New York Times*, Jan. 13, 1920.
56. *Times of London*, 13 Jan. 1920.
57. "Dr. Shelton Held for Ransom," *World Call* (February 1920): 2.
58. John Nelson postcard, Shelton Files, 1918–1928 Missionary Correspondence, Disciples of Christ Historical Society, Nashville, Tennessee.
59. Acting Secretary of State Frank Polk to Senator Charles Curtis, Mar. 9, 1920; Acting Secretary of State Frank Polk to Congressman James G. Strong, Mar. 12, 1920; Naomi Shelton to W. E. Blackburn, Mar. 2, 1920, noted from Kansas Governor Allen's letter to the State Department. Blackburn Collection, Kansas State Historical Society, Topeka, Kansas.
60. "Latest News of Dr. Shelton," *West China Missionary News* (April 1920): 38.
61. "Coast of China Speeds Yankees on Rescue Trip," undated, unidentified clipping with Smith's dispatch datelined Hong Kong March 1 via *Chicago Tribune* Foreign News Service.
62. UCMS to Naomi Shelton, March 5, 1920, Shelton Files, 1918–1928 Missionary Correspondence, Disciples of Christ Historical Society, Nashville, Tennessee.
63. *Papers Relating to Foreign Relations of the United States, 1920*, vol. 1, 800–801.
64. Flora B. Shelton, *Shelton of Tibet*, 235.
65. Ibid., 238.
66. Ibid., 238.
67. Ibid., 239.
68. Albert Shelton called the village Tang Laü. Osgood termed it Ta-la-wu. Tanao is Gowman's name for the village. Theoretically, as the CIM missionary posted closest to the place, Gowman had the best chance of correctly transliterating the name. *Papers Relating to Foreign Relations of the United States,1920*. vol. 1, 800–801.
69. Flora B. Shelton, *Shelton of Tibet*, 240.
70. Ibid., 241.
71. Shelton named the village as Toogu.
72. Flora B. Shelton, *Shelton of Tibet*, 232.
73. "How Smith Went After Shelton," *World Call* (August 1920): 6.
74. "Missionary Prisoner of Chinese Bandits," *Chicago Tribune* clipping, Shelton Files, 1918–1928 Missionary Correspondence, Disciples of Christ Historical Society, Nashville, Tennessee.
75. "How Smith Went After Shelton," *World Call* (August 1920): 6.
76. "Rescue Caravan Quits Yunnanfu for Bandit Lair," undated and unidentified clipping, Shelton Files, 1918–1928 Missionary Correspondence, Disciples of Christ Historical Society, Nashville, Tennessee.

77. "Brigands Firm," undated clipping from Cincinnati paper, Shelton Files, 1918–1928 Missionary Correspondence, Disciples of Christ Historical Society, Nashville, Tennessee.
78. "Acts to Free Dr. Shelton," *Newark News,* Mar. 2, 1920 clipping, Shelton files, Newark Museum, Newark, New Jersey.
79. Flora B. Shelton, *Shelton of Tibet,* 243. "Two Months in Bondage," *South China Morning News,* undated clipping, Blackburn Collection, Kansas State Historical Society, Topeka, Kansas, noted Shelton was less than six feet tall and weighed 239 pounds at the time of his capture.
80. Flora B. Shelton, *Shelton of Tibet,* 242–243.
81. Albert Shelton, *Pioneering in Tibet,* 203. Shelton stated that the official was investigating the Taku kidnapping, while Drysdale stated it was one of the Wuting magistrate's runners looking for Shelton and Yang. *Papers Relating to Foreign Relations of the United States, 1920,* vol. 1, 802.
82. Albert L. Shelton, *Pioneering in Tibet,* 204–205.
83. Shelton called the village Yenmo. Dr. Osgood termed it Yien-mo.
84. Albert L. Shelton, *Pioneering in Tibet,* 206.
85. "How Captured Workers Were Delivered from Robbers," *World Call* (October 1920): 39.
86. Flora heard through one of the couriers who carried letters between Yang and the governor that Albert was bearded. "One of her requests," Dr. Shelton recalled, "was that they be disposed of at once; so by the help of Osgood's scissors and Thornton's razor, I was again transformed from a Bolsheviki into an American." Albert Shelton, *Pioneering in Tibet,* 210.
87. Ibid., 211.
88. Ibid., 211.
89. U.S. State Department telegram to UCMS, Mar.10, 1920, Shelton Files, 1918–1928 Missionary Correspondence, Disciples of Christ Historical Society, Nashville, Tennessee.
90. "Bandits Free Dr. Shelton," *New York Times,* Mar. 16, 1920.
91. "Chinese Troops Find Dr. Shelton in Bleak Stable," *Chicago Tribune,* Mar. 16, 1920; "Outrages by Chinese Bandits," *Times of London,* Mar. 25, 1920.
92. Flora B. Shelton, *Shelton of Tibet,* 244.
93. Albert Shelton to Abraham Corey, Mar. 20, 1920, Shelton Files, 1918–1928 Missionary Correspondence, Disciples of Christ Historical Society, Nashville, Tennessee. The nature of Shelton's tumor was unclear. He termed it alternately benign or a sarcoma, a malignant growth arising in connective tissue that was aggravated by his three months of constant flight. Marian L. Duncan, *Flame of the Fire,* 53–54, stated that it was a goiter. In any case, the tumor pressed on a major nerve in Shelton's neck, numbing his head and almost paralyzing his arm. From his repeated use of opium in the last days of kidnapping, Shelton shifted to an ongoing use of morphine for the pain.

Chapter 13

1. "Dr. Shelton to Speak," *South Bend* [Indiana] *Tribune,* Sept. 29, 1920.
2. Flora Shelton to FCMS, Mar. 20, 1920, Shelton Files, 1918–1928 Missionary Correspondence, Disciples of Christ Historical Society, Nashville, Tennessee. E. I. Osgood, "Dr. Shelton's Experience Among the Bandits," manuscript, Shelton Files, 1918–1928 Missionary Correspondence, Disciples of Christ Historical Society, Nashville, Tennessee.
3. Albert L. Shelton, *Pioneering in Tibet, A Personal Record of Life and Experience in the Mission Fields* (New York: F. H. Revell and Company, 1921), 214.
4. Henry R. Davies, *Yün-nan, the Link Between India and the Yangtze* (Cambridge: Cambridge University, 1909), 330–331.

5. Customs Documents, Apr. 7, 1920, Shelton Files, Newark Museum Archives, Newark, New Jersey.

6. Albert Shelton to J. C. Dana, Apr. 20, 1920, Shelton Files, Newark Museum Archives, Newark, New Jersey.

7. Missionary child John Espey recalled landing in Vancouver after his China years, when distant America was wholly romanticized: "Are those white men doing that coolie work American?' I asked pointing to some stevedores. 'Why yes,' she answered. Utopia threatened to collapse." John Espey, *Minor Heresies, Major Departures* (Berkeley, California: University of California Press, 1994), 78, 81.

8. http://www.mayo.edu/general/history.html

9. Marian L. Duncan, *A Flame of the Fire* (Spring Hill, Tennessee: Marian L. Duncan, 1999), 54.

10. The Mayo doctors thought the tumor related to a bout of influenza that Shelton suffered a year before. Albert Shelton to J. C. Dana, May 18, 1920, Newark Museum, Shelton Files, Newark Museum, Newark, New Jersey. Rosboro stated Shelton still had six weeks' recuperation though he was heading directly to the Newark and the National Geographic. O. E. Rosboro to J. O. LaGorce, June 5, 1920, National Geographic Archives, Washington, D.C.

11. Naomi Shelton to W. E. Blackburn, May 26, 1920, Blackburn Collection, Kansas State Historical Society, Topeka Kansas.

12. O. E. Rosboro to J. O. LaGorce, June 5, 1920, National Geographic Archives, Washington, D.C.

13. It was Shelton's second visit with John LaGorce, as he also called on the National Geographic Society during his first furlough. J. O. LaGorce to Albert Shelton, May 5, 1919, National Geographic Archives, Washington, D.C., referred to a previous visit when LaGorce discussed his weaponry collection.

14. J. O. LaGorce to G. H. G., June 22, 1920, National Geographic Archives, Washington, D.C.

15. "Early Newspaper Clippings," Box 2, Newark Museum Archives, Newark New Jersey.

16. Flora B. Shelton, *Shelton of Tibet* (New York: George Doran, 1923), 252–253.

17. In August 1921, Shelton sent the *National Geographic* a list of 59 colleagues, supporters and friends for complimentary copies of the issue of the National Geographic with his article. The list included people such as Abe Cory and Colonel Drysdale. Included among them was P. H. Gray at the Osteopathic Hospital in Detroit, possibly where Shelton had his treatment. To the disgust of Dr. William Hardy, Shelton returned to Batang with an effusive enthusiasm for osteopathy. Albert Shelton to J. O. LaGorce, Aug. 15, 1921, National Geographic Archives, Washington, D.C.

18. Berthold Laufer to J. C. Dana, July 12, 1920, Field Museum Library Archives, Chicago, Illinois.

19. "Tibetan Collection. Cost to date. August 3, 1920." Shelton wrote the Newark in September 1919 that he wanted a minimum of $3,500 for the artifacts. At that time the museum trustees huffed about acquiring more *Kanjurs*—they wanted Tibetan jewelry. AWK, Newark Museum Association to J. C. Dana, Sept. 19, 1919, Shelton Files, Newark Museum Archives, Newark New Jersey. The 1920 $3,000 purchase represented about $25,650 in 2000 purchasing power. http://woodrow.mpls.frb.fed.us/economy/calc/cpihome.html

20. J. C. Dana to J. O. LaGorce, Sept. 20, 1920, National Geographic Archives, Washington, D.C.

21. Marian L. Duncan, *Flame of the Fire*, 59. Rupees, both Indian and Chinese, were the currency in common use on the border. In 1917, the exchange rate was four rupees to one U.S. dollar. "Estimates Allowed, 1917," Foreign Christian Missionary Financial Records, "Tibet. Ledger, 1914–1930," Disciples of Christ Historical Society, Nashville, Tennessee.

22. Albert Shelton to Plopper, Nov. 5, 1919, instructing him to send $1,000 to his family in the U.S. and send the balance of $500 to him. When the Hardy and Shelton families met in Yunnan, the FCMS salary increase was a notable source of discussion. While in captivity in January 1920, Albert Shelton wrote to FCMS Treasurer Plopper thanking him for the undisclosed increase. Albert Shelton to C. W. Plopper, Jan. 24, 1920, Shelton Files, 1918–1928 Missionary Correspondence, Disciples of Christ Historical Society, Nashville, Tennessee. In 1917, Shelton listed his salary as $1,200 per year with the mission society paying housing on a China Medical Board data sheet. "Data Regarding Physicians and Nurses," RG 4 (China Medical Board) Box 21, folder 409, Foreign Christian Missionary Society Hospital Batang, Szechwan. The Rockefeller Archive Center, North Tarrytown, New York.

World War I reversed a normal two-to-one exchange of U.S. dollars to Chinese dollars—that is, one U.S. dollar brought two Chinese dollars, or "Mexican dollars" as the Chinese currency as Mexico was the origin of the coined currency in circulation. The *yuan* was the official name for Chinese currency, though few foreigners used the term. During the war, the exchange rate was 1 U.S.$ = Chinese .80. This meant $5,000 Chinese would yield U.S. $6,500, a potential source of exchange profit some missionaries utilized to their benefit. While the borderland of Kham experienced different monetary convulsions (and even currencies), most of the missionary funds were in Shanghai banks where the exchange rates prevailed. Grace Service, *Golden Inches: The China Memoir of Grace Service* (Berkeley, California: University of California Press, 1989), 98n.

23. One of Shelton's Living Link churches, Detroit's Central Christian Church, gave $1,000 to Shelton in 1919. D. K. Stewart to Archibald McLean, 21 Jan. 1920, 1918–1928 Missionary Correspondence, Disciples of Christ Historical Society, Nashville, Tennessee. Before Shelton's return to Tibet in 1921, the Bakersfield Christian Church also agreed to be a Living Link Church for Dr. Shelton. Marian L. Duncan, *Flame of the Fire*, 62.

24. The 1920 census listed Pomona with 13,505 inhabitants; Los Angeles had 576,673. *Abstract of the Fourteenth Census of the United States 1920* (Washington, D.C., Government Printing Office, 1923), 58, 59.

25. The first Shelton document with 381 N. Gibbs as the return address was late August 1920. Pomona property records and city directories listed the previous owner, J. H. Hopkins, as the resident on May 20, 1920, and Dr. Albert Shelton as the resident by the next record on November 20, 1920. The First Christian Church was located at Center and Main streets. Pomona, California Public Library Archives.

26. He listed in an UCMC questionnaire requesting "facts you deem important," his memberships in the Royal Geographic Society and the Royal Asiatic Society and his fifteen thousand miles on muleback in Kham. "Who's Who Among Our Missionaries," Shelton Files, Missionary Archives, Disciples of Christ Headquarters, Indianapolis, Indiana. Flora B. Shelton, *Shelton of Tibet*, 141, also added his honorary doctorate from Gotner University and his Masonic Degrees to the geographic society memberships.

27. Albert Shelton to J. C. Dana, Sept. 14, 1920, Shelton Files, Newark Museum Archives, Newark, New Jersey.

28. Dan Bryant, *In Mission and Service: Disciples in Pomona, 1883–1983* (Pomona, California: First Christian Church, 1983), 55.

29. "Dr. A. L. Shelton to Speak Tonight at Christian Church," *State Normal Bulletin*, Oct. 6, 1920; "Dr. Shelton Gives Talk on Foreign Work," *State Normal Bulletin*, Oct. 13, 1920.

30. "Expected to Die in Orient," *Indianapolis News*, Mar. 6, 1922, An Oregon mission official, C. F. Swander, stated Shelton expected to die carrying on the work of the Christian church: "When he left he never expected to return to this country."

L. C. Rudolph, *Hoosier Faiths: A History of Indiana Churches & Religious Groups* (Bloomington, Indiana: Indiana University Press, 1995), 71. The Disciples' founder Alexander Campbell celebrated the martyrs: "John the Harbinger of the Messiah, lost his head. The Apostles were slaughtered. The Saviour was crucified. The ancient confessors were slain. The reformers all have been excommunicated. I know that we shall do little good if we are not persecuted." Campbell concluded by writing, "There are many with whom it shall be my honor to live and labor, and my happiness to suffer and die."

31. "Dr A. L. Shelton K.S.N. Graduate Killed in Tibet," *State Normal Bulletin,* Mar. 16, 1922.

32. "International Convention of Disciples of Christ . . . Minutes," 1920 St. Louis Convention Files, Disciples of Christ Historical Society, Nashville, Tennessee. Shelton was not given to the formal style of Christian preaching, but rather was more extemporaneous in his speeches, with a passionate espousal of the role of Westernism and the gospel in Tibet.

33. The St. Louis papers were generous in their coverage of Shelton, conjecturally because of the UCMS headquarters in the city.

34. "Dr. A. L. Shelton Tells of Experiences When Chinese Brigands Kidnap Him," *St. Louis Post-Dispatch,* Oct. 19, 1920.

35. "Preacher Relates Trials as Captive of Chinese Bandits," "Woman Who Spent Seventeen Years Translating the Bible, and Her Family," October 20, 1920; "Dr. A. L. Shelton Plans to Go Back to Orient Where He Was Kidnapped," *St. Louis Times,* Oct. 23, 1920.

36. Flora B. Shelton, *Shelton of Tibet,* 263.

37. E. H. Kann to S. J. Corey, May 5, 1920; S. J. Corey to E. H. Kaan, May 8, 1920, Shelton Files, 1918–1928 Missionary Correspondence, Disciples of Christ Historical Society, Nashville, Tennessee.

38. S. J. Corey to Albert Shelton, Shelton Files, May 8, 1920, 1918–1928 Missionary Correspondence, Disciples of Christ Historical Society, Nashville, Tennessee. There is no record of Shelton's reply or whether the project happened.

39. The American Museum of Natural History, one of the great collecting institutions, hosted the Second International Congress of Eugenics in 1921. Donna Haraway, "Teddy Bear Patriarchy: Taxidermy in the Garden of Eden, New York City, 1908–1936," *Social Text* (Winter 1984–1985), 21. Haraway noted the link between the museum-funded expeditions and the ongoing drive to maintain white male dominance in an unsure world. What Haraway wrote of the AMNH building was indicative of the institution of the Western museums in general, "One is entering a space that sacralizes democracy, Protestant Christianity, adventure, science, and commerce."

40. John F. Kasson, *Houdini, Tarzan, and the Perfect Man: The White Male Body and the Challenge of Modernity in America* (New York: Hill and Wang, 2001), 10, 13, 159.

41. Ibid., 221.

42. In 1885, the Cambridge Seven, C. T. Studd, M. Beauchamp, S. P. Smith, A. T. Podhill-Turner, D. E. Hoste, C. H. Polhill-Turner, W. W. Cassels, took up the goal of Christianizing China. The British press lionized the young toffs and they became great popular heroes. Arthur H. Smith, *Rex Christus: An Outline Study of China* (New York: The Macmillan Company, 1904), 150–152;

43. Albert L. Shelton, *Pioneering in Tibet,* 214.

44. Marian L. Duncan, *Flame of the Fire,* 60–61.

45. Polygamy was part of the Tibetan culture, particularly among the noble families. Tea traders such as those in Tachienlu often had wives and families at both ends of their trading routes, both aware of the other. "There were no recriminations," traveler Peter Goullart wrote, "and the children of both families were happy for, having reached the traveling age, were taken for a visit from one family to another, getting a warm welcome."

Polyandry was also common in Tibet. It took various forms, including women living with more than one husband and women who married temporarily or serially. For the most part, polyandry of the first part was confined to the nomads in the high grasslands. The latter type of polyandry was common in the commercial centers and trading posts on the borders of Tibet. E. H. Wilson, the naturalist who visited the Sheltons, wrote about the institution, "The past hints, and the present proves that indifference to female virtue connotes the people known as Thibetans and tribes of common origin, and I understand it to be the indirect cause of polyandry." Not all Westerners viewed the institution in such a harsh light. When Andrew Wilson toured the Himalayas in 1875, he encountered Moravian missionaries who perceived polyandry differently. He wrote, "I was a little surprised to find that one of the Moravian missionaries defended the polyandry of the Tibetans, not as a thing to be approved of in the abstract, or tolerated among Christians, but as good for the heathen of so sterile a country. . . . a superabundant population in an unfertile country must be a great calamity." Goullart, *Princes of the Black Bone: Life in the Tibetan Borderland* (London: J. Murray, 1959), 31; E. H. Wilson, *A Naturalist in Western China*, 214; Andrew Wilson, *The Abode of Snow: Some Observations on a Tour from Chinese Tibet to the Indian Caucasus, Thorough the Upper Valleys of the Himalayas* (London: Cadogan Books, [1913] 1986).

46. Marian L. Duncan, *Flame of the Fire*, 78.

47. While the missionaries had to make their ameliorations in the field, they remained resolute in their desire to bring Christianity to Tibet. Their writings for the supporters back home remained adamantine. Consider the 1929 writing of Marion H. Duncan, *The Mountain of Silver Snow* (Cincinnati, Ohio: Powell & White, 1929), 49, "Mumbling and stumbling, the Tibetan pilgrim circles hoary mountain passes seeking for that which he knows not and which he fears he cannot find. He gropes in the everlasting circle of desire."

48. Mary M. Rhie and Robert A. F. Thurman, *Wisdom and Compassion: The Sacred Art of Tibet* (New York: Harry Abrams, Inc., 1996), 39–62; "Lost Treasure from Tibet," *New York Times*, Apr. 20, 2001; Robert E. Fisher, *Art of Tibet* (London: Thames and Hudson, 1997), 13, 22, 29, 168, 207. Fisher noted the artistic importance of the Karmapa branch of the Kagyupa sect in eastern Tibet, where the Chinese-influenced landscapes and interest in embroidered silk of the Karma Gadri school reflected China's increasing engagement with Tibetan culture from the late sixteenth century forward. A number of Shelton's *tangkas* used the Karma Gadri's bright palette and extensive use of blues and greens.

49. "Check list of Second Tibet Collection. Received, July 1920." Shelton Files, Newark Museum Archives, Newark New Jersey.

50. Janet Gyatso, "Image as Presence," in Valrae Reynolds, *From the Sacred Realm: Treasures of Tibetan Art from the Newark Museum* (Munich: Prestel Verlag, 1999), 172.

51. Fisher, *Art of Tibet*, 67, 73, 74.

52. Flora B. Shelton, *Shelton of Tibet*, 186–187.

53. Dr. Albert Shelton Invoice to Newark Museum, Nov. 1, 1919, Notes, pages 1–2.

54. Fisher, *Art of Tibet*, 116, noted Tibetan sculptures termed bronzes should be understood to be part of a generic grouping of metal images. The images are often crafted of brass and copper. Metallurgical testing indicated that half of the so-called Tibetan bronzes are actually brass, which is copper alloyed with zinc. Bronze, which constituted only 10 percent of the objects tested, is copper alloyed with tin. Both tin and zinc needed to be imported into Tibet.

55. "Check list of Second Tibet Collection. Received, July 1920," 19, Shelton Files, Newark Museum Archives, Newark New Jersey. Reynolds, *From the Sacred Realm*, 218. The "rodent" in the 1920 checklist description is the wealth-giving mongoose.

56. Fisher, *Art of Tibet*, 56; Phillip Rawson, *The Art of Tantra* (London: Thames and Hudson, 1978), 36.

57. "Dana Appeals to Missionaries to Send Articles to Museum," *Newark News*, May 23, 1921, "Early Newspaper Clippings," Box 2, Newark Museum Archives, Newark New Jersey. Marian l. Duncan, *Flame of the Fire*, 28, termed the Shelton-Newark association to be "long and mutually profitable." The Newark was not the only museum to utilize missionaries. Beyond the overweening example of the Vatican Museum, the American Museum of Natural History purchased "a rather important collection from Tibet," from a sixteen-year veteran of the Moravian missions on the Tibetan border, Dr. H. B. Marx, Ephrata house, Nazareth, Pennsylvania. AMNH Director F.A. Lucas to J. C. Dana, June 30, 1920, Shelton Files, Newark Museum Archives, Newark, New Jersey. In time James Ogden collected material for the Newark Museum, as did Christian missionaries to Amdo, Rev. M. G. Griebenow, Robert Ekvall, and Carter D. Holton. A YMCA official in Chengdu, Robert Roy Service, who was the husband of missionary writer Grace Service, also provided Tibetan artifacts to the Newark. Roderick MacLeod later served as a consultant to the Newark Museum's curator, Eleanor Olson. Reynolds, *From the Sacred Realm*, 13–14, 18–19.

58. Louise Connolly to J. C. Dana, Dec. 1, 1920, Shelton Files, Newark Museum Archives, Newark, New Jersey.

59. Raymond Blaine Fosdick, *John D. Rockefeller, Jr., A Portrait* (New York: Harper and Brothers, 1956), 24, 33. Rockefeller's connection to China missions dated back to his boyhood support of a Sunday school in China. Rockefeller organized the China Medical Board in 1914 as part of a campaign against tropical diseases plaguing the country, and he and his wife sailed for China in August 1921 to visit their missions. In 1923 their daughter Lucy was kidnapped by Chinese bandits on the Shanghai-Beijing railroad line, later to be released unharmed. For decades she relieved boring upper-crust dinner parties with the line, "Oh, I must tell you about the time I was captured by Chinese bandits." Bernice Kert, *Abby Aldrich Rockefeller: The Woman in the Family* (New York: Random House, 1993), 191–196; Peter Collier and David Horowitz, *The Rockefellers: An American Dynasty* (New York: Holt, Rinehart, and Winston, 1997), 104–105.

60. November 29, 1920, J. D. Rockefeller, Jr. to A. E. Cory, Rockefeller Archive Center, North Tarrytown, New York.

61. Undated, Albert Shelton to J. D. Rockefeller, Jr.; J. D. Rockefeller, Jr. to Albert Shelton, Dec. 7, 1920, Rockefeller Archive Center, North Tarrytown, New York

62. Abby Rockefeller to Albert Shelton, undated, Still Family Archives, Scottsdale, Arizona.

63. Albert Shelton to J. D. Rockefeller, Jr., Dec. 30, 1920, Rockefeller Archive Center, North Tarrytown, New York.

64. Louise Connolly, "Tibet," Exhibit catalogue, ii, The Newark Museum, 1921–1922. Newark Museum Archives, Newark, New Jersey.

65. James Clifford, *The Predicament of Culture: Twentieth-century Ethnography, Literature, and Art* (Cambridge, Massachusetts, Harvard University Press, 1988), 189–251. The appreciation of American folk art mirrored the shift that non-Western art experienced in the first third of the twentieth century. Coincidentally, the Newark Museum was also became instrumental in this metamorphosis, when it opened Holger Cahill's seminal folk art exhibitions, "American Primitives," in 1930, and "American Folk Sculpture" in 1931. "Collectors See a Flurry of Folk Art," *New York Times*, Feb. 16, 2001.

66. "Dr. Shelton before the National Geographic Society," *World Call* (January 1921): 51. Quoted in Marian L. Duncan, *Flame of the Fire*, 61–62,

67. "Tibetans Play Bagpipes," *Washington Post*, December 4, 1920, 8.

68. Albert L. Shelton, "Life Among the People of Eastern Tibet." *National Geographic* 40, no. 3 (September 1921): 324.

69. Albert Shelton to J. O. LaGorce, July 17, 1921, National Geographic Archives, Washington, D.C.

70. The National Geographic-sponsored expedition to Alaska added a Lake Grosvenor and a Mount La Gorce to the map. "Our Greatest National Monument," *National Geographic* (September 1921): 222.

71. Flora B. Shelton, *Shelton of Tibet*, 253.

72. Louise Connolly to J. C. Dana, Dec. 1, 1920, Shelton Files, Newark Museum Archives, Newark, New Jersey.

73. Albert Shelton to A. E. Cory, Shelton Files, Apr. 13, 1921, 1918–1928 Missionary Correspondence, Disciples of Christ Historical Society, Nashville, Tennessee.

74. Flora B. Shelton, *Shelton of Tibet*, 267.

75. Albert Shelton to Archibald McLean, Sept. 21, 1920, Shelton Files, 1918–1928 Missionary Correspondence, Disciples of Christ Historical Society, Nashville, Tennessee; Flora B. Shelton, *Shelton of Tibet*, 266.

76. "Lead On, O King Eternal," *World Call* (August 1921): 26. Marian L. Duncan, *Flame of the Fire*, 62 n38.

77. Roderick MacLeod to Albert Shelton, Aug. 11, 1920, Still Family Archives, Scottsdale, Arizona.

78. "Report of a Trip Thru Yunnan, Eastern Tibet, and Szechuan, by Major John Magruder, F.A., Ass't Military Attache, Jan.17-July 11, 1921," Appendix 7, 2, Reel 2—U.S. War Dept. Military Intelligence Division China, 1918–1941.

79. Esther MacLeod to Flora Shelton, Sept. 21, 1920, Still Family Archives, Scottsdale, Arizona.

80. Nina Hardy to Flora Shelton, Feb. 4, 1921, Still Family Archives, Scottsdale, Arizona.

81. Ibid.

82. "Tibetan Affairs," May 7, 1921, *Records of the Department of State Relating to Internal Affairs of China, 1910–1929* (Washington, D.C.: National Archives and Records Service, 1973).

83. Marian L. Duncan, *Flame from the Fire*, 56, 59, stated James Ogden helped negotiate a cease-fire after the Chinese shelled the town. Marion H. Duncan, *The Mountain of Silver Snow*, 105, 144 stated that in 1923 the renegade monk Ranalama leading the Hsiangch'eng raiders issued a statement to the TCM missionaries guaranteeing safety. He wrote, "You are doing a good work. Not a hair on your head will be touched." Four years later, some of Ranalama's former men broke into their former leader's house and cut off his head with a hand axe, ending that particular chapter of rebellion in western Kham. Louis Magrath King, *China in Turmoil: Studies in Personality* (London: Heath, Cranton, Limited, 1927), 38–39. During the same 1920–1921 period of disorder, British Consul Louis King reported brigands attacked Tachienlu and a battle raged all day and into the night, Chinese soldiers in puttees, Sam Browne belts, and crisp service hats fighting the armed nomads clad in animal skins.

84. "Report of a Trip Thru Yunnan, Eastern Tibet, and Szechuan, by Major John Magruder, F.A., Ass't Military Attache, Jan.17-July 11, 1921," Appendix (7), 3–4, Reel 2—U.S. War Dept. Military Intelligence Division China, 1918–1941.

85. Missionary letters, May 7 and 15, 1921 and Aug. 20, 1921, U.S. State Dept Reviews 1921, *Records of the Department of State Relating to Internal Affairs of China, 1910–1929* (Washington, D.C.: National Archives and Records Service, 1973).

86. Marian L. Duncan, *Flame of the Fire*, 56–57.

87. Albert Shelton to Abraham Cory, Aug. 29, 1920, Shelton Files, 1918–1928 Missionary Correspondence, Disciples of Christ Historical Society, Nashville, Tennessee.

88. Marian L. Duncan, *A Flame of the Fire,* 58.

89. Flora Shelton to S. J. Corey, July 21, 1921 [received], Shelton Files, 1918–1928 Missionary Correspondence, Disciples of Christ Historical Society, Nashville, Tennessee. In July 1921, the College of Missions bought two Tibetan costumes for a hundred dollars for its Foreign Day and permanent collection. Flora Shelton wrote, "We are sending the two costumes, which will be of service to the Society a long time after we are not. Also sending a Litang headdress of greasy strings & silver & beads."

90. Flora Shelton to C. W. Plopper, Apr. 26, 1920, Shelton Files, 1918–1928 Missionary Correspondence, Disciples of Christ Historical Society, Nashville, Tennessee.

91. Flora B. Shelton, *Shelton of Tibet,* 253.

92. The woman was Mrs. W. H. Archers. Marian L. Duncan, *Flame of the Fire,* 62.

93. Dorris Shelton Still, *Beyond the Devils in the Wind* (Tempe, Arizona: Synergy Books, 1989), 107.

Chapter 14

1. Albert Shelton to daughters, Dec. 26, 1921, quoted in *Pomona Progress,* Mar. 30, 1922. Albert Shelton to S. J. Corey, Dec. 26, 1921 Shelton Files, 1918–1928 Missionary Correspondence, Disciples of Christ Historical Society, Nashville, Tennessee.

2. Flora B. Shelton, *Shelton of Tibet* (New York: George Doran, 1923), 253.

3. Ibid., 253.

4. Gertrude Morse (Helen M. Morse, ed.), *The Dogs May Bark, But the Caravan Moves On* (Joplin, Missouri: College Press Publishing Co. 1998), 50. Except for itinerations and promotional campaigns, the Sheltons had never been separated in nineteen years. A few days later, Albert wrote S. J. Corey, "Mrs. S. left us at Shanghai—I never knew it could be as hard as it was." Albert Shelton to S. J. Corey, Shelton Files, Sept. 4, 1921, 1918–1928 Missionary Correspondence, Disciples of Christ Historical Society, Nashville, Tennessee.

5. The UCMS funded $2,175 for travel expenses for each of the Morse and Duncan families, plus a $950 outfitting expense. S. J. Corey considered approaching Columbus, Indiana industrialist Will Irwin for the money. Tibet Files, Disciples of Christ Historical Society, Nashville, Tennessee.

6. *The Evening Star* [China], Mar. 6, 1922, 1918–1928 Shelton Files, 1918–1928 Missionary Correspondence, Disciples of Christ Historical Society, Nashville, Tennessee. Roderick and Esther MacLeod to Flora Shelton, May 26, 1922. Still Family Archive, Scottsdale, Arizona, noted the jewels were stolen during the attack in February 1922. Presumably the items in his baggage included trade goods. *St. Louis Post-Dispatch,* Mar. 5, 1922, stated Shelton gained passage through the Sangen by distributing "presents to the women of the first mirrors they had ever seen—souvenirs given away by a malted milk producer and brought from the United States."

7. Morse, *The Dogs May Bark, But the Caravan Moves On,* 25

8. Marion H. Duncan, *The Mountain of Silver Snow* (Cincinnati, Ohio: Powell & White, 1929), 17.

9. Flora Shelton to FCMS, Shelton Files, Mar. 20, 1920, 1918–1928 Missionary Correspondence, Disciples of Christ Historical Society, Nashville, Tennessee.

10. Dr. E. I. Osgood, "Dr. Shelton's Captivity and Escape," *World Call* (June 1920): 12.

11. Albert Shelton to Dorothy Shelton, Sept. 27, 1921, Oct. 11, 1921, Still Family Archives, Nashville, Tennessee.

12. Flora B. Shelton, *Shelton of Tibet,* 277.

13. "Strangers in a Strange Land are Compatriots," *World Call* (November 1920): 54.

14. Albert Shelton to Shelton daughters, Sept. 27, 1921, Still Family Archive, Scottsdale, Arizona.
15. Albert Shelton to S. J. Corey, June 20, 1921; S. J. Corey to Albert Shelton, June 24, 1920, Shelton Files, 1918–1928 Missionary Correspondence, Disciples of Christ Historical Society, Nashville, Tennessee. Dr. Shelton Returns to Thibet," Miscellaneous Shelton Clippings, Disciples of Christ Historical Society, Nashville, Tennessee.
16. Marion H. Duncan, *The Mountain of Silver Snow*, 30.
17. Flora B. Shelton, *Shelton of Tibet*, 279.
18. Marion H. Duncan, *The Mountain of Silver Snow*, 27.
19. Marian L. Duncan, *A Flame of the Fire* (Spring Hill, Tennessee: Marian Duncan, 1999), 62.
20. Marion H. Duncan, *The Mountain of Silver Snow*, 30.
21. Flora B. Shelton, *Shelton of Tibet*, 280.
22. Marion H. Duncan, *The Mountain of Silver Snow*, 35.
23. Ibid., 38.
24. Ibid., 39.
25. Mrs. A. E. Morse postcard to C. W. Plopper, May 22, 1922, Shelton Files, 1918–1928 Missionary Correspondence, Disciples of Christ Historical Society, Nashville, Tennessee.
26. Ibid., 58.
27. Ibid., 49.
28. Flora B. Shelton, *Shelton of Tibet*, 278.
29. Marion H. Duncan, *The Mountain of Silver Snow*, 58–59.
30. Ibid., 69.
31. Ibid., 66.
32. T. T. Cooper wrote about Khuyuk La pass, "The banditti of this neighborhood are famous throughout Thibet, and defy alike the Chinese and Thibetan authorities. Living in the fastnesses of the mountains, they hold the more peaceable inhabitants in complete terror." On his return from Batang, Cooper encountered a band of "sturdy Mongols," who confronted him. "Suddenly several dismounted Mongols stepped out from behind a pile of granite boulders; and with long matchlocks (on which the matches were burning) thrown over their arms, stationed themselves across the path." Cooper managed to bluff his way through, but the pass remained a passage of fear for travelers in the intervening decades. T. T. Cooper, *Travels of Pioneer of Commerce* (New York: Arno Press, [1871] 1967), 276–277, 401–402.
33. Phillip Ho (Hodabah) and Marguerite Fairbrother, *Wandering Tibetan* (Long Beach, California: Christian Press, 1966), 3, wrote of his Chinese-Tibetan family being paid to climb into the high mountains to gather snow for the missionaries' ice cream. As testimony to the violence of the Batang area, Ho, who became a Christian missionary, wrote that his family was robbed eleven times before he was born.
34. Details of the journey and route are from Marion H. Duncan, *The Mountain of Silver Snow*, 15–71; and Morse, *The Dogs May Bark, But the Caravan Moves On*, 21–42.
35. Albert Shelton to daughters, Dec. 26, 1921, quoted in *Pomona Progress*, Mar. 30, 1922; Albert Shelton to S. J. Corey, Dec. 26, 1921, Shelton Files, 1918–1928 Missionary Correspondence, Disciples of Christ Historical Society, Nashville, Tennessee.
36. Marion H. Duncan, *The Mountain of Silver Snow*, 71.
37. Flora B. Shelton, *Shelton of Tibet*, 281.
38. James Ogden had acquired more than forty acres from General Liu in payment for the loans he extracted from the missionaries during the 1919 tumult. As owning private property was clearly forbidden by U.S.-China law, the ownership created a long-lived imbroglio until Ogden deeded the land to the mission orphanage. Marion H. Duncan, *The Mountain of Silver Snow*, 92–93.

39. Marian L. Duncan, *A Flame of the Fire,* 59.

40. U.S. Minister in China Schurman memorandum to Chinese Minister of Foreign Affairs W. W. Yen, June 17, 1922, *Papers Relating to the Foreign Relations of the United States, 1922,* 2 vols. (Washington, D.C.: United States Printing Office, 1938), vol. 1, 863.

41. By the 1920s there were over five thousand Protestant missionaries scattered across China, serving in missions, churches, schools, colleges, and hospitals. The 1920s were to be the peak of foreign mission work in China. In Britain and America, fund-raising continued to set records as the mission societies honed their public relations and fund-raising skills. By 1920, the United States outstripped Britain as the largest source of mission donations, contributing $29 million. Among the Chinese, Christian conversion appeared to be an easier goal. In 1911 there were half a million Chinese Christians. By 1920 there were two million Chinese Roman Catholics, and over six hundred thousand Protestants. J. W. Gregory, *To the Alps of Chinese Tibet* (London: Seeley, Service & Co., 1923), 124. In the period since Albert Shelton arrived in Kham, America had overtaken Britain as the primary homeland of Protestant missionaries. In 1905, 45 percent of the Protestant missionaries came from Great Britain and 35 percent from the United States. By 1922, 51 percent of the missionaries hailed from American and only 18 percent from Great Britain. Kenneth S. Latourette, *A History of the Christian Missions in China* (London: Society for Promoting Christian Knowledge, 1929), 769.

42. Marion H. Duncan, *The Mountain of Silver Snow,* 75.

43. Flora B. Shelton, *Shelton of Tibet,* 281–282.

44. William Hardy to J. W. Hardy, Jan. 24, 1922, Hardy Files, 1918–1928 Missionary Correspondence, Disciples of Christ Historical Society, Nashville, Tennessee.

45. Marian L. Duncan, *A Flame of the Fire,* 68.

46. Louis King despatches to H.B.M. Minister at Peking, Sir Beilby Alston, Aug. 24, 1921, No. F 4594/59/10 Oriental and India Office Collections, British Library, London.

47. "Mrs. Shelton, Wife of Dr. Shelton, Slain Missionary, Tells of Terrors Caused by Drought in China," *The Bulletin* [Pomona, California], Apr. 16, 1922.

48. "Strange Coincidence Told In Letter From Mrs. Shelton, Wife of Slain Missionary," *The Bulletin* [Pomona, California], Apr. 9, 1922.

49. "Wife of Dr. Shelton, Slain Missionary, Writes Interesting Account of Visit to Penang," *The Bulletin* [Pomona, California], Apr. 2, 1922.

50. The press published Flora Shelton's books as a 124-page geography, a 240-page storybook, and a 174-page hymn book.

51. "Letter Tells of Loneliness of Dr. Shelton," *Pomona Progress,* Apr. 10, 1922.

Chapter 15

1. Marion H. Duncan, *Love Songs and Proverbs of Tibet* (London: Mitre Press, 1961), 175.

2. Flora B. Shelton, *Shelton of Tibet* (New York: George Doran, 1923), 294.

3. Ibid., 297–298.

4. "Say Shelton Was Warned," *The New York Times,* Mar. 31, 1922.

5. Surkhang Depon to Olsen, Aug. 12, 1948, Newark Museum, Newark, New Jersey. The Tibetan official indicated that the scion of the prince's Tibetan name was Kesang Namgyal.

6. Former Disciple of Christ missionary Joe Smith to author, June 14, 2000 phone interview.

7. A Batang photo of the 1919–1920 era of a group of Chinese, Tibetans including Gezong Ongdu and the Jo Lama, showed the growing preference for Western-style hats, and borderland mixtures of Chinese and Tibetan clothes. Shelton Files, Disciples of Christ Historical Society, Nashville, Tennessee. J. W. Gregory, *To the Alps of Chinese Tibet* (London:

Seely, Service & Company, 1923), 209. Also *World Call* (March 1920): 47, ran a photo of a TCM 1919 baptism with a number of local Chinese and Chinese-Tibetan men with fedoras. Gezong Ongdu favored a fedora with the brim reshaped into a rakish Robin Hood-style chapeau. J. W. Gregory, a University of Glasgow geology professor who traveled in the Tibetan marches in the early 1920s, corrected his original statement in *To the Alps of Chinese Tibet* to write that Shelton, at the time of his death, was wearing a long khaki sheepskin-lined Tibetan-style coat. "The Death of Dr. Shelton," *Geographical Journal* 65 (January 1925): 87–88.

8. The Chinese name for the pass is Sa Swei San.

9. Marion H. Duncan, *The Yangtze and the Yak* (Alexandria, Virginia: Marion H. Duncan), 117.

10. Dr. Hardy wrote, "Dr. Shelton did not know whether he could, at this time, open medical, or other mission work in Lassa or not." Hardy File, 1918–1928 Missionary Correspondence, Disciples of Christ Historical Society, Nashville, Tennessee.

11. *Papers Relating to the Foreign Relations of the United States, 1922,* 2 vols. (Washington, D.C.: United States Printing Office, 1938), vol. 1, 861.

12. This account of Dr. Shelton's ride between Batang and the Tibetan border utilizes material from the following sources: Dorris Shelton Still, *Beyond the Devils in the Wind* (Tempe, Arizona: Synergy Books, 1989), 108–110; Flora B. Shelton, *Shelton of Tibet,* 256; Valrae Reynolds and Barbara Reynolds, *The Museum New Series* (Newark, New Jersey: Newark Museum, 1972), 42–48; Marian L. Duncan, *A Flame from the Fire* (Spring Hill, Tennessee: Marian L. Duncan, 1999), 68–69; February 17, 1922 William Hardy letter to Stephen J. Corey, Albert Shelton Files, 1918–1928 Missionary Correspondence, Disciples of Christ Historical Society, Nashville, Tennessee.

13. Gertrude Morse (Helen M. Morse, ed.), *The Dogs May Bark, But the Caravan Moves On* (Joplin, Missouri: College Press Publishing Co.1998), 47–52.

14. Hardy to S. J. Corey, quoted in *Pomona Progress,* Feb. 17, 1922.

15. There were discrepancies between Hardy's and Demnbajangtsen's accounts, particularly regarding the amputation. According to TCM missionary child and author Marian L. Duncan, Hardy edited his report with the thought that Flora Shelton would be reading it and he didn't want to upset her. Marian L. Duncan, *A Flame from the Fire,* 68–69; interview with Marian L. Duncan, Nov. 14, 1999.

16. William Hardy to Bert Wilson, July 27, 1922, Disciples of Christ Historical Society, Nashville, Tennessee.

17. Ibid.

18. Flora B. Shelton, *Shelton of Tibet,* 287–288.

19. William Hardy to Dr. H. G. Thompson in Yunnanfu, Feb. 26, 1922, was copied in a British despatch: April 25, 1922 F. Lewison to Foreign Secretary to the Government of India, (P 2292 1922), Oriental and India Office Collections, British Library, London.

20. Flora B. Shelton, *Shelton of Tibet,* 294.

21. Ibid., 290.

22. Still, *Beyond the Devils in the Wind,* 111.

23. William Hardy to UCMS, Mar. 4, 1922, Shelton Files, 1918–1928 Missionary Correspondence, Disciples of Christ Historical Society, Nashville, Tennessee.

24. Local Disciple of Christ member Eva Pye chided the mission society about the insensitive press release that led to the subsequent United Press bulletin the next day. She wrote, "The word came to Pomona the same way before your telegram [to the Shelton daughters] but fortunately it did not reach the Sheltons altho it was even posted on a bulletin board." Eva Pye to UCMS, Mar. 5, 1922, Shelton Files, 1918–1928 Missionary Correspondence, Disciples of Christ Historical Society, Nashville, Tennessee.

25. *The Bulletin* (Pomona, California), Mar. 5, 1922.

26. Eva Pye to UCMS, Mar. 5, 1922, Shelton Files, 1918–1928 Missionary Correspondence, Disciples of Christ Historical Society, Nashville, Tennessee.

27. O. A. Rosboro to J. O. LaGorce, May 25, 1922, Shelton Files, National Geographic Archives.

28. S. J. Corey to A. E. Cory, Shelton Files, 1918–1928 Missionary Correspondence, Disciples of Christ Historical Society, Nashville, Tennessee.

29. "Heart Touching Scene as Mrs. Shelton, Wife of Slain Missionary Returns," *The Bulletin* (Pomona, California), May 18, 1922

30. *Biography Set, Series Five: Our Workers in Jamaica, Tibet, Philippine Islands* (Indianapolis, Indiana: The United Christian Missionary Society, 1937), Leaflet Seven.

31. "The Death of Dr. Shelton Near Batang," Shelton Files, 1918–1928 Missionary Correspondence, Disciples of Christ Historical Society, Nashville, Tennessee.

32. "Dr. Shelton Slain by Chinese Bandits," *New York Times,* Mar. 5, 1922.

33. "Dr. Shelton Killed By Chinese Bandits in the Wilds of Thibet," *New York World,* Mar. 5, 1922. There is no evidence that Shelton sold material to the AMNH, though the Newark Museum did trade some of Shelton's collection to the AMNH decades later.

34. *The China Press,* Mar. 5, 1922; *Evening Star,* Mar. 6, 1922, clippings, Shelton Files, 1918–1928 Missionary Correspondence, Disciples of Christ Historical Society, Nashville, Tennessee.

35. "Indianapolis Missionary Slain by Chinese Bandits," and "Expected to Die in Orient," *Indianapolis Star,* Mar. 5, 1922.

36. "Dr. Shelton Killed Near Batang, China," *Anthony Republican,* Mar. 9, 1922.

37. "Dr. Shelton Slain By Chinese Bandits At Climax of a Notable Career," *St. Louis Post-Dispatch,* Mar. 5, 1922.

38. "Deaths," *West China Missionary News,* May 1922.

39. "Life on the Roof of the World," September 2, 1922; Buddhism Blended With Devil-worship: Tibetan Monastic Art," Sept. 9, 1922, *The Illustrated London News.*

40. "American Murdered By Chinese Bandits," *Newark Call,* Mar. 5, 1922.

41. Newark Museum Grateful Debtor of Dr. Shelton," *New York World,* Mar. 12, 1922.

42. J. O. LaGorce to O. A. Rosboro, Mar. 28, 1922; F. L. Fisher to O. A. Rosboro, May 6, 1922; J. C. Dana to O. A. Rosboro, May 14, 1922, Shelton Files, 1918–1928 Missionary Correspondence, Disciples of Christ Historical Society, Nashville, Tennessee.

43. O. A. Rosboro to J. O. LaGorce, May 4, 1923, Shelton Files, 1918–1928 Missionary Correspondence, Disciples of Christ Historical Society, Nashville, Tennessee.

44. O. A. Rosboro to HBH, Mar. 15, 1922; O. A. Rosboro to S. J. Corey, Mar. 31, 1922; S. J. Corey to O. A. Rosboro, Apr. 4, 1922, Shelton Files, 1918–1928 Missionary Correspondence, Disciples of Christ Historical Society, Nashville, Tennessee.

45. L. F. Kirby to UCMS, Mar. 5, 1922, Shelton Files, 1918–1928 Missionary Correspondence, Disciples of Christ Historical Society, Nashville, Tennessee.

46. "Church Honors Dr. A. L. Shelton Sunday Morning," *Pomona Progress,* Mar. 6, 1922.

47. *St. Louis Post-Dispatch,* May 6, 1922. R. H. Miller to UCMS, May 7, 1922, Shelton Files, 1918–1928 Missionary Correspondence, Disciples of Christ Historical Society, Nashville, Tennessee.

48. Ch'en Tung Chi to American Consulate at Chungking, Mar. 6, 1922 [received], Shelton Files, 1918–1928 Missionary Correspondence, Disciples of Christ Historical Society, Nashville, Tennessee.

49. March 9, 1922 N. F. Allman letter to Ch'en Yung Chi. The acknowledgement was dated Jan. 12, 1920, addressed to Liu Chao-ching, Commissioner for Foreign Affairs, Shelton Files, 1918–1928 Missionary Correspondence, Disciples of Christ Historical Society, Nashville, Tennessee.

50. A. B. Ruddock to N. F. Allman, Apr. 3, 1922, Shelton Files, 1918–1928 Missionary Correspondence, Disciples of Christ Historical Society, Nashville, Tennessee.

51. *Papers Relating to the Foreign Relations of the United States, 1922,* vol. 1, 861–862.

52. Ibid., 862–863.

53. Ibid., 862–863.

54. Ibid., 863.

55. Ibid., 864.

56. "Imperial and Foreign News Items," *Times of London,* Apr. 1, 1922; "Say Shelton Was Warned," *New York Times,* Mar. 31, 1922.

57. Colonel W. S. Drysdale memorandum, no. 77, Feb. 5, 1920, U.S. War Department Military Intelligence Division, Correspondence of the Military Intelligence Division relation to the general, political, economic, and military conditions in China 1918–1941.

58. "Hughes Gives Out Report on Death of Dr. Shelton," *St. Louis Post-Dispatch,* Mar. 30, 1922.

59. Gregory, *To the Alps of Chinese Tibet,* 255

60. The British despatch quoting missionary B. G. Lewer was copied in the Apr. 6, 1922 Ottewill to H.B.M. Minister at Peking (No. 205/137). Lewer stated that Shelton said he expected to be "plugged" for his opium-suppression campaign in Batang.

61. *The Bulletin* (Pomona, California), Mar. 5, 1922.

62. *The Chinese Recorder* (May 1922): 356. *The Bulletin* (Pomona, California), Mar. 5, 1922. *The Chinese Recorder* also recorded the theory that Yang's band killed Shelton in revenge for the execution of their leader. "Gleanings from Correspondence and Exchanges," *The Chinese Recorder* (May 1922).

63. "Kansas Doctor Who Opened the Gates of Lhasa With a Scalpel," *St. Louis Post-Dispatch,* Apr. 16, 1922.

64. James Huston Edgar, *The Land of Mystery, Tibet* (Melbourne: China Inland Mission, 1939), 22.

65. Flora Shelton to missionary publications, June 25, 1922, Shelton Files, 1918–1928 Missionary Correspondence, Disciples of Christ Historical Society, Nashville, Tennessee.

66. O. A. Rosboro to S. J. Corey, Sept. 7, 1922; S. J. Corey to O. A. Rosboro, Sept. 11, 1922, Shelton Files, 1918–1928 Missionary Correspondence, Disciples of Christ Historical Society, Nashville, Tennessee.

67. Flora Shelton to Berthold Laufer, Aug. 29, 1922; Berthold Laufer to Flora Shelton, Sept. 5, 1922; Flora Shelton to Berthold Laufer, Sept. 12, 1922, Field Museum Archives, Chicago, Illinois.

68. S. J. Corey to Flora Shelton, Dec. 13, 1922; S. J. Corey to James Ogden, Mar. 21, 1923, Shelton Files, 1918–1928 Missionary Correspondence, Disciples of Christ Historical Society, Nashville, Tennessee.

69. Flora B. Shelton, *Shelton of Tibet,* 170, 256.

70. Julian Pettifer and Richard Bradley, *Missionaries* (London: BBC Books, 1990), 175.

71. Alastair Lamb, *The McMahon Line: A Study in the Relations Between India, China, and Tibet, 1904–1914,* 2 vols. (London: Routledge and Kegan Paul, 1966), vol. 1, 60. Hardy stated that British Consul Eric Teichman was behind Shelton's rebuff at the border: "When Teichman saw the reply [invitation], he said that it was only a polite letter without any meaning, and that Shelton could never make the trip. Shelton told the Consul to attend to his consular business, while he would carry on his missionary work. Teichman, I think, proceeded to attend to consular business by blocking Shelton . . . Not that Teichman had anything to do with the arrival of robbers on the road the day Shelton was coming back to Batang . . . but Teichman saw to it that Shelton was not to enter Tibet, and the result was, according to the runner that came to Shelton from the Tegi, that word

had come from England to Lassa, and from Lassa to the Galong Lama, and then to the Governor, that no foreigner was to enter Tibet without the Galong's permission." William Hardy to Bert Wilson, July 27, 1922, Shelton Files, 1918–1928 Missionary Correspondence, Disciples of Christ Historical Society, Nashville, Tennessee.

72. Louis King to Denys Bray, Mar. 9, 1922 (2737/1922), Oriental and India Office Collections, British Library, London.

73. B. Alston to Marques Curzon of Kedleston, Apr. 25, 1922 (F 1986/607/10), Oriental and India Office Collections, British Library, London.

74. Major F. M. Bailey to Secretary to the Government of India, Oct. 25, 1922 (stamped 532/P and P 4712/1922) Oriental and British Office Collections, British Library, London.

75. J. W. Gregory, *To the Alps of Chinese Tibet,* 209; "The Death of Dr. Shelton," *Geographical Journal,* vol. 65 (January 1925): 88. William Hardy wrote, "I believe I am safe in saying that I have treated an average of a case every two months and more than that number have been killed at this place within six or seven miles of Batang, but the officials and soldiers roll another opium pill every time a fight takes place on the pass and say it is too bad." Marian L. Duncan, *A Flame of the Fire,* 70. This quote was part of the Hardy death report that was widely circulated and quoted in media accounts of the time.

76. There seemed to be consensus among the missionaries about Shelton's killers. Roderick MacLeod talked to a reporter about the "little tribe near their mission station in Batang that had been the cause of Dr. Shelton's tragic death." "The Blood and Faith of the Old Covenanters Still Tell," *Christian-Evangelist* (July 17, 1924): 975. Morse, *The Dogs May Bark, But the Caravan Moves On,* 47–52, called the tribe Geh-mo. Marion H. Duncan, *The Yangtze and the Yak* (Alexandria, Virginia: Marion H. Duncan, 1952), 165, transliterated the tribe as Kemo. In the mid-1930s, Duncan encountered the entire Kemo tribe in winter camp, which consisted of forty black tents stretched for two miles in a grassy valley not far from the pass where Shelton was shot. Like Morse and MacLeod, Duncan held the Kemo tribesmen accountable for the murder of Albert Shelton. Though diminished by a twenty-year war with the Hsiang-ch'eng tribe, the Kemo remained a "defiant group," who still were "not adverse to robbing a passing caravan." Ever resourceful, the missionaries hired the Kemo as bodyguards, both to strengthen the caravan against other brigands and to avoid having the Kemo steal their horses.

  Shelton's death gave rise to some interesting local folklore. Phillip Ho, a Batang native who later became a Christian evangelist, wrote a tale of Shelton taking his pistol and handing it to the bandit with the muzzle facing himself, "taking death himself rather than taking the lives of others to save himself." Phillip (Hodabah) Ho and Marguerite Fairbrother, *Wandering Tibetan* (Long Beach, California: Christian Press, 1966), 24.

77. Marian L. Duncan, *Flame from the Fire,* 69.

78. J. W. Gregory to Flora Shelton, Dec. 15, 1924, Still Family Archives, Scottsdale, Arizona.

79. Nina Hardy to S. J. Corey, Mar. 2, 1922, Shelton Files, 1918–1928 Missionary Correspondence, Disciples of Christ Historical Society, Nashville, Tennessee.

80. S. J. Corey to O. A. Rosboro, Sept. 11, 1922, Shelton Files, 1918–1928 Missionary Correspondence, Disciples of Christ Historical Society, Nashville, Tennessee.

81. S. J. Corey to Flora Shelton, May 30, 1923, Shelton Files, 1918–1928 Missionary Correspondence, Disciples of Christ Historical Society, Nashville, Tennessee.

Epilogue

1. Marion H. Duncan, *Love Songs and Proverbs of Tibet* (London: Mitre Press, 1961), 179.

2. "The Kansas Doctor who opened gates of Lhasa with a scalpel," *St. Louis Post-Dispatch,* Apr. 16, 1922.

3. On February 23, 1923 the Disciples held a nationwide program to raise $100,000 for the Shelton Memorial Fund. Across the country, thousands filed into church to sing "Sweet Bye and Bye," Shelton's favorite hymn and contribute to the cause. Each person contributing a dollar received a certificate and a large photo of Dr. Shelton. Shelton Files, Disciples of Christ Historical Society, Nashville, Tennessee.

4. Still Family Archives, Scottsdale, Arizona.

5. "Pension Fund of Disciples of Christ" flyer, Shelton Files, Disciples of Christ Historical Society, Nashville, Tennessee.

6. J. B. Hunley, *Shelton and the Crimson Trail: A Missionary Drama* (Cincinnati, Ohio: Powell and White, 1924); Nina Millen, ed. *Missionary Hero Stories* (New York: Friendship Press), 1948.

7. The College of Missions operated in Indianapolis from 1911 to 1928, when the college moved to Hartford, Connecticut. Paul Diebold and Julia Fangmeier, *Mission Accomplished: The Missions Building, Its History and Its People* (Indianapolis, Indiana: Irvington Historical Society, 1995), 10.

8. Douglas Wissing, "Area's Tibetan presence has roots in Cold War," *Indianapolis Star,* Aug. 25, 2003; "Tibetan Adventure," *Indianapolis Star,* Jan. 28, 2000; "Old Mission Building finds new purpose," *Indianapolis Star,* Jan. 29, 2000.

9. Since 1948, when the first Tibetans to live in America, the Tibetan Trade Delegation, visited the Newark Museum to view the holdings, the Newark Museum has forged ongoing relationships with Tibetan Buddhist notables and scholars. After World War II, Geshé Wangyal, the first lama with full Tibetan monastic training to form a Buddhist monastic center in America (in central New Jersey), began serving as an advisor to the Newark. Following the Dalai Lama's flight from Tibet in 1959, scholars from the Tibetan community in exile have provided extensive assistance to the museum's research efforts. Valrae Reynolds, *From the Sacred Realm: Treasures of Tibetan Art for The Newark Museum* (Munich: Prestal Verlag, 1999), 11–21.

10. "Bible Concordancy," written by Flora Shelton and Minnie Ogden, Disciples of Christ Historical Society, Nashville, Tennessee. James Hilton to Flora Shelton, Sept. 15, 1942, Still Family Archives, Scottsdale, Arizona.

11. Flora Shelton to Newark Museum, Nov. 7, 1950, Shelton Files, Newark Museum Archives, Newark, New Jersey.

12. Marion Duncan, *The Mountain of Silver Snow* (Cincinnati, Ohio: Powell & White, 1929), 130–144; Marian Duncan, *A Flame of the Fire* (Spring Hill, Tennessee: Marian Duncan, 1999), 105; Corey to Flora Shelton, Jan. 16, 1924, Missionary Correspondence, Shelton File, Disciples of Christ Historical Society, Nashville, Tennessee. Intelligence reports from Dr. William Hardy to Consul, Aug. 3, 1923 and July 23–24, 1924, Records of the Department of State Relating to Internal Affairs of China, 1910–1929. Washington, D.C.: National Archives and Record Service, 1973, Roll 34, 893.00/5205 and Roll 37, 893.00/5534.

13. Eric Teichman, *Travels of a Consular Officer in Eastern Tibet* (Cambridge, England: Cambridge University Press), 1922.

14. Marian Duncan, *A Flame of the Fire,* 87–91.

15. Ibid., 196–197, 202–262.

16. Ibid., 190. Flora wrote the Duncans that Ongdu's death was a terrible blow to her.

17. Missionary Correspondence, Ogden Files, Disciples of Christ Historical Society, Nashville, Tennessee.

18. Marian Duncan, *A Flame of the Fire,* 229–238.

19. Minnie Ogden, "An Account of the War at Batang, 1932," Tibetan Christian Mission Files, Disciples of Christ Historical Society, Nashville, Tennessee.

20. Marian Duncan, *A Flame of the Fire,* 234, 243. There were about twenty-five converts in the TCM congregation in 1922. Flora B. Shelton, *Shelton of Tibet* (New York: George Doran, 1923), 305.

21. The revolt against the Chinese Communist rule in Tibet began in Kham and Amdo in the mid-1950s, a resistance movement known as Chushi Gangdruk. After the Dalai Lama fled Tibet in 1959 with a Khampa bodyguard, the CIA began funding a secret war against the Chinese Communists in Tibet with a Tibetan guerilla army based in the remote region of Mustang in western Nepal. Lasting until 1969, it was one of the CIA's longest-running covert operations. At one point, seventy percent of the secret Tibetan army was Khampa. John Kenneth Knaus, *Orphans of the Cold War: America and the Tibetan Struggle for Survival* (New York: PublicAffairs, 1999), 69–82, 127–136, 165, 239, 296.

22. Author research trip to Kham, September 1999.

SOURCES

General References

Achinstein, Asher. *American Economic History* (Seymour E. Harris, ed.). New York: McGraw-Hill Book Company, 1961.

Adams, Brooks. *America's Economic Supremacy.* New York: MacMillan, 1900.

Alley, Rewi, trans. *Tu Fu Selected Poems.* Peking: Foreign Language Press, 1962.

Andreas, A. T. *Illustrated Historical Atlas of the State of Indiana.* Indianapolis, Indiana: Indiana Historical Society, [1876] 1968.

———. *History of the State of Kansas.* Chicago, 1883.

Arnold, Anna E. *A History of Kansas.* Topeka: State of Kansas, State Printing Plant, 1914.

Austin, Alvyn J. *Saving China: Canadian Missionaries in the Middle Kingdom, 1888–1959.* Toronto: University of Toronto Press, 1986.

Bacot, Jacques. *Dans les Marches Tibetains.* Paris: Plon, 1909.

———. *Le Tibet Révolté.* Paris: Hachette et cie, 1912.

Bailey, Lt. Col. F. M. *China-Tibet-Assam; A Journey, 1911.* London: J. Cape, 1945.

Bangs, Richard, and Christian Kallen. *Riding the Dragon's Back.* New York: Laurel Books, 1992.

Banwart, Don. *Rails, Rivalry, and Romance.* Fort Scott, Kansas: Historical Preservation Organization of Bourbon County, Inc.,1982.

Barnett, Robert, ed. *Resistance and Reform in Tibet.* Bloomington, Indiana: Indiana University Press, 1994.

Barr, Patt. *To China with Love: The Lives and Times of Protestant Missionaries in China 1860–1900.* London: Secker & Warburg, 1972.

———. *The Memsahibs: The Women of Victorian India.* London: Secker & Warburg. 1976.

Barrows, Robert G. *A Demographic Analysis of Indianapolis, 1870–1920.* Bloomington, Indiana: Indiana University Dissertation, 1977.

Batchelor, Stephen. *The Tibet Guide.* London: Wisdom Publications, 1987.

Beckwith, Christopher. *The Tibetan Empire in Central Asia.* Princeton, New Jersey: Princeton University Press, 1987.

Berthoff, Rowland. *An Unsettled People: Social Order and Disorder in American History.* New York: Harper & Row, 1971.

Bhabha, Homi K. *The Location of Culture.* London: Routledge, 1994.

Bishop, George. *Travels in Imperial China: The Explorations and Discoveries of Père Armand David.* London: Cassell, 1990.

Bishop, Isabella Bird [nee Isabella L. Bird]. *Among the Tibetans.* New York: Fleming H. Revell Company, 1894.

———. *Isabella Lucy Bird's A Lady's Life in the Rocky Mountains: An Annotated Text* (Ernest S. Bernard, ed.). Norman, Oklahoma: University of Oklahoma Press, [1879] 1999.

———. *The Yangtze Valley and Beyond: An Account of Journeys in China.* Boston: Beacon Press, [1899] 1987.

Blakiston, Thomas W. *Five Months on the Yang-Tsze, and Notices of the Present Rebellions in China.* London: J. Murray, 1862.

Blanchard, Charles, ed. *Counties of Morgan, Monroe, and Brown, Indiana: Historical and Bio-graphical.* Mt. Vernon, Indiana: Windmill Publications, [1884] 1993.

Blanchard, Leola H. *Conquest of Southwest Kansas.* Wichita, Kansas: Wichita Eagle Press, 1931.

Bodard, Lucien. *The French Consul.* New York: Knopf, [1973] 1977.

Bodenhamer, David J., Robert G. Barrows, and David Gordon Vanderstel, eds. *The Encyclopedia of Indianapolis.* Bloomington, Indiana: Indiana University Press, 1994.

Bower, Hamilton, Sir. *Diary of a Journey Across Tibet.* Kathmandu, Nepal: Ratna Pustak Bhandar, [1893] 1976.

Brackenbury, Wade. *Yak Butter & Black Tea: A Journey into Forbidden China.* Chapel Hill, North Carolina: Algonquin Books of Chapel Hill, 1997.

Bray, John. *The Himalayan Mission: Moravian Church Centenary, Leh, Ladakh, India: 1885–1985.* Leh, Ladakh: Moravian Church, 1985.

Broomhall, B. *The Evangelisation of the World: A Missionary Band: A Record of Consecration, and an Appeal.* London: Morgan & Scott, 1889.

Bryant, Dan. *In Mission and Service: Disciples in Pomona, 1883–1983.* Pomona, California: First Christian Church, 1983.

Buddhist Monasteries of Ganzi Tibetan Autonomous Prefecture, Western Sichuan, China. Los Angeles: China Exploration and Research Society, 1992.

Bull, Geoffrey T. *When Iron Gates Yield.* Chicago: Moody Press, 1955.

Butchart, Reuben. *The Disciples of Christ in Canada Since 1830.* Toronto: Canadian Headquarters' Publications, 1949.

Cannadine, David. *Ornamentalism.* New York: Oxford University Press, 2001.

Carey, William. *Travel and Adventure in Tibet, Including the Diary of Miss Annie R. Taylor's Remarkable Journey from Tau-Chau to Ta-Chien-Lu through the Heart of the Forbidden Land.* London: Hodder and Stoughton, 1902.

Carlsen, William D. *Tibet: In Search of a Miracle.* Nyack, New York: Nyack College, 1985.

Carlson, Lillian. *If the Vision Tarry.* Minneapolis: World Mission Prayer League, 1988.

Carr, Floyd L. *Albert L. Shelton, Martyr Missionary of Tibet.* New York: Baptist Board of Education, 1929.

Carson, Gerald. *Cornflake Crusade.* New York: Rinehart & Company, Inc., 1957.

Carter, Paul A. *The Spiritual Crisis of the Gilded Age.* DeKalb, Illinois: Northern Illinois University Press, 1971.

Castleton, A. G. *Rough, Tough, and Far Away: James Edgar of Tibet.* New York: Friendship Press, 1948.

Catalogue of Kentucky University, Session of 1902–1903. Lexington, Kentucky: Transylvania Company, 1903.

Cathcart, Charlotte. *Indianapolis from Our Old Corner.* Indianapolis, Indiana: Indiana Historical Society, 1965.

Cather, Willa. *My Àntonia.* Boston: Houghton Mifflin Company, 1918.

Cauble, Commodore Wesley. *Disciples of Christ in Indiana.* Indianapolis, Indiana: Meigs Publishing Company, 1930.

Central Christian Church (Indianapolis). *125 Significant Years: The Story of Central Christian Church, 1833–1958.* Indianapolis, Indiana: Central Christian Church, 1958.

The China Mission Hand-book. Shanghai, China: American Presbyterian Mission Press, 1896.

Clifford, James. *The Predicament of Culture: Twentieth-Century Ethnography, Literature, and Art.* Cambridge, Massachusetts: Harvard University Press, 1988.

Coates, P. D. *The China Consuls: British Consular Officers, 1843–1943.* Hong Kong: Oxford University Press, 1988.

Cohen, Paul. *China and Christianity.* Cambridge, Massachusetts: Harvard University Press, 1963.

———. *History in Three Keys: The Boxers as Event, Experience, and Myth.* New York: Columbia University Press, 1997.

Collier, Peter, and David Horowitz. *The Rockefellers: An American Dynasty.* New York: Holt, Rinehart and Winston, [1976] 1997.

Connell, Evan S. *Son of the Morning Star.* New York: Harper & Row, 1984.

Cooper, Thomas T. *Travels of a Pioneer of Commerce.* New York: Arno Press, [1871] 1967.

Cordier, Georges. *La Province du Yunnan.* Hanoi: Impr. Mac-Dinh-Tu, 1928.

Cotton, James. *Asian Frontier Nationalism: Owen Lattimore and the American Policy Debate.* Atlantic Highlands, New Jersey: Humanities Press International, 1989.

Courtright, David T. *Dark Paradise: Opiate Addiction in America before 1940.* Cambridge, Massachusetts: Harvard University Press, 1982.

Crisler, Clarence C. *China's Borderlands and Beyond.* Takoma Park, Maryland: Review and Herald Publishing Company, 1937.

Cronk, Mrs. Katharine Scherer. *Under Many Flags.* New York: Board of Foreign Missions and the Woman's Board of Foreign Missions of the Presbyterian Church in the U.S.A., 1921.

Cronon, William, George Miles, and Jay Gitlin, eds. *Under an Open Sky: Rethinking America's Western Past.* New York: W. W. Norton & Company, 1992.

Crossette, Barbara. *The Great Hill Stations of Asia.* New York: Basic Books, 1999.

———. *So Close to Heaven: The Vanishing Buddhist Kingdoms of the Himalayas.* New York: Vintage Books, 1996.

Crow, Carl. *The Traveller's Handbook for China.* Shanghai, China: Hwa-Mei Concern, 1913.

Dary, David. A. *The Buffalo Book.* Chicago: Sage Books, 1974.

Das, Sarat Chandra. *Journey to Lhasa and Central Tibet* (W. W. Rockhill, ed.). New Delhi: Manjusri Publishing House, [1902] 1970.

Davies, Henry R. *Yün-nan, the Link between India and the Yangtze.* Cambridge: Cambridge University, 1909.

Davis, A. R. *Tu Fu.* New York: Twayne, 1971.

Davis, Kenneth S. *Kansas: A History.* New York: Norton, 1984.

D'Elia, Pasquale M. *The Catholic Missions in China.* Shanghai, China: The Commercial Press, Ltd., 1941.

Dejnozka, Edward L., David E. Kapel, Charles S. Gifford, and Marilyn B. Kape. *American Educators' Encyclopedia.* New York: Greenwood Press, 1991.

De Filippi, Filippo, ed. *An Account of Tibet: The Travels of Ippolito Desideri of Pistoia, S. J., 1712–1727.* London: George Routledge & Sons, 1937.

Derks, Scott, ed. *The Value of a Dollar.* Lakeville, Connecticut: Grey House Publishing, 1999.

De Rosthorn, A. *On the Tea Cultivation in Western Ssuch'uan; and, the Tea Trade with Tibet viâ Tachienlu.* London: Luzac & Co., 1895.

Desgodins, C. H. *La Mission Du Thibet de 1855 à 1870.* Verdun, France: C. Laurent, 1872.

———. *Le Thibet d'apèrs la Correspondance des missionaires.* Paris: Librairie Catholique de l'oeuvre de Saint-Paul, 1885.

Diamond, Jared M. *Guns, Germs, and Steel: The Fates of Human Societies.* New York: W. W. Norton, 1997.

Diebold, Paul, and Fangmeier, Julia. *Mission Accomplished: The Missions Building, Its History and Its People.* Indianapolis, Indiana: Irvington Historical Society, 1995.

Divita, James J. *Ethnic Settlement Patterns in Indianapolis.* Indianapolis, Indiana: Marian College, 1988.

Doherty, William J. *Indianapolis in the 1870s: Hard Times in the Gilded Age.* Bloomington, Indiana: Unpublished Dissertation, Indiana University, 1981.

Dönden, Dr. Yeshi. *Health Through Balance: An Introduction to Tibetan Medicine.* Ithaca, New York: Snow Lion Publications, 1986.

Dong, Stella. *Shanghai: The Rise and Fall of a Decadent City.* New York: William Morrow, 2000.

Dorje, Rinjing. *Food in Tibetan Life.* London: Prospect Books, 1985.

Draegert, Eva. *Indianapolis: The Culture of an Inland City.* Bloomington, Indiana: Unpublished Dissertation, Indiana University, 1952.

Duncan, Marian L. *A Flame of the Fire.* Spring Hill, Tennessee: Marian Duncan, 1999.

Duncan, Marion H. *Love Songs and Proverbs of Tibet.* London: Mitre Press, 1961.

———. *Customs and Superstitions of the Tibetans.* London: Mitre Press, 1964.

———. *The Mountain of Silver Snow.* Cincinnati, Ohio: Powell & White, 1929.

———. *The Yangtze and the Yak.* Alexandria, Virginia: Marion H. Duncan, 1952.

Dunn, Jacob Piatt. *Greater Indianapolis: The History, the Industries, the Institutions, and the People of a City of Homes.* 2 vols. Chicago: Lewis Publishing Company, 1910.

Dymond, M. M. *Yunnan.* London: Marshall Brothers, 1929.

Easton, Robert. *China Caravans.* Santa Barbara, California: Capra Press, 1982.

Eberle, Edith. *They Went to China: Biographies of Missionaries of the Disciples of Christ.* (Lois Anna Ely, rev.). Indianapolis, Indiana: Missionary Education Department, United Christian Missionary Society, 1948.

Edgar, James Huston. *The Land of Mystery, Tibet.* Melbourne: China Inland Mission, 1930.

———. *The Marches of the Mantze.* London: Morgan & Scott, 1908.

Ekvall, David P. *Outposts, or, Tibetan Border Sketches.* New York: Alliance Press Co., 1907.

Ekvall, Robert L. *Cultural Relations on the Kansu-Tibetan Border.* Chicago, Illinois: University of Chicago Press, 1939.

———. *Fields on the Hoof: Nexus of Tibetan Nomadic Pastoralism.* New York: Holt, Rinehart and Winston, 1968.

———. *Gateway to Tibet.* Harrisburg, Pennsylvania: Christian Publications, Inc., 1938.

Encyclopedia Britannica. Vol. 12. Cambridge, England: Cambridge University Press, 1910.

Encyclopedia of Indianapolis. Bloomington, Indiana: Indiana University Press, 1994.

Espey, John. *Minor Heresies, Major Departures: A China Mission Boyhood.* Berkeley, California: University of California Press, 1994.

Ewing, Elizabeth. *History of Twentieth Century Fashion.* Totawa, New Jersey: Barnes and Noble, 1986.

Fairbank, John K. *The Missionary Enterprise in China and America.* Cambridge, Massachusetts: Harvard University Press, 1974.

Fairbank, John K., and Denis Twitchett, eds. *The Cambridge History of China.* vol. 10. Cambridge, England: Cambridge University Press, 1978.

Fairbrother, Marguerite. *Eight Little Americans in Tibet.* Kearney, Nebraska: Morris Publishing, 1999.

Faragher, John Mack, ed. *Rereading Frederick Jackson Turner: The Significance of the Frontier in American History and Other Essays.* New York: H. Holt, 1994.

Federal Writers' Project of the Works Project Administration for the State of Kansas. *Kansas: A Guide to the Sunflower State.* New York: Viking Press, 1939.

Finer, S. E. *The Man on Horseback: The Role of the Military in Politics.* New York: Praeger, 1962.

Fischer, David Hackett. *Albion's Seed: Four British Folkways in America.* New York: Oxford University Press, 1989.

Fisher, Robert E. *Art of Tibet.* London: Thames and Hudson, 1997.

Fleming, Peter. *Bayonets to Lhasa: The First Full Account of the British Invasion of Tibet in 1904.* New York: Harper, 1961.

Ford, Robert. *Wind Between the Worlds.* New York: David McKay, 1957.

Forsythe, Sidney A. *An American Missionary Community in China, 1895–1905.* Cambridge, Massachusetts: East Asian Research Center, Harvard University, 1971.

Fosdick, Raymond Blaine. *John D. Rockefeller, Jr., A Portrait.* New York: Harpers and Brothers, 1956.

Foster, Barbara M. and Michael Foster. *Forbidden Journey: The Life of Alexandra David-Neel.* San Francisco: Harper & Row, 1987.

————. *The Secret Life of Alexandra David-Neel: A Biography of the Explorer of Tibet and Its Forbidden Practices*. Woodstock, New York: Overlook Press, 1998.

Frawley, Maria H. *A Wider Range: Travel Writing by Women in Victorian England*. Rutherford, New Jersey: Fairleigh Dickinson University Press, 1994.

French, Patrick. *Younghusband: The Last Great Imperial Adventurer*. New York: HarperCollins, 1995.

Fu, Tu. *Thirty-six Poems* (Kenneth Rexroth and Marden Brice, trans.). New York: Peter Blum Edition, 1987.

Fuller, Wayne E. *The Old Country School*. Chicago, Illinois: University of Chicago Press, 1982.

Garrett, Shirley S. *Social Reformers in Urban China: The Chinese Y.M.C.A., 1895–1926*. Cambridge, Massachusetts: Harvard University Press, 1970.

Gertz, Clifford. *Agricultural Involution: The Process of Ecological Change in Indonesia*. Berkeley, California: University of California Press, 1963.

Gesar: The Wondrous Adventures of King Gesar. Berkeley, California: Dharma Publishing, 1991.

Ghose, Indira. *Women Travelers in Colonial India: The Power of the Female Gaze*. Delhi: Oxford University Press, 1998.

Gibb, George Sweet, and Evelyn H. Knowlton. *History of Standard Oil Company (New Jersey): The Resurgent Years 1911–1927*. 4 vols. New York: Harper & Brothers, 1956.

Gill, William John. *The River of Golden Sand*. 2 vols. London: John Murray, 1880.

Gillin, Donald G. *Warlord: Yen Hsi-shan in Shansi Province, 1911–1949*. Princeton, New Jersey: Princeton University Press, 1967.

Goldstein, Melvyn C. *The Snow Lion and the Dragon: China, Tibet, and the Dalai Lama*. Berkeley, California: University of California Press, 1997.

Goldstein, Melvyn C., and Gelek Rimpoche. *A History of Modern Tibet, 1913–1951: The Demise of the Lamaist State*. Berkeley, California: University of California Press, 1989.

Goldstein, Melvyn C., William R. Siebenschuh, and Tashi Tsering. *The Struggle for Modern Tibet: The Autobiography of Tashi Tsering*. Armonk, New York: M. E. Sharpe, 1997.

Gore, Francis. *Trente Ans aux Portes du Thibet Interdit*. Hong Kong, China: Maison de Nazareth, 1939.

Goullart, Peter. *Forgotten Kingdom*. London: John Murray, Butler & Tanner, 1955.

————. *Princes of the Black Bone: Life in the Tibetan Borderland*. London: J. Murray, 1959.

Grand Rapids & Indiana Railroad Company. Grand Rapids: Michigan: H. M. Clark & Co., 1874.

Gratuze, Gaston. *Un Pioneer de la Mission Tibétaine: Le Père Auguste Desgodins (1826–1913)*. Paris: Apostalate des Éditions, 1968.

Gray, Jack, ed. *Modern China's Search for a Political Form*. London: Oxford University Press, 1969.

Gray, Ralph, ed. *The Hoosier State: Readings in Indiana History*. Grand Rapids, Michigan: W. B. Eerdmans Publishing Company, 1980.

Greeley, Horace. *An Overland Journey, from New York to San Francisco, in the Summer of 1859*. New York: C. M. Saxton, Barker and Company.

Greene, James. *The Personal Diary of James Greene: A Record of Life in Indianapolis, Indiana during 1875*. Indianapolis, Indiana: Manuscripts Collection, Indiana Division, Indiana State Library, 1979.

Gregory, J. W. *To the Alps of Chinese Tibet*. London: Seely, Service & Company, 1923.

Grunfeld, A. Tom. *The Making of Modern Tibet*. Armonk, New York: M. E. Sharpe, 1987.

Guinness, M. Geraldine. *The Story of the China Inland Mission*. 2 vols. London: Morgan & Scott, 1893–1894.

Hanbury-Tracy, John. *Black River of Tibet*. London: Travel Book Club, 1940.

Harris, Seymour, ed. *American Economic History*. New York: McGraw-Hill Book Company, 1961.

Haywood, C. Robert. *The Merchant Prince of Dodge City: The Life and Times of Robert M. Wright*. Norman, Oklahoma: University of Oklahoma Press, 1998.

Heat Moon, William Least. *PrairieErth*. Boston: Houghton Mifflin, 1991.

Hedin, Sven Anders. *Through Asia.* 2 vols. London: Methuen and Co., 1899.

———. *Trans-Himalaya: Discoveries and Adventures in Tibet.* 2 vols. New York: Macmillan, 1909.

Hedtke, Charles Herman. *Reluctant Revolutionaries: Szechwan and the Ch'ing Collapse, 1898–1911.* Berkeley, California: Unpublished dissertation, University of California, 1968.

Heinrich, Thomas R. *Ships for the Seven Seas: Philadelphia Shipbuilding in the Age of Industrial Capitalism.* Baltimore: Johns Hopkins University Press, 1997.

Hendrickson, Robert. *The Grand Emporiums: The Illustrated History of America's Great Department Stores.* New York: Stein and Day, 1979.

Hersey, John. *A Single Pebble.* New York: Knopf, 1965.

Hershatter, Gail. *Dangerous Pleasures: Prostitution and Modernity in Twentieth-Century Shanghai.* Berkeley, California: University of California Press, 1997.

Hewlett, William Meyrick. *Forty Years in China.* London: Macmillan, 1943.

Historical Atlas of Harper County, Kansas. Chicago: Davy Map and Atlas Co, 1886.

A Historical Collection of Harper County Churches. Anthony, Kansas: Harper County Religious Heritage Committee, 1961.

Historical Statistics of the U.S.: Colonial Times to 1970. Washington, D.C.: Bureau of the Census, 1975.

History of Shelton Memorial Christian Church. Ulysses, Kansas: Shelton Christian Church, 1965.

Ho (Hodabah), Phillip and Marguerite Fairbrother. *Wandering Tibetan.* Long Beach, California: Christian Press, 1966.

Ho, Ping-ti. *Studies on the Population of China, 1368–1953.* Cambridge: Harvard University Press, 1959.

Hobhouse, Henry. *Seeds of Change: Six Plants that Transformed Mankind.* London: Papermac, 1999.

Holdsworth, May. *Sichuan.* Lincolnwood, Illinois: Passport Books, 1993.

Holloway, H. R. *Indianapolis: A Historical and Statistical Sketch of the Railroad City.* Indianapolis, Indiana: Indianapolis Journal Print, 1870.

Holy Bible. Ashland, Ohio: Landoll's, Inc., 1994.

Hope, Holly. *Garden City: Dreams in a Kansas Town.* Norman, Oklahoma: University of Oklahoma Press, 1988.

Hopkirk, Peter. *The Great Game: The Struggle for Empire in Central Asia.* New York: Kodansha, 1992.

Hosie, Alexander Sir. *On the Trail of the Opium Poppy; a Narrative of Travel in the Chief Opium-Producing Provinces of China.* 2 vols. Boston: Small Maynard & Company, 1914.

Houston, G. W., ed. *The Cross and the Lotus: Christianity and Buddhism in Dialogue.* Delhi: Motilal Banarsidass, 1985.

Howe, Christopher. *Wage Patterns and Wage Policy in Modern China, 1919–1972.* Cambridge: Cambridge University Press, 1973.

Hoy, Suellen. *Chasing Dirt: The American Pursuit of Cleanliness.* New York: Oxford University Press, 1995.

Hsüeh, T'ao. *Brocade River Poems: Selected Works of the Tang Dynasty Courtesan Xue Tao* (Jeanne Larsen, trans.). Princeton, New Jersey: Princeton University Press, 1987.

Huc, Evariste Regis. *Lamas of the Western Heavens.* London: The Folio Society, [originally published 1851–54 as *Souvenirs d'un Voyage dans la Tartarie et le Thibet*],1982.

———. *Travels in Tartary, Thibet, and China, 1844–1846.* New York: Harper & Brothers, 1928.

———. *Recollections of a Journey through Tartary, Thibet, and China, during the Years 1844, 1845, and 1846* (Mrs. Percy Sinnett, trans.). Taipei: Ch'en Wen Publishing Company, [1852] 1971.

Hunley, J. B. *Shelton and the Crimson Trail: A Missionary Drama.* Cincinnati, Ohio: Powell and White, 1924.

Huntington, Ellsworth. *The Pulse of Asia: a Journey in Central Asia Illustrating the Geographic Basis of History.* Boston: Houghton, Mifflin and Company, 1907.

Hutchison, William R. *Errand to the World: American Protestant Thought and Foreign Missions.* Chicago: University of Chicago Press, 1987.

Ibbotson, R. M. A. *Adventures of Missionary Explorers.* London: Seeley, Service, 1915.

Illustrated Historical Atlas of the State of Indiana. Chicago: Baskin, Forster, & Company, 1875 [reprinted Indianapolis, Indiana: Indiana Historical Society, 1968].

Indiana Writers' Program. *Indiana, a Guide to the Hoosier State.* New York: Oxford University Press, 1941.

Ise, John. *Sod and Stubble.* Lawrence, Kansas: University Press of Kansas, 1996.

Issacs, Harold. *Images of Asia: American Views of China and India.* New York: Capricorn Books, 1962.

Jack, Robert Logan. *The Back Blocks of China.* New York: Greenwood Press, [1904] 1969.

Jeffrey, J. H. *Khams or Eastern Tibet.* Ilfracombe, Devon: Arthur H. Stockwell, Ltd., 1974.

Johnson, Paul. *A History of the American People.* New York: HarperCollins, 1997.

Johnson, Tess, and Deke Erh. *Near to Heaven: Western Architecture in China's Old Summer Resorts.* Hong Kong: Old China Hand Press, 1994.

Kapp, Robert A. *Szechwan and the Chinese Republic: Provincial Militarism and Central Power, 1911–1938.* New Haven: Yale University Press, 1973.

Kasson, John K. *Houdini, Tarzan, and the Perfect Man: The White Male Body and the Challenge of Modernity in America.* New York: Hill and Wang, 2001.

Kert, Bernice. *Abby Aldrich Rockefeller: The Woman in the Family.* New York: Random House, 1993.

Kilborn, Dr. O. L. *Heal the Sick: An Appeal for Medical Missions in China.* Toronto: Missionary Society of the Methodist Church, 1910.

King, Louis Magrath. *China in Turmoil, Studies in Personality.* London: Heath, Cranton, Limited, 1927.

King, Rin-chen Lha-Mo. *We Tibetans: An Intimate Picture.* London: Seely Service & Company, Limited, 1926.

Knaus, John Kenneth. *Orphans of the Cold War: America and the Tibetan Struggle for Survival.* New York: PublicAffairs, 1999.

Kvaerne, Per. *A Norwegian Traveler in Tibet: Theor Sörensen and the Tibetan Collection at the Oslo University Library.* New Delhi: Manjusri Publishing House, 1973.

Lamar, Howard, and Leonard Thompson. *The Frontier in History: North America and Southern Africa Compared.* New Haven: Yale University Press, 1981.

Lamb, Alastair. *The McMahon Line: A Study in the Relation between India, China, and Tibet, 1904–1914.* London: Routledge and Kegan Paul, 1966.

Lambert, John C., *Missionary Heroes in Asia: True Stories of the Intrepid Bravery and Stirring Adventures of Missionaries with Uncivilized Man, Wild Beasts, and the Forces of Nature.* London: Seeley and Co. Limited, 1908.

Landon, Perceval. *Lhasa: An Account of the Country and People of Central Tibet, and of the Progress of the Mission Sent There by the English Government in the Year 1903–04.* 2 vols. London: Hurst and Blackett, 1905.

———. *The Opening of Tibet.* New York: Doubleday, Page & Company, 1906.

Latourette, Kenneth S. *A History of Christian Missions in China.* London: Society for Promoting Christian Knowledge, 1929.

Lattimore, Owen. *Studies in Frontier History; Collected Papers, 1928–1958.* London: Oxford University Press, 1962.

Laufer, Berthold. *Kleinere Schriften von Berthold Laufer* (Hartmut Walravens, ed.). Wiesbaden, Germany: Steiner, 1976.

Launay, Adrien. *Histoire de la Mission du Thibet,* 2 vols. Paris: Desclee de Brouwer & Cie, 1902.

Leary, Edward A. *Indianapolis, A Pictorial History.* Virginia Beach, Virginia: Donning, 1980.

Lens, Sidney. *The Labor Wars: From the Molly Maguires to the Sitdowns.* Garden City, New York: Anchor Press/Doubleday, 1974.

Lerman, Leo. *The Museum: One Hundred Years and the Metropolitan Museum of Art.* New York: Viking Press, 1969.

Lewis, Norman. *The Missionaries: God Against the Indians.* New York: Penguin Books, 1988.

Lhalungpa, Lobsang Phuntshok. *Tibet, the Sacred Realm: Photographs, 1880–1950.* Millerton, New York: Aperture, 1983.

Lilly, Eli, ed., and Heinrich Schliemann. *Schliemann in Indianapolis.* Indianapolis, Indiana: Indiana Historical Society, 1961.

Ling, Chuke. *China's Railway Rolling Stock.* Seattle: University of Washington Press, 1946.

Lipin, Lawrence M. *Producers, Proletarians, and Politicians: Workers and Party Politics in Evansville and New Albany, Indiana, 1850–87.* Urbana, Illinois: University of Illinois Press, 1994.

Liu, Wu-chi, and Irving Yucheng Lo, eds. *Sunflower Splendor: Three Thousand Years of Chinese Poetry.* Garden City, New York: Anchor Books, 1975.

Lodwick, Kathleen L. *The Chinese Recorder Index: A Guide to Christian Missions in Asia, 1867–1941.* Wilmington, Delaware: Scholarly Resources Inc., 1986.

———. *Crusaders Against Opium: Protestant Missionaries in China, 1874–1917.* Lexington, Kentucky: The University Press of Kentucky, 1996.

Loewe, Michael. *Imperial China.* London: Allen & Unwin, 1966.

Loftis, Z. S. *Message from Batang.* New York: Fleming H. Revell, 1911.

Logan, Pamela. *Among Warriors: A Woman Martial Artist in Tibet.* New York: Vintage Books, 1998.

Lomazzi, Brad S. *Railroad Timetables, Travel Brochures and Posters: A History and Guide for Collectors.* New York: Golden Hill Press, 1995.

Long, Clarence Dickinson. *Wages and Earnings in the United States, 1860–1890.* Princeton, New Jersey: Princeton University Press, 1960.

Lopez, Donald S. *Prisoners of Shangri-La: Tibetan Buddhism and the West.* Chicago: University of Chicago Press, 1998.

Loup, Robert. *Martyr in Tibet; The Heroic Life and Death of Father Maurice Tornay, St. Bernard Missionary to Tibet.* New York: D. McKay, Inc., 1956.

Lutz, Jessie Gregory. *Christian Missions in China; Evangelists of What?* Boston: Heath, 1965.

Maberly, Allan. *God Spoke Tibetan.* Mountain View, California: Pacific Press Publications Association, 1971.

MacGregor, John. *Tibet: A Chronicle of Exploration.* New York: Praeger Publishers, 1970.

Maclaren, Ian, *Beside the Bonnie Briar Bush.* Fleming H. Revell Toronto 1894.

Madison, James H. *The Indiana Way: A State History.* Bloomington, Indiana: Indiana University Press, 1986.

———. *Heartland: Comparative Histories of the Midwestern States.* Bloomington, Indiana: Indiana University Press, 1988.

Malin, James Claude. *A Concern about Humanity: Notes on Reform, 1872–1912, at the National and Kansas Levels of Thought.* Lawrence, Kansas: James C. Malin, 1964.

Marrin, Albert. *Sitting Bull and His World.* New York: Dutton Children's Books, 2000.

Martin, Christopher. *The Boxer Rebellion.* London: Abelard-Schuman, 1968.

Martin, John Bartlow. *Indiana, An Interpretation.* New York: Alfred A. Knopf, 1947.

May, Henry Farnham. *Protestant Churches and Industrial America.* New York: Harper, 1949.

McCutcheon, Marc. *The Writer's Guide to Everyday Life in the 1800s.* Cincinnati, Ohio: Writer's Digest Books, 1993.

McGovern, William Montgomery. *To Lhasa in Disguise.* New York: Grosset & Dunlap, 1924.

McKenna, Richard. *The Sand Pebbles, a Novel.* New York: Harper & Row, 1962.

McLean, Archibald. *The History of the Foreign Christian Missionary Society.* New York: Fleming H. Revell, 1919.

McNeill, William Hardy. *The Great Frontier: Freedom and Hierarchy in Modern Times.* Princeton, New Jersey: Princeton University Press, 1983.

Mecham, Kirche, ed. *Annals of Kansas*. Vol. 1. Topeka, Kansas: Kansas State Historical Society, 1954.

Mémoires de la Société Académique Indo-Chinoise de France. Paris: Challamel aîné et Ernest Leroux, 1877.

Meyer, Karl Ernest, and Shareen Blair Brysac. *Tournament of Shadows: The Great Game and Race for Empire in Central Asia*. Washington, D. C.: Counterpoint, 1999.

Michael, Charles D. *Missionary Heroes: Stories of Heroism on the Mission Field*. Kilmarnock: John Ritchie Limited, 1905.

Michie, Alexander. *Missionaries in China*. London: Edward Stanford, 1891.

Migot, Andre. *Tibetan Marches*. New York: Dutton, 1955.

Millen, Nina, ed. *Missionary Hero Stories*. New York: Friendship Press, 1948.

Miller, Hunter, ed. *Treaties and Other International Acts of the United States of America*. Vol. 7. Washington, D.C.: United States Government Printing Office, 1942.

Miller, Lillian B., T. K. Walter, H. Nugent, and Wayne Morgan. *1876: The Centennial Year: Indiana Historical Society Lectures*. Indianapolis, Indiana: Indiana Historical Society, 1973.

Miller, Nathan. *Theodore Roosevelt: A Life*. New York: Morrow, 1992.

Miller, Nyle H., and Joseph W. Snell. *Great Gunfighters of the Kansas Cowtowns, 1867–1886*. Lincoln, Nebraska: University of Nebraska Press, 1967.

Miner, H. Craig. *West of Wichita: Settling the High Plains of Kansas, 1865–1890*. Lawrence, Kansas: University Press of Kansas, 1986.

Monroe, Paul, ed. *A Cyclopedia of Education*. New York: The Macmillan Company, 1913.

Morgan, H. Wayne, ed. *The Gilded Age, a Reappraisal*. Syracuse, New York: Syracuse University Press, 1963.

Morgan County Scrapbooks. 2 vols. Mooresville, Indiana: Morgan County History-Genealogy Club, 1985.

Morrison, John H. *History of American Steam Navigation*. New York: W. F. Sametz, 1903.

Morrow, Barbara O. *From Ben-Hur to Sister Carrie*. Indianapolis: Guild Press of Indiana, 1995.

Morsberger, Robert E. *Lew Wallace, Militant Romantic*. New York: McGraw-Hill, 1980.

Morse, Eugene. *Exodus to a Hidden Valley*. New York: E. P. Dutton, 1974.

Morse, Gertrude. *The Dogs May Bark, But the Caravan Moves On* (Helen M. Morse, ed.). Joplin, Missouri: College Press Publishing Co., 1998.

Mosely, George. "The Frontier Regions in China's Recent International Politics," in Jack Gray (ed.), *Modern China's Search for Political Form*. London: Oxford University Press, 1969.

Mott, John R. *The Evangelization of the World in this Generation*. New York: Arno Press, [1900] 1972.

Myres, Sandra L. *Westering Women and the Frontier Experience, 1800–1915*. Albuquerque, New Mexico: University of New Mexico Press, 1982.

Nash, Roderick. *Wilderness and the American Mind*. New Haven: Yale University Press, 1973.

Nelson, Daniel. *Farm and Factory: Workers in the Midwest, 1880–1990*. Bloomington, Indiana: Indiana University Press, 1995.

Nichol, C. R. *Gospel Preachers Who Blazed the Trail*. Austin, Texas: Firm Foundation Publishing House, 1911.

Nolan, Jeannette Covert. *Hoosier City; The Story of Indianapolis*. New York: J. Messner, 1943.

Norbu, Jamyang. *Warriors of Tibet: The Story of the Aten and the Khampas Fight for the Freedom of the Country*. London: Wisdom Publications, 1986.

O'Connor, Richard. *The Spirit Soldiers: A Historical Narrative of the Boxer Rebellion*. New York: G. P. Putnam's Sons, 1973.

O'Connor, William Frederick Travers. *Folk Tales from Tibet*. London: Hurst and Blackett, 1907.

Olson, Eleanor. *Catalogue of the Tibetan Collection and other Lamaist Articles in The Newark Museum*. 5 vols. Newark, New Jersey: The Newark Museum, 1950–1971.

Osborn, J. S. *Memories [by] Jennie Stoughton Osborn*. Medicine Lodge, Kansas: Press of the Barber County Index, 1935.

Osborne, Milton E. *The Mekong*. New York: Atlantic Monthly Press, 2000.

Pai, Chü-i. *The Selected Poems of Po Chü-I* (David Hinton, trans.). New York: New Directions, 1999.

Parmee, Edward A. *Kham and Amdo of Tibet*. New Haven, Connecticut: Human Relations Area Files, 1972.

Pascoe, Peggy. *Relations of Rescue: The Search for Female Moral Authority in the American West, 1874–1939*. New York: Oxford University Press, 1990.

Patterson, George N. *Patterson of Tibet: Death Throes of a Nation*. San Diego, California: ProMotion Publishing, 1998.

———. *Requiem for Tibet*. London: Aurum Press, 1990.

Peissel, Michel. *The Cavaliers of Kham: The Secret War in Tibet*. London: William Heinemann, 1972.

Penick, Douglas J. *The Warrior Song of King Gesar*. Boston: Wisdom Publications, 1996.

Peniston, William A., ed. *The New Museum: Selected Writings by John Cotton Dana*. Newark, New Jersey and Washington, D.C.: The Newark Museum Association and the American Association of Museums, 1999.

Petech, Luciano. *China and Tibet in the Early Eighteenth Century*. Leiden, Netherlands: E. J. Brill, 1972.

Pettifer, Julian, and Richard Bradley. *Missionaries*. London: BBC Books, 1990.

Phillips, Clifton Jackson. *Indiana in Transition*. Indianapolis, Indiana: Indiana Historical Bureau, 1968.

Pollock, J. C. *The Cambridge Seven*. London: Inter-Varsity Fellowship, 1955.

Polo, Marco. *The Travels of Marco Polo*. (Teresa Waugh, trans.). New York: Facts on File Publications, 1984.

———. *The Travels of Marco Polo*. Ware, England: Wordsworth Editions Limited, 1997.

Preston, Diane. *The Boxer Rebellion: The Dramatic Story of China's War on Foreigners That Shook the World in the Summer of 1900*. New York: Walker & Company, 2000.

Preston, Douglas J. *Dinosaurs in the Attic: An Excursion into the American Museum of Natural History*. New York: St. Martin's Press, 1986.

Probst, George Theodore. *The Germans in Indianapolis, 1840–1918* (Eberhard Reichmann, rev). Indianapolis, Indiana: German-American Center & Indiana German Heritage Society, 1989.

Przheval'skii, Nikolai Mikhailovich. *Mongolia, the Tangut Country, and the Solitudes of Northern Tibet Being a Narrative of Three Years' Travel in Eastern High Asia*. London: S. Low, Marston, Searle, and Rivington, 1876.

Pye, Lucian W. *Warlord Politics: Conflict and Coalition in the Modernization of Republican China*. New York: Praeger, 1971.

Rawson, Phillip. *The Art of Tantra*. London: Thames and Hudson, 1978.

Reade, Charles. *The Cloister and the Hearth: A Tale of the Middle Ages*. London: Oxford University Press, [1859] 1923.

Rexer, Lyle, and Rachel Klein. *American Museum of Natural History: 125 Years of Expedition and Discovery*. New York: Harry N. Abrams, Inc., 1975.

Reynolds, Valrae. *From the Sacred Realm: Treasures of Tibetan Art from the Newark Museum*. Munich: Prestel Verlag, 1999.

Reynolds, Valrae, and Amy Heller. *Catalogue of the Newark Museum Tibetan Collection*. 5 vols. Newark, New Jersey: Newark Museum, 1983–1986.

Reynolds, Valrae, and Barbara Lipton. *The Museum New Series*. Newark, New Jersey: Newark Museum, 1972.

Rhie, Mary M., and Robert A. F. Thurman. *Wisdom and Compassion: The Sacred Art of Tibet*. New York: Harry Abrams, Inc., 1996.

Richmond, Robert W. *Kansas: A Land of Contrasts.* Wheeling, Illinois: Harland Davidson, 1999.

Ridgely-Nevitt, Cedric. *American Steamships on the Atlantic.* London: University of Delaware Press, 1981.

Rijnhart, Susie. C. *With the Tibetans in Tent and Temple.* Chicago: Fleming H. Revell Company, 1901.

Riley, Glenda. *The Female Frontier: A Comparative View of Women on the Prairie and the Plains.* Lawrence, Kansas: University of Kansas Press, 1988.

Robert, Dana L. *American Women in Mission: A Social History of Their Thought and Practice.* Macon, Georgia: Mercer University Press, 1997.

Rock, Joseph Francis Charles. *The Ancient Na-Khi Kingdom of Southwest China.* 2 vols. Cambridge, Massachusetts: Harvard University Press, 1947.

Rockhill, W. W. *Diary of a Journey through Mongolia and Tibet in 1891 and 1892.* Washington, D.C.: Smithsonian Institution, 1894.

———. *Land of Lamas: Notes of a Journey through China, Mongolia and Tibet.* San Francisco: Chinese Materials Center, [1891] 1976.

Ross, Steven Joseph. *Workers on the Edge: Work, Leisure, and Politics in Industrializing Cincinnati, 1788–1890.* New York: Columbia University Press, 1985.

Rudolph, L. C. *Hoosier Faiths: A History of Indiana Churches & Religious Groups.* Bloomington, Indiana: Indiana University Press, 1995.

———. *Religion in Indiana: A Guide to Historical Resources.* Bloomington, Indiana: Indiana University Press, 1986.

Rydjord, John. *Kansas Place-Names.* Norman: University of Oklahoma Press, 1972.

Said, Edward W. *Orientalism.* New York: Vintage Books, 1979.

Samuel, Geoffrey. *Civilized Shamans: Buddhism in Tibetan Societies.* Washington, D.C.: Smithsonian Institution Press, 1993.

Sandberg, Samuel Louis Graham. *The Exploration of Tibet: Its History and Particulars, from 1623–1904.* Calcutta: Thacker, Spink & Co., 1904.

Sanders, Gwendoline, and Paul Sanders. *The Harper County Story.* North Newton, Kansas: The Mennonite Press, 1968.

Schenkel, Albert F. *The Rich Man and the Kingdom: John D. Rockefeller, Jr., and the Protestant Establishment.* Minneapolis, Minnesota: Fortress Press, 1995.

Schurmann, Franz and Orville Schell. *Imperial China.* Harmondsworth, England: Penguin Books, 1967.

Serrell, Jeanne M. *Tales of Modern Missionaries for Young People.* New York: Fleming H. Revell Co., 1929.

Service, Grace. *Golden Inches: The China Memoir of Grace Service* (John S. Service, ed.). Berkeley, California: University of California Press, 1989.

Shakya, Tsering. *The Dragon in the Land of Snows: A History of Modern Tibet since 1947.* New York: Columbia University Press, 1999.

Shaw, Henry K. *Hoosier Disciples.* St. Louis, Missouri: Bethany Press for the Association of the Christian Churches in Indiana, 1966.

Shelton, Albert L. *Pioneering in Tibet, A Personal Record of Life and Experience in Mission Fields.* New York: F. H. Revell Company, 1921.

———. *Tibetan Folk Tales.* St. Louis, Missouri: United Christian Missionary Society, 1925.

Shelton, Flora Beal. *Chants from Shangri-La* (Dorris Shelton Still, ed.). Palm Springs, California, 1939.

———. *Geography.* Calcutta: Baptist Mission Press, 1922.

———. *Shelton of Tibet.* New York: George Doran, 1923.

———. *Songs of Service.* Calcutta: Baptist Mission Press, 1922.

———. *A Story Book for Tibetan Boys and Girls.* Calcutta: Baptist Mission Press, 1922.

————. *Sunshine and Shadow on the Tibetan Border.* Cincinnati, Ohio: Foreign Christian Missionary Society, 1912.

Sheridan, James. E. *Chinese Warlord: The Career of Feng Yu-hsiang.* Stanford, California: Stanford University Press, 1966.

Shortridge, James R. *Peopling the Plains: Who Settled Where in Frontier Kansas.* Lawrence, Kansas: University Press of Kansas, 1995.

Simmonds, Stuart, and Simon Digby, eds. *The Royal Asiatic Society: Its History and Treasures.* Leiden, Netherlands: E. J. Brill, 1979.

Smith, Arthur Henderson. *Chinese Characteristics.* New York: Fleming H. Revell, 1894.

————. *A Manual for Young Missionaries to China.* Shanghai, China: Christian Literature Publishing House, 1918.

————. *Rex Christus: An Outline Study of China.* New York: The Macmillan Company, 1904.

Small Towns of Bourbon County. Fort Scott, Kansas: Old Fort Geneological Society of Southeastern Kansas.

Smith, Page. *America Enters the World.* New York: McGraw-Hill Book Company, 1985.

Smith, Paul H. *Taxing Heaven's Storehouse: Horse, Bureaucrats, and the Destruction of the Sichuan Tea Industry, 1074–1224.* Cambridge, MA: Council of East Asian Studies, Harvard University, 1991.

Smith, William Edward. *A Canadian Doctor in West China: Forty Years under Three Flags.* Toronto: Ryerson Press, 1939.

Solverson, Howard M. *The Jesuit and the Dragon: The Life of Father William Mackey in the Himalayan Kingdom of Bhutan.* Montreal: Robert Davies Publishing, 1995.

Spence, Jonathan. *The Chan's Great Continent: China in Western Minds.* New York: W. W. Norton, 1998.

Spence, Jonathan, and Ann-Ping Chin. *The Chinese Century.* New York: Random House, 1996.

Stanford, Edward. *Atlas of the Chinese Empire.* London: Morgan & Scott, 1908.

Stanley, Henry M. *The Autobiography of Sir Henry Morton Stanley* (Dorothy Stanley, ed.). Boston: Houghton Mifflin, 1909.

Stephens, Harrison. *A Song of Home: The First Seventy-Five Years of Pilgrim Place in Claremont, California.* Claremont, California: Pilgrim Place Diamond Jubilee Committee, 1989.

Still, Charles E. *Frontier Doctor-Medical Pioneer: The Life and Times of A. T. Still and His Family.* Kirksville, Missouri: The Thomas Jefferson University Press at Northeast Missouri State University, 1991.

Still, Dorris Shelton. *Beyond the Devils in the Wind.* Tempe, Arizona: Synergy Books, 1989.

————. Flora Beal Shelton, trans. *Chants from Shangri-La.* Self-published, 1939.

————. *Sue in Tibet.* New York: John Day, 1942.

Stover, John F. *American Railroads.* Chicago: University of Chicago Press, [1961] 1997.

Sulgrove, Berry R. *History of Indianapolis and Marion County, Indiana.* Philadelphia: L. H. Everts & Company, 1884.

Sutton, Donald S. *Provincial Militarism and the Chinese Republic: The Yunnan Army 1905–1925.* Ann Arbor, Michigan: University of Michigan Press, 1980.

Sutton, S. B. *In China's Border Provinces.* New York: Hastings House, 1974.

Swanson, Leslie C. *Rural One-Room Schools of Mid-America.* Moline, Illinois: Self- published, [1976] 1984.

Swisher, Earl. *China's Management of the American Barbarians; A Study of Sino-American Relations, 1841–1861, with Documents.* New Haven, Connecticut: Far Eastern Publications, Yale University, 1953.

Taylor, Annie R. *Pioneering in Tibet.* London: Morgan and Scott, 1895.

Taylor, Howard Mrs. *The Call of China's Great North-West or, Kansu and Beyond.* London: China Inland Mission, 1926.

Taylor, Robert M., Jr., and Connie A. McBirney, eds. *Peopling Indiana: The Ethnic Experience.* Indianapolis, Indiana: Indiana Historical Society, 1996.

Taylor, Robert M., Jr., Errol Wayne Stevens, Mary Ann Ponder, and Paul Brockman. *Indiana: A New Historical Guide.* Indianapolis, Indiana: Indiana Historical Society, 1989.

Teichman, Eric. *Travels of a Consular Officer in Eastern Tibet.* Cambridge, England: Cambridge University Press, 1922.

————. *Travels of a Consular Official in North-West China.* Cambridge, England: Cambridge University Press, 1921.

Theobald, Paul. *Call School: Rural Education in the Midwest to 1981.* Carbondale, Illinois: Southern Illinois University Press, 1995.

Thornbrough, Emma Lou. *Indiana in the Civil War Era, 1850–1880.* Indianapolis, Indiana: Indiana Historical Bureau, 1965.

————. *The Negro in Indiana Before 1900: A Study of a Minority.* Bloomington, Indiana: Indiana University Press, [1957] 1993.

Thurman, Robert A. F. *Essential Tibetan Buddhism.* San Francisco: Harper San Francisco, 1995.

Tolley, Kemp. *Yangtze Patrol: The U.S. Navy in China.* Annapolis, Maryland: Naval Institute Press, 1971.

Tomes, Nancy. *The Gospel of Germs: Men, Women, and the Microbe in American Life.* Cambridge, Massachusetts: Harvard University Press, 1998.

Torjesen, Edvard P. *Fredrik Franson: A Model for Worldwide Evangelism.* Pasadena, California: William Carey Library, 1983.

Treistman, Judith M. *The Early Cultures of Szechwan and Yunnan.* Ithaca, New York: China-Japan Program, Cornell University, 1974.

Tsering, Marku. *Sharing Christ in the Tibetan Buddhist World.* Upper Darby, Pennsylvania: Tibet Press, 1988.

Tuchman, Barbara. *Stillwell and the American Experience in China, 1911–45.* New York: Macmillan, 1970.

Tucker, William Edward, and Lester G. McAllister. *Journey in Faith: A History of the Christian Church (Disciples of Christ).* St. Louis, Missouri: Bethany Press, 1975.

United States Bureau of the Census. *Historical Statistics of the United States, Colonial Times to 1970.* 2 vols. Washington, D.C.: United States Department of Commerce, Bureau of the Census, 1975.

Van Dyck, Howard. *William Christie: Apostle to Tibet.* Harrisburg, Pennsylvania: Christian Publications, Inc., 1956.

Van Slyke, Lyman. *Yangtze: Nature, History, and the River.* Reading, Massachusetts: Addison-Wesley Publishing Co., 1988.

Varg, Paul A. *Missionaries, Chinese, and Diplomats: The American Protestant Missionary Movement in China, 1890–1952.* Princeton, New Jersey: Princeton University Press, 1958.

————. *Open Door Diplomat.* Urbana, Illinois: University of Illinois Press, 1952.

Wallace, Archer. *Blazing New Trails.* New York: Doubleday, Doran & Co., 1928.

Wallace, Lew. *An Autobiography.* New York: Harper & Brothers Publishers, 1906.

————. *Ben-Hur: A Tale of Christ.* New York: Dodd, Mead & Company, [1880]1953.

Waller, Derek J. *The Pundits: British Exploration of Tibet and Central Asia.* Lexington, Kentucky: University Press of Kentucky, 1990.

Walravens, Hartmut, ed., *Kleinere Schriften/von Berthold Laufer.* In *Sinologica Coloniensia.* Vol. 1. Weisbaden: Franz Steiner, 1976.

Wang, Y. C. *Chinese Intellectuals and the West, 1872–1949.* Chapel Hill, North Carolina: The University of North Carolina, 1966.

Ward, Francis Kingdon. *The Land of the Blue Poppy: Travels of a Naturalist in Eastern Tibet.* Cadogan Books, London, [1923] 1986.

————. *The Mystery Rivers of Tibet.* London: Cadogan, [1923] 1986.

Ward, James Arthur. *Railroads and the Character of America, 1820–1887.* Knoxville, Tennessee: University of Tennessee Press, 1986.

Weale, B. L. Putnam. *The Fight for the Republic in China.* New York: Dodd, Mead and Company, 1917.

Wellby, Capt. Montagu Sinclair. *Through Unknown Tibet.* New Delhi: Asian Educational Services, 1996.

Wessels, Cornelius. *Early Jesuit Travellers in Central Asia, 1603–1721.* The Hague: Martinus Nijhoff, 1924.

Wheeler, Marcia Ann. *A Journey of Faith in the Hoosier Heartland: A History of the First Christian Church.* Noblesville, Indiana: First Christian Church, 1999.

Wiebe, Robert. *The Search for Order, 1877–1920.* New York: Hill and Wang, [1967] 1999.

Wilder, Daniel Webster. *The Annals of Kansas: 1886–1925.* Topeka, Kansas: Kansas State Historical Society, 1954.

Williams, D. Newell. *A Case Study of Mainstream Protestantism: The Disciples' Relation to American Culture, 1880–1989.* St. Louis, Missouri: Wm. B. Eerdmans Publishing Co., 1991.

Williamson, Alexander. *Journeys in North China, Manchuria, and Eastern Mongolia with Some Account of Corea.* 2 vols. London: Smith, Elder and Company, 1870.

Wilson, Andrew. *The Abode of Snow: Observations on a Tour from Chinese Tibet to the Indian Caucasus, Through the Upper Valleys of the Himalaya.* New York: G. P. Putnam's Sons, 1875.

Wilson, Ernest Henry. *A Naturalist in Western China.* London: Cadogan Books, [1913] 1986.

Winchester, Simon. *The River at the Center of the World.* New York: H. Holt, 1996.

Woodrooffe, Thomas. *River of Golden Sand.* London: Faber and Faber, 1936.

Woodward, David B. *Aflame for God: Biography of Fredrik Franson.* Chicago: Moody Press, 1966.

————. *Detour from Tibet.* Chicago: Moody Press, 1975.

Wyman, Andrea. *Rural Women Teachers in the United States: A Sourcebook.* Lanham, Maryland: The Scarecrow Press, Inc., 1997.

Xu Feng-Xiang and Zheng Wei-Lie. *Wild Flowers of Tibet.* Beijing: Zhongguo lü you chu ban she, 1999.

Yanyun, Xian. *In Search of the Ancient Tea Caravan Route.* Hong Kong: Hong Kong China Tourism Press, 1995.

Yin, Ma, ed. *China's Minority Nationalities.* Beijing: Foreign Languages Press, 1994.

Yule, Henry Sir. *Cathay and the Way Thither.* Vols. 1, 37, 41. Nendeln, Litchenstein: Kraus Reprint Limited, 1967 (originally published London: Hakluyt Society, 1913–1916).

Articles

Amundsen, Edward. "A Journey Through South-West Sechuan." *Geographical Journal* 15, no. 5 (May 1900) and 15, no. 6 (June 1900).

Beckwith, Christopher. "The Impact of the Horse and Silk Trade on the Economies of T'ang China and the Uighar Empire." *Journal of the Economic and Social History of the Orient* 34 (June 1991).

Beech, Joseph. "University Beginnings: A Story of the West China Union University." *Journal of the West China Border Research Society* 6 (1933–34).

Berquist, James M. "Tracing the Origins of a Midwestern Culture: The Case of Central Indiana." *Indiana Magazine of History* (March 1981).

Bloch, Kurt. "Warlordism: A Transitory Stage in Chinese Government." *The American Journal of Sociology* 13, no. 5 (March 1938).

Bray, John. "Christian Missions and the Politics of Tibet, 1850–1950," Wilfred Wagner (ed.), *Kolonien & Missionen, Referate des. 3. Internationalen Kolonialgeschichten Symposiums 1993 in Bremen.* Munster; Hamburg: Bremen Asien Pazifik Studien, 1993.

———. "Heinrich August Jaeschke: Pioneer Tibetan Scholar," *The Tibet Journal* 8, no. 1 (Spring 1983).

———. "The Moravian Church in Ladakh: The First Forty Years: 1885–1925," *Recent Research in Ladakh,* Schriftenreiche Internationales Asienforum, vol. 1, Detlef Kantowsky and Reinhard Sander (eds.). Munich: Weltformum Verlag, 1983.

Bruce, A. J. "Some Secret Societies in Szechwan." *Journal of the West China Border Research Society* 8 (1936).

Brysac, Sharlee Blair. "The Last of the Foreign Devils." *Archeology,* 50, no. 6 (Nov./Dec. 1997).

Calder, Kent. "Growing up in the Christian Church." *Encounter* 60 (Spring 1998).

Ch'en, Jerome. "Defining Chinese Warlords and Their Factions." *Bulletin of Oriental and African Studies* 31 (1968).

Coales, Oliver. "Eastern Tibet." *Geographical Journal* 53, no. 4 (January-June 1919).

Dehergne, Joseph. "La Chine du Sud-Ouest: Le Swechwan, Le Kweichow, Le Yunnan," *Achiuum Historicum Societatus Jesu,* Anno XLII, Fasc. 84 (July-December 1973).

Desgodins, M. L'Abbé. "Notes Ethnographiques sur le Thibet," *Mémoires de la Sociétié Académique Indo-Chinoise de France,* vol. 1, années 1877–1878 (Paris: Challamel Aine, 1879).

"Dr. A. L. Shelton K.S.N. Graduate Killed in Tibet." *State Normal Bulletin* (Mar. 16, 1922).

Dye, D. S. "James Huston Edgar, Pioneer." *Journal of the West China Border Society* 8 (1936).

Edgar, James Huston. "The Great Open Lands." *Journal of the West China Border Society* 4 (1930–1931).

———. "Hsiang Ch'eng or Du Halde's 'Land of the Lamas.'" *Journal of the West China Border Research Society* 7 (11935).

———. "Litang: or Missionary Problems in the Highest Town on Earth." *The Chinese Recorder* (May 1915).

Ekvall, Robert L. "Nomadic Patterns of Living among the Tibetans as Preparation for War." *American Anthropologist* (1961).

———."Peace and War Among the Tibetan Nomads." *American Anthropologist* (1964).

Elder, Chris. "The Man Who Found Shangri-La: James Edgar Huston [sic]." *New Zealand Journal of East Asian Studies,* 1, no. 2 (1993).

"Gesar." *Journal* 4, no. 1 (Winter 1977).

Gregory, J. W. "The Death of Dr. Shelton," *Geographical Journal* 65 (January 1925): 87.

Hall, Norman. "The U.S., Tibet, and China—A Study in American Involvement in Tibet." *Tibetan Review* 13, no. 1 (January 1978).

Haraway, Donna. "Teddy Bear Patriarchy: Taxidermy in the Garden of Eden, New York City, 1908–1936." *Social Text* (Winter 1984–1985).

Holdrich, Col. Sir T. H. "Sven Hedin and Dutreuil De Rhins in Central Asia." *Geographical Journal* 13 (February 1899).

Houston, G. W. "Jesus and His Missionaries in Tibet." *Tibet Journal* 16 (Winter 1991).

Hughes, Richard T. "The Apocalyptic Origins of the Churches of Christ and the Triumph of Modernism." Religion and American Culture (Summer 1992).

Lang, Elfrieda. "Southern Migration to Northern Indiana Before 1850." *Indiana Magazine of History* 50 (December 1954).

Martin, William S. "A Bibliographic Essay on American Missionaries to the Tibetans Prior to 1950." *Lungta* 11 (Winter 1998).

MacKinnon, Stephen R. "The Peiyang Army, Yüan Shih-k'ai, and the Origins of Modern Chinese Warlordism," *Journal of Asian Studies* 32, no. 3 (May 1973).

"Memorial Service for Dr. A. L. Shelton." *The Emporia Daily* (Apr. 10, 1922).

Miller, Beatrice D. "American Popular Perceptions of Tibet from 1858–1938." *Tibet Journal* 13 no. 3 (Autumn 1988): 3–20.

"Mission Dream Team." *Christianity Online Magazine* 52 (Christian History).

Rijnhart, Susie. "Tibet." *Missionary Tidings* 20, no. 7 (November 1902).

Rockhill, W. W. "The Dalai Lamas of Lhasa and the Relations with the Manche Emperors of China, 1644–1908." T'oung Pao 11 (1910).

————. "Tibet: A Geographical, Ethnographical, and Historical Sketch, Derived from Chinese Sources." *Journal of the Royal Asiatic Society of Great Britain and Ireland* 28 (1891).

Shelton, Albert L. "Life Among the People of Eastern Tibet." *National Geographic* 40, no. 3 (September 1921).

Shelton Exhibit Catalogue Descriptions. *The Newark Museum* 2, 3 (July 1912).

Siu, Paul C. P. "The Sojourner." *American Journal of Sociology* 58, no. 34 (July 1952).

Sperling, Elliot. "The Chinese Venture in K'am, 1904–1911, and the Role of Chao Erh- Feng." *The Tibet Journal* 2, no. 2 (April/June 1976).

Stansell, Christine. "Women on the Great Plains, 1865–1890."*Women's Studies* 4 (1976).

Tarkington, Booth. "As I Seem to Me." *Saturday Evening Post* (July 5, 1941).

Templeman, David. "J. H. Edgar, an Australian Missionary in the Tibetan Marches." *Lungta* (Winter 1998).

Vogelgesang, Susan. "Zerelda Wallace: Indiana's Conservative Radical." *Traces* 4 (Summer 1992).

Wissing, Douglas. "Area's Tibetan presence has roots in Cold War." *Indianapolis Star,* Aug. 25, 2003.

————. "Old Mission Building finds new purpose." *Indianapolis Star,* Jan. 29, 2000.

————. "Tibetan Adventure." *Indianapolis Star,* Jan. 28, 2000.

Pamphlets, Papers, and Miscellaneous Sources

Bronson, Bennet. "Berthold Laufer at the Field Museum." Unpublished manuscript.

"Diplomatical Archives of Nantes, Pekin 37, extract *Peking Gazette,* appended to the report number 99 from M. Bons d'Anty, French Consulate at Chengdu to M. Dubail, French Ambassador at Pekin, Chengdu, 25th/05/1905." Email message from Laurent Deshayes, Feb. 7, 2001.

"Diplomatical Archives of Nantes, Pekin 37, First petition presented to the Imperial Authorities by the Samkiengtsong of Bathang, dated 3rd moon of the 31st year of Guangxu appended to the report number 99 from M Bons d'Anty, French Consualte at Chengdu to M. DUBAIL, French Ambassador at Pekin, Chengdu, 25th/05/1905." Email message from Laurent Deshayes, Feb. 7, 2001.

Indianapolis City Directories, 1875–1880.

"Lower Cimarron Springs" [flyer]. Archives of Historic Adobe Museum, Ulysses, Kansas.

"The Men and Millions Movement, History and Report, 1913–1919." United Christian Missionary Society Archives, Yale Divinity School Library Special Collections, New Haven, Connecticut.

"Old Church" [flyer]. Archives of Historic Adobe Museum, Ulysses, Kansas.

Our History. Archives of the Historic Adobe Museum, Ulysses, Kansas.

Papers Relating to the Foreign Relations of the United States (1920). 3 vols. Washington, D.C.: Government Printing Office, 1935.

Papers Relating to the Foreign Relations of the United States (1921). 2 vols. Washington, D.C.: Government Printing Office, 1936.

Papers Relating to the Foreign Relations of the United States (1922). 2 vols. Washington, D.C.: Government Printing Office, 1938.

Paul, C. T. "Brown Churches of Christ." Biography of Dr. Susie Rijnhart, in Rijnhart Files, Disciples of Christ Historical Society, Nashville, Tennessee.

Records of the Department of State Relating to Internal Affairs of China, 1910–1929. Washington, D.C.: National Archives and Record Service, 1973.

"Report of a Trip Thru Yunnan, Eastern Tibet, and Szechuan, by Major John Magruder, F.A., Ass't Military Attache, Jan.17-July 11, 1921." Reel 2. U.S. War Dept. Military Intelligence Division China, 1918–1941.

"Small Towns of Bourbon County" [booklet]. Fort Scott, Kansas: Old Fort Genealogical Society of Southeastern Kansas, Inc.

"Soldier vs. Settler" [flyer]. Fort Scott National Historic Site, Fort Scott, Kansas.

"The State Normal School" [brochure], Academic year 1895–1896. In files, Emporia State University Library, Emporia, Kansas.

Tarbet, Lena. "History of Shelton Memorial Christian Church." Ulysses, Kansas: Shelton Christian Church, 1965.

United States, National Archives and Records Service. *Records of the Department of State Relating to Internal Affairs of China, 1910–29*. Washington, D.C.: National Archives, National Archives and Records Service, General Services Administration, 1967.

United States War Department, Military Intelligence Division. *Correspondence of the Military Intelligence Division Relating to General, Political, Economic, and Military Conditions in China 1918–1941* (reels 1–4, 1918–1923). Washington, D.C.: National Archives and Records Administration, 1986.

U.S. Census. Provided by Kansas State Historical Society, Topeka, Kansas. "Who's Who in Our Missionaries" [questionnaire], filled out by Dr. Albert Shelton. Files of Disciples of Christ Overseas Ministries Office, Indianapolis, Indiana.

Journals and Magazines

The Chinese Recorder
The Christian-Evangelist
Journal of the West China Border Research Society
Newark Museum Quarterly
The Tibet Journal. Dharamsala, India: Library of Tibetan Works & Archives.
West China Missionary News
World Call

Newspapers

Anthony Republican. Anthony, Harper County, Kansas
The Bulletin [Pomona, California]
The Chicago Tribune
Emporia Daily
Indianapolis Star
Indianapolis Tribune
The Kodak [Kansas State Normal College, Emporia, Kansas]
The New York Times
Pomona Progress
The Republican [Grant County, Kansas]
State Normal Bulletin [Kansas State Normal College, Emporia, Kansas]

These Indianapolis newspapers were examined for the year 1875. They are available from the newspaper microfilm collection at Indiana University-Bloomington's Main Library.
Evening News
Journal Sentinal
Weekly News
Saturday News
Sunday News

Archives

American Natural History Museum, New York
Battye Library, State Library of Western Australia

Bourbon County, Kansas Recorder of Deeds
British Library, Political and Secret Files, London
British Public Records
Christian Theological Seminary, Indianapolis, Indiana
Diplomatic Archives of Nantes
Disciples of Christ Historical Society, Nashville, Tennessee
Disciples of Christ Overseas Ministries Office, Indianapolis, Indiana
Emporia State University, Emporia, Kansas
Field Museum Archives, Chicago, Illinois
Grant County, Kansas Recorder of Deeds
Harper County, Kansas Recorder of Deeds
Historic Adobe Museum, Ulysses, Kansas.
Indiana Historical Society Archives, Indianapolis, Indiana
Indiana State Library, Indianapolis, Indiana
John Basmajian Film Archives, Los Angeles, California.
Kansas Collection at the Kansas University Library, Lawrence, Kansas
Kansas State Historical Society, Topeka, Kansas
Los Angeles County, California Recorder of Deeds
National Geographic Society Archives, Washington, D.C.
Newark Museum Archives
The Rockefeller Archive Center
Royal Asiatic Society, London
Royal Geographical Society Archives, London
Still Family Archives, Scottsdale, Arizona
Transylvania College, Lexington, Kentucky
University of Chicago Archives
Yale University School of Divinity

INDEX